WILLIAM SHERIDAN ALLEN

THE NAZI SEIZURE OF POWER

THE EXPERIENCE OF A SINGLE GERMAN TOWN 1922-1945

REVISED EDITION

A GROLIER COMPANY

FRANKLIN WATTS
NEW YORK LONDON TORONTO SYDNEY

FRANKLIN WATTS, INC.
387 PARK AVENUE SOUTH
NEW YORK, NEW YORK 10016

Library of Congress Cataloging in Publication Data

Allen, William Sheridan.
The Nazi seizure of power :
the experience of a single
German town 1922–1945.
Includes index.
1. Germany—Politics and governnment—1918–1933.
2. Local government—Germany—Case studies.
3. National socialism. I. Title.
DD256.5.A58   1984   943.086   83-27340
ISBN 0-531-09935-0
ISBN 0-531-05633-3 (pbk.)

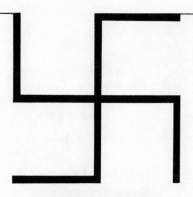

CONTENTS

TO MY MOTHER

and to the
memory of my father,
who taught me
love of learning

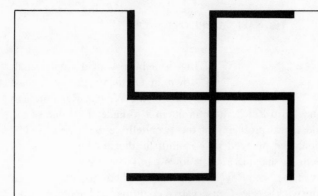

PREFACE
TO THE
FIRST
EDITION

This is a history of a single small town in Germany during the last years of the Weimar Republic and the first years of the Third Reich. It is an attempt to understand one of the central political and moral problems of the twentieth century: how a civilized democracy could be plunged into a nihilistic dictatorship. I chose to approach this problem by studying a single town partly because no close study of the local aspects of the Nazi Revolution existed. A book has been written on the State of Brunswick's Nazi-Conservative coalition, and another on the Nazification of the Schleswig-Holstein provinces* (both halting before the actual seizure of power), but before I undertook this present study there was nothing written to cover the entire period of the Nazi Revolution or that focused on a limited locality.

Yet Nazi measures on the local level were a key to the establishment of the Third Reich in Germany. Before Hitler came to power he gained great support through the virtuosity and adaptability of his local party organizations. The actual seizure of power in the spring of 1933 occurred largely from below, though it was facilitated and made possible by Hitler's position as Chancellor of Germany. The *Fuehrer* reached the pinnacle of power because his followers were successful at the lowest level, at the base.

A single unit can never adequately reflect the whole. The subject of this book was not, in many ways, an average German town. It was heavily middle class; it was more closely tied to the countryside and less to industry than most German towns; it was overwhelmingly Lutheran; it turned to Nazism earlier and more strongly than most of the rest of Germany. Yet it does show representative characteristics: in the activism of the Nazi party, in the sociological strengths and weaknesses of the Social Democrats, in the attitudes of the nationalistic middle class, in voting trends, in the growth of political activity and partisan violence, and perhaps in other ways that will become apparent only when other towns are studied in similar detail. In this sense it is not a true microcosm, though it can be instructive of broader trends. I offer it as at least one concrete example of what the Nazi Revolution meant in all its varied aspects in one confined area.

If a microcosm has the drawback of being nonrepresentative, it has the advantage of permitting a close and detailed study. The smaller number of actors makes it possible for the historian to come near to knowing them all. Variables are limited and there is a comprehensible and relatively constant

---

*Ernest-August Roloff, *Bürgertum und Nationalsozialismus: Braunschweigs Weg ins Dritten Reich* (Hannover, 1960): Rudolf Heberle, *From Democracy to Nazism* (Baton Rouge, 1945).

background. Immediacy and reality are enhanced. One can fit actions into the pattern of daily life and thus determine why individuals acted as they did, why Germans made the kind of choices that let Hitler into power. It was this possibility, more than anything else, that led me to research into the fate of a town which would otherwise not deserve even a footnote in a general study of the rise of Nazism.

The ravages of revolution, terror, war, and occupation severely limited the number and type of source materials available for this study. Thanks to the cooperation of the townspeople, however, most of the public and private documents that survived were put at my disposal. Enough of the people of the town agreed to be interviewed so that I was able to interrogate most leading figures and also obtain an acceptable general cross-section. Their recollections and impressions were then checked against the contemporary documents and newspaper accounts. The result was a considerable collection of detail, much of which had to be omitted from this book but which is to be found in my doctoral dissertation.*

When the idea for this study first came to me, I was given essential encouragement by Dr. Harry Marks of the University of Connecticut, for which I thank him. The research was made possible by a grant from the Federal Republic of Germany. Dr. Heinrich Eggeling gave me valuable advice and practical aid, while Dr. Karl Roskamp provided me with the benefit of his experience in the labyrinth of German tax statistics. Various revisions were suggested by my two excellent teachers at the University of Minnesota, Professor Harold Deutsch and Professor William Wright, by my two kind colleagues at the University of Missouri, Professor David Pinkney and Professor Roderick McGrew, by Professor Gerhard L. Weinberg, and by Professor Raul Hilberg. My wife, Luella S. Allen, lent a critical ear and much moral support. While I acknowledge their separate kindnesses gratefully and affirm the collective nature of whatever insights this work may possess, the actual formulation and therefore the responsibility for any defects rests with myself alone.

Small towns the world over have two aspects in common: little privacy and much gossip. Before I ever began my research I came to the conclusion that not only should the names of informants and other principal characters be kept secret but the actual name of the town would have to be disguised. Consequently anyone who looks on a map or in an encyclopedia for "Thalburg" will not find it. This precaution was also part of a promise which I made to the city fathers and to all those interviewed. Scholars who want to

*Available from University Microfilms, Inc., Ann Arbor, Michigan, No. 63-1188.

pursue the matter will find the identity of the town plus a list and identification of sources on file at the History Department of the University of Minnesota.

There is a descriptive list of persons interviewed appended for reference. In addition, each person interviewed will be described in a note on the page where he first appears. No person from Thalburg mentioned in this study has been given his true name. Inventing so many names taxes the imagination; should any reader find his name in these pages I hope he will understand that it is pure coincidence.

W.S.A.
Columbia, Missouri
1965

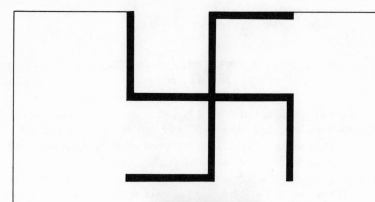

PREFACE TO THE REVISED EDITION

When my publisher first suggested that I revise this book in time to mark the fiftieth anniversary of Hitler's seizure of power in Germany, I had some doubts. It seemed to me that as it stood the book had worn well: reviewers had been very positive about it, none of its major interpretations had been seriously questioned, and its methodology was accepted as valid and emulated by numerous scholars. Most satisfying to me, as a teacher, was that the book proved useful for undergraduate courses. In fact it has become, over the past seventeen years, the most widely assigned book in German History classes in America, largely, I think, because students feel unintimidated by the prospect of trying to understand one town rather than an entire nation. What may appear impossibly complex as a problem involving sixty million people seems more comprehensible in a small community, even if most of the same elements of complexity are there—or so many American students have felt. In short, I accepted the wisdom of the old adage: "If it isn't broken, don't fix it."

Also, I doubted that I could find enough new information to justify a revision. Not that new things have not become known about the rise of Nazism in general, but the whole point of a microcosmic study is to limit it to what can be established about a particular confined locality. And so, while it is valid to use the insights developed from other studies, it would not be proper to borrow their information. Much comparable data has come from other local studies since 1965, so that it might be instructive to discuss the various findings from different German towns. But we all seem to have reached the same major conclusions. An exhaustive analysis of the fine shadings produced by microcosmic research on Nazism would make a good review article for a scholarly journal but probably not an interesting book for the general reader.

The publication in 1971 of an extremely instructive regional study of the Nazi organization directly above that which I had analyzed* made me want

---

*Jeremy Noakes, *The Nazi Party in Lower Saxony: 1921–1933* (Oxford University Press, 1971). Noakes wrote (p. 1) that his investigation was stimulated by the hope of answering questions I had raised but was not in a position to answer, primarily those concerning the extent of local vs. higher initiative in the Nazi movement. His book answered many questions but not, I believe, that one. Since he concentrated on the regional Nazi organization and had no intensive knowledge of the underlying locales, he neglected the bottom end of a bipolar relationship (as I had previously neglected the upper end). I hope that now, with both sets of sources under scrutiny, I have answered that key question more adequately. But clearly I could not have attempted this without the benefit of his pioneering and meticulous work, to which I am thus heavily indebted.

to meld its findings with mine, but to do this adequately I would have needed new information at my level to match its data. Since I was convinced that I had exhausted all the available documentary records at the time of my original research and since no new discoveries had been announced in the interim, I did not believe that there was any new material. (What was to happen constitutes, therefore, a cautionary tale for historical researchers.)

Nevertheless I took the occasion of a research trip to Germany in 1979 to investigate whether there was any new data on the rise of Nazism in Northeim (the town that was the subject of my original study). I went through the governmental and Party records at the Federal Archives in Koblenz, the Prussian Privy State Archives in Berlin-Dahlem, and the Berlin Document Center. In each depository I found a few interesting but minor bits of information. What I really needed were the actual files of the Nazi Party of Northeim and those, I had been told long ago, were burned at the collapse of the Third Reich.

However, as other scholars had long since discovered, the records of the Nazi district to which Northeim belonged, *Gau* South Hanover-Brunswick, were largely intact. In the Nazi Party's organizational structure Germany was divided into some thirty-five districts, each called a *Gau*. Each *Gauleiter,* or Nazi district leader, was responsible for the Local Groups within his region and thus I hoped to find correspondence between Local Group Northeim and the *Gauleitung* of South Hanover-Brunswick. If there were any such letters, they would be in the State Archives of Lower Saxony, in Hanover.

In Hanover the archivist rapidly detailed the files where I might find letters between Northeim and its *Gauleitung* and then said he also had some other documents from Northeim that might interest me. They had never been cataloged, had never even been assigned archival numbers, had never been seen by other researchers, and would fill about eight large wash baskets. This new material turned out to be carbon copies of the correspondence of the Nazi Party of Local Group Northeim, 1929–1938! There were also other items reaching into the early 1940s including about a thousand "Evaluations of the Political Reliability of Individual Persons" from Northeim, with an archivist's penciled notation on the cover: "Not very interesting." All this had been transferred to the *Gau* archives during World War II, had been more or less buried as being inconsequential, and had thus escaped the fate of the originals of Northeim's Nazi records at the end of the war. Clearly this was the material that would not only justify but would require a revision of *The Nazi Seizure of Power.*

Analysis of these documents showed that most of them confirmed rather than contradicted my original conclusions. But they also supplied extensive additional data: on the inner workings of the Nazi Party in the town, on its financing and propaganda techniques, on the control methods it used to exercise power over the townspeople during the Third Reich, on the extent of the assistance and direction given to the local Nazis by the Party's regional and national offices. There was enough material on the early history of Nazism in Northeim (1922–1929), and on the period 1935–1945, so that I could add several new sections to the book and could also extend its parameters to cover the town's whole experience of Nazism—from the beginning to the end.

Some of this material has already enabled me to contribute to the debate over theories about the nature of Hitler's regime.* Other data is valuable mainly for the specific details it provides about the day-to-day doings of the Nazis. It should help students understand that the rise of the Nazis to power, with all that that implies and led to, was not some mysterious plague that could creep up again with little warning. Analyzed in detail, the Nazi victory is quite explicable as a consequence of clever (but comprehensible) techniques under conditions that were terribly conducive to their success (but which are also avoidable). Knowing how it happened once can arm us all against letting something similar happen again—which was what led me to write this book in the first place.

Readers familiar with the first edition will find one other major difference in this revision. In the first edition I tried to protect the privacy of the townspeople by referring to their city pseudononymously as "Thalburg." Reviewers in America and England (who undoubtedly identified the actual town easily enough, as any specialist in German History could) respected my attempt. But the West German magazine *Der Spiegel* "exposed the secret" shortly after the German translation appeared,** and for good measure also identified most of the individuals mentioned in my book. So there is no longer any reason not to use the name of Northeim and, since many of the persons mentioned in the first edition have since died, I have used their real names, too. Others, to whom I promised anonymity and who were not listed in the *Spiegel* article, will continue to be identified by pseudonyms (see Appendix A). Additionally, I have integrated my original sources, with full identification, into the footnotes for the use of future researchers.

The research for this revised edition was materially aided by a fellow-

---

*See "Totalitarianism: The Concept and the Reality" in Ernest A. Menze, ed., *Totalitarianism Reconsidered* (National University Publications, Port Washington, N.Y., 1981), pp. 97–108, parts of which I have also incorporated into this book.
**"Unsere kleine Stadt," *Der Spiegel*/49, Nov. 28, 1966, pp. 59ff.

ship from the National Endowment for the Humanities. In addition to restating my gratitude to those who gave me critical advice when I was writing the first edition, I would like to thank two scholars whose ideas have stimulated me very much in the years since then: Professor Henry Ashby Turner of Yale and Dr. Timothy W. Mason of Oxford. I also want to thank Karen for clarifying my sometimes turbid prose and Will Davison for being so patient.

W.S.A.
Buffalo, New York
1983

PART ONE

THE DEATH OF DEMOC- RACY

1922 TO JANUARY 1933

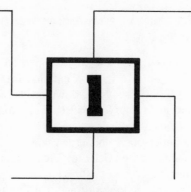

THE
SETTING

Drink and Eat
Forget not God
Protect your Honor
No one will ask more of you than that.

**Medieval Inscription
on a Northeim House**

If you open an atlas to the map of Central Europe and put your thumb down on the center of prewar Germany, the chances are good that you will land on Northeim, a town in the former Kingdom of Hanover. In the days of the Weimar Republic it was still a small town, with a population of about ten thousand. There were close to a thousand towns of this size in Germany then; about one of every seven Germans lived in them.[1]

In 1930 Northeim was the kind of town that English tourists were fond of discovering: provincial and off the beaten track, semimedieval, set in quiet and pleasant surroundings. It nestled against one of the many low, wooded foothills that frame the valley of the Leine River. Since the valley was only a few miles wide and very flat, a person standing in the slanting fields above Northeim could see across to the hills on the other side; it gave the town a sense of being snug, enclosed, protected from the outer world. The placid Leine River was joined at Northeim by a smaller river, the Ruhme, which had carved out a narrow valley immediately north of the town. The confluence of the rivers and their valleys created the town, for from the days of the Hanseatic traders this place had been a minor east-west, north-south junction point. From the hills above the town in 1930 you could see the main railroad line stretching up and down the Leine River Valley toward Munich or Hamburg, just touching against the perimeter of Northeim, and the spur-line swinging around the city walls to follow the Ruhme Valley toward Berlin.[2]

There actually were walls around part of the town. They enclosed the medieval inner core of Northeim. Here, within an oval about six hundred yards long, was a neat but imprecise jumble of half-timbered houses with steep red-tiled roofs along winding cobblestone streets. One street that ran through the town was three lanes wide (and therefore called "Broad Street"): the main commercial avenue with shops in every house. In the middle of the town was a large square, used for the weekly produce market and also suitable for open-air mass meetings. The only other clear areas within the walls were a small War Memorial on one side of Broad Street, a small space in front of the Town Hall, and another in front of the great sixteenth-century Lutheran church. The rest of the inner town was filled with narrow streets, with houses built to the very edges, jammed side by side, the front of each decorated with timbered beams of various geometric patterns, the upper stories marked by irregular, small-paned windows, the whole surmounted by steep roofs in a skyline diversified by angular gables and chimneys. There

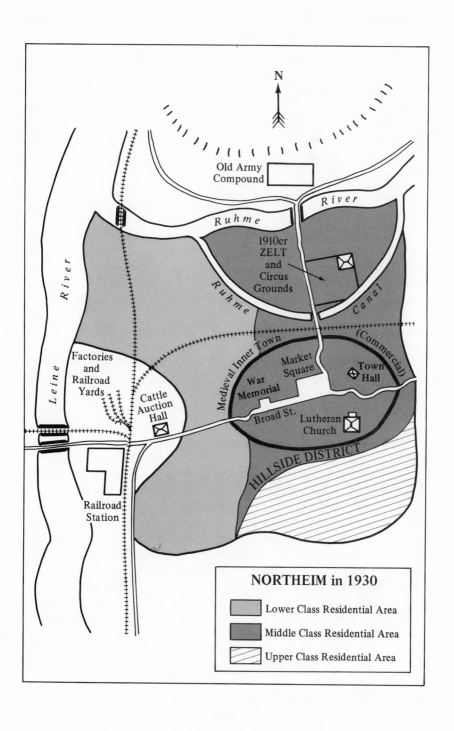

N

Old Army
Compound

River

Ruhme

Ruhme

1910er
ZELT
and
Circus
Grounds

Canal

Leine

River

Factories
and
Railroad
Yards

Cattle
Auction
Hall

Medieval Inner Town

(Commercial)

War
Memorial

Market
Square

Town
Hall

Broad St.

Lutheran
Church

HILLSIDE DISTRICT

Railroad
Station

NORTHEIM in 1930

Lower Class Residential Area

Middle Class Residential Area

Upper Class Residential Area

were over five hundred houses in the old part of Northeim; almost half of the townspeople lived there.[3]

Outside the medieval oval were various residential areas, built mainly in the period from 1870 to 1914. The most desirable district was on the hillside above the old town. There one found large, one-family dwellings, schools, broad asphalt streets, spacious lawns, shade trees, and shrubbery. From these houses there was a good view of town and valley and the summer breezes kept this area cooler than the rest of Northeim. Here dwelt the town's upper class.

On the other side of the medieval section, across the spur-line of the railroad, was the Ruhme Canal, dug in the Middle Ages to power a grain mill. This narrow strip of water created an island closed off by the Ruhme River. There were apartment houses, small dwellings, and a large circus grounds on it. At one corner of the circus grounds was a large meeting hall, called the *1910er Zelt,* suitable for dances, festivals, and mass meetings. A bridge, called the "Long Bridge," spanned the Ruhme River. On the other side lay a former Army compound backed up against foothills. In 1930 the compound housed a variety of state houses, including the employment office, a factory, emergency low-rent dwellings, and a youth hostel.[4]

On the side of the town toward the Leine River were nondescript residential dwellings, a few industrial plants and a sugar beet refinery whose ugly smokestacks spoiled the skyline, and the railroad station with extensive yards and maintenance buildings.

Thus around the old inner city were three areas where the town had expanded: up the hill and toward each of the two rivers, one district for the rich and two for the lower classes. But the center and essence of Northeim remained the old medieval city surrounded by the slowly crumbling walls.

The history of the town, like its physical setting, showed an interplay between isolation and involvement. Northeim was founded in the time of Charlemagne, but from then to the thirteenth century it was little more than a blockhouse, a monastery, and an appended village. In those early days Northeim enjoyed some moments of national eminence, for one of its counts was a military leader strong enough to do battle with the Holy Roman Emperor himself, though with disastrous results to his own family's fortunes.

The future of the town lay in more prosaic areas of endeavor. Beginning in the twelfth century merchants settled before the monastery walls, and it was under their leadership that Northeim was granted a city charter by the Guelph Dukes in 1252. In subsequent years the town grew rapidly. A town wall was built with battlements, towers, and moat; immigration swelled the population; the Ruhme Canal was dug; and Northeim joined the Hanseatic

League. By the fifteenth century the town was almost completely independent of the Guelph Dukes and even coined its own money. This was the
period of Northeim's flowering. An ancient engraving shows it to be one of
the richer and larger cities of that era.

The period of medieval splendor and independence for Northeim came
to an end with the Thirty Years War. The town had become Lutheran during
the Reformation, and when it was ordered to open its gates to the Catholic
Army under Tilly, the city council refused. A bitter two-year siege followed. Within Northeim there was an intense factional fight. The upper classes
favored surrender while the lower classes chose to resist the Catholic Army.
In 1627 the peace party turned the town over to General Tilly, who punished
Northeim severely for its former resistance.

Northeim emerged from the Thirty Years War small and weak: "The
shadow of its former strength."[5] It had been occupied by both sides, belea-
guered, plundered, and burned. In 1648 over three hundred houses were empty
and only about seven hundred inhabitants were left in the town. The Duke
had revoked its rights, stripped away all vestiges of independence, and placed
a permanent garrison in the town to intimidate the burghers.

Recovery came very slowly; it was not until the time of the French Revolution that Northeim regained the number of inhabitants it had had in the
fourteenth century—about 2,500. Though the merchants still predominated,
economically and politically, the town had become only a local market center, exchanging handicraft products for agricultural ones.[6] It was not until
1817 that the first house was built outside the city walls. The mainline railroad was built through Northeim in 1857, and ten years later the east-west
line through the mountains turned the town into an important traffic point.
Now government offices began to find it a convenient location. The former
Kingdom of Hanover was incorporated into Prussia, bringing new uniforms
to the garrison troops and laying the basis for more rapid development. By
the 1870s the town had acquired a variety of technical academies and college preparatory schools. In 1886 it was named a county capitol. Railroad
maintenance shops were built and several small factories were founded. The
town acquired a working class who brought with them the new doctrines of
Karl Marx. Owing to the influx of teachers, artisans, government officials,
and railroad personnel, a Catholic church could be opened in Northeim. Those
thin iron rails had brought the outer world with them.

The last vestige of medieval ways ended in 1900 when a sewage system
was introduced. Prior to that, Northeim had cleaned its streets by opening
the upper moat every Saturday. The waters would flow down the slight in-
cline, coursing over the cobblestones toward the Ruhme Canal, and house-

wives or maids would follow with their brush-brooms. The new sewage system was expensive, but the Germany of Kaiser Wilhelm II was prosperous and required symbols of prosperity. In Northeim a fountain was built on the Market Square with a copper statue of the ancient Count of Northeim, at a cost of 9,000 marks. The War Memorial, built to commemorate those Northeimers who had fallen in the short war between Prussia and Hanover in 1866, was now crowned with a bronze "Germania."

Both of these symbols of present affluence and past military glory were soon to be lost, though, and many more names were to be added to the War Memorial. When World War I erupted, the statues were melted down to help supply Germany's need for metal. In return, the central government provided the town with an Army school for noncommissioned officers, with a permanent compound located across the "Long Bridge." Two hundred and fifty-three Northeimers gave their lives to defend the Reich.

Yet despite these efforts, and for reasons mysterious to many Northeimers, the war was lost, and with it also a whole way of life, for in the wake of defeat came a revolution led by the working class which overthrew the Kaiser and established a democratic republic in Germany. In Northeim the revolution of 1918 was accomplished peacefully, since the troops negotiated directly with the officers. The following year, however, the local workers-and-soldiers soviet forced the commander of the garrison to resign, and in November 1920, the Army withdrew from the town completely.[7]

There were Northeimers who refused to accept the new state of affairs; the town soon became a relatively strong center for the violently rightist organization, *Jung deutsche Orden*. In 1922, shortly after nationalistic terrorists assassinated the Republic's Foreign Minister, Walther Rathenau, the *Jung deutsche Orden* decided to stage a nationalistic drama (Kleist's *Hermannschlacht*) in Northeim. Socialists from Northeim and neighboring areas determined to stop the play. In response, nationalist-minded farmers flocked to Northeim and a column of students from a nearby university also marched on the town. When they met they fought wildly, using cobblestones and beer bottles as weapons. The police were roughly handled before the town was restored to order, and practically every shop window on Broad Street was broken in the mêlée.[8]

As in the Thirty Years War the town was rent by strife and inner cleavage. An indication of Northeim's political division, even in the settled middle years of the Weimar Republic, comes from election statistics. In the presidential election of 1925, the Socialist-Catholic candidate received 2,080 votes; Hindenburg (running for the Rightists) got 3,375 votes; the only other candidate, a Communist, polled 19 votes.[9]

THE SETTING

Despite its Grimm's Fairy Tales appearance and apparent remoteness, Northeim contained all the conflicting loyalties and tensions of Weimar Germany. Within a few years, and under special circumstances, the town would experience the death agony of German democracy. Inside a whirlwind there is no escape from devastation.

THE ANATOMY
OF THE TOWN

*"Then," said I, "suppose we should
imagine we see a city in the making;
we might see its justice, too, in
the making, and the injustice?"*

**Socrates, in
Plato's** *Republic*

Even such a small and apparently integrated community as Northeim has its elements of strain and disintegration. In normal times these may balance; in times of stress they may pull the community apart. A demagogue may exploit them, driving wedges into existing social gaps.

Northeim was a remarkably complex community for its size and some of its sociological and economic features facilitated the growth of Nazism in the years after the onslaught of the depression, and also promoted the eventual ease with which the Nazis introduced dictatorial reorganization.

There were political divisions between Left and Right; there were class lines between worker and bourgeois; there were occupational lines between the stable and the insecure; there were areas of segregation between the relative newcomers and the old families; there were religious and social divisions. There were also areas of common interest, such as city government; and instruments of cohesion, such as schools, clubs, and interest groups; and there were primary loyalty groups—from families to circles of close friends.

Despite its antiquity, Northeim was essentially a product of the nineteenth century. In 1871 the town had 4,700 inhabitants; by 1930 it reached exactly 10,000. Half the increase came from an increased birthrate, but the other half came from immigration. In the late 1930s, the composition of Northeim was estimated as follows, counting back two generations:[1]

Born in Northeim	25 percent
From rural Northeim County	26 percent
From the rest of Hanover	34 percent
From all other parts of Germany	15 percent

The rural hinterland, with its strongly traditionalistic prejudices, had made a considerable impression on the town. But more important was the natural division between these newcomers and those whose families were Northeimers running back for several generations. Most of the "old Northeimers" lived in the inner town. A list compiled in 1932 of the most common family names in Northeim shows how interwoven these families were. Excluding the usual "Muellers," "Meyers," and "Schmidts," one finds 109 names, each of which was shared by five to ten families. Some twenty-five names were each shared by ten or more families. Three particularly localized names were shared respectively by twenty-two, nineteen, and eighteen families each.[2] The "old Northeimers" knew each other quite well since most of them had become related by marriage down through the centuries. There was thought to be neither special fellowship nor common political outlook among them, though they might present a common front against "outsiders."[3]

The whole area where Northeim was situated has a reputation for being what Germans call *stur:* stubborn and reserved, as New Englanders are said to be. One man who first came to Northeim in 1930 found that it took him two years to get to know anyone well and to be accepted in social circles, even though he was fairly extroverted and held a job of high prestige.[4]

If Northeimers were divided as to origin, they were united in religion. Despite changes wrought by the nineteenth-century influx, 86 percent of the townspeople were Lutheran, only 6 percent Catholic, and the rest consisted of various sects and those of no faith. This was substantially the same proportion that existed at the turn of the century and that was to be found in Northeim County. In 1930 there were only 120 Jews in Northeim, approximately the same percentage as the national average for urban areas.[5]

In occupation, Northeim looked upon itself as a city of civil servants: about one-third of its seven thousand adults were in the public employ, most working for the railroad. An additional fifth were widows or pensioners, so that close to half the townspeople had fixed incomes. One out of every seven persons was a higher civil servant. Stability and dependence on the state ran high, a factor that was to have considerable effect on the town's experience with the Third Reich.[6]

The large proportion of civil servants conditioned the town's economic structure. There was little industry, and what there was depended either on the rural hinterland or the railroad. The government offices brought farmers to town and Northeim's merchants and artisans supplied them with goods. As long as farmers prospered and as long as the government kept its offices in Northeim the town could expect to maintain economic equilibrium. Furthermore, the cost of living was low in Northeim: in 1931, per capita expenditures for staples were 25 percent less than the national average.[7] Many Northeimers kept pigs or other animals and many had small vegetable gardens. Barring catastrophe, Northeim was economically secure.

In 1930 the depression had just begun and its economic effects were scarcely noticed in Northeim. The number of motor vehicles in the town increased by about 15 percent between the summer of 1929 and the summer of 1930. Savings deposits in the City Savings Bank rose by almost a half-million marks in 1930, and the number of accounts was increased by about five hundred. In that bank alone there were close to 3,600 savings accounts with an average of 537 marks per account. The average per capita savings in Northeim was 20 percent greater than the average for all Prussia.[8] Northeim was at the top of its class of cities in new dwellings constructed for 1930. Alarmists might note that there were 329 registered unemployed at the beginning of 1930, but that was less than the average in Northeim's governmental subdistrict as a whole.[9]

If the town seemed sound even in the face of depression it was because there was so little industry. A sugar beet refinery, a dairy products plant, a grain mill, a brewery, two sawmills, and a cannery made up the industries dependent on the rich land of the Leine Valley. In addition, there was a construction firm, two brick factories, a road building company, a cigar manufacturing plant, a paper sack factory, and a tiny cement works. None of these were large undertakings. At a moment when all were operating at once they could employ about 1,125 people. But between one-third and one-half of the work force depended on seasonal employment; when the sugar beet factory shut down in December of each year, for example, almost three hundred people were thrown out of work. Over three hundred more depended upon construction, and an equal number, employed by the cigar factory and the cannery, were women. Industry was the weakest factor in Northeim's economy, but it was also the smallest factor.

The rural-connected industries, the many governmental offices, and the good road and railroad connections all drew farmers to Northeim and made the town a center for retail trade. In 1930 there were about a hundred shops with perhaps five hundred employees. The largest was a dry-goods store employing about thirty people. Most were small family shops, with very moderate incomes, passed on from father to son.

The artisan shops were also family businesses. In 1930 one ironworker celebrated the 300th anniversary of the founding of his smithy; he was the tenth generation of his family to serve the town.[10] It was a rare artisan who could not trace his shop back at least three generations. Northeim's artisans were organized in "guilds," which were mere shadows of their medieval precursors, being essentially professional societies. There were seventeen guilds in 1930, representing about 150 small shops.

The artisans and retail traders dominated the commercial life of the town, although there were also several credit institutions: branches of three national banks, a local bank owned by a Jew named Müller, a local stock bank, a County Savings Bank, and the City Savings Bank.

Most of Northeim's middle class consisted of government civil servants. The list of government offices in Northeim in 1930 was extensive, the most important being the County Prefecture which administered the eighty towns and villages of Northeim County for the Prussian government. The Reich and State governments maintained nine other offices in Northeim such as the post office, district court, employment office, etc., which employed about four hundred persons and served several counties. But the government service with the largest number of employees was the railroad, with its switchyards, maintenance shops, tie-dip, and bus system. Altogether, the railroad station gave work to about a thousand people and was the dominant economic force in the town.

The city itself maintained a considerable bureaucracy. In addition to the customary functions such as police and fire departments, street cleaning, and garbage disposal, it produced gas, electricity, and water for the town and maintained a construction office and a hospital. It owned numerous nongovernmental enterprises such as a slaughterhouse, an icehouse, a cemetery, and a brewery. These were money-making enterprises and they tended to spawn others. The city owned considerable forest land in the hills above the town and so maintained a forest administration, which ran a gravel pit that then led to a small cement-making plant. The welfare office not only supplied payments to the disabled, the poor, and the unemployed, but also operated two small old-age homes, a soup kitchen, and emergency low-rent housing units for those who would otherwise be shelterless. Also under control by municipal authorities was the local Health Insurance Office which, since its director happened to be a Social Democrat, was known as the ''red'' Health Insurance Office.[11]

In this way the city added over two hundred civil servants, not counting the seasonally recruited casual laborers. There were so many employees of central and local government that they formed their own political party for local elections, the Civil Servants party, which held the balance of power in the City Council. Not all were of the middle class, though a civil servant of full rank was well paid and occupied an enviable position in German society. A worker, on the other hand, even if employed by the government, was viewed by others and by himself as a proletarian. The railroad workers formed the core of the Socialist vote in Northeim and the bulk of the city workers were also Social Democrats.

Class structure, though strongly affected by income, is really contingent on an attitude of mind. Every year the city published an address book, and from the titles individuals gave themselves, one can make the following calculation:[12]

Lower class   37 percent
(unskilled and semiskilled workers)

Lower middle class   32 percent
(skilled workers, white-collar workers,
farmers, and pensioners)
Upper middle class   27 percent
(craft masters, civil servants, and busi-
nessmen)
Upper class   4 percent
(businessmen, self-employed, and profes-
sionals)

Though this is a very rough approximation it leads to the conclusion that Northeim had an exceedingly strong *petite bourgeoisie:* the raw material from which Hitler forged his movement. The relatively even distribution does not mean that great differences in income were nonexistent. One laborer at the city gas works with over fifteen years' seniority earned 1,500 marks a year in 1932.[13] A man in the medical profession had an annual income of 9,600 marks that same year.[14] When a worker with a good job saw a rather ordinary professional man earning six times as much as he did, he was bound to reaffirm whatever concepts of class struggle the Social Democratic party might have instilled in him.

In Northeim, as in most other places in the Germany of the Weimar Republic, the working class formed a definite community, almost a subculture. Workers had their own social clubs, economic organizations, and their own party: the Social Democratic party *(Sozialdemokratische Partei Deutschlands).* The SPD's organization was complex. It consisted of a number of different groups, all nominally independent of one another, but all facets of the working class and all actually working together. A list of the leaders of the various organizations showed so many duplications that for all practical purposes one composite committee could have been made of about fifteen persons, which would have included the key officers of all the groups. It would have included union secretaries (especially of the railroad workers' union), chairmen of sport societies, the workers' first-aid society, workers' choral groups, workers' shooting societies, and the like. There were officers of the "Common Good Construction Club" and the "Householders Consumers' Cooperative," the latter with a membership of 1,275 families and gross annual sales of a third of a million marks.[15] The former built low-rent housing; with 128 members it did over 600,000 marks worth of business in the depression year of 1932.[16] Then there were the direct adjuncts to the SPD: the youth group ("Young Socialist Workers"), the children's group ("Red Falcons"), the Women's Auxiliary, and proliferating committees of all kinds. There was the *Reichsbanner*, a paramilitary corps for the defense of the Republic, which though theoretically open to all, was actually staffed and peopled almost exclusively by Socialists. From the Infants' Aid Society to the Workers' Funeral Savings Association, the SPD permeated and unified the working class of Northeim.

Class consciousness was not the only unifying bond, for the SPD also provided a common ideology—essentially, commitment to democracy. This, plus overlapping leadership, made it possible for the SPD's minor solar system to revolve smoothly. Each organization had its own needs and aspirations, however, so that cooperation necessitated compromise and adjustment. Since the nineteenth century, when it was founded, Northeim's SPD had not only provided excellent practical training for democracy; it had become a way of life to the working class of the town.

For Northeimers who were neither workers nor Socialists, the real social cohesion was supplied by clubs. There is a proverb: "Two Germans, a discussion; three Germans, a club." This was almost true of Northeim where, in 1930, there were no fewer than 161 separate clubs, an average of about one for every sixty persons in town. There were twenty-one sport clubs, forty-seven with an economic or occupational function, twenty-three religious or charitable societies, twenty-five veterans' or patriotic associations, and forty-five special interest and hobby groups. With hardly an exception, they followed the town's class lines. Of the two soccer clubs, one was middle class and one was composed mainly of workers.[17] Of the gymnastic clubs, two were middle class and one was worker. In the economic or occupational associations the class line was even clearer and occasionally became political. The thousand-member Railroad Club, with a social as well as an occupational function, was SPD-oriented. The County Farmers' League and the County Artisans' League, on the other hand, both sponsored Rightist speakers and eventually gave open backing to the Nazis and the Nationalist party, respectively.[18] Most were not so openly political, however, and one economic club deriving from medieval customs even cut across class lines.

Traditionally, Northeimers who owned houses within the walls had certain privileges, such as free wood to repair their timber beams or a small amount of free beer from the brewery in compensation for the loss of private brewing rights. In the revolutionary atmosphere of the early twenties, which seemed to threaten these privileges, the house owners formed the "Club for the Defense of Old Northeim Privileges" and took legal action to maintain and extend their rights. In 1930, for example, they used old documents to win a case for a free chimney cleaning once a year. Without political or class orientation, this was another instance of cohesion among the "old

Northeimers'' who intermarried and stuck together, at least against the outside world.[19]

There was a bewildering array of militaristic and nationalistic organizations in Northeim. This was not unusual for the area and the times, as comparison with neighboring towns shows. Many of the militaristic societies were affiliated with a specific branch of the armed services, such as the "Society of Former Reserve Ninety-Firsters" or the "Cavalry Association." Others were general, such as the "Warriors League," or else derived from specific experiences, such as the "League of the War Wounded." There were also nationalistic societies such as the "Association for Germandom in Foreign Lands," or youth groups such as the "Schill Free-Band."[20] When one adds to this list the organizations that were adjuncts to the German Nationalist party or the Nazis, such as the "Steel Helmet" and the "Queen Luise Society," or the "National Socialist Women's Club" and the "Hitler Youth," one can see to what extent Rightist organizations dominated the social life of Northeim's middle classes.

All of these organizations had considerable membership. The smallest ("Society of Former Artillerists") had thirty members. The "Warriors League" had over four hundred in 1930, and the twenty-three others ranged between.[21] Their activities included speeches, parades, and social gatherings, and were marked by orgies of nationalism. On occasion they joined for a "nonpartisan" political effort; in 1930, for example, they petitioned the Prussian Minister of Education to ban *All Quiet on the Western Front* from school libraries.[22]

Spectacles were a definite part of the military clubs' activities. Three or four times a year one of the veterans' organizations could be counted on for a parade with bands, uniforms, and participation by all the other organizations. All gave service to the nationalist cause, and a few even came to espouse the Nationalist party, and later the Nazis, publicly. Taken as a whole, the nationalistic and veterans' clubs formed an important social element in the town. Their "stag evenings," dances, and theatrical presentations kept them in the public eye. They were primarily responsible for whipping up patriotic fervor and keeping militarism popular and vital in Northeim.

The most clearly social group of clubs in Northeim were the special interest and hobby groups. Despite their specific purpose they functioned essentially as occasions for social gatherings, and consequently followed class lines. Choral societies are a case in point. Northeim had eight such clubs: seven middle class and one worker, the "Northeim People's Choir." The upper-class club was clearly the "Song Stave." In the words of a nonmember, it was "really a social club composed of the better elements."[23] A former member of the "Song Stave," who admitted that he joined for professional reasons rather than from a love of singing, described its members as "directors, professional men, and entrepreneurs of larger enterprises."[24]

The size of these singing clubs varied from sixty-five to twenty-five; close to four hundred Northeimers belonged to one or another in 1930. They met frequently to practice, with beer afterward to cool the throat. Five or six times a year wives were brought to a concert, and occasionally the club traveled to a regional singing festival. Only the "People's Choir" had a political orientation; it performed at Republican festivals and Social Democratic gatherings.

Another vehicle for good fellowship and social intercourse was the "shooting society," a relic of Northeim's medieval past. In those days all burghers had been mustered through their guilds to man the city walls. An annual shooting festival kept these part-time soldiers effective. When the old guilds were dissolved, five shooting societies took their place. In 1930 they held regular practice sessions, and their three-day shooting festival with parties, dances, prizes, and parades was the social event of the year. One member described the class structure: "The 'Gun Club of 1910' was for the broad masses; the 'Hunters' were mostly middle class; the 'Free-hand Shooters' were the upper 10 percent."[25]

While these were strictly apolitical, many of the most innocent clubs became infused with nationalism. Thus the "Gardeners' Club" gave a garden-products show in 1930 at which the speaker attacked foreign competition: "It must be hammered into every German: Eat German fruit! Eat German vegetables! Buy German flowers!"[26]

Whatever social cohesion was not provided by the various formal clubs of Northeim came from two informal types of social gatherings. One was the *Stammtisch;* the other could be called the "beer club." The *Stammtisch* was a group of men who ate lunch together on a specified day every week at the same restaurant around the same table (hence the name). They were closed and definite groups, some lasting the lifetime of the members, all marked by close friendship and free discussion. The "beer clubs" were similar; they consisted of regular meetings at some tavern for talk, beer, and possibly card playing. Given the town's political division, one result of these "beer clubs" was that taverns tended to become politically segregated; a Socialist was not welcome in a Nazi tavern, or vice versa. The "beer clubs" involved mainly lower-class people, while the *Stammtische* were generally middle and upper class in composition. Together, these groups were the most common and closest social organizations in the town. Mutual trust was a prerequisite for their flourishing.

The many clubs and societies cemented individual citizens together. Without them Northeim would have been an amorphous society. Yet few of them cut across class lines.

The institution which most clearly embraced the various divisions of the town was the public school system, a part of Northeim's remarkable educational facilities. There were three public primary schools with 1,200 pupils, arranged so that children could also secure religious orientation. *Bürgerschule I* was Lutheran, the *Katholische Volksschule* served Catholic children, and *Bürgerschule II* was nondenominational. Each school had its own Advisory Council, elected by the pupils' parents. By prior discussion with Social Democratic leaders, working-class parents were assured representation on these councils.

The secondary system involved a boys' *Gymnasium* and a girls' *Lyzeum,* both of which had college preparatory curricula and charged tuition. Together they enrolled about five hundred pupils, half of whom were from Northeim. Most of these students were from the middle classes and most were strongly nationalistic.[27] For children who wanted vocational training there was a Business School with over three hundred pupils, mainly apprentices from artisan shops; a Merchants' Vocational School with fifty-five pupils, maintained by the Northeim Merchants' Association; an Agricultural School which served several countries and was controlled by the Farmers' League, and a Home Economics School which was financed by the County Prefecture and graduated twenty-five girls a year.

These various schools minimized some of Northeim's provincialism. Their teachers, according to a former newspaper reporter from the town, "controlled, shaped, and directed the intellectual and spiritual life of Northeim."[28] But teachers also depended on the government for their income and position, with the City Council and the Provincial Ministry of Education dividing the functions of a school board.

Northeim possessed other cultural facilities, though much depended on private groups such as the Lecture Society or the Museum Society. The town sponsored a city band which gave weekly concerts on the Market Square and joined in public festivals. There was a public library with over two thousand volumes, but it was not much used. Workers preferred their own library at the Union Hall. There were two motion picture theaters and, for a while, a local operetta company.

The most important cultural institutions were the three daily newspapers. The oldest was the *Göttingen-Grubenhagensche Zeitung,*[29] founded in 1831 as the town's first newspaper. According to its editor-publisher it "put itself completely at the service of the National German."[30] In point of fact it was an organ of the German Nationalist party, and its editor was on the right wing of that party. Bias found its way into every article and, in addition, it was often a day or two late with the news. It had a small but stable readership of about six hundred subscribers in Northeim and probably considerably more in the county. The GGZ made a definite attempt to appeal to the farming community.

At the other end of the political spectrum was the *Göttinger Volksblatt*. Though published in a neighboring town, it carried enough local news to compete with other Northeim newspapers. It was an organ of the Social Democratic party and made no pretense of neutrality. More than any other newspaper (except the Nazis') it was a scandal sheet, full of scathing attacks and red ink. About two thousand Northeimers read it. Also printed on the *Volksblatt* press was the weekly pep sheet of the *Reichsbanner*, called the *Northeimer Echo*, with a circulation of three thousand for Northeim County.[31]

The local Nazi publication began in the summer of 1931 and was called *Hört! Hört!* ("Hear! Hear!"). It consisted of two pages, letter-sized, mimeographed on both sides, and used brown paper (the hue evoking scatological speculations from the *Volksblatt*). Its stated purpose was to provide news of Nazi doings and to "combat the lies of the reds which the bourgeois press seems incapable of doing."[32] It was slanderous, constantly under libel action, and periodically suppressed.

The third major newspaper was the *Northeimer Neueste Nachrichten*, founded in 1909 and primarily a business venture. Its editor was a member of the People's party and national news was often taken from the People's Party Press Service; but it tried to remain as moderate as possible so as to retain a large circulation. It was always first with the news, generally accurate, and gave the most complete coverage. Its circulation in Northeim was close to four thousand. Middle-class calm and efficiency were the outstanding characteristics of the NNN; its chief editorial concern was that city government operate in a businesslike manner.[33]

The government of Northeim was in the tradition of efficient city government that in Germany dates from the reforms of Baron vom Stein. The constitution represented a cross between aldermanic and city manager governments. Voters elected a twenty-member council which then elected four senators. All laws were passed by the council, which also formed committees to supervise administration.

A senator was chairman of each committee and could intervene in the administration of its area of competence (for example: police, brewery, welfare department). The formal work of running the city rested upon the mayor, or *Bürgermeister*, a professional administrator. He was chosen by the senators for a term of twelve years and could expect to be continually reelected, the fixed tenure protecting him from the council's extreme powers. As a professional the mayor was expected to be impartial and was paid an exceedingly high salary. In 1930 Northeim's mayor had been in office for twenty-seven years.

This carefully balanced system plus the long tradition of self-administration resulted in a smoothly functioning city government for Northeim. It was with sober pleasure that the NNN reported, in August of 1930, that while in fifty-six German towns with a comparable population there was an average public debt of 7.74 marks per person, Northeim had no deficit at all. The budget for 1930 balanced at 1,385,000 marks.[34]

Indeed, when one surveys Northeim's economic, cultural, and governmental structure the impression is that of a balanced, self-contained entity. The one way in which the town was not integrated harmoniously was socially, where there were distinct class divisions in almost every sphere of activity. This disunifying factor grew to be politically important, and under the impact of steadily declining economic conditions, politics became radicalized. In the years after 1930 this flaw split Northeim wide open, led to bloody riots and the deterioration of the democratic mood, and culminated in the Nazi seizure of power. The Nazi answer to the problem of class division was to abolish its expression by force.

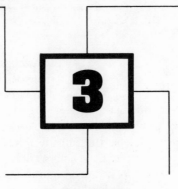

ENTER
THE NAZIS

SPRING-
SUMMER
1930

*The evil which you fear becomes
a certainty by what you do.*

Goethe, *Egmont*

Mass extremism, intolerance, a desperate desire for radical change—all factors that make a stable democracy impossible—are difficult to evoke. When the community is secure, political agitators find themselves ranting in near-empty halls. It takes a haunting fear, a sudden awareness of hitherto unsuspected dangers, to fill the halls with audiences who see the agitator as their deliverer.

The average Northeimer looked upon himself as a *Spiessbürger:* calm, oblivious to great problems, satisfied with life, pleasantly filled with good food, modest hopes, and a sense of simple order. On Sunday afternoon Northeimers are wont to take family walks in the neat and ancient woods above the town, slowly strolling along the well-kept paths to points where they can look across the Leine Valley to the misty western hills. And then, Sunday dinner digested, they return to the snug town with its medieval houses. The setting gives a sense of continuity to life; the old ways can be trusted; stability is both desirable and inherent.

But in 1930 new fear began to haunt the town, for the world depression was spreading and cascading quotations on the New York Stock Exchange affected even his remote valley in central Germany. It was the depression, or more accurately, the fear of its continued effects, that contributed most heavily to the radicalization of Northeim's people. This was not because the town was deeply hurt by the depression. The only group directly affected were the workers; they were the ones who lost their jobs, stood idle on the corners, and existed on the dole. Yet, paradoxically, the workers remained steadfast in support of the status quo while the middle class, only marginally hurt by the economic constriction, turned to revolution.[1]

The economic structure of Northeim kept the middle classes from being hard pressed. Merchants lost only a small portion of their trade. Artisans, apart from those in the building trades, found plenty of work. Civil servants had their wages reduced, but none of them lost their jobs, and if their pay was less, prices also dropped so that their relative position was not weakened. Total savings increased slightly during the years of the depression in Northeim, and the number of savings accounts also rose. By 1933 over half of the adult population of Northeim had savings accounts, and almost half of these were for substantial amounts: from 100 to 500 marks.[2]

But the depression engendered fear. Businessmen whose own enterprises were doing well worried about the general situation in Germany. Banks that had no difficulty collecting on loans began to reduce all credit allotments.[3] Only the workers were directly hurt, but the rest of the townspeople, haunted by the tense faces of the unemployed, asked themselves, "Am I next?'' ''When will it end?'' Because there were no clear answers desperation grew.

In this situation, the voice of the Nazi began to be heard. Northeim had previously ignored the NSDAP* (as it had ignored other extremist groups after the *Jung deutsche Orden* battle which was largely the work of outsiders); in the national elections of 1928 the total vote for the Nazi party in Northeim was 123, or 2⅓ percent of the votes. In the local elections of November 1929, the Nazis received only 213 votes out of 5,133 cast.[4] Before the depression they were an insignificant fringe in Northeim.

In fact, at the beginning of 1929 there were just five members of the Nazi party in Northeim, too few to even constitute a ''Local Group,'' the lowest formal unit of the NSDAP.[5] That there were any at all was largely a carry-over from the turbulent events immediately following World War I.

In Northeim, as elsewhere in Germany during the first years of the Weimar Republic, there were people who could not accept Germany's defeat, revolution, and the resultant democracy. Often they opposed modernity altogether: liberalism, cosmopolitan culture, an open society, a competitive industrialized economy, a powerful labor movement. Collectively, such people constituted a radical right wing, but they had no effective organization to express their often inchoate and even contradictory antipathies. More precisely, they had too many organizations—none of them effective—as radical Rightist grouplets sprang up all over the country.[6] Among the many was the infant Nazi party, which grew rapidly in southern Germany but hardly at all in the North, including the area around Northeim.

To the north of the town, in the industrial city of Hanover, a former policeman who had developed anti-Semitic paranoia during World War I while stationed in Poland, joined the NSDAP after discovering that Hitler's ideas about Jews paralleled his own. An unemployed businessman, who had sat out World War I in neutral Spain and compensated by becoming a supernationalist after returning to Hanover, joined the ex-policeman in founding a Nazi Local Group in the summer of 1921.[7] To the south of Northeim, in the university city of Göttingen, a group of students led by one who later became a medical quack, also formed a branch of the party in February 1922.[8] The Göttingen recruits were attracted by another aspect of Nazism: its vague ideology of a new society in which patriotic solidarity would supplant Germany's rigid class distinctions. Both branches were strongly middle class and both were suffused with missionary zeal. In 1921 and 1922, Nazi preachers from Göttingen and Hanover traveled up and down the railroad along the

---

Nationalsozialistische deutsche Arbeiterpartei (National Socialist German Workers' Party).

Leine River in quest of converts. Some stopped in Northeim where, though they found no recruits yet, they convinced at least a few of the townspeople that among the various right wing radicals of Germany, the Nazis were the most *Konsequent* (i.e., willing to pursue their ideas to the extremes).

Perhaps the Nazi missionaries from neighboring towns might have gradually gained a permanent beachhead in Northeim by preachments alone. Those were the years of Germany's hyper-inflation, national humiliation, and incessant political upheavals. As it happened, however, a series of local crises forced events.

By 1922 both ends of the German political spectrum were stretching toward the Weimar Republic's first great crisis. Militants of the radical Right were given open support by the traditional conservatives. The Göttingen Nazis got both funds and publicity from the previously sedate Rightists of their city; the Hanoverians were financed by the old Pan German League.[9] More significantly, the formerly respectable Right also applauded the series of political assassinations of Republican leaders carried out by underground *Freikorps* terrorists. The conservatives were becoming identified with the fanatics.

Meanwhile, the extreme Left, led by the Communists, fostered a series of uprisings that proved abortive but also terrifying to the middle classes. Formerly moderate workers also grew frantic as they watched the gains of their 1918 revolution peter out and saw the leaders of their republic murdered by right wing thugs. Many of the early Hanoverian Nazis were intimidated by the hostility of workers; others became more fanatical.[10]

The culmination of this dialectic came in June 1922, when *Freikorps* gunmen murdered the Republic's Foreign Minister, Walther Rathenau. Workers in the entire region around Northeim exploded in fury. To them the fine ideological gradations among the multiform segments of Germany's Right were irrelevant; the whole right wing seemed like allies of the assassins. In the wake of the Rathenau murder an anti-Rightist lynch atmosphere pervaded the Leine Valley. In Northeim's neighboring towns conservative leaders were beaten, threatened with death, or had to flee to police stations for safety. In Northeim itself, as mentioned in Chapter 1, there was a pitched battle in the streets between workers from Einbeck and students from Göttingen.[11] After this battle some Nazis began carrying pistols.[12] To a few Northeimers the moment had come for the most extreme option and they organized the town's first "Local Group" of the Nazi Party—chartered in autumn 1922.

It was a tiny group of young, middle-class men. The leader who emerged for Northeim, Ernst Girmann, was typical of these first Nazis. He was an "outsider," as they were reckoned in the town, since his father (a hardware store owner) had been born in Helmstedt. Girmann was born in Northeim in 1896, had been educated through the upper forms of the *Gymnasium*, but instead of going to the university had received business training. His real education was the war. He served in the Germany army from age nineteen to twenty-two (1915–1918) in France, Galicia, and Russia; he was shot in the chest and earned the Iron Cross, second class; he ended the war as a First Lieutenant. In 1919 he joined the *Jung deutsche Orden* and the Nationalist Party. He had been baptized a Lutheran but later described himself as "Gottgläubig" (believer in a deity). A contemporary photograph of him shows a cleft chin, thin lips, snapping grey eyes, an embittered but very youthful face (he was twenty-six when he joined the Nazi Party and became its leader in Northeim). His dark blonde hair was parted exactly in the middle and slicked down firmly. He held membership card number 4,294.[13]

Along with Ernst Girmann, his brother Karl (three years older) joined; so did the bookseller Wilhelm Spannaus (aged thirty-five), the accountant Heinrich Böhme (aged nineteen), and a small businessman, Rudolf Ernst (aged thirty-three). They recruited one or two others, but there are no records of them.[14]

No sooner had this first Nazi organization in Northeim been founded than the entire party was banned in Prussia, on November 17, 1922. Of course the Nazis continued to meet secretly, but they could no longer collect dues or agitate publicly and so the party began to atrophy. Then came Hitler's "Beer Hall Putsch" of November 1923, and the Nazi Party was outlawed all over Germany. Hitler went to prison, the party split into competing factions that spent more time on dreary doctrinal disputes than on recruitment, and worst of all, Germany recovered from its many-leveled crises. The inflation was stopped, political stability returned, and the stable period of the Weimar Republic (1924–1929) began. The Nazi leader from Hanover spoke twice in Northeim in June 1924, first on "Duty as the Basis of the Nazi Program" and then on "Germany Bartered by the Experts' Testimony," but there was little response.[15] One of the faction leaders (from the National Socialist Liberation Party) visited Northeim in June 1924, and reported that the Nazis there were firmly under the control of Ernst Giermann (sic).[16]

Hitler was released from prison and, in February 1925, refounded the Nazi Party. Local Group Northeim reconstituted itself shortly thereafter, with 12 members.[17] But the initial enthusiasm had no momentum behind it and the party stagnated—not just in Northeim but over the entire region. On January 1, 1926, *Gau* Hanover had 1,860 members; a year later the total was 2,441. Throughout 1927 and 1928 the membership in the *Gau* was virtually stagnant, hovering around 2,500. An average of about 100 a month joined, but about half as many also quit: in November 1927, 34 joined and 65 quit. But what it came down to was a no-growth situation, or at least nothing to fulfill the millenialist hopes on which Nazism fed.[18]

In Northeim it was the same story. As the years went by, the membership dropped off. Girmann was no longer the Local Group's leader; his place was taken by another small businessman, Rudolf Ernst, who was on his way to a nervous breakdown, bankruptcy, and removal fron Northeim to Berlin (in 1930). A contemporary photograph shows him to have been fat, bull-necked, bald, and round-headed, with a prominent Hitler moustache.[19] He was not energetic. For most Northeimers the Nazi Party hardly existed; one nodded away their occasional emergence as a remnant from the turbulent past, which was what the NSDAP really was in those placid middle years of the Weimar Republic.

Yet behind the façade of calm prosperity, conditions were developing that would stimulate a regrowth of Nazism in the region. Even before the depression the middle classes, especially small farmers, felt themselves to be in trouble; increased taxes, tight credit, competition from a modernizing economy, and the perception that the government was in the hands of the Left were components of this sentiment.[20] Moreover, the traditional middle-class political parties were in disarray.[21] For the area around Northeim, the largest pool of conservative voters adrift from their traditional party were the "Guelphs," the *Deutsch-Hannoversche Partei*. This was a states' rights, possibly separatist, movement left over from the nineteenth century. Its supporters were mainly "the rural middle class—peasantry, shopkeepers, and artisans—particularly in the oldest Guelph lands" (which included the area around Northeim).[22] Amazingly, they had considerable support: approximately one quarter of all the voters in Hanover Province voted, in 1924, for a Guelph-sponsored referendum to separate the former Kingdom of Hanover from Prussia, and as late as the 1928 Reichstag elections the Guelphs got 20.4 percent of the vote in Northeim County (in 1930 they were to get 5.3 percent there; in 1932, 0.5 percent).[23] The "Guelph" party was becoming irrelevant but the resentments of its followers remained. Their votes were up for grabs. So, at least in the villages around Northeim, by 1929 a potential Nazi constituency was appearing.

Moreover, the Nazis had used the fallow years to tune up their propaganda machine and redirect it toward the middle classes who were now becoming ripe for a radical mobilization.[24] Through most of the period 1925–1928, Nazi propaganda had been mainly aimed toward the working class and was predominantly anti-Semitic in content. That had helped recruit the extant pool of bigots, but as the membership figures showed, there just were not enough of them for a real mass movement. The 1928 national election was the first real test, since 1924, of these tactics. In Lower Saxony the NSDAP got 4.5 percent of the vote. In Northeim County they got 4.2 percent; in the town itself, 2.3 percent.[25]

Recruitment and voting figures might reflect a variety of factors, but attendance at meetings and responses to speeches were fairly precise tests of the effectiveness of the meetings' subjects and the speakers' themes. The Nazis kept accurate records of attendance, since admission was by ticket only. The level of enthusiasm produced by the speaker could be gauged from the proceeds of the collection taken up at every meeting. After the 1928 election campaign *Gau* South Hanover-Brunswick found profits from meetings to be meager. One local leader reported on five speeches given in his town. Four lost money, while the fifth earned a profit (excess over the cost of advertisement, hall rental, and speaker's fee) of just two marks, fifty *Pfennig*. The writer requested a subsidy of RM 113.22, which the *Gau* found abhorrent since it expected to receive money from the Local Groups, not give any to them.[26]

So there were strong reasons for the Nazis to change the targets and content of their propaganda by the end of 1928, and on Hitler's orders they did. Though there would be a continued attempt to win workers, and though anti-Semitism would not be abandoned, the new emphasis would be on groups that *were* responding to Nazism and on propaganda themes that produced results. That meant primarily appeals to small businessmen, shop clerks, and the rural population, with a primary content of anti-Marxism plus attacks on the economic policies of the Weimar Republic.[27]

As for the methods to be used, there was also a change in emphasis rather than fundamental technique. Speeches at meetings continued to serve as the main vehicle of propaganda; getting the speakers before audiences involved methods developed over the whole period since 1925. The *Gau* provided a stable of potential speakers, each with a specific set of topics, and arranged their arrival at the localities on dates requested by local leaders. The local leaders picked a speaker and topic according to their estimation of what would produce a good turnout. Since the local leaders also had to pay for the speaker's transportation, food and lodging, and his fee of RM 10–20 per speech, they were deeply interested in getting a speech that would be a success. The profit or loss from the meeting was the bottom line on what was successful and what was not.

This sytem provided local flexibility and constant feedback so that even as doctrinaire a movement as Nazism became very adaptable. Almost everything depended on able and energetic local leaders. The *Gauleitung* maintained its "speakers' bureau" but otherwise gave no direct help to the local organizations apart from an occasional conference for leaders. What the *Gau* did primarily was regulate internal organization in the Local Groups and districts and collect money from them.[28] But the entire system of propaganda by speeches at meetings became highly sensitized to what worked well: it was self-correcting.

Thus, beginning in 1929, the Nazi Party started to grow in *Gau* South Hanover-Brunswick, thanks to a newly receptive constituency, a propaganda emphasis directed toward them, and a system of propaganda delivery finetuned in adversity. In the first six months of 1929 the *Gau* lost only 184 members while recruiting 1,166, for a net gain of 982—a substantial increase in their total membership (from 2,268 to 3,250).[29]

In Northeim the Nazi revitalization began in the summer of 1929. On May 22 four of the members decided to take the initiative rather than wait for the torpid Rudolf Ernst to accomplish something. They engaged a Nazi from Göttingen to speak every Monday at semiprivate meetings to be held in Northeim's Cattle Auction Hall, whose sympathetic owner offered them a rent-free room. Ernst would preside, but the effort would be a collective one. Beginning on May 27 and continuing to July 29, eight "discussion evenings" were held. At first only fifteen people came, then attendance rose to an average of forty, of whom fifteen applied for party membership while even more took out subscriptions to the *Gau*'s newspaper. The topics of these meetings were basic Nazi ideology:

May 27:	"Why Do We Call Ourselves the National Socialist German Workers Party?"
June 3:	"The Program of the Nazi Party, Part One."
June 10:	"The Program of the Nazi Party, Part Two."
June 17:	"Breaking the Serfdom of Interest."
July 1:	"Supranational Powers."
July 8:	"The Protocols of the Wise Men of Zion."
July 22:	"Nazism, Liberalism, and Marxism."
July 29:	"The Young Plan."

The day after the last meeting Rudolf Ernst sent a jubilant report to the *Gauleiter*, requesting propaganda pamphlets, application forms, and (since Northeim now had more than the minimum fifteen members) reinstatement as a Local Group.[30] Nazism had come alive in Northeim, three months before the stock market crash on Wall Street, on the initiative of its own members.

With two exceptions (a locomotive engineer and a chauffeur) all the new members were small businessmen or artisans, and most of them were in their twenties.[31] They brought to the party their middle-class skills and their youthful energies. The *Gauleitung* was bombarded with requests for speakers and for information as to how to operate a Local Group of the Nazi Party. It responded with the speakers on hand, though it explained that schedules were tight because of increased demand, and promised a folder containing instructions and the forms needed for a Local Group. The speakers came but the folder never arrived until late autumn, by which time the Local Group was flourishing on its own.[32] By October, Local Group Northeim had recruited twenty-four more members and lost only a few who moved or stopped paying dues.[33] In November there were sixteen more applicants and the Local Group was frantically asking for propaganda placards. (The *Gau* had none and told them to improvise.)[34] A public meeting held on November 11 ("The Marxist Betrayal of German Workers") drew 120 people who paid RM 22.90 to the collection. Six of the audience decided to join the Nazi Party.[35] But by this time also, the Local Group's files were in disorder and its members were beseeching the *Gauleitung* for some permanent person to serve as a speaker and organizer.[36] The porcine Rudolf Ernst was clearly in over his head and the others all had full-time jobs.

Thus by the end of 1929 things had changed quite a bit since the previous December, when there were only five Nazis and no meetings. Even so, Northeim's Nazi movement was still less than a mass organization; though 120 people at a meeting was something, it was clearly not an accomplishment that would bring Hitler's ideas before the rest of Northeim, which was still largely ignoring the Nazis.

This was not for want of Nazi effort, for the new Local Group was relentlessly thrusting Nazi ideas before the public. In the early months of 1930 the NSDAP held a meeting roughly every other week, advertised with such titles as "The German Worker as Interest-Slave of Big International Capitalists" or "Saving the Middle Class in the National Socialist State." Like most Nazi meetings, each of these featured an outside speaker, promised a discussion after the speech, and charged an admission price of about thirty *Pfennig* (the price of two loaves of bread). The meetings were held in the Northeim Cattle Auction Hall which, according to the Socialists, simply exemplified the Nazi slogan "To Each His Own." But the hall was well suited to Nazi needs; it was cheap to rent, emphasized Nazi connections with the rural population, and was small enough so that a poor turnout would not be conspicuous. This was important, because, in these early months of 1930, attendance at the meetings continued to be relatively small.[37]

But the meetings were not without effect, for they created an image of

the Nazis. To the average Northeimer the Nazis appeared vigorous, dedicated, and young. A housewife put it clearly:

> The ranks of the NSDAP were filled with young people. Those se-
> rious people who joined did so because they were for social justice,
> or opposed to unemployment. There was a feeling of restless en-
> ergy about the Nazis. You constantly saw the swastika painted on
> the sidewalks or found them littered by pamphlets put out by the
> Nazis. I was drawn by the feeling of strength about the party, even
> though there was much in it which was highly questionable.[38]

Thus one function of the constant Nazi activity was to demonstrate to Northeimers that Nazis really believed in the ideas they preached. But who were
the Nazis? Most Northeimers would have found it difficult to answer this
question in 1930, for individual Nazis were rarely in the public eye. Yet
most Northeimers could have identified at least one member of Hitler's party:
Wilhelm Spannaus, the owner of a bookstore on Broad Street. Wilhelm
Spannaus came from an old Northeim family; his father owned the town's
first bookstore. One of his brothers fought and died in World War I and another became a university professor. Wilhelm became a high school teacher
in a German school in South America, where he lived from 1912 to 1921,
when he returned to take over the bookstore:

> It was shortly after the *Spartakus* uprising in the Rhineland; prac-
> tically every windowpane was broken on the train in which I re-
> entered Germany, and the inflation was reaching fantastic propor-
> tions.
>   I had left Germany at the height of the power and glory of the
> Wilhelmine Reich. I came back to find the Fatherland in shambles,
> under a Socialist republic.[39]

In his years abroad Spannaus had come to admire the writings of Houston
Stewart Chamberlain. Shortly before the Munich *Putsch* he heard, at a literary tea, that Chamberlain had said of Hitler, "There's a man I could follow with my eyes shut," and consequently Spannaus joined the NSDAP as
the first member in Northeim.

Wilhelm Spannaus was exceedingly well liked in Northeim. A spare,
lively man, he was gentle and kindly, friendly to everyone yet thoughtful
and reserved enough to hold people's respect. His bookstore was the intellectual center of the town, for he was acquainted with many of the writers

and poets the town admired, and he was chairman of the Northeim Lecture Society. In addition, he was a prominent member of the Lutheran church. "Wilhelm Spannaus bears a heavy burden, for it was mainly his example that led many people to join the NSDAP," remarked one Northeimer. "People said, 'If he's in it, it must be all right.' "[40]

Most of the other local Nazis were simply unknown to Northeimers at that time. By January 1930, the Local Group had 58 members, but most of them were residents of villages near Northeim.[41] The rural area was the real locus of Nazi growth in these months: there were over 230 Nazi members in Northeim County in January 1930, who did not belong to the Local Group but who clamored for speakers.[42] Also the Local Group's membership was fluid. They were adding a score of members each month but losing half again as many for nonpayment of dues, changes of residence, etc.[43] Keeping track of all this was beyond the abilities of Local Group Leader Rudolf Ernst and his volunteer assistants. In response to frantic requests, the *Gau* finally supplied a Nazi "business director" for Northeim County in February 1930 (to whom Northeim's Nazis had to pay RM 100 per month), but he proved incompetent and by April he was fired.[44] Finally the Northeimers picked one of their own, Walter Steineck, whom the *Gauleiter* appointed "County Leader and Acting Local Group Leader" in May. Ernst Girmann stepped in as Steineck's assistant for Northeim and effectively ran the town's organization while Steineck concentrated on the more lucrative county.[45]

Walter Steineck was another "outsider" (born in Dortmund, in 1889). He had become a Nazi during the revival of Local Group Northeim in June 1929. He was a dealer in agricultural implements and consequently knew his way around the rural hinterland from sales trips. Thus he was well-suited to be County Leader and his business experience made him effective as an organizer of meetings, a wholesaler of Nazi propaganda materials, and a keeper of the membership rosters and dues records. Both the *Gau* and the Local Group were pleased with his work; additionally he had enough income from his business so that he was unpaid by the NSDAP.[46] On the other hand, people in Northeim hardly knew Steineck. They knew Girmann from his father's hardware store and they knew another local businessman who joined in 1930, Hermann Denzler. Denzler, then thirty years old, had a small dry goods store on Broad Street. He had served in a prestigious Guards Regiment in the last year of World War I, and shortly after becoming a Nazi he joined the Stormtroopers and became their leader for Northeim. He was later to become an SS Leader and ultimately joined the Gestapo.[47] He looked and acted like a bullyboy and was associated by Northeimers with Ernst Girmann, whose violent temperament also made the townspeople uncomfortable with him. They were of the type that Northeimers thought belonged to the fringes of the Nazi movement. But since Nazism had sprung up in the town overnight, most Northeimers initially had difficulty knowing who the real Nazis were. It was easiest to identify the movement with a serious person like Wilhelm Spannaus; everyone knew him.

What were the ideas that drew men like Wilhelm Spannaus into the Nazi movement? To most Northeimers the NSDAP was first and foremost an anti-Marxist party.[48] When a Northeimer thought of Marxism he was not likely to think of the Communists, who in 1928 had received only 28 of the 5,372 votes cast in the town. The "Marxist" party in Northeim was the Social Democratic party, the SPD, the Socialists. The Socialists were the dominant political force in Northeim. In the 1928 elections they cast almost 45 percent of the town's votes—more than the next three largest parties combined.

That the SPD was a non-revolutionary party (espousing, in fact, the status quo) and "Marxist" only in rhetoric probably did not matter to most of the town's burghers. The Socialists carried a red flag. They sang the *Internationale*. There had been laws against them in the days of Germany's glory. They were associated with the cataclysm of 1918. They represented the proletarians, the unwashed workers, the restive unemployed. They preached Marxism and class struggle. Their leaders who sat in the city council were cited by improbable occupations: "oiler," "union secretary," "track-walker." One never met them socially, yet there they were in the City Hall—touchy, aggressive, demanding. To oppose these radical apostles of equality was of paramount importance in a depression environment.

This was an element in middle-class thinking which the Nazis understood clearly. The Socialists, for their part, appreciated the Nazi threat very early. In March 1930 their militia organization, the *Reichsbanner,* passed a resolution at their Northeim County conference that called for "an energetic stand against . . . the ruffianly behavior of the NSDAP" and demanded action, "otherwise the comrades will turn to their own solutions."[49] A month later the *Reichsbanner* combined with the unions, the SPD, and the tiny Democratic party to sponsor a mammoth rally in opposition to the Nazis. Plans called for a series of parades, a demonstration on the Market Square, and a speech in the huge shooting hall, *1910er Zelt,* on the subject "Dictatorship or Democracy?" The affair was planned for April 27, a Sunday. This was what the Nazis were waiting for, and three days after the Socialists' announcement, Northeim's Local Group of the NSDAP advertised that they would hold a meeting on the same day with a parade led by a band, a speech on the Market Square, and a "Gigantic Meeting in the Cattle Auction Hall" featuring a Nazi Reichstag representative. Moroever, the Nazi program was geared to conflict directly with the SPD's; both parades were to start at one in the afternoon, both demonstrations on the Market Square were set for two o'clock.[50]

This confluence was too much for the police. Because of previous outbreaks of violence, Prussia had prohibited all open-air meetings and processions of a political character for a three-month period which had just ended on March 30, 1930.[51] In the week of the two announcements there had been two outbursts of violence in Northeim. In one, which occurred in front of a tavern on Broad Street, ten Nazis and Socialists had a short fight which sent one of the participants to the hospital in an ambulance. In the other fight, which took place in the woods above the town, eleven people were involved and one emerged with a broken nose.[52] In view of the tense situation the police forbade both April 27 meetings.

This provided the Nazis with another opening. In an advertisement emblazoned *"Trotz Verbot—Nicht Tot!"* ("Despite Prohibition—Not Dead!") they announced that their demonstration would be held as planned, but in a village about two miles from Northeim. To the meeting the Nazis brought over two thousand people, drawing on the entire district. Eight hundred Stormtroopers marched in what the GGZ called "a powerfully impressive recognition of Nazi ideas." After the event three truckloads of Stormtroopers passed through Northeim scattering leaflets.[53] By this demonstration of organizational agility the Nazis had not only blocked the Socialist meeting; they had dominated the press and "powerfully impressed" Northeimers with their size and determination. Their mood was so exultantly bellicose that at a County Council meeting the following day, they heckled the Socialist speaker to a point almost precipitating a brawl. The Nazi image was projecting itself upon Northeim. Perhaps for this reason, May Day of 1930 was celebrated in full strength. Workers from all areas, especially the railroad workers, were present for the march through town in closed ranks. There was much drinking, many speeches, and of course the sentimental singing of the *Internationale*.[54]

The second idea of Nazism that Northeimers recognized clearly in these early days was its claim to fervent patriotism and avid militarism. This was a foot in the door of respectability, as the number and nature of the town's nationalistic social organizations shows. The extent to which the people of Northeim accepted these values was demonstrated by the big event of May 1930—a visit to Northeim by Field Marshal von Mackensen. The occasion was the fortieth anniversary of the founding of the Northeimer "Militia and Reservist Club."

The Field Marshall arrived on the morning of May 17, by special train, and was greeted by about a thousand people at the Northeim station. A small girl presented him with flowers while the Northeim city band played a stirring march. After inspecting the local veterans' clubs, drawn up in uniform on the platform, the Field Marshal mounted a white horse and rode up Broad Street followed by the band and the clubs, including contingents from neighboring towns. Crowds lined his route, many houses were bedecked with the old Imperial colors, and roses were strewn in his path at the Market Square, where a rousing cheer welcomed him. His brusque speech on the importance of a strong army led to the general singing of *Deutschland über Alles*. Three days of parades and festivities followed.[55]

This spectacle could hardly be matched by the Nazis, who were still reveling in their triumph of April 27 over the Socialists. The day before the Field Marshal arrived the Nazis held another of their small meetings in the Cattle Auction Hall, entitled "What's Going on in Northeim? Confusing Newspaper Reports, Deliberate Errors, and the Forbidding of the Demonstration of April 27."[56] In the ensuing weeks of May and June the Nazis kept plugging away with meetings on unemployment, on the "Protocols of the Wise Men of Zion," and on youth in Germany.[57] But such meetings lacked the spark of controversy and the pageantry needed to impress the public.

In 1930 the Prussian Ministry of the Interior was trying a variety of expedients to limit the violence that was corroding German life. The main contributors to street fights were Hitler's Brownshirts, the SA.* The shirt was significant, for it emboldened its wearer and was a provocation to others. Hence, in 1930 the wearing of uniforms by political groups was prohibited in Prussia. This provided the Nazis with a new propaganda tool. In the last week of June the Northeim NSDAP again drew on neighboring areas to stage a protest march over the Prussian uniform prohibition. About four hundred SA men marched (all wearing white shirts instead of brown), accompanied by a fife-and-drum corps from a larger town about ten miles from Northeim. On the Market Square a vitriolic speech was given by a Nazi imported from Hamburg, featuring the slogan: "Heads Will Roll in the Sand." The rest of the afternoon was given over to speechmaking in the Cattle Auction Hall.[58]

This spurred the Socialists to counteraction. On June 26 the SPD sponsored a meeting in the spacious *1910er Zelt* on "The Crimes of the National Socialists." Over a thousand people heard what the NNN called "an objective and calm" analysis of Nazism. There were some catcalls but no violence, and when a Nazi attempted a rebuttal he was "easily dispatched by reference to his personal record," according to the NNN. The experience

---

Sturmabteilung, literally "Storm Section," commonly known as Stormtroopers.

must have cut the Nazis, for the following day they distributed one-page leaflets attacking the SPD's speaker.[59]

A second event growing out of the Nazi demonstration against the uniform prohibition shows how seriously the Socialists took the Nazi threat. The Deputy Chief of Police for Northeim was Senator Wilhelm Mahner, leader of the Rightist faction in the City Council. He had been present at the Market Square meeting where the Nazi speaker promised that "heads will roll in the sand." Northeim's Socialists thought that Senator Mahner should have had the police arrest the speaker for inciting to violence. Mahner's failure to act was taken as a sign that he was partial to Nazism. Consequently the *Reichsbanner* called a special public meeting at which it was determined to send a complaint to the Prussian Minister of the Interior and the Provincial Governor (both, providentially, Socialists). Mahner was then stripped of his police powers by the provincial authorities, and Senator Carl Querfurt, the leader of the SPD faction in the city council, was made Deputy Police Chief in his stead.[60]

About the same time, the *Volksblatt* began to report incidents which suggested that the Nazis were violent and vicious. For example, it reported that when a Nazi leader told some of his SA men, marching in the parade in Northeim that they looked like "a herd of sheep," bystanders who had laughed were threatened with assault. It later recounted that a Nazi from Northeim, while hitchhiking into town, showed the driver his revolver, fired two shots into the air, and then fled before the driver could call a policeman.[61] Thus even before the Reichstag election campaign of 1930, the political atmosphere in Northeim was tense and the lines were drawn between the Nazis and the Social Democrats.

The Socialists had long since evolved a method of electioneering; they had been fighting election campaigns in Northeim since the 1870s. The method was to make every effort to fuse the working class into a solid bloc by big, impressive demonstrations and meetings, and at the same time to give evidence to voters on the periphery that the SPD was solid, effective, and responsible. In August of 1930, when the campaign for the September Reichstag elections began, the SPD was favored by the coincidence that the opening of the campaign came about the time of the annual Constitution Day holiday, August 8. This was the chief festival of the Weimar Republic, with which the Social Democrats were so closely identified.

As early as June of 1930 the *Reichsbanner* announced that it would hold a torchlight parade and a dance in the *1910er Zelt* in support of the holiday. In addition they pressured other organizations to support Constitution Day by publicly excoriating clubs which refused to participate and promising "certificates of honor" to those who cooperated in the celebration. To assure a large crowd, teachers and pupils from the schools were required to attend. The torchlight parade involved over eight hundred torches and twenty-one clubs, including the Military Club and the Naval Society. In the words of the NNN, it was "the first really successful Constitution Day celebration in Northeim."[62]

The SPD was also active on the legislative front. By June 1930, there were 272 registered unemployed in Northeim, a matter of obvious concern to the Socialists, who therefore presented the City Council with petitions and concrete plans for a limited public works project. In August these efforts paid off when the council adopted the SPD's program and voted funds for the lengthening of a few streets, the construction of a playground, and the erection of two extra sets of emergency barracks for the "shelterless."[63] The SPD could now enter the election campaign counterposing constructive action to Nazi demagoguery.

This was important, for the Nazis, spurred by the election campaign, became increasingly active. On August 10 they held their first election meeting, with an outside speaker, on the subject: "Eleven Years Republic—Eleven Years Mass Misery." A week later there was a second Nazi meeting featuring a *Gauleiter* who spoke on: "Down to the Last Tax Penny." This drew such a large crowd that many had to be turned away from the Cattle Auction Hall. Five days later there was a meeting featuring a member of the Prussian Diet, with standing room only, and a week after that yet another.[64]

The Social Democrats held fewer campaign meetings but strove to make them more impressive. On August 24 the SPD staged a "County Party Festival" involving six hundred *Reichsbanner* men who converged in four columns upon the Market Square. After numerous speeches there was a second parade through Northeim with 1,200 participants and five bands. The parade wound up at a beer garden where there were speeches, songs, acrobatic acts, and, in the evening, a dance. Ten days later the SPD held a second mass rally in the *1910er Zelt*. Admission was only 20 *Pfennig* (unemployed free) and the hall was jammed. A series of speeches defended Social Democratic policies and attacked the Nazis, a few of whom were on hand to heckle.[65]

The efforts of other parties were far less strenuous. The German Nationalist party held only one meeting, a small one. The GGZ was their main campaigning instrument; in the last two weeks before the voting it ran at least five advertisements a day for Alfred Hugenberg and the DNVP.* By

---

Deutschnationale Volkspartei (German Nationalist People's Party).

election eve the paper was filled almost exclusively with Nationalist party propaganda. Page one, for example, was completely taken up with a picture of Hugenberg, a poem in honor of the party, and an appeal to vote DNVP. The People's party also made extensive use of the NNN for election advertisements, with at least one a day for the three weeks preceding the voting. The general line of the DVP* was "Order, law, morality, and unity," which left it free to attack both the SPD (for "causing the depression") and the Nazis (for "destructive radicalism"). This was also the theme of the DVP's one meeting during the campaign, at which the Nazis were condemned in astringent terms while the People's party was extolled as the carrier of the spirit of the late Gustav Stresemann** and the solid core of the middle class. It was well attended by a quiet crowd.[66] The only other election campaign meeting was held under the auspices of the *Staatspartei*, a reactionary successor to the defunct Democratic party. The speaker called for orderly, middle-class parliamentary rule, and for laws by which "Jews would be allowed citizenship only according to their character and accomplishments."[67] There was sparse attendance.

At the climax of the campaign there occurred an event which, though not directly related to the electioneering, must have aided the cause of nationalism, and thus probably the Nazis. In the last days of August the Seventeenth Infantry Regiment, one of the crack units of Germany's tiny *Reichswehr*, passed through Northeim on its way to fall maneuvers. One company was quartered in the town for a night and the regimental band gave a concert on the Market Square which drew a large crowd and much applause. Both newspapers gave considerable space to the event, and the NNN noted slyly that the soldiers got along well with the local girls. Many children were up with the troops at six the following morning to watch the regiment march out, band still playing.[68]

The last days of the campaign were hectic, with all parties pasting up posters and distributing leaflets. Inevitably, violence flared. Five days before the voting three Communists beat up a *Reichsbanner* man because he refused to accept a propaganda leaflet they were handing out. Shortly thereafter, another *Reichsbanner* man was beaten by two Nazi Stormtroopers. Feeling ran so high that it became necessary for the leaders to insist that *Reichsbanner* men not carry canes in their demonstration parades. The state

---

Deutsche Volkspartei (German People's Party).
**Stresemann, one of the few charismatic political leaders of the Weimar Republic, won the Nobel Prize for Peace and led the DVP until his death in October 1929.

authorities had also issued ordinances requiring all meetings to close by ten
o'clock and providing stiff penalties for anyone found with a knife or cane
on his person at a campaign meeting.[69]

On election eve the SPD held a final mass meeting in the *1910er Zelt*
with a direct appeal to its followers to vote Socialist and do away with the
"unsocial bourgeois-bloc cabinet." For their last meeting the Nazis appealed to the religious element in Northeim by bringing in a Lutheran minister as a speaker. The Cattle Auction Hall was overflowing and the speaker
assured his audience that Nazis were neither economic nor antireligious radicals.[70]

On Sunday, September 14, 1930, Northeimers cast their first ballots of
the depression period. The voting was extremely heavy: 6,235 people voted,
94 percent of those eligible. In Northeim as all over Germany the most amazing
result of the election was the meteoric rise of Nazi strength. In the Reichstag, Nazi representation went from 12 to 107 seats. The NSDAP in Northeim went from 123 votes (in 1928) to 1,742 votes, or 28 percent of the
electorate. Nazi gains did not come at the expense of the SPD (with 2,246
votes the Social Democrats actually gained slightly) or at the expense of the
People's party (which, with 788 votes, showed a net loss of only 46 compared to the 1928 elections). But 805 "new" votes were cast, and the various splinter parties lost over 1,000 votes; it was here that the Nazis gar-
nered support.[71] At least three-quarters of the new voters voted NSDAP; at
least half of the Nazi vote gain came from those who had previously voted
for another party. Votes were taken especially from the Nationalist party and
the *Staatspartei*. Since there were fewer than 350 newly qualified voters, the
Nazi gain had to come from those who were not especially young but had
either voted for another party in 1928 or had not bothered to vote at all.

Regardless of the origin of its votes, it was clear that the NSDAP had
increased its backing by fifteen-fold. Over one-quarter of the adult population of Northeim now placed its hopes with Adolf Hitler. The radicals, the
extremists, the advocates of dictatorship had arrived in force.

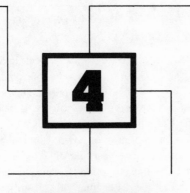

EXPLOITING VICTORY

AUTUMN–WINTER 1930–1931

*Democracies are most commonly
corrupted by the insolence of demagogues.*

Aristotle, *Politics*, Book V

Every week in September 1930, about six thousand men came to Northeim. They came from four counties to look for jobs or to receive their dole at the Northeim District Employment Office. The Employment Office was located in one of the barracks of the old Army compound north of town. The other barracks served as emergency housing for the most destitute citizens of Northeim—the "shelterless." The barracks of the compound formed a quadrangle, and it was within this small area that the bitter unemployed milled about while waiting their turn at the Employment Office windows. Inevitably there were jostlings, arguments, eruptions of the pent-up energy of idle men. Most of the jobless belonged to the SPD but there were enough Nazis and Communists to guarantee frequent fights. In the supercharged political atmosphere, the Army compound, with its daily influx of hungry and worried men, was a concrete example to Northeimers of what the deepening depression could bring.

Burghers who watched the unemployed pass through Northeim saw them as more than the symbol of economic catastrophe and potential social degradation. The misery of the jobless evoked suspicion and disgust more often than compassion. One teacher recalled primarily that "Masses of young men stood idle on corners and made a lot of noise, often insulting people who were passing by." A housewife had similar reactions: "There were great numbers of unemployed who just stood around—the bulk of them were just lazy and didn't want to work—theirs was a sad case."[1]

There were those who did look for work, though—for example at Northeim's sugar beet refinery, which needed an additional two hundred men each fall after the crop was in. In September 1930, over nine hundred applied for these jobs. The *Volksblatt* claimed that the refinery favored Nazi sympathizers because they were not organized in unions. It predicted gloomily that previous gains in wages and working conditions at the refinery would now be lost.[2] Even if wages were lower, the jobs were still desired, since they reestablished the worker's right to regular unemployment benefits. The maximum period a worker could receive these was one year—less depending on how long he had previously been employed. After the regular payments were exhausted, the jobless could draw "emergency" payments for an additional thirty-five weeks. After that the unemployed worker came under the care of the city Welfare Office, which ordinarily supported orphans, cripples, and the aged. There was no limit to the length of time a worker could stay on the Welfare Office rolls, as long as he had no other income.

Normal wages of a semiskilled worker were about 30 marks per week; regular unemployment pay was 15 marks per week, and "emergency" benefits were only slightly less. But the welfare dole was only 8.75 marks per week for a married man, and half as much for a single man. The process of moving downward through the grades was accelerated when it was decided in November 1930 that "emergency" payments would be made only to those who could "prove need." This dismal and elastic concept was the first of many expedients designed to ease the strains caused by unemployment on the state and local budgets. As for the jobless, a class structure had developed among them by autumn 1930, with those receiving regular unemployment compensation being the uneasy elite.[3]

Shopkeepers and other previously self-employed persons were excluded from the stages of degradation; if they lost their income they went directly on the welfare dole. In 1930, three of Northeim's artisan shops went bankrupt, two of them about the time of the September elections.[4] Though each was a marginal enterprise to begin with, every case must have caused reflection among the townspeople. The Artisans' League believed its members' troubles stemmed from illegal competition from unemployed journeymen. In November 1930, it ran advertisements beseeching Northeimers to contract immediately for any repair work they were planning, and to abstain from hiring illegal workers.[5]

The SPD, instead of commiserating with the burghers, exploited these bankruptcies. One of the September failures, a locksmith, happened to be a Nazi. The *Volksblatt* reveled in the gory details. According to its account, the locksmith's "property was in . . . a horrible situation. There were enormous and illegal debts." The final blow came when one of the locksmith's employees absconded with the remainder of the shop's money and also with a young lady. The *Volksblatt* described the whole event as "a good example of Nazi business methods."[6]

There were other ways in which the Socialists rubbed salt in the wounds of the middle class. At the time of the visit of the troops to Northeim, the army had advertised payments for quarters, but with few takers. The *Volksblatt* exposed this shortly after the September elections. It thought it strange that "the Rightists with big houses" did not offer their extra rooms to the soldiers, many of whom had to sleep in halls. It asked: "Where are the four hundred members of the Warriors' League? The four hundred men of the Militia and Reservists Club? And the countless hurrah-patriot clubs?"[7] Nor did the SPD hesitate to attack leading nationalists openly, to the extent of provoking feckless denials. This was the case with a Nationalist leader from Northeim County, Count von Strahlenheim, who wrote to the GGZ in September 1930 to say that he hired only a few foreign workers on his estate, that his pension was a small one which he deserved since he was wounded in the war, and that the SPD was responsible for high taxes and unemployment.[8] Nor did the touchiness of the Socialists themselves when attacked endear them to Northeimers. In 1930, for example, Senator Querfurt sent a mimeographed copy of the Uniform Prohibition Decree to all SA men in Northeim County and received a bitter reply from one Stormtrooper. Querfurt took it to court where it was found slanderous; he was awarded 50 marks.[9]

Thus many Northeimers felt there were good reasons to oppose the SPD, some obvious and rational, others stemming from general disquietude over the threatening economic situation. If the burghers wanted the Socialists cut down they could argue that they were simply restoring the traditional order. In Prussia, prior to 1918, towns like Northeim were run by a closed clique of wealthy people. The instrument of exclusion was the "three class" voting system by which those individuals who paid the highest taxes controlled the City Council. The revolution of 1918 swept away all monetary suffrage distinctions and introduced direct, equal, and secret balloting. It was this that suddenly enabled the SPD, with its mass backing, to have a dominant voice in the Northeim City Council for the first time in the town's history.[10]

The political vehicle used to combat the Socialists prior to the rise of Nazism was the Civic Association *(Bürgerliche Vereinigung).** If the bewildering variety of national parties had competed independently in local elections, the Socialists, with their solid block of votes, would have controlled the city governments completely. To prevent this, all those who stood to the right of center joined in support of a common list of candidates. But the Civic Association was more than a local political alliance; it was also an independent entity with its own officers, treasury, and division of candidates by occupation: artisans, retail merchants, etc. The cement of the organization was, nonetheless, antipathy to the SPD.[11]

The chairman of the Civic Association was Senator Mahner, owner of a small business and a member of the DNVP. He was staunchly Lutheran and unabashedly reactionary. From 1924 to 1929 the Civic Association had the largest representation on the Northeim City Council, which was divided among eight Civic Association councilmen, seven Social Democrats, and five from the Civil Servants party. In November 1929, the SPD increased its representation to nine while the other two parties each lost a seat. Had the Socialists won two more seats they would have had an absolute majority.

Bürgerlich is impossible to translate in one word, since it means "civic," "bourgeois," and "conservative" in German. Henceforth *Bürgerliche Vereinigung* will be rendered Civic Association, but the reader must bear in mind that the term also had the connotations of political and economic conservatism as well as social exclusiveness.

In the September 1930 Reichstag elections, Northeim's Social Democrats increased their vote slightly again. The leaders began to consider new areas of activity, but the choice they made refocused the antipathy of the town's middle classes. Due in October was the election of elders for Northeim's Lutheran church. Like the rest of the townspeople, nine-tenths of the Social Democrats were Lutherans. Yet they had hitherto been unrepresented on the Church Board and felt, moreover, that Northeim's ministers emphasized nationalism far too much. Hence the Socialists prepared a list of candidates for the Elders' election.

The burghers saw this as an intolerable challenge. The Civic Association called a meeting on October 23 where Senator Mahner attacked the SPD as antireligious. He demanded a heavy vote to defeat the "Marxists." Advertisements by the Civic Association and the Evangelical Men's Club charged that "For the first time, the anti-church SPD wants to drag the hate and agitation of partisan politics even into church. . . ."[12]

Most Socialists were embarrassed by this attack. In their own meeting, held shortly before the election, the speaker began by expressing his regrets that politics had entered the church, where it did not belong. He insisted, nonetheless, that since most Social Democrats were Lutherans, they had a right to representation. The sharpness of the campaign could have been avoided if the Rightists had been willing to make a compromise list of candidates with the SPD. He hoped that nothing like this would occur in the future.[13]

If the Socialists were embarrassed and the Rightists outraged, the Nazis were delighted, for this gave them a new chance to portray themselves as effective opponents of "Marxism." They had by no means been inactive since their election victory in mid-September. Ten days after the election they held a discussion evening and five days after that a member of the Reichstag was brought in for a speech. A few days later, there were two showings of the film "The Growth of National Socialism," each with a speaker afterward. Finally, on October 12, a meeting featured the chief candidate in the previous elections, now a member of the Reichstag. Thus in the month following the election, Northeim's Nazis held as many public functions as they had in the month preceding the election—a prime example of their tactics of perpetual campaigning.[14]

This incessant agitation was at least partly stimulated by directives from the Nazi *Gau* offices. On September 15 its propaganda division ordered the Local Groups to continue the election campaign that had ended the day before without any letup. Local Groups were required to hold at least one meeting per month or else submit a detailed explanation as to why they had not done so.[15]

The September election campaign taught Northeim's Nazis that their best drawing cards were religion and nationalism, preferably combined. This lesson was now put to work to exploit the middle-class uproar over the SPD's entry into the Church Elders' election. The day before the voting the NSDAP staged a rally featuring a Lutheran pastor who was also a Nazi member of the Reichstag. The announced topic was "Marxists as Murderers of the German *Volk* in the Pay of the Enemy." Confident of a mass audience, the Nazis rented the *1910er Zelt*, which could contain 1,200 people. Fifty *Pfennig* admission was charged, and since the meeting was aimed directly at the middle class, no reduction in price was offered to the unemployed.

Nazis expectations were fully justified; so many people came to the meeting that there was standing room only. The pastor's main topic was the nature of the NSDAP, which he likened to the old Imperial Army in that both represented the whole of the German people and not any specific group. Near the close of his speech he dwelt on the Elders' election in Northeim, which he said proved the SPD's tyrannical motives. He exhorted the audience to vote the "Non-Partisan" ticket.[16]

The following day, a Sunday, the elections were held. In earlier church elections only 17 percent of the Lutheran community had voted; this time about 60 percent voted. The heavy voting was aided by a Civic Association transportation service to bring voters to the polls. The SPD mustered only a quarter of its usual voting strength and its candidates were defeated by a margin of five to one. A solidly conservative set of Elders was elected.

Though they had not run candidates, the Nazis could be well satisfied. The campaign had exacerbated the burghers' repugnance for the SPD. The Nazis could claim a heavy contribution to the defeat of the Socialists through their meeting, which was also their first real mass meeting in Northeim. Best of all, the burghers had been taught that the SPD could be beaten. To rub in the lesson, the Stormtroopers thenceforth held a march through the town every Thursday and Sunday.

The remainder of 1930 was filled by the Nazis with frequent but fairly ordinary meetings, all held at the Cattle Auction Hall. On November 9 the Nazis commemorated those who had died in Hitler's abortive "Beer Hall" *Putsch* of 1923. Four days later there was a discussion evening and two days after that a speech on "The Echo in Foreign Lands of the September 14 Elections." Early in December a speech on economics emphasized Nazi ties to the lower middle class, and a week before Christmas another speech attacked the SPD. The year 1930 closed with a Nazi Christmas party for children and an "Evening of Entertainment" for the adults.[17]

Yet by the end of 1930 the higher offices of the Nazi party were gearing up for more extensive and more refined propaganda campaigns, fueled by the funds and the mass backing generated from their September election triumph. Regular monthly circulars from the *Gau* propaganda section were now supplying Local Groups with guidelines for coordinated activities, lists of available speakers (with topics), and whole catalogs of leaflets and pamphlets for a variety of specific needs. Slide shows and films could also be rented, including one "talkie." All these were to be ordered directly from the national headquarters in Munich, payment in advance.

Furthermore, the "speakers bureau" system was tightened up. Beginning Jan 1, 1931, no one could be an official speaker at a Nazi meeting without a special identification card issued by the *Gau,* and the card was issued only after the speaker had passed a test. Since those who passed could then earn the standard fee of seven marks per speech—good money in those depression years—plus transportation, meals, and lodging, many Nazis strove to obtain the official certification, and the *Gau* could be selective. Fewer than one-third of the applicants were certified. After that, of course, if they hoped to be asked to speak repeatedly, their future employment depended upon success on the circuit. Thus the Nazis' proven system of propaganda was being further honed. In addition, the list of printed propaganda was growing constantly, at reasonable prices. A four-page pamphlet cost a Local Group one *Pfennig,* quantity discounts available. The number of posters had increased to the point where the printer's catalog of them alone cost a Local Group one mark. Finally, the *Gau* propaganda section was supplying Local Groups with brief summaries of the latest arguments used by opposition parties, plus recommended counterarguments.[18]

Local Group Northeim by now had its own propaganda specialist: one member was responsible for collecting, digesting, and further disseminating the information sent down from the *Gau* propaganda section. In Northeim the Nazis expressed particular need for speakers and posters to combat the SPD, which was holding constant propaganda marches not just through Northeim, but through the surrounding villages, too.[19]

For the SPD there was work to be done beyond propaganda activity and forays into church politics. In October the SPD faction in the City Council proposed an extensive public works project to get the unemployed off the streets. The plan, sections of which were used by the Nazis after they came to power, involved improvements in Northeim's parks and streets. Its main feature was that it would provide much work and little expenditure for tools or materials. Only one measure of this ambitious program was passed—the widening of a forest path in the town-owned woods—but it was the first project to use unemployed workers exclusively.[20]

In the County Council, where the SPD held ten of the twenty-one seats and, thanks to a coalition with the two "Middle Party" delegates, controlled the council, the whole SPD program was voted. By October, 180,000 marks were allocated for works projects. But it was of no benefit since by December rising welfare costs from unemployment put the county so deeply in debt that nothing could be carried out.[21] In the two years to follow, the County Council was impotent because of financial weakness. Since the voting was predictable after the formation of the SPD coalition, the Council became a sounding board for the participating politicians. In December of 1930, for example, the right faction expostulated against the *Volksblatt* and in the ensuing debate Carl Querfurt attacked the Nazis so vehemently that the entire Rightist faction left the session in protest.[22] The possibility of increasing taxes was limited. The mere mention of this brought a protest meeting by the Civic Association in December 1930, which declared that higher taxes would be "unbearable." At this meeting Heinrich Voge, a Northeim teacher who was a Nazi, gave the Civic Association a long lecture establishing that the Treaty of Versailles was the root of Northeim's financial problems.[23]

The growing Nazi threat caused as much concern to the Social Democrats as the depression. On November 22, the *Reichsbanner* held a crowded meeting on the subject of Mussolini's Italy. The speaker compared German democracy to the Italian dictatorship, with direct allusions to the Nazi program. Many Northeimers sensed the danger. The *Reichsbanner,* which had numbered one hundred members before the September elections, reported that seventy new members had joined in the interim. A few weeks later, on a gray Sunday afternoon, the *Reichsbanner* held another meeting, this time on the Market Square. A parade with five flags and a fife-and-drum corps brought out a large audience. The speaker's theme was the Nazi slogan, "Heads Will Roll in the Sand." He declared that the *Reichsbanner* was ready to fight in defense of the Republic, but that it would not strike the first blow. Two days later, a members' meeting reported thirty-nine new *Reichsbanner* men in the past few weeks.[24] By the beginning of 1931, Northeim's *Reichsbanner* counted three hundred members, including fifty-six in the Youth Section.[25] Democracy would not go without a fight in Northeim.

Social Democratic determination did not deter Nazi intentions, nor did it lessen political tension, which rose sharply with the coming of the new year. New Year's Day, 1931, saw the first incident of violence. Three Nazis, apparently drunk, dragged Carl Querfurt's teenage son into the men's room of one of the town's hotels and beat him. Several *Reichsbanner* men rushed to the rescue and only the coolness of the hotel owner averted a general mêlée.[26] Also within the first week of 1931, the SPD held a mass rally to point up the Nazi threat. The *1910er Zelt* was filled to hear a Socialist Reichstag member insist that everything must be done to keep the Nazis from getting into the government. He predicted accurately: "If that bunch ever once gets in, democracy will be lost."[27]

Northeim's Nazis began 1931 with a Sunday afternoon meeting in the Cattle Auction Hall. It was similar to those held in early 1930. The speaker was from Hanover and the topic typical: "Enchained Justice—German Law in the Straitjacket of a Party-State?"[28] Such meetings had become unsatisfactory to Northeim's Nazis after their experience with mass audiences the previous year and in view of the SPD's recent rally. What was needed to fill halls was an appeal to nationalism. On January 16, 1931, the NNN reported excitedly: "The NSDAP has been able to get the well-known U-Boat Captain Hersing to come to Northeim for a speech. Hersing is the second most famous U-Boat hero of the World War and sank innumerable ships."[29] Nazi advertisements were exultant:

GERMAN PEOPLE AWAKEN!   ON TO NORTHEIM!
Sunday, January 25
at 3 P.M. in the *1910er Zelt* there will speak Party Comrades:
1. Corvette-Captain (Ret.) *Hersing*, commander of U-Boat 21.
2. The famous agrarian revolutionary *Blankenmeyer* (of Oldenburg).
    Expense-contribution: Advance sales 50 *Pfennig* at Spannaus's Bookstore; at the box office, 60 *Pfennig*.
FREE DISCUSSION!   OUT WITH THE MASSES!
NSDAP, *Ortsgruppe* Northeim.[30]

To add spice to the affair the Nazis told a leading figure of the Northeim SPD that he could have forty-five minutes' time to speak at the Nazi meeting and could bring *Reichsbanner* men with him if they paid 30 *Pfennig* admission. Before the meeting the SA from the whole of Northeim County marched through the town, with the *Reichsbanner* marching behind them. Ten minutes before the Nazi meeting began, 150 *Reichsbanner* men appeared at the *1910er Zelt*. Walter Steineck, the Nazi leader in charge of the Hersing meeting, was somewhat shocked by this and declared he would admit only twenty *Reichsbanner* men at 30 *Pfennig*—the rest would have to pay the full price. This touched off a heated argument during which an additional 150 *Reichsbanner* men materialized. The Nazis hurriedly got the police to close the doors, whereupon the Socialists repaired to the Market Square and held a counterdemonstration. When both meetings broke up, tempers were still high, and a brawl between the SA and *Reichsbanner* was only narrowly averted.[31]

In the two weeks that followed, two more battles almost broke out when *Reichsbanner* men tried to stop Nazi parades.[32] On February 8, the SPD held another mass rally featuring Professor Eric Noelting on the subject, "National Socialism: Its Beginning and Its End." Over a thousand republicans crowded the hall and heard an exact description of what Hitler intended to do: "Whoever wants to make a successful *Putsch* in Germany must also hold the power of the state in his hands. Therefore Hitler wants to get *into* the government, but never *out*."[33]

The Nazis were beginning to feel oppressed by Socialist militance. Shortly after the Noelting meeting, one Nazi tore the cockade off the hat of a *Jungbanner* member and was promptly knocked flat by nearby *Reichsbanner* men. There was also a rash of incidents at the Employment Office, the victims being Nazis from other places who had come to Northeim to collect their compensation payments.[34] In the City Council, the SPD moved that the town no longer buy its schoolbooks through Wilhelm Spannaus's bookstore, since Spannaus was a Nazi. Fortunately for him, the Civil Servants partly joined with the Civic Association to defeat the motion. A conservative councilman lamented even the suggestion, "since politics change every day in our world."[35]

The Nazi response to the Noelting meeting was to change the title of a previously planned meeting from "The Politicos into the Bacon, the Folk into the Pigsty," to "A Correction of the Announced Noelting Theme, namely, 'National Socialism at Its Beginning, the SPD at Its End.' " Furthermore, they cut their admission price for unemployed persons from 15 *Pfennig* to nothing.[36] But neither this meeting, nor one held a week later directed to "young workers of the hand and brain," drew much of a crowd, and so the Nazis turned to another of Northeim's peculiarities, its high proportion of government employees, for a mass meeting. The theme was to be "The Civil Service and National Socialism" and the speaker a railroad man, "the famous old fighter, Locomotive-Engineer Dreher, a Reichstag representative." The *1910er Zelt* was rented and the admission price was cut to 30 *Pfennig*.

The meeting drew a crowd in excess of 1,200. A strong contingent of SA was on hand and thus the atmosphere became tense when a body of *Reichsbanner* men entered the hall in closed formation, with flags flying, and proceeded to heckle the speaker, dwelling particularly on the fact that he never touched on his preannounced theme. According to the NNN, which covered the matter in an editorial appealing for political moderation, "a great tumult ensued and only the reasonableness of the leaders on both sides kept order."[37]

Socialist political activity kept pace with the Nazis during this hectic February. The *Reichsbanner* was engaged in preparing itself to thwart a Nazi *Putsch*. Shortly before the incident described above, a test alarm was held when the *Reichsbanner* District Commander made a surprise visit to Northeim. With only one hour's notice, one hundred *Reichsbanner* men were assembled at the Market Square to hear their commander give a pep talk and to make a propaganda parade. The following week the county organization of the SPD met and were told that now was the time to defeat the Nazis. Every Socialist was exhorted to recruit one more man. A few days later, the whole county organization of the *Reichsbanner* gathered to celebrate the seventh anniversary of its founding. There was a parade of nine hundred *Reichsbanner* men, all from Northeim County, with twenty flags, two bands, and two fife-and-drum corps. There were speeches at the Market Square and on the circus grounds, and a dance at the *1910er Zelt*. The theme expressed prevailing fears of a Nazi *Putsch:* "The *Reichsbanner* will be strong enough to protect the Republic." As though to punctuate this, a contingent of SA crashed the dance and, after they were expelled by the police, threw a chair leg through a window of the hall.[38] Nor did the Socialists during these days forget their antipathy to capitalism. This was the subject of a play put on by the Free Unions on Valentine's Day, which drew an audience of four hundred.[39]

Not to be outdone, the Nazis staged another mass rally at the *1910er Zelt,* on Feburary 26, with a former Army lieutenant and another speaker on "Twelve Years of Republic—Where's the Freedom?"[40] The town was becoming saturated with political activity. In the thirty-one days since the Nazi meeting that featured the U-boat hero, there had been twelve different political events: parades, rallies, meetings—six by the Social Democrats and six by the Nazis. The *1910er Zelt* was in almost constant use, and most of the events had been tinged with violence or at least extreme tension. Charges of political malpractice were also in the air. On February 27, the GGZ, quoting from a Nazi newspaper article, charged that "scandalous conditions . . . rule at the Northeim City Construction Office." The article alleged that workers who would not march in an SPD parade were "unbelievably terrorized" and that one worker had to quit his job to protect himself. Since the Construction Office was in an SPD senator's area of competence, the GGZ demanded investigations and suspensions. Unfortunately for the Nationalists, the City Council had already investigated the matter and found the Nazi allegations to be devoid of fact. The *Volksblatt* was happy to report this the day after the GGZ's editorial, and went on to label the editorial "another blatant bourgeois swindle."[41]

The Socialists undoubtedly felt, by the end of February 1931, that they were successfully meeting the Nazi challenge. The arrogance of the SA had been matched by the militancy of the *Reichsbanner*. Nazi charges were refuted, Nazi plots exposed. Every Nazi meeting or rally was countered by a Socialist rally. But in the half-year since the September elections the whole political atmosphere of the town had changed. Politics was becoming radicalized, with mass meetings, demonstrations, and street clashes replacing the rather sleepy provincial approach that had been the norm in Northeim except during election campaigns.

This shift was bound to have its effect upon the watching burghers. The times were changing drastically. In the game of matching radicalism with the Nazis, the SPD could not hope to win, for they lacked the brutality and irrationality of their opponents. Furthermore, every move in the game simply added to the troubled spirit of Northeim's middle classes, making them more vulnerable to extremist appeals.

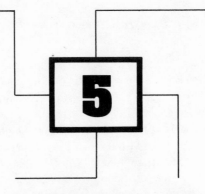

AUTHORITARIANS UNITE

SPRING-SUMMER 1931

Nazi propaganda consists entirely of a perpetual appeal to whatever is swinish in man.

**Dr. Kurt Schumacher (SPD):
Reichstag speech,
February 23, 1932**

To the Socialists the Nazis were a threat only insofar as they might attempt an armed *coup d'état*. Serious politics was a matter of rational appeals and positive results. Since the NSDAP seemed incapable of either, they could not constitute a political threat. Nazi propaganda seemed to illustrate this, for it consistently pinned two labels on the SPD: *"Marxisten"* and *"Bonzen"* (approximately, "ward-heelers," with overtones of corruption). The labels are of course contradictory; it is difficult to conceive of fervid radicals who are simultaneously comfortably venal. But effective propaganda need not be logical as long as it foments suspicion, contempt, or hatred. The choice of the two words not only had that effect upon the bourgeoisie, it summed up the dilemma of the Social Democrats precisely.

The SPD was not "Marxist," though it used language that made it appear so. Thus it was doubly encumbered, for it was unwilling to be a revolutionary party at a time when the best defense of democracy may have been social revolution, and secondly, its revolutionary tradition made it incapable of seeking or receiving the support of any but the working class. Furthermore, the SPD's defense of democracy meant, in practical terms, defense of a status quo which was identified in the minds of most Northeimers with national humiliation and economic ruin.[1]

The SPD's tradition as a proletarian party was the most serious impediment to a *modus vivendi* with Northeim's middle classes. The town's class structure and the social antipathies felt by the middle classes contributed to this: Northeimers resented the Social Democrats' insistent class consciousness even though it was largely a reflection of that of the bourgeoisie. Townspeople who had working contact with individual Socialists conceded that they were good and able men, but still distrusted the SPD in general.[2]

From the Socialist point of view there seemed to be little to gain from an alliance with Northeim's middle classes. The town had a permanent Rightist majority and the SPD often felt oppressed by it. Especially after 1930, the bourgeois elements in Northeim seemed bent on weakening the SPD and willing to back the Nazis to accomplish this. To Northeim's workers, the town's businessmen seemed exclusively Nazi.[3] By tradition, organization, and ideology, the workers expected to rely upon themselves alone. Why should the SPD appeal to the middle classes at the risk of losing the allegiance of their main support, the workers? If the SPD relaxed its ritualistic radicalism, the Communists were there to lure off dissidents. Thus neither the Socialists nor the moderate middle class worked for a rapprochement.

As the depression deepened, it was no longer radicalism that alienated burghers from the SPD but the rhetorical quality of that radicalism. No one believed that the Socialists would really attempt fundamental economic changes. Many blamed the Social Democrats for not being radical enough (in economic matters) while still resenting their social composition and "leveling" goals.[4] Thus the SPD could not keep the middle classes from flocking to the banners of the NSDAP, for the Nazis were known as real radicals. It was not enough to preach loyalty to democracy or to the Republic. Most Northeimers obviously felt no reason to respond to such an appeal. The way to undercut the Nazis was not by blind opposition but by a counterprogram sufficiently attractive to awaken in the hearts of the bourgeoisie the kinds of hopes that the Nazis were able to arouse.

Instead, the Social Democrats concentrated on holding the loyalty of the working class and saw the Nazi threat in terms of armed rebellion. Thus, no matter how hard they tried, Northeim's Socialists did not provide effective opposition to the Nazis.

Most of Northeim's SPD members were born into the working class. Belief in Socialism tended to come more from family background than from subsequent conviction. The typical SPD member's father had worked at the town's railroad yards, had been a follower of the SPD since before the turn of the century, and had reared his children as Socialists. Thus the average Social Democrat had the almost unconscious commitment to Socialism that the average American worker seems to have to trade unionism.[5] Nazism made few gains among these people. Almost all Northeimers knew this and voting statistics demonstrate it.[6] Far from joining or backing the Nazis, Northeim's workers were known for their extreme anti-Nazism. As one SPD leader put it when his wife questioned him about the dangers of his opposition to Nazism, "I'd rather lose everything than my freedom."[7]

This sober determination characterized most Social Democratic leaders. They were not flamboyant men. They rose through the ranks to posts as union secretaries, consumers' cooperative chairmen, and other roles in the Socialist *Apparat* on the basis of their ability and seriousness, not because of charismatic qualities. When they were young men, one of the key slogans of the Socialist movement was: "Knowledge Is Power!" In toilsome hours after the regular workday, the youthful energy of the aspiring Socialist leader was spent in studying economics, history, or social welfare laws. To those whose social position made them disparage the proletarian party, these men might easily appear to be *Bonzen,* for they were certainly not revolutionaries.

Three of Northeim's SPD leaders stood out among their quiet colleagues—Karl Deppe, Friedrich Haase, and Senator Carl Querfurt. Karl Deppe the *Reichsbanner* leader, was described by a nonadmirer as "a brutal and inconsiderate man."[8] He was short and powerful with a voice that had been made hoarse and weak by a gassing in World War I. Though his official occupation was *Krankenbesucher* (i.e., he investigated insurance-receivers in the town hospital), he was essentially a politician. In addition to his work with the *Reichsbanner* and the offices he held in the SPD Local and other worker organizations, he was speaker of the City Council and a delegate to the County Council. Touchy and aggressive, he alienated many people by his roughness, but he was very much respected by the workers and was cool in a fight.

His assistant and leader of the *Reichsbanner* youth section, Friedrich Haase, was just the opposite. Tall, slim, and exceedingly boyish, he had a clear and winning speaking voice. He had once intended to be a singer and had received vocal training, but he gave it up to become a clerk in the county administration. While the County Prefect was a Social Democrat, Friedrich Haase was given as much free time as he wanted to work for the *Reichsbanner,* though this ended when the county received a conservative Prefect in 1932. Honesty, modesty, and kindliness shone from Friedrich Haase's face; most Northeimers liked him.

The real leader of Northeim's SPD was Carl Querfurt. He was chairman of the Northeim SPD Local and of the county organization, too. He was senator in the Northeim city government and SPD majority leader in the County Council. He was also delegate to the Hanoverian Provincial Legislature and a member of its twelve-man executive committee. To many he was the embodiment of the Social Democratic party in Northeim.

Carl Querfurt was not a worker. He owned a small tobacco shop in the heart of the old town. He was rather distinguished looking, with sandy hair and a florid face. The conservative County Prefect, von der Schulenberg, described him as "a man of great natural talent, but violent; he imparted a violent character to the whole SPD Local."[9]

Senator Querfurt was that rarity, the completely partisan man. He was capable of the most oily political double-talk but managed to make it sound forthright and honest. He had great self-confidence, courage, and presence of mind (his record in the war was distinguished), but could also use refined invective and vituperation. With all this he was a good judge of character and believed in the ultimate triumph of rationality and love, though only in the misty future and not without a struggle. Most Northeimers accepted him for what he was—the complete politician—but the town's workers idolized him. Finally, he possessed two other attributes: full commitment to democracy and considerable common sense. He was superbly fitted to lead Northeim's SPD but totally incapable of building a supra-Socialist alliance. His opponents hated him but gave him grudging admiration. Few underestimated Carl Querfurt.

This, then, was Northeim's Social Democratic party, the town's only defenders of democracy and its only bulwark against Nazism. They failed the test they were put to in the years before 1933. That they were incapable of victory did not mean, however, that they were without courage and dignity.

After its vigorous efforts in January and February of 1931, the SPD no longer attempted to match the Nazis meeting for meeting, though in Northeim County they held sixteen public meetings while the Nazis held eight. In the town the Nazis kept up a stronger agitational pace. In the first week of March they held a different type of meeting, an "SA Recruitment Evening with Theatrical Presentations and a German Dance."[10] Five days after that, another famous personage was brought in for a speech that drew an audience of eight hundred: "Edmund Heines (Member of the Reichstag), the Chief Defendant in the . . . Stettin Feme Murder Trial." Heines had been in the highly nationalistic Free Corps in the early twenties, where he had "executed" a "traitor" after a kangaroo-court trial, and had gone unpunished in a trial before Rightist judges. This meeting was held in the *1910er Zelt,* and according to the GGZ, the audience all cheered when Heines got to the point in his story where he shot his victim, and after that, there was a mounting wave of applause, culminating in a final storm of hand-clapping, cheers, and the "Horst Wessel Song."[11]

By way of contrast to such bloodthirstiness, the Nazis next decided to arouse the populace against Orthodox Jewish methods of cattle slaughtering. Consequently they sponsored a speech on this subject, with color slides, by the chairman of a Hanoverian society for the prevention of cruelty to animals. At the speech, Northeim's Nazi leaders put themselves on record as being opposed to such practices.[12]

The *Volksblatt* was quick to point out the almost comical irony of "the Nazis screaming about 'cruel Jewish slaughtering methods as the greatest cultural disgrace of the twentieth century,' " while they were also "constantly talking about 'heads rolling in the sand.' " But apparently some people took the Nazi charges seriously, for the *Volksblatt* also devoted a long article to refuting the specific charge that animals were being cruelly handled by the rabbi in the town slaughterhouse. It also noted that "Nazi elements frequently hang around the slaughterhouse and are discourteous to Jews there." This brought results; the SPD senator in charge of the slaughterhouse brought suit against the Nazi newspaper which made the original charge of "Gruesome Torture of Animals at the Northeim Slaughterhouse," while the Northeim Senate issued a warning to two Nazis that if they were discourteous to Jews again they would be forbidden to enter the slaughterhouse.[13]

During this period Local Group Northeim also continued to hold biweekly semiprivate "discussion evenings" in the Cattle Auction Hall, for the indoctrination of new members and the recruitment of others. Topics included such themes as "Our Program" and "Nationalism and Socialism," the discussion leaders were local Nazis such as Ernst Girmann, and the attendance averaged about 85. By the end of April membership in the Local Group was up to 191, but as before they were overwhelmingly from Northeim County and as soon as a particular village reached the minimum of 15 members it would split off to form its own Local Group. Thus the figures for Local Group Northeim were constantly growing and shrinking around the core of town resident members. There were enough, however, for constant meetings, leafletings, and demonstration marches.[14]

The incessant agitation drew other parties into activity, especially the Nationalists, who felt that Nazi success could be matched by a similar appeal. Already in February, the *Stahlhelm* (which locally stood in the same relationship to the DNVP as the SA to the Nazis) held its first meeting in Northeim in over a year, featuring "His Excellency von Henning auf Schoenhott." As was to be the case with almost all Nationalist functions, the affair held in the town's best hotel, the Sonne, and admission was free. (The hotel was owned by a member of the DNVP.) The speaker, in addition to attacking Liberals, Marxists, Jews, and the SPD, proclaimed that Hitler was the "drummer of Nationalist ideas" and that "Bismarck was the first National Socialist." Thirty new members joined the *Stahlhelm*. A month later the DNVP held a meeting featuring a Nationalist party Reichstag member. Three weeks after that there was another *Stahlhelm* meeting, this time with a motion picture as a drawing card.[15] Furthermore, the Civic Association held an open-air meeting in March at which Senator Mahner attacked the Treaty of Versailles and prophesied that when Germany became internally united she would once again become a world power. A band was present to lead the crowd in singing *Deutschland über Alles.*[16]

The Communists also were active, holding their first parade and meeting in Northeim. For their meeting they rented the Riding Hall, which, while it was mammoth, was not really a meeting hall. Fewer than one hundred people came to the Communist meeting.[17]

Northeim was beset by so many differing political points of view that it is hard to imagine anything approaching common political action. Yet in March 1931, an event was at hand which would show that the Communists and the Nazis, the Nationalists and the People's party could all join hands—at least for purposes of opposing the SPD.

The bastion of democracy in Weimar Germany was the State of Prussia, which in Germany's peculiar federal system constituted three-fifths of the population and land area of Germany. Prussia was ruled by a coalition of the Catholic Center, which drew its strength from the Roman Catholic Rhineland provinces, and the SPD, whose support came from the industrial areas of the Ruhr, Silesia, Berlin, and the Hanseatic harbor towns. As long as the SPD-Center coalition conducted the government in Prussia, democracy was safe.

After the first hard winter of the depression, both the Nazis and the Communists believed they had enough increased support to break the coalition's majority, if elections were held. To have elections, however, the Prussian Parliament would have to be dissolved, which the governing coalition refused to do. The Weimar Constitution provided another way. If enough signatures could be gathered on a petition, a referendum could be held, and if enough votes were gained on the referendum, dissolution of the Prussian Parliament would be forced despite the government's majority within the Parliament.

The Nazis conceived the idea, and the Communists were quick to support them (following the Comintern's tortured thinking that defeat of the Social Democrats was the prime goal). The Nationalists, the Hanoverian "Guelph" party, and the People's party also pledged aid, though at least one Northeim People's party leader refused to join in this purely negative maneuver.[18] Most of the welter of splinter parties followed suit. The Civic Association also participated; Senator Mahner explained that while it existed for local politics, a change in the Prussian government would have a decisive effect on local government too.[19]

Nazi meetings slowed down during the petition campaign, which absorbed most of their energies. To be effective the campaign required an actual gathering of signatures; propaganda would not have been enough. Nevertheless, the Nazis found time to hold at least one public function, a speech at the Cattle Auction Hall on "Position of Civil Servants and Government Employees on the Petition to Dissolve the Prussian Parliament; also, The End of Unemployment." The speaker was a former Prussian civil servant who was now a Nazi Reichstag delegate.[20] The Civic Association's meeting during the campaign was a larger one, held at the *1910er Zelt*. Senator Mahner attacked the SPD and its government in Prussia as "dictatorial." He urged all Northeimers to sign the petition and "break the power of the SPD."[21]

The Socialists were concerned by the petition campaign, primarily because they feared Nazi pressure tactics. No ballot booths were involved and the voter, confronted with a Stormtrooper on his doorstep, had to say "yes" or "no" openly. The *Volksblatt* charged that the Nazis were using the petition lists to boycott any businessman who did not sign. The SPD was especially concerned about Nazi intimidation in the somewhat isolated villages of Northeim County. Later, when the referendum was held, the *Volksblatt* was able to show that in some villages in Northeim County fewer people voted "yes" than had signed the petition.[22]

The Social Democrats' answer to this was to increase the activity of the *Reichsbanner*. On March 24, a week before the campaign opened, the *Reichsbanner* held a meeting in the Market Square. Deppe was the speaker, and he pulled out all stops. He referred to Hitler's cowardice at the time of the Munich *Putsch,* reviewed Nazi political assassinations, and castigated the murderer Heines, whom the Nazis had featured as a speaker. Two days thereafter, one hundred Northeim *Reichsbanner* men undertook a thirty-five kilometer march through the county with speeches afterward in the Market Square. A few days later it was announced that the *Reichsbanner* had acquired twenty-two additional members and expelled one who was a spy for the Nazis.[23]

In the very midst of the signature-gathering for the petition, on April 10, the *Reichsbanner* made another demonstration. About two hundred *Reichsbanner* men marched, with a fife-and-drum corps in the van. The parade was led directly through the hillside residential district and also stopped twice in front of the offices of the Civic Association to hoot and shout. Behind this was the anger of SPD leaders over the conservatives' collaboration with the Nazis. In the Market Square, Deppe gave what the NNN called an "incendiary speech" against the Nazis and the Nationalists. A second speech, before the Town Hall, commemorated the fall of the Spanish dictator, Primo de Rivera.[24] The *Reichsbanner* was making its presence felt.

The *Volksblatt* also charged that Nazis were violating the uniform prohibition decree and provoked the government to a reiteration of the ban on brown shirts. The Socialist Governor of Hanover Province, Noske, prohibited the transporting of participants for political gatherings in trucks or buses, since it had been noted that fighting elements (especially the SS) were frequently brought to political meetings and inclined more to street fights than the local contingents. Noske also—acting on the basis of a private theory—forbade the use of the color red in all posters except official ones.[25]

Despite these measures, the increased tension inevitably led to violence. On April 8, there was a fight between two Nazis and four *Reichsbanner* men, with the Nazis getting the worst of it. A week later the *Volksblatt* reported that a Nazi had slapped the wife of a *Reichsbanner* man; it threatened to take matters into its own hands if more police protection were not forthcoming. At the climax of the campaign the NNN reported that two young Nazis mishandled a woman Socialist, that two *Reichsbanner* men ripped the swastika insignia from the coat of a lady who was a member of the Nazi Women's Auxiliary, and that members of the youth section of the *Reichsbanner* jeered at some children on their way to church. The *Volksblatt* denied the latter two incidents.[26]

The campaign atmosphere also led to some scatter-shot propaganda by the *Volksblatt*. On April 1, it reported that the son of a pastor from Northeim County received a scholarship intended to enable poor but gifted students to attend the *Gymnasium*. It pointed out that the pastor earned 800 marks per month while an unemployed worker got 60 marks a month at the highest; readers were then invited to draw their own conclusions. Two days later it noted that three copies of the Nazi *Völkischer Beobachter* were found on a table in the Northeim City Library. It thundered editorially: "What is this subversive newspaper doing in the public library?"[27]

If the Socialists were seeing Nazis everywhere it was because of the extent of middle-class collaboration with the Nazis in the petition campaign. On April 19, 1931, all groups supporting the petition joined for a mass rally. Official sponsorship was given to the *Stahlhelm,* and the speaker of the evening was a member of its youth section. But the meeting was also backed by all political parties involved (except the Communists) and by almost all right-wing organizations in Northeim: the County Agricultural Society, the Pan-German League, the National Association of German Officers, the Savings Depositors' League, the German National Apprentices' Society, and finally, the Civic Association. The *1910er Zelt* was packed. The *Stahlhelm* provided a band from a neighboring town and its own Northeimer fife-and-drum corps, while the Nazis provided SA contingents. The main speaker pronounced a lengthy curse on the "godless movement," by which he meant the SPD, and went on to say that the SPD-Center party coalition was a league between "Rome and the Reds." The meeting closed with the enthusiastic singing of "The Watch on the Rhine" and the national anthem.[28]

The gathering of signatures lasted only two weeks and demonstrated considerable organizational ability on the part of the Nazis, who were the driving force behind the campaign. In the first ten days almost one-fifth of Northeim's qualified voters (1,275) signed up. Then the Nazis put on a spurt of energy and in the last four days collected almost as many signatures again to bring the total up to 2,246, one-third of the town's voters. In the rest of Prussia enough signatures were gathered to insure that the referendum would be held, with the date set for August of 1931.

Certainly many Northeimers signed the petition because of the concurrent signs of economic constriction. On April 2, Northeim's branch office of the *Commerz und Privatbank* closed permanently. A week later occurred the worst calamity to befall the town's middle class during the depression: the collapse of the Enterprise Bank, a locally financed cooperative bank which was the pride of the lower middle class. Bankruptcy was declared on April 9, 1931, although the liquidation extended into 1933 and caused considerable bitterness. The collapse of the Enterprise Bank was not due to the general economic situation, but was the result of poor management, especially in interest policy. Meetings of the creditors were acrimonious and the matter became a political issue. The Nazis claimed that the bankruptcy was due to the Versailles Treaty and the republican form of government, while the Socialists gleefully pointed out that the board of directors was composed of Nationalists and Nazis, and listed some of the blunders which had caused the bank's failure. After 1933 the Nazis tacitly acknowledged the element of mismanagement by instituting legal action against the former director.

About 15 percent of the town's small businessmen were decisively affected by the incident and at least one man later declared himself bankrupt because of it. Many others had to struggle for existence thereafter.[29]

Under these circumstances, protests became more bitter. At a meeting of the Northeim Housewives' Club held on April 7, the speaker ranted against "the Americanization of the economy" and against department stores, consumers' cooperatives, and foreign imports. He exhorted women to buy only from small dealers.[30] The Nazis, in their catchall propaganda, promised to aid the small businessman, but until the millennium arrived businessmen were pressed hard to contribute to the Nazi cause. By the end of April 1931, the *Volksblatt* charged that Northeim's Nazis had not paid their bills and had no money to pay them. It warned businessmen not to extend credit to the NSDAP, but suggested that the Nazis frequently threatened businessmen with boycotts in order to extort credit or contributions. At least one Northeim businessman later verified the charge.[31]

Businessmen were the last to suffer from the depression; by April 1931, the number of unemployed registered at the Northeim District employment office reached twelve thousand—double the number of the previous autumn. Other workers suffered pay cuts or shortened hours. The town's cigar factory (with 250 employees) had been on a reduced workweek for over four months.[32] The *Volksblatt,* in reporting the death in a farm machinery accident of a ten-year-old boy from Northeim County, noted parenthetically that the boy had been earning more than his father.[33] Under these circumstances hardly any workers left their jobs for the May Day celebration, which in 1931 fell on a Friday. There was a pitifully small parade led by only three red flags and a placard inscribed "We demand the 40-hour week." The town band played a few marches in the Market Square, but that was all.[34]

In general, political activity abated after the petition campaign, though the Nazis attempted to keep up the pressure. On May 2 they brought in a Reichstag delegate for a speech that drew 260 people and a few weeks later staged a parade with 600 Stormtroopers, a concert, and a meeting in the *1910er Zelt.* About 900 people attended, and the only thing to mar what the GGZ called "one of the greatest successes of the NSDAP" was actually the sort of thing the Nazis felt added spice: a short fight with some *Reichsbanner* men during the parade.[35] Early in June there was another varied program in the *1910er Zelt* with a concert, dramatic presentations, speeches, a raffle, and dancing. This also drew a large crowd (650) which apparently enjoyed itself, though the "dramatic presentations" consisted solely of scenes of SA men beating up Communists.[36] Four weeks after that the president of the Prussian Parliament spoke in Northeim for the Nazis and a week later, in keeping with the relaxed summer atmosphere, the SA band gave a concert at the ruins of an old castle outside Northeim.[37]

The Nationalists also relaxed. Apart from a recruitment evening in May, which gave the *Stahlhelm* ten new members, their only other activity in the early summer of 1931 was a June garden party in honor of their national commander's fiftieth birthday, with a concert and other light entertainment.[38] There was only one unpleasant incident to bother the conservatives. In May, Senator Mahner had charged that the SPD used Welfare Office funds to show one of their propaganda films to some pensioners. Mahner was promptly sued by an SPD leader and was required to publish an advertisement in the NNN declaring that: 1) he had not really made the accusation; 2) he took it all back with an expression of deep sorrow; and 3) he would pay all the costs of the trial.[39]

The pace of SPD activity also slowed in the late spring and early summer. In early June the *Reichsbanner* staged a demonstration parade and in a speech at the Town Hall Friedrich Haase dwelt on the miseries of the Italian working classes and emphasized that Socialist ideology thrives only in a democracy. A few days later the SPD sponsored a mass meeting in the *1910er Zelt* featuring the exiled Italian anti-fascist, Professor Mario Cofi. A good-sized crowd heard him talk on "the bloody and shameful regime of Italian Fascism." The lecture was significantly entitled "Swastika Wonderland." Some Nazis were present but none tried to speak.[40]

A few days after that Northeim was invaded by groups of "Young Socialist Workers" for a two-day conference. The SPD Local took advantage of their presence for a parade and meeting on the Market Square. The NNN thought the boys and girls made a handsome parade with their blue blouses and red ties, their songs, and their bright red flags.[41] Another pleasant interlude was provided a week later by the celebration of "Workers' Sport Day" on June 15. Proletarian sport clubs paraded with the city band and the *Reichsbanner* fife-and-drum corps, and then held a variety of athletic contests. At night there was a torchlight parade, songs by the People's Choir, and a speech on the Socialist import of sport. The day ended with cries of *"Hoch der deutschen Republik!"* and the singing of the *Internationale.* A few days later the SPD tried more low-pressure propaganda as it sent a loudspeaker truck through Northeim with only a few slogans and mostly light, nonpolitical airs.[42] The depression even abated during June of 1931; unemployment in the Northeim District dropped to eight thousand, the lowest it had been since the previous October.

As the heat of the summer bore in, though, there was a new economic crisis. The American stock market crash led U.S. banks to call in loans they had made to Germany. The credit crisis became acute by mid-1931, and in July the major German banks began to close. The government declared a bank holiday on July 14. In Northeim there was no real run on the banks. A former director of one of the banks recalled that "only a few people came in to withdraw their money, and they later returned it with sheepish excuses."[43] Yet the town's leaders were concerned. The City Council decided unanimously not to attend the annual festival of the shooting societies. Its reasoning was that the general economic misery made festivals inappropriate. This decision was extremely unpopular, since the populace took the opposite view, holding that beer and skittles were especially needed to take one's mind off the depression. The Council did not repeat its mistake the following year, though the economic crisis was even graver by then.[44]

The Social Democrats also displayed concern, especially over the possibility that the Communists might make inroads among the unemployed. In

June the Free Unions called a special meeting to discuss countermeasures against KPD* activity among the jobless. Within a week the *Volksblatt* was able to report that through SPD city councillors the town of Northeim had made potatoes and other food available to the Free Unions for distribution and had also arranged the free use of the town's swimming pool for jobless persons. The *Volksblatt* also issued a vehement denial that the Communists were making inroads among Northeim's "Young Socialist Workers."[45]

Along with economic concern came rising political tension, especially with the August 8 "Referendum for the Dissolution of the Prussian Parliament" in the offing. In mid-July there was a rumor of a Nazi *Putsch* and the Northeim *Reichsbanner* was mobilized, but the evening passed with nothing more than a parade and a speech on the Market Square. A week later the *Reichsbanner* was called out again to hold a protest demonstration over the murder of a *Reichsbanner* man in Hanover. The Northeimers probably remembered a nasty incident that had occurred in their own town in June when two Stormtroopers had trampled a Socialist with their boots and then cut off his fingers with a sickle. In their protest demonstration the *Reichsbanner* marched to the Market Square, led by their fife-and-drum corps, to hear Friedrich Haase promise that they would defend the Republic and to have Deppe lead them in a *"Frei Heil!"* for democracy.[46]

The August referendum drew together all the anti-Socialist forces that had backed the April petition. Nationalist propaganda became the prime content of the GGZ, while the NNN ran a *Stahlhelm* advertisement for twelve consecutive days preceding August 9, calling on people to vote "yes." As before, the Nazis were the driving force. On August 1 they held a meeting in the Cattle Auction Hall preceded by a parade of about six hundred SA, SS, and Hitler Youth, plus a band. They also had the honor of the election-eve rally. Seven to eight hundred people came to each meeting.[47] The Civic Association's turn came on August 5, when Mahner called for a "common front against Bolshevism" (ignoring the fact that the Communists were also supporting the referendum). At this meeting a car pool was arranged to help get out the vote.[48]

Again the *Reichsbanner* focused its efforts on the remote villages of Northeim County, using trucks for transportation. Meetings were held in each village under the slogan "Republicans are ready to fight." One trip ended with a march past the Cattle Auction Hall, prompting admonitions from the NNN. In repeated speeches on the Market Square, "against the destruction

Kommunistische Partei Deutschlands, Communist Party of Germany.

of Prussia,'' Deppe emphasized that Nazis and Communists were working together to break the SPD supremacy.[49] The SPD also held meetings in out-lying areas of the county, places with a thoroughly Nazified peasant popu-lation. The *Reichsbanner* from Northeim usually went along to provide pro-tection, and wives of Socialist speakers waited up until their men came home.[50] On one occasion Carl Querfurt was able to save himself from a beating only by prolonging his speech until *Reichsbanner* reinforcements arrived from town. As it was, the SA was just beginning to interrupt when police and *Reichs-banner* arrived simultaneously.[51] In other parts of the county Socialists were living in a virtual state of terror. In one village a twenty-two-year-old worker died as a result of a beating given him by Nazis in the spring, and in Au-gust, Nazis led a mass assault on a few *Reichsbanner* men in the same vil-lage. The event was carefully noted in Northeim, especially when some thirty Nazis received fines and prison sentences totaling 128 months for their part in the attack.[52]

There were also rumors of an impending Nazi *Putsch*. Rumors of this sort were frequently spread. A year before, after the September 1930 elec-tions, the NNN took pains to point out that rumors about a Hitlerian *Putsch* were false and that the Defense Minister had said he was prepared to nip any revolution in the bud.[53] Behind it all was the fact that Hitler had one attempted *Putsch* on his record—the Munich ''Beer Hall'' fiasco of Novem-ber 1923.

A few days before the election Northeim's *Reichsbanner* took to patrol-ing the streets in groups of five. The Mayor, as chief of police, immediately warned the *Reichsbanner* not to do this. In reply, the *Volksblatt* published a belligerent open letter demanding better police protection and refusing to stop the patrols[54] The Northeim police also prohibited a planned Nazi parade on election eve, fearing it would ''pose a danger to the public peace.''[55]

In the last few days before the election, haying was completed in the rural areas around Northeim, enabling numerous SA men to come into town and thus raising the political temperature. Tempers were honed to the point where the slightest incident became a cause for violence. The day before the election, for example, an SA man entered a tavern and announced ''Make way—the SA is here!'' A *Reichsbanner* man immediately knocked him un-conscious. No wider violence came of this episode at the time, though it helped set the stage. That same day, a Northeim Nazi named Tumpelmann hit a member of the Workers' First Aid Society on the head with brass knuckles, sending him to the doctor for stitches.[56]

In short, everything was conducive to a major battle, which occurred the evening of election day, August 9. During the day both *Reichsbanner* and SA were in a state of full alert. In the subsequent trial the Nazi attorney produced the following secret order which indicates the mood of the day:

Reichsbanner Black-Red-Gold. 10th District
To all Local Groups of the 10th District

Comrades:
All local Groups of the 10th District will place themselves in full alert. Any moves of the enemy which indicate *Putsch*-intentions are to be reported immediately to the District Leader. Local Groups [X, Y, and Z] shall each provide a motorcyclist to maintain contact with the District Leader. These contact-people are to present themselves on Sunday the 9th at 7 P.M. at the residence of the District Leader. They are to appear completely in civilian dress without any insignia. All other Local Groups are to make certain that they have further motorcyclists or bicyclists ready so that in the event of a disruption of telephone communications, contact will be maintained with the District Leader. For security reasons all orders will be delivered orally. Telephone calls from Sunday evening after seven o'clock only at the Northeimer *Ratskeller,* Number 204. After 10 o'clock that evening, at the City Construction Office, Number 357.

Frei Heil!
Deppe, District Commander,
the 10th District.[57]

In Northeim the *Reichsbanner* gathered in uniform at the *Ratskeller* café, while the SA maintained headquarters at another tavern two blocks up Broad Street. Dusk came at eight o'clock, and both groups began their patrols through town. Inevitably the two patrols met head-on between the two cafés. In the Nazi group were Ernst Girmann, Deputy Leader for Northeim and Tumpelmann, about whom the *Reichsbanner* had been talking all day because of his brass-knuckles attack the previous evening. Words were exchanged, and the Nazis struck the first blow. The noise attracted attention in both cafés and in a minute Broad Street was filled with fighting men. Leaders on both sides wanted to halt the battle, but when the *Reichsbanner* saw two of their comrades lying on the ground bleeding while Girmann, who had suffered a knife wound, was beating one with a cane and shouting ''I'll beat you to death,'' there was no holding them back. The Nazi leader phoned the state police, who arrived ten minutes later and broke it up. Men from both sides were hospitalized with knife wounds and broken heads; many were cut and bruised.

Investigation by the police led to the indictment of the three Nazis in the original patrol on charges of assault with a deadly weapon. Two trials were necessary because of the confused and contradictory testimony. The court found all three Nazis guilty. Ernst Girmann was given two months in prison, a fine of 300 marks, and three years' probation. Tumpelmann was given four months in prison, as was the third Nazi, who had been indicted for a murder in the interim and had fled the country. In its decision the court declared that the *Reichsbanner* was not entirely without guilt for the "Referendum Day Battle," as it came to be called.[58]

The actual referendum was a failure throughout Prussia, and the SPD-Center coalition continued to govern. In Northeim the SPD made no effort to "get out the vote" since not voting was equivalent to voting "no." The Nazis had worked hard, and over a thousand more Northeimers voted for the referendum than had signed the petition. Yet the total "yes" votes barely exceeded the total vote that parties supporting the dissolution had won in September 1930.

While the vote was not a Nazi victory, since it failed to topple the government, the NSDAP could be well pleased with the atmosphere created by the spring and summer campaigns. Not only had all parties succumbed to Nazi leadership; the political process had been further radicalized, and by means of a constitutional provision designed to assure maximum democracy. The violence in Northeim was especially gratifying since it was another step toward bringing the town's troubled burghers over to Hitler's side. Dictators are nothing if not good policemen.

THE DEPTHS OF THE DEPRESSION

AUTUMN-WINTER 1931-1932

*No higher being will come to save us,
No God, no Kaiser, nor Tribune.
If we want freedom from our misery,
We'll get it only by ourselves, alone.*

**German Socialist version
of the *Internationale***

The split lips and broken heads, the ragged cuts and throbbing lumps that were the heritage of the "Referendum Day Battle" had at least one beneficial consequence. They cleared the air of violence and sated the hotheads on both sides. There were no more incidents of physical violence in Northeim for almost three months following August 9.

This does not mean that all tensions abated immediately, for there was still a backwash of accusations and suspicion left from the campaign. Three days after the referendum the GGZ charged that Carl Querfurt, as chairman of the vote-watching committee, had permitted voters to use a booth in which an election slogan had been scrawled. The City Council investigated the charge, found it incorrect, and the GGZ withdrew its accusation and apologized. A relatively mild riposte from the *Volksblatt* followed.[1] Actually the GGZ was routed from the field of polemics less by the *Volksblatt's* barbs than by the appearance of a competitor whose attacks were without restraint: the Nazi weekly newsletter *Hört! Hört!*, the first issues of which appeared in early August at a cost of 66 *Pfennig* a month. Every issue contained furious attacks on the SPD, especially upon city operations within areas of competence covered by SPD senators, and above all upon the "red" Health Insurance Office. The weapon was the same type of rhetorical question that the *Volksblatt* used so skillfully. For example: "How can the Health Insurance Office send *three* men and a car to a convention? Or are they incapable of saving money?"[2]

The *Volksblatt*, for its part, focused most of its efforts upon Senator Mahner because of his collaboration with the Nazi effort to dissolve the Prussian Parliament. It charged that Mahner was a Nazi dupe and that the Civic Association's election-day car pool was used by the Nazis to build up their own prestige. It accused Mahner of writing articles for *Hört! Hört!* and of diverting funds from the Civic Association's treasury into Nazi hands. This was the beginning of a campaign to destroy Mahner, which eventually succeeded.[3]

Another by-product of the bitterness engendered by the referendum campaign was the neglect of the annual Constitution Day celebration. The public meeting was held in one of the schools and the assembly hall was only two-thirds full. The *Volksblatt* complained that very few civil servants, who presumably owed allegiance to the Republic, were present. In the evening there was a torchlight parade with only the *Reichsbanner* and the Free Unions marching. The GGZ charged that because the Socialists had insisted on having the *Reichsbanner* head the parade, none of the clubs or guilds would join.[4]

There were other signs of the ominous effects of the "Referendum Day Battle." At the next meeting of the City Council the SPD demanded an annual subsidy of 25 marks for the Workers' First Aid Society. Northeim was already subsidizing the Voluntary First Aid Society of the Red Cross, but Carl Querfurt threatened to block further grants to that organization if the Council did not pass his motion. The Civil Servants group reluctantly helped the SPD override the Civic Association and the subsidy was passed.[5]

Measures of a preparatory nature were also taken by the *Stahlhelm*. At a meeting in September, featuring two outside speakers, a *Stahlhelm* leader declared that there would soon be civil war in Germany "between the Bolsheviks and the National Opposition" in which "there will be no neutrality." The following morning the youth section of Northeim's *Stahlhelm* held "defense-sport" exercises. A week later, a thousand *Stahlhelm* men were expected in Northeim for similar activities, but the police were afraid of trouble and forbade it. By now the *Volksblatt* was aroused and reported that "some *Stahlhelmern* practiced hand-grenade throwing Sunday morning in the Northeim park and called it 'sport.' Also at 2 A.M. they marched through the streets singing songs. Will the police do something about this?"[6]

As the first autumn winds swept over the north German plains these matters were thrust aside, for another depression winter was moving upon the town. Unemployment figures followed the seasons, cresting in the winter. By October there were over 9,000 registered unemployed coming to the Northeim Employment Office each week. In the town itself there were 418 unemployed. This was not many more than there had been the previous year at the same time, but whereas in October 1930, two-thirds of the town's unemployed were still on regular unemployment compensation, by October 1931, only about a third were; the rest were drawing emergency benefits or the welfare dole. The difference was the measure of despair.

Again there was an enormous press of applicants at the sugar beet factory. The *Volksblatt* reported that a worker who had been employed every harvest season for the past twenty years was now turned down because he was a Republican. The worker stated that the employment chief told him he would have to change his politics if he wanted work.[7]

As the misery of the unemployed increased, there were attempts to mitigate it through private charity. In October 1931, all of Northeim's charitable organizations (Nazis and *Stahlhelm* excepted) decided to work together with a common treasury. This *Hilfsbund* included Lutheran, Catholic, and Jewish charities, organizations of the Left, such as the Socialists' Workers' Welfare, and of the Right, such as the Fatherland's Women's Club. It also received public support from the County Prefect and the mayor of Northeim. The *Hilfsbund* undertook street collections and distributed food, clothing, and fuel. By the end of November 1,350 marks had been collected. In addition, merchants contributed clothes, while grocers, bakers, and butchers promised weekly deliveries of food. The Jewish merchants in the town were among the heaviest contributors. The Free Unions sponsored a Welfare Party which drew a large crowd at 75 *Pfennig* per person. There was music by the People's Choir and the city band. Various local comedians performed and the Workers' Gymnastic Society gave a show. From this alone 350 marks was earned for the *Hilfsbund,* and the Workers' Welfare Society also held a sale of homemade Christmas presents, with proceeds going to the unemployed. By November 27, 1931, 250 unemployed had applied for help. They also asked for four representatives from their own ranks to help supervise the distribution of aid, but this was unanimously refused.[8]

In support of the general effort, coal dealers reduced the price of lignite bricks for all unemployed and the Northeim Bakers' Guild cut the price of bread by 8 percent. It was more than altruism that prompted the bakers, for the *Volksblatt* had conducted a relentless attack against their pricing policy, comparing it unfavorably to that of neighboring towns. When the December 1931 price cut came, the *Volksblatt,* instead of applauding, simply noted that the price of bread in bakery shops was now the same as that of the consumers' cooperative. Since Northeim's bakers "made Nazi propaganda," workers were advised to shop at the cooperative even without the advantage of lower prices.[9]

The city also helped to mitigate the lot of the unemployed. Beginning in February 1931, free "cultural" movies were shown at one of the public schools. The following autumn the town began vocational training courses for young unemployed persons and also offered to lease several acres of city-owned garden land to unemployed families. During the winter of 1931–1932, needy unemployed were issued certificates enabling them to buy up to two hundred pounds of coal a month at 30 *Pfennig* a sack less than normal prices.[10]

Despite all these measures, the pace of the depression increased. There were six bankruptcies in 1931, double the number of 1930, and in December 1931 one of the town's larger businesses, a paper sack factory, closed down and prepared to move from Northeim.[11] By the end of the winter there were 704 unemployed in Northeim. There were over 13,000 in the Northeim Employment Office District, which meant an average of 2,000 a day tramping through Northeim to the old Army barracks. To complete the misery created by the economic situation, nature added woes. In January of 1932 the Ruhme river flooded, doing great damage to the workers' district north of the railroad tracks. Even the emergency dwellings for the shelterless in the old Army compound were flooded. Total damage in Northeim County was estimated at a quarter of a million marks.[12]

Banking began to show signs of constriction also. With the bank holiday of the previous summer, the City Savings Bank lost 50,000 marks' worth of accounts. This was less than 3 percent of the total, but it was enough to make Senator Mahner urge that members of the Civic Association keep their money in the City Savings Bank, since the bank was perfectly safe "despite vicious rumors." He was speaking to the right people, since it was the large accounts, those over 500 marks, that had left the bank. By the end of 1931 the City Council, County Prefect, and twelve economic organizations signed a large advertisement telling Northeimers not to hoard their money but to put it in banks, where it would be safe.[13] Though it was not reported in the press, this worked; by the end of 1932 not only had the large accounts returned, but many new small accounts were opened, so that the City Savings Bank showed a net increase over the three years of the depression. At least a quarter of the town's adult population had savings accounts of over 100 marks in the City Savings Bank, and this did not include money put in other Northeim banks or invested in stocks and bonds. The middle classes were hardly touched by the depression in Northeim, except psychologically.[14]

The Nazis, with their feel for effective agitation, moved to exploit the deepening of the depression. In the wake of the referendum there had been a reversion to old-style meetings. One at the end of August, held in the Cattle Auction Hall, featured a former army officer and a former Communist who spoke on "Our Gigantic Advance to the Great Victory! The Red Terror!" A week later a Hitler Youth Leader spoke on "The Murder of the Youth." Shortly thereafter the Nazis rented the *1910er Zelt* for a theatrical presentation: "National Socialism is trying to rescue German art and make it German again. Therefore the N.S. Stage Group will present the play 'Poison Gas 506'. . . ." Attendance was not noteworthy despite the bait of "Famous Actors; Cheap Prices." Apparently the town could stand only so many "evenings of entertainment," for later in September the Nazis took part in one put on by the *Stahlhelm* rather than give their own.[15]

In October the Nazis began to work on the town's concern over economic matters. During the first week there was a speech on "What Will Winter Bring Us?" A fortnight later, the chief Nazi economic theorist, Gottfried Feder, came to Northeim to speak on "Financial and Economic Policy in the National Socialist State." He drew an enormous crowd to the *1910er Zelt,* including many middle-class people who were interested in the Nazi economic program. They got, instead, such generalities as "no nationalization of the productive free economy" and "organic economic leadership." Nevertheless, this was one of the Nazis' most effective meetings.[16]

The rest of 1931 was filled by the Nazis with fairly ordinary events: a play, the annual commemoration of the Munich *Putsch,* a welfare concert, and the Christmas party. The only mass meeting was held on November 26, featuring a Prussian Parliament member who attacked the SPD as responsible for the current economic distress and promised that when the Nazis came to power they "would not use soft gloves."[17]

The Nazis also went beyond propaganda in exploiting the depression. In the late fall of 1931 they opened a soup kitchen to feed the unemployed. It was located in the former factory of a canning company that had gone bankrupt in 1929; the owner supplied the rooms free. Hitler had formed an alliance with the Nationalist party—the so-called "Harzburg Front"—in October 1931. Hence the way was open for closer cooperation on the local level and the soup kitchen was a joint Nazi-*Stahlhelm* venture. Since it was in competition with the *Hilfsbund,* the Nazis attempted to discredit the town's general relief effort:

> The worst winter in 100 years! State and Reich refuse to help! Germany will only be saved from all misery when no heart closes itself to this cry of need! Every man must give as much as he can spare. The majority of the *Volk,* represented by the National Opposition, will master the distress by standing together, all for all. Contributions may be given only to the representatives who have our card.
>
> Stahlhelm (League of Front Soldiers)
> NSDAP, County Northeim[18]

Enough contributions came in so that by mid-December the kitchen was feeding two hundred people per day, including forty families, twenty single people, and numerous SA men. Most of the food was donated by peasants (sometimes extorted from them) and by some of Northeim's grocers, bakers, and butchers. The Nazis claimed that they charged only those who could pay and gave food to all regardless of party affiliation, but at least one worker was refused food because he was a "Leftist" and the *Volksblatt* claimed only unemployed Nazis were fed.[19]

By the end of 1932 the Nazi kitchen had given out twelve thousand dinners, but welfare operations were not its only function. Some rooms were set aside for the SA (the *Stahlhelm* was elbowed out early in 1932 after the "Harzburg Front" collapsed) and the factory became Northeim's SA headquarters and "barracks." Within a fortnight of its opening, a swastika flag waved from the highest chimney of the factory. Since the Nazis were forbidden to display party symbols in Prussia, the *Volksblatt* was quick to ask what the police intended to do about it. Nothing was done, however, until the short-lived dissolution of the SA in the late spring of 1932, when the flag came down upon police order, but only for a few days. In a country preoccupied with symbols, the constant flying of a swastika over Northeim must be counted as another step toward convincing the wavering middle class that the Nazis were the party of the future.[20]

By the end of 1931, Northeim's Nazis could look back on a busy year. The number of meetings was not greater than in the previous year, but their character had changed. In the first place, the NSDAP was able to draw upon the pool of Reichstag delegates elected the previous year, for local meetings. No fewer than five Reichstag delegates appeared on Nazi platforms in Northeim in 1931, in addition to the president of the Prussian Parliament and the Nazi parliamentary leader of that body. This was a rich selection of speakers for a town of ten thousand, especially since it also included Gottfried Feder, who in the eyes of the general public was a top Nazi leader. Furthermore, the NSDAP was beginning to play upon the militaristic yearnings of Northeim's citizens. During the year they provided three former officers as speakers and staged five paramilitary parades. But the most striking difference was the size of Nazi meetings. The Nazis had been able to rent the *1910er Zelt* only once in 1930; in 1931 they filled it no fewer than ten times—true mass meetings, with about a thousand people on each occasion. There were also fourteen meetings in the Cattle Auction Hall. In other words, almost every other meeting was planned for a mass audience. Finally, 1931 also saw the beginning of Nazi "evenings of entertainment": infused with as much pageantry as politics, but of varied appeal and a distinct change of pace from the usual three to five hours of speeches.

The Nazi record of activity becomes even more astounding when one considers that Northeim had only about sixty actual members of the NSDAP prior to 1933. They were aided by many party members from the county, and also by many fellow-travelers, but the core was a strictly limited one. A limited core was not a limiting factor once the movement achieved a mass following, which it clearly did in Northeim by mid-1930. And there were many party members just outside the town. The rural areas around Northeim continued to be the strongest source of Nazi members and Local Group Northeim continued to include all those from the county who did not have their own Local Groups. In 1931 Walter Steineck spent much of his time (every night during the spring, he claimed) converting all county localities with over fifteen members to independent Local Groups. By December 1931, there were twenty-three Local Groups in Northeim County. In August of that year the enrollment in Local Group Northeim went from 184 to 82 because of losses to new Local Groups (plus others who moved away or stopped paying dues). There were so many farmers in the Nazi Party that Steineck reported to the *Gau* that activities in Northeim County virtually ceased in the fall because of harvesting. Not all farmers were Nazis by conviction; the police had evidence that farmers around Northeim were being forced into the Nazi Party under threat of boycott and that farm workers were told they would be fired unless they joined the Party or the SA. Farmers also paid their hired hands' dues.[21] So there was an extensive group of outsiders to help the Local Group's activities in the town. Furthermore, not many Northeimers suspected how few dues-paying members there were in the town. The townspeople believed that the Nazis were numerous and that most of them were young.[22]

As far as the youthful aspect is concerned, this was probably correct. Students at the Northeim *Gymnasium* were strongly attracted to Hitler. Most of the work done in public was done by young people in the SA or the Hitler Youth. A former member of the Hitler Youth in Northeim still has vivid recollections of painting swastikas and slogans on sidewalks and walls and distributing leaflets and pamphlets.[23] Despite their reliance on the spoken word, the Nazis often distributed such literature, and especially at election times delivered party newspapers, broadside leaflets, and free tickets to their meetings to almost every house in Northeim.[24] Though the Hitler Youth was used for this, most of its program was not directly tied into Nazi party activity. A former member described Northeim's Hitler Youth in the years before 1933 as follows:

> There was no pressure put on me by my father or anyone else to join the Hitler Youth—I decided to join it independently simply because I wanted to be in a boys club where I could strive towards a nationalistic ideal. The Hitler Youth had camping, hikes, and group meetings. I was number 9 in the Northeim group when I joined in 1930. There were boys from all classes of families though mainly middle class and workers. There were no social or class distinctions, which I approved of very much. There was no direct or obvious political indoctrination until later—after Hitler came to power. Without really trying to get new members, the Northeim Hitler Youth grew rapidly. I think most of the other boys joined for the same reason I did. They were looking for a place where they could get together with other boys in exciting activities. It was also a depression time and there were many evil influences abroad from which decent boys wished to escape. In any event, I don't think the political factor was the main reason boys joined. We did march in parades and hated the SPD, but that was all general, not specific—it

was all a part of it. We weren't fully conscious of what we were doing, but we enjoyed ourselves and also felt important.[25]

By the end of 1932 the Northeim Hitler Youth had grown to about seventy-five members.

The female counterpart to the Hitler Youth was the League of German Girls, open to those aged ten to eighteen. The Northeim branch was led by SS leader Hermann Denzler's wife, Claire. Though it stressed practical activities such as first-aid training, it was also used for propaganda work: the girls were displayed in parades and at mass meetings. By the end of 1932 there were ninety-two members of Northeim's League of German Girls, though not all were residents of the town.[26]

The Nazis also had an organization for women, set up early in 1931 with a starting membership of twenty-two. Most, but not all, of its members were the wives of Nazi party members. Internal bickering characterized the Women's Auxiliary in Northeim, primarily because of the personality of the chairwoman, Frau Meyer, and consequently the organization was never effective. Despite her unpopularity, Frau Meyer was perversely supported by Ernst Girmann and kept in office until early 1933, when he finally ordered her dismissal because the uproar over her leadership had become a threat to his own position.[27]

The real workhorses of Northeim's Nazi organization were the members of the "Storm Section": the SA, or "Brownshirts." Not all members of the party were in the SA, nor were all Stormtroopers party members, though there was some crossover. In Northeim there were not more than fifty members of the SA before 1933, though it seemed to most townspeople that there were anywhere from three to eight times as many. Whenever the Nazis held a public function in Northeim they called in SA men from the rural countryside for protection and to impress the populace. Much of the day-to-day work of the SA was also done by these men from the farming villages of Northeim County. Whenever they came to town they gathered either at the soup kitchen or at Northeim Nazi headquarters (in a tavern on Broad Street), and in addition to drinking and talking politics they were available for any tasks. It was an open secret that the SA was receiving military training (mostly drill) every Friday night in the Cattle Auction Hall, whose owner let them use the rooms rent-free.[28] They were frequently seen on the streets and made themselves conspicuous by shouting insults at Social Democrats or *"Heil Hitler!"* to one another. Thus there appeared to be many more Stormtroopers than there actually were.[29]

There was much for the SA to do. Many Nazi meetings were held under their auspices and almost all functions required their participation for protection, music, or entertainment. It was their job to put up posters and in general to conduct publicity. The SA also undertook all sorts of actions as a result of either boredom or animal energy. Thus in 1931, two SA men crept up to the house of a Northeim SPD leader and painted a swastika on his door with the words, "Under this sign you'll bleed, you red pig." [30] Northeimers frequently saw slogans painted on walls or telephone poles, "Throw the Jews out!" or "The Jews are our misfortune!" and these too were the casual work of the SA. [31]

If there was nothing else for the SA to do, there were always lists of potential pro-Nazis to work on. The Nazis kept close track of whoever came to their meetings and afterward worked hard to get such people to join, contribute to, or at least vote for, the NSDAP.

Many Stormtroopers were rough types, and at least some were former Communists. Northeim's workers were likely to beat them up, and furthermore, SA discipline systematically promoted nihilistic brutality. The SA generally incorporated weapons into their uniforms. Leather shoulder straps were made detachable and the buckles were weighted. Many SA men carried blackjacks, brass knuckles, or *Stahlruten*. These last were ingenious weapons consisting of a short length of pipe open at one end, inside of which was a spring with steel balls attached. The pipe was the handle; the spring and balls the weapon. When swung, the balls came out on the spring and struck with the leverage of their extended length, yet the whole contraption fitted neatly into a pocket. The presence of a group of rough, armed, and bored SA men, many of whom came from outside Northeim, was the prime cause of violence in the town. [32]

Northeimers saw the SA most frequently when the Nazis held parades. The newspapers generally commented favorably on their drill order. But the SA was determined to be more than good parade soldiers. Already in 1931 the *Volksblatt* reported that people passing by the Cattle Auction Hall could hear the sounds of military exercises. By autumn 1932, Northeim's SA members engaged in extensive public maneuvers in a nearby forest, followed by a "Maneuver Ball." By late 1932 training courses were instituted, and the SA was able to set up its own *Standarten-Heim* in an abandoned factory, moving from the soup kitchen. [33] In short, by the end of 1932, Northeim's SA, composed mainly of young farmers' sons, had developed into a formidable instrument: well trained, equipped, and housed; spirited and under the iron discipline of the Nazi party. The knowledge that people had of the existence of this corps was to be an important factor in the opening months of the Third Reich.

Many SA men were unemployed and could not afford to buy a Storm-trooper uniform. The Nazi solution to this was, like all their financial ar-rangements, ingenious, flexible, and decentralized. Uniforms could be bought on credit; more frequently local party members were asked to donate the money on an *ad hoc* basis; no doubt it was gratifying to them to "adopt" a specific Stormtrooper. Or a wealthy Nazi from Northeim might fit out five or six SA men.[34] In no instance did money for this come from outside the town and any money the SA itself might collect (in the streets or at meetings) had to be turned over to the Local Group of the party, which was then responsible for all the SA's expenses.[35] Like the whole of Nazi operations in Northeim, the SA was financed exclusively from local resources. Far from receiving money from the national NSDAP, the Local Group was constantly called upon to make contributions to it. The money Local Group Northeim used for its own operations came from a variety of expedients. At the core of the whole financing system was the ever-growing mass backing for Nazism, a fanatically self-sacrificial cadre of members, and a number of sharp practices deriving from the small-business background of so many Nazi leaders.

A constant source of income was the dues paid by each member, which were fixed at about RM 1.40 per person per month. Of this sum, 30 *Pfennig* could be retained by the Local Group, while the rest had to be turned over to the *Gau* (which in turn had to give half of what it got to the national headquarters in Munich).[36] The requirement of making these fixed monthly remittances kept every level in the Nazi party keenly interested in accurate membership records and made the upper levels determined to get prompt payments in accordance with membership figures. Any Nazi who missed three dues payments was automatically expelled from the party—it was by far the most common reason for the membership's high turnover rate. New mem-bers also had to pay an "initiation fee" ranging from zero to 3 marks, ac-cording to the individual's income. In addition, members were assessed pe-riodic "campaign contributions" of up to 15 marks per person. For example, thirty-nine members admitted to Local Group Northeim in 1933 paid a total of 202 marks in these two categories. In initiation fees two paid none, six paid 2 marks apiece, and the rest each paid 3 marks. Their campaign con-tributions totaled 97 marks: one paid 15, two paid 10, thirteen paid nothing, and the rest paid 1 to 3 marks each.[37]

Other special contributions were frequently demanded of the members. For Reichstag elections every member was required to pay 1 mark extra dues. In March 1931, each party member in *Gau* South Hanover-Brunswick had to buy 10 marks' worth of shares in the *Niedersächsische Tageszeitung* so that the *Gau* could have a daily newspaper (to which, of course, every Nazi was then expected to subscribe). The following month each member was assessed a fixed contribution to buy the Hitler Youth some capital equipment. These were just the formal exactions levied by the national and district leadership; there were innumerable similar but informal demands made by the local leaders. All this was based on the idea that a Nazi should sacrifice for the cause. In short, the members of the Nazi party were exploited for all they could bear.[38]

Yet the party also operated in a very businesslike manner: cash in advance was the rule for everything the Local Group received from the *Gau*, from bundles of printed propaganda to speaker's fees. Not even the printed receipt forms given to townspeople who made contributions to the Local Group were free. Called *Bausteine* ("building blocks"), these were color-coded for varying sums from 50 *Pfennig* to 5 marks, and the *Gau* charged Local Group Northeim for their printing costs, the cost of mailing them, and then expected a strict accounting of the proceeds from their sale.[39]

The Local Group was equally stingy about its own operational expenses. Wherever possible, people were asked to pay for the leaflets and pamphlets the Nazis pressed upon them. For each meeting Local Group Northeim held it paid an insurance fee of 1 mark for every two hundred persons attending, to protect itself against any damage suits that might arise. All Northeim's County and Local Group officials were unpaid volunteers; the only salary paid was 45 marks a month to a typist. The party's offices, above a tavern on Broad Street, cost them 25 marks a month to rent. But they sublet space in the anteroom to a small businessman who used it to sell Nazi postcards, stationery, and greeting cards and paid 10 marks a month to the Local Group for this privilege. When the Local Group had to contract for outside services, such as legal representation, the provider's bill might be returned to him with a polite suggestion that he consider making his fee a campaign contribution.[40] Virtually no chance was missed to save or earn a few *Pfennige*.

The main source of income came from mass meetings: from the ticket sales for admissions and the collection taken up after the speaker's performance. Consequently, meetings were very carefully tailored to the town's tastes; from a profit-making point of view these meetings may be compared to revival meetings held in the American Midwest at about the same time. Certainly the Nazis became very conscious of the entertainment value of their mass meetings in small towns like Northeim.[41] They had also discovered that one meeting with a famous speaker would earn enough to finance a second one and the take from that second meeting was thus pure profit. Since the tickets and the collection usually yielded an average of 1 mark per person, two full-house meetings in the *1910er Zelt* cleared well over 1,000 marks. Of course it rarely worked out so neatly and often things went wrong (a rainy night, for example). But the vision of getting their hands on vast funds, even in a depression environment, was held by many Nazi leaders.[42]

It was important enough so that the *Gau* propaganda section formulated exact rules on how to stage a meeting, with a checklist for everything from the advertising to the use of the SA. There was even a model script with the actual words to be used at all points in the meeting plus blank spaces for the name of the town, the speaker, etc. The model meeting always included a collection. Appended to this memorandum was a lengthy section on the literal care and feeding of the speaker: he was to be assured periods of quiet and therefore must not be "entertained" or socially lionized; he must not be paid his fee in the small coins collected at meetings; his schedule must be punctually kept so that he could maximize his speaking engagements; in general he was a valuable asset whose careful treatment would bring commensurate rewards.[43] Thus, Nazi meetings not only paid for themselves, they financed other propaganda activities that increased attendance at future meetings. By 1931 the Nazi party had become a kind of "pyramid club" and as long as the momentum could be sustained it seemed that the profits would grow limitlessly.

Although the local leaders did not personally get to keep the profits generated from meetings and other sources, profits meant that funds were then available to be applied locally for further recruiting activity, and the leader who was successful in building backing for Nazism could expect promotion within the Nazi hierarchy. The *Gau* was tireless in pressing recruitment materials on the Local Groups (on a cash-in-advance basis, of course). There were guidelines and pamphlets for door-to-door campaigning, slides and films, leaflets to pass out at meetings or stuff into mailboxes, posters for billboards (red was the preferred color according to the party's propaganda technicians), and gummed stickers to be pasted onto walls and fences. Themes and contents were so numerous that almost any combination could be created to suit particular needs. There was also advice on how to compose personal invitations to "discussion evenings" and even a breakdown of the expected costs for staging a mass march.[44] The more a Local Group held profitable meetings, the more it would be able to buy the materials to recruit new members and supporters, which in turn led to more meetings and more profits. The payoff was in the swelling ranks of members and the mounting numbers of Nazi votes, both of which were frequently verified in firm statistics. Growth redounded to the glory, within the Nazi movement as a whole, of the responsible local leader. Success was quite easily measured, as was failure. Thus there was not only constant pressure for activity but also constant feedback as to what sorts of activities worked. This self-reinforcing system was a major cause for the growing power of Hitler's movement in the period from 1930 to 1933.

But the key to the system, the base factor in the whole process, was the method of adapting mass meetings, with appropriate speakers, to local interests and concerns. Again, what worked was immediately measurable in terms of attendance and contributions, so that effective themes and speakers could be repeated while ineffective combinations could be discarded. Had the Nazis not found it necessary to finance themselves from the bottom up, they probably never would have produced such a self-regulating propaganda mechanism.

The burden of operating this system fell equally on the Local Group's leaders and the *Gau* offices (though specific propaganda materials and themes were devised and produced at the national Nazi headquarters). Yet the *Gauleitung* provided hardly any actual direction. Most of the correspondence between the local Nazis and the *Gauleitung* was about propaganda (getting the locally requested speakers and printed materials to the local units), money (mostly whether the dues remitted were correct, sometimes about debts), and organization (verifying who was a member and assuring that all local party positions were properly filled). For the rest, the *Gau* depended overwhelmingly on the energy and skill of its local leaders and gave them almost complete freedom of action as long as they produced money, members, and votes.[45]

In Northeim the Nazi effort was supervised by two officials: the County Leader, Walter Steineck, who was also titular Local Group Leader for the town until late 1932, and the Deputy Local Group Leader of Northeim, Ernst Girmann, who actually ran the town's Nazi party. While Girmann was theoretically subordinate to Steineck, in practice they were equals because Steineck simply did not have the time to control day-to-day operations in the town and therefore had to give Girmann a free rein. Since Girmann was both extremely assertive and power hungry, he took full advantage of this situation with respect to Steineck and operated as Local Group Leader for Northeim, in all but name, from 1930 on.

Walter Steineck, the County Leader, had first joined the Nazi party in June 1929, at the time of the revival of Nazism in Northeim. He was of the lower middle class, a marginally successful salesman of agricultural implements, and had just moved to Northeim that year. His great weakness was alcohol, which he consumed prodigiously and which finally killed him during World War II. He often spent time sitting around the baggage room of the Northeim railroad station, drinking from his private flask and telling the workers Rabelaisian jokes. Yet he also devoted considerable time and effort to the Nazi cause, neglecting his own business (which had declined because of the depression, anyway) to the point where he was on the verge of bankruptcy by 1933. After the first Nazi leader for Northeim, Rudolf Ernst, was eased out of the job in the spring of 1930, Steineck took over as County Leader and proved to be a success at it. Supervising the County organization was an increasingly heavy task, but Steineck approached it in an easygoing way, aided by his business background. It was only in late 1932 that his health began to break down under the strain. A sentimentalist, he was at his best when joking with SA men. He never was much of an orator and often lamented the passing of the old intimate meetings in the Cattle Auction Hall. Though capable of ruthlessness, he was not a brutal man and even his opponents conceded that he had a warm heart beneath his crude manner.[46]

Ernst Girmann was a different sort of person altogether. Chunky, with fair hair, a ruddy complexion, and pale gray eyes, he was energetic and fanatical. The kindest thing said of him was that he was "an unpleasant contemporary," which at the least was the reaction of most Northeimers, including Walter Steineck. Girmann, too, had business experience from working in his father's hardware store, though it was his brother, Karl, who actually managed the business. Another brother had died in World War I, in which Ernst had also fought and been wounded. In fact, Ernst Girmann never lost the bitterness he acquired as an army officer during that war, and possibly also the contempt for his fellow man that he brought home from the war. He was cold, cynical, crude, ruthless, and brutal. He was never much interested in a business career but showed enormous talent as an administrator and a politician. Being a Nazi became his life work: he joined the party in 1922 and was to become mayor of Northeim for the duration of the Third Reich. Perhaps because of the long years during which Northeim had ignored the Nazis, Girmann frequently expressed contempt for the townspeople. He drank heavily and when drunk was generally morose. His most common emotion was anger, which could develop into furious rage. Long after the Nazi years were over, many Northeimers still quailed at the recollection of his pulsing red face and mordant language. Devoid of other sentiment and consumed by ambition, Girmann was chiefly responsible for the driving energy of Local Group Northeim of the Nazi party.

Though Ernst Girmann had been a Nazi since 1922, and the town's leader in those early years, he had drifted away from a leadership role and it was not until 1930 that he took over as Deputy Local Group Leader for Northeim. Generally unknown, even to some of the town's party members, he rapidly imposed his cold and driving personality upon the organization. His success in turning the town into a Nazi stronghold was rewarded by the *Gauleitung* in November 1932, when he was officially appointed Local Group Leader for Northeim. By then he also had many enemies among the town's members of the NSDAP. To those who were not Nazi party members, Ernst Girmann was frequently identified with the rough, undesirable side of Nazism.[47]

"There were two groups of Nazis in Northeim," said a former civil servant, "the decent ones and the gutter type. In the end the gutter won out."[48] This was the feeling of many Northeimers, for even those who voted for the NSDAP had mixed emotions. But then there were Nazis like Wilhelm Spannaus, and indeed many respectable Northeimers were Nazis: the owner of one of the town's hotels, the director of the *Lyzeum,* about three teachers, the owner of the cigar factory, the owner of the movie theater on the Market Square, both judges at the County Court, and several high officials of the railroad directory. And of course a leading Nazi who lived in Northeim County was Count von Strahlenheim, a man of impeccable credentials—nobleman, landowner, and major in World War I. When he quit the Nationalists to join the Nazis, it was page one news for both the GGZ and the NNN.[49]

Another ambivalent aspect of Nazism for most Northeimers was the party's anti-Semitism. Social discrimination against Jews was practically non-existent in the town. Jews were integrated along class lines: the two wealthy Jewish families belonged to upper-class circles and clubs, Jews of middling income belonged to the middle-class social organizations, and working-class Jews were in the Socialist community. Yet abstract anti-Semitism in the form of jokes or expressions of generalized distaste was prevalent, approximately to the extent that these things existed in America in the 1930s. If Nazi anti-Semitism held any appeal for the townspeople, it was in a highly abstract form, as a remote theory unconnected with daily encounters with real Jews in Northeim. Northeim's NSDAP leaders sensed this, and in consequence anti-Semitism was not pushed in propaganda except in a ritualistic way. (The chief exceptions to this were the chalked or shouted slogans of the SA and their acceptance by peasants and by some of the rowdier employees of the artisan shops.) Northeimers were drawn to anti-Semitism because they were drawn to Nazism, not the other way around. Many who voted Nazi simply ignored or rationalized the anti-Semitism of the party, just as they ignored other unpleasant aspects of the Nazi movement.

Northeimers joined the NSDAP for many reasons in the years before Hitler came to power. One man and his wife were moved by "social" reasons: "We believed the common people should have a better life and that socialism was essential. We were idealists. In fact we were among the few people who had something to lose, for my business was successful.''[50] Another, the principal of the girls' high school in Northeim, was motivated primarily by anti-Communism. He joined in 1932, quickly got into a struggle over Ernst Girmann's ''corrupt doings,'' and was forced to leave the town after the Third Reich was established. After the war he wrote:

> I came to Northeim in 1925 from Berlin, where I had lived for thirty years and where I returned for a few weeks during my vacation every year. I observed many things in Berlin which could not be noticed—or only to a lesser degree—in small towns. I saw the Communist danger, the Communist terror, their gangs breaking up ''bourgeois'' meetings, the ''bourgeois'' parties being utterly helpless, the Nazis being the only party that broke terror by anti-terror. I saw the complete failure of the ''bourgeois'' parties to deal with the economic crisis (6 to 7 millions out of work, the Reichsbank discount up to 15 percent). Only national socialism offered any hope. Anti-Semitism had another aspect in Berlin; Nazis mostly did not hate Jews individually, many had Jewish friends, but they were concerned about the Jewish problem: Most Jews, though ready for complete assimilation, willing to be 100 percent Germans, persisted in being loyal to their Jewish fellows (mostly coming in from Poland and Russia), helping them, pushing them on, so that more and more Jews got positions not only in trade, banking, theater, film, the newspapers, etc., whole branches of the economy and key positions being in the hands of Jews, also doctors, lawyers, etc. (The direct influence of Jews in politics was greatly overestimated by the Nazis.) Many people saw the danger of that problem. Nobody knew of any way to deal with it, but they hoped the Nazis would know. If they had guessed how the Nazis did deal with it, not one in a hundred would have joined the party.[51]

Others joined the NSDAP for simpler reasons: because it looked as though the Nazis would be victorious and they hoped to profit. This was notoriously the case with a teacher at the *Gymnasium,* and indeed, when the Nazis came to power he was promoted.[52] Another man, who owned a printing shop, joined for business reasons:

> It was the depression and business was bad. The Nazis used to ask my father for contributions and he refused. As a consequence of

this he lost business. So he joined the Nazi party. But this lost him other customers, so he was discouraged by the whole situation. He probably wouldn't have joined of his own choice.[53]

In the opinion of a keen observer, "Most of those who joined the Nazis did so because they wanted a radical answer to the economic problem. Then, too, people wanted a hard, sharp, clear leadership—they were disgusted with the eternal political strife of parliamentary party politics."[54]

Yet most Northeimers were dubious. "My previous experience showed me that the ranks of the NSDAP were mostly filled with incompetents and bankrupts."[55] This was the opinion of the conservative Prefect of Northeim County (an opinion he later changed). "The Nazis were bankrupt people prior to 1933—full of the poor, the thieves, and the morally and financially bankrupt," said another who later joined the NSDAP.[56] And of course the Social Democrats were uniformly of this opinion.

Most Northeimers had little idea what the Nazis would really do after they achieved power. Even Jews had no notion that the Nazis really meant what they said.[57] This was not for lack of information. Anyone who went regularly to Nazi meetings, or read the pamphlets, or even the slogans chalked on the walls, should have been able to discern the vulgar and violent aspects of the NSDAP. Northeimers could find out directly by reading the Nazis' own publication for Northeim: *Hört! Hört!* Every article in it derided some individual, and it was readable only because of variety in the forms of derision. Sarcasm and gutter language were the rule. Not one single issue of the paper contained a positive idea. And its editor was a crook.[58]

One series of opinions on what kinds of individuals were Nazis was available to Northeimers through the columns of the *Volksblatt*. Nor did Northeimers have to read the SPD paper to hear the stories, for they were generally so juicy that they went around by word of mouth. The *Volksblatt's* stories attempted to show that Northeim's Nazis were ridiculous, crude, venal, and brutal. If a delivery boy fell off his bicycle while trying to manage the Nazi salute, that made the *Volksblatt*.[59] If the SA put swastika stickers on the tombstones of the cemetery, the headline was "Nazi Respect for the Dead."[60] Since the *Volksblatt* believed most Nazis were thieves, it always reported stories like "B——, writer for *Hört! Hört!* . . . and pillar of the Nazi party in Northeim, who was recently given a three-month sentence for libel against Governor Noske, has now betrayed the confidence of his landlady and stolen money from her. Another Nazi has thus proved himself a common crook. Who'll be next?"[61]

In addition to seeing the Nazis as foolish, crude, and greedy, the *Volks-*

blatt portrayed them as violent and vicious. Story after story built up this image: of a four-year-old boy admitted to the Northeim hospital after having been beaten by his Nazi stepfather, of a sixteen-year-old Hitler Youth member who shot his grandmother while trying to rob her, and, most scabrous of all, of a Nazi carpenter in a neighboring town who tried to rape a married woman who was dusting the altar in the town church.[62] The other newspapers did not report incidents of this sort. The editor of the GGZ, though a Nationalist, was favorably disposed toward Nazism. The NNN considered such stories in bad taste; if it had to report unpleasant incidents it avoided mentioning names but used the person's occupation and first initial of his last name. The worst one could read about the Nazis in the NNN were reports of their being jailed for violating the uniform prohibition, or of the suppression of *Hört! Hört!* for libel (both frequent occurrences). By late 1932 the editor of the NNN became increasingly anti-Nazi, but he was also a careful businessman with no desire to lose circulation or advertising, with so many people voting Nazi.

Thus unless Northeimers believed the Socialist press, which was probably the case only for those townspeople who were already Socialist, they had little chance to acquire unfavorable opinions of the NSDAP. Enough of the character of the Nazis was apparent in their words and actions to make even those who voted for them dubious, but the fact remains that few Northeimers had any real conception of what the Nazis would do if they ever came to power. Northeimers were mainly aware that conditions were currently very bad and that the Nazis were a young, energetic group pledged to rectify the situation.

The only Northeimers who clearly apprehended the Nazi threat were the Social Democrats. After the August 1931 referendum, the Socialists were relatively inactive. In October the *Reichsbanner* staged another march through the county and in December held a public meeting with about six hundred attending. The speaker attempted to show that a Nazi-bourgeois coalition in Braunschweig worked to the disadvantage of the middle classes, but his only recommendation was that the middle class join the SPD. One final event of the year was the showing of an anti-Communist film.[63]

But public meetings were not the only work of the SPD in 1931. During that year the Socialists held seven membership meetings in Northeim and sixty-three in the county. Finances came from dues and the small admission fee charged for some public meetings. Income of the Northeim Social Democratic party in this depression year was 1,841 marks; expenditures, 1,762 marks. In addition, the Workers' Welfare section was active with four meetings, three children's excursions, 206 Christmas packages to poor families,

67 packages to old folks, and 350 articles of clothing made by workers' wives. It took in 2,125 marks and disbursed 1,859 marks, an effort which put it ahead of all other private welfare organizations in town. The Socialist Women's Group held fifty meetings over the year and increased its membership to 130. The Young Socialist Workers held eighty-five meetings, showed films, and gave a "parents' evening" in addition to working for the party. The SPD Children's Friends Movement visited thirty-five children to make sure they were well cared for. Politics was almost a sideline for the SPD.[64]

The year 1932 was the last year of democracy in Germany. Northeim's Social Democrats could not know this, but they did have a sense of crisis. An indication of this was the decision, made nationally in response to the Nazi-Nationalist "Harzburg Front," to amalgamate all anti-Nazi groups into one organization to be named the "Iron Front." In Northeim a new executive committee representing all workers' organizations called a mass meeting in late January in the *1910er Zelt*. The hall was so crowded that many had to stand. The black-red-gold flag of the Weimar Republic was prominently displayed and music was supplied by the *Reichsbanner* fife-and-drum corps and two workers' choral societies. A cartoon film, "In the Third Reich," was shown. There were four speakers, including Deppe and Carl Querfurt. The speeches were militantly anti-Nazi, though one also emphasized SPD achievements and Nazi-capitalist connections. Three weeks later another mass meeting heard a general denunciation of the NSDAP and a promise that the Iron Front would be victorious. At the SPD County General Meeting on February 16, all agreed that Nazism was the prime foe, and that it was "do or die" this year against Hitler.[65]

With the beginning of 1932 the Nazis also moved into high gear. On January 25 they held a "Big Army March and Concert Evening" with gymnastic presentations and an SA *Oberfuehrer* as speaker. The *1910er Zelt* was full until one in the morning. The very next day there was another mammoth rally with three speakers including a member of the Reichstag and of the Prussian Parliament. For five hours the audience heard speeches on agriculture, the middle class, and the "the struggle against Marxism and Liberalism."[66]

The Nazis did not neglect their appeal to the religious element in Northeim, either, in which they were aided by Lutheran fears of the SPD. The previous autumn the county church convention had heard a pastor from Hanover warn the faithful against the Social Democratic party, which he characterized as "fundamentally antichurch." His speech was seconded by the Count von Strahlenheim, who directed the assembled ministers to struggle against "Bolshevism." At a meeting of the Northeim Lutheran parish in

February 1932, another pastor linked the SPD with the Communists as the chief force behind atheism and "free-thinkerdom."[67] The SPD simply ignored such charges, but the Nazis moved to exploit them. On February 12, 1932, they brought in a minister to lecture before a select list of "preachers, church elders, teachers, and school committeemen" on "National Socialism and Christianity" at one of the town's hotels. The speaker declared that German Christianity had received a blow from the Weimar Constitution, which he said pointed directly toward Bolshevism. He described the Nazi goal as "the folkish, organic, God-fearing man." At least one pastor challenged the speaker by asserting that the Nazi racial program would lead to "national idolatry and mass-hatred." But "when the speaker denied this heatedly, the audience applauded warmly."[68]

Nationalism was also promoted. On February 12, a packed *1910er Zelt* heard the Braunschweig Nazi Minister of the Interior spend two hours attacking the "Pan-Europe" movement.[69] The DNVP pushed a similar theme at a meeting in the Hotel Sonne where a retired lieutenant general described how the German army would have won World War I if it had not been stabbed in the back by traitors at home. Nineteen new members of the *Stahlhelm* youth section were sworn in and the meeting closed with the singing of *Deutschland über Alles* and an oath of allegiance to the black-white-red Imperial flag.[70]

Against this background the SPD could score one success. Since the August referendum, the *Volksblatt* had been relentless in its attacks on Senator Mahner of the Civic Association. Among the senator's areas of competence in the city government was the Northeim Brewery. Late in 1931, the *Volksblatt* reported persistent rumors that the brewery's bookkeeper had embezzled funds. The editorial queried gleefully: "Can it be that Senator Mahner has not kept careful watch?" Within a few months the whole story was out: since 1924 the bookkeeper had stolen 90,000 marks. The *Volksblatt* warmed to its task: "Were there no auditings of the books? Did Senator Mahner take adequate precautions against embezzlement? When will there be a public hearing?" A few weeks later the *Volksblatt* reported with unspeakable joy that the bookkeeper was a member of the German Nationalist party, just like Senator Mahner.[71]

The senator was eventually driven to despair by the *Volksblatt*'s incessant attacks. At practically every Civic Association meeting he railed against the paper and tried to get Northeim's businessmen to stop advertising in it. He vigorously denied that he was a member of the NSDAP, saying that he was above parties *("Bürgerlich und daher überparteilich")*. He explained to the general meeting of the Civic Association of February 26, 1932, that the brewery bookkeeper had repaid all that he had embezzled and the City Council had unanimously decided not to prosecute. After this explanation, Senator Mahner declared that he could no longer bear the attacks of the *Volksblatt* and that he was therefore resigning as chairman of the Civic Association. His fellow members defended him and later tried to reelect him, but he refused to serve any longer. The fight had gone out of him; he never made another speech and was inactive thereafter.[72]

Even this did not mollify the *Volksblatt*. As long as Mahner continued to hold his senatorship, the assaults upon his character continued. In April it was charged that the brewery supplied free beer to a Nazi Stormtroopers' school in a neighboring town. In August the *Volksblatt* charged that the brewery automobile had been given a faulty repair job but that 1,000 marks had been paid to the garage owner anyway. In December 1932, Mahner was charged with hiring "double earners" instead of unemployed persons for some city work.[73]

All of this made interesting reading for Northeimers and possibly increased the *Volksblatt's* circulation. In some cases it might even have affected votes. But its chief effect was to debase the nature of politics and to destroy the foundation of trust and mutual respect without which democracy cannot succeed. When politics becomes a matter of vilification and innuendo, then eventually people feel repugnance for the whole process. It is the beginning of a yearning for a strong man who will rise above petty and partisan groups. The Nazis were to exploit this feeling fully, and though they contributed richly to the rise of partisan acrimony, they were also the first to pronounce "politician" with every possible tone of scorn and sarcasm.

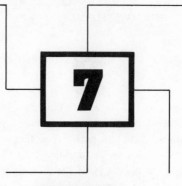

POLITICAL CRESCENDO

SPRING 1932

Elect Hindenburg! Elect our best.
He is not the servant of any party—
he follows only God and his conscience.

Advertisement of the German
People's Party (DVP), Northeim
in the *Northeimer Neueste Nachrichten*
on March 11, 1932

By the end of the winter of 1931–1932, conditions in Northeim were favorable to the rapid advance of Nazism. The depression was at its worst, violence was becoming more frequent, and the twin passions of nationalism and class antagonism were at their height. Northeim's Nazis had established themselves as both respectable and radical. They were seen as patriotic, anti-Socialist, and religious. They enjoyed the apparent blessings of the conservatives. But at the same time the Nazis appeared to be vigorous, determined and, above all, ready to use radical means to deal with the crucial problem—the depression. Ordinary measures had been proved sufficient for welfare efforts, but only extreme measures would end the depression and only the Nazis were thought of as sufficiently extreme. All that was needed to complete the favorable situation was the whip of new election campaigns.

The propitious circumstances were not, of course, predominantly local. Despite its constant activity in Northeim, the NSDAP won its first successes there only after democracy deteriorated on the national level. Beginning in 1930, a stable majority was unobtainable in the Reichstag and the chancellor, Brüning, began to issue laws over the head of the parliament by using Hindenburg's presidential emergency powers. Though Brüning's decrees were unpopular with the SPD, the Socialists refused to topple him because they feared that the turmoil of elections would result in further Nazi and Communist gains. Hence a queasy stalemate existed in Germany from the spring of 1930 to the spring of 1932: the country was ruled by unpopular laws, issued not on the authority of a democratic parliament, but on that of the aging Field Marshal who had been elected president in 1925.

The only justification for such a debilitating procedure would have been success in dealing with the depression. But Brüning's harsh deflationary measures, based on economic orthodoxy, actually intensified the effects of the depression, and the Nazis successfully labeled him the "Hunger Chancellor." The only benefit of Brüning's semi-authoritarian rule was political stagnation in the sense that new elections were avoided. In 1932 even this came to an end as Hindenburg's term ran out. The final condition for Nazi growth in Northeim was thus present.

The presidential election was set for March 13, 1932. Hindenburg stood for reelection and was backed by Republican parties from the SPD to the People's party. The Nazis ran Hitler, and the Communists also entered a candidate—the veteran Stalinist Ernst Thaelmann. The Nationalists, unwilling to support Hindenburg because he had not subverted the Republic, and not yet willing to throw in their lot with Hitler, nominated the deputy commander of the *Stahlhelm,* Duesterberg. There was also a crackpot named Winter who managed to get on the ballot. But almost every German saw the essential contest in terms of Hitler *versus* Hindenburg.

In Northeim the first, almost predictable sign of the impending election was an upsurge of violence. Since the "Referendum Day Battle" of the previous August, there had been no political fights in the town, except a minor tavern brawl in early December.[1] In the last week of February 1932, however, there was a knife fight near the railroad station and two other fights on Broad Street between Nazis and *Reichsbanner* men.[2] A week later an irate Northeimer wrote to the NNN to say that even children were becoming involved. He had observed a group of boys describing Hitler in filthy terms (with the encouragement of their parents) before the newly opened Nazi election headquarters. The *Volksblatt* countered this by reporting that three Nazi youths followed some working women home shouting foul language at them. It identified one of the boys as a clerk at Hermann Denzler's store. It also reported that a woman taking her child to church on a Sunday morning was struck in the face by a bundle of political leaflets when she refused to accept one from a young *Stahlhelm* member.[3] These incidents found their way into the newspapers, but exchanges of taunts and insults between *Reischsbanner* men and Nazis were daily occurrences.

Behind part of the bitterness was the economic distress, since the election campaign came at a time when the greatest number of Northeimers were unemployed during the entire depression era. In the town there were over seven hundred registered unemployed in March and April of 1932, an increase of almost 50 percent over the previous year at the same time. Furthermore, from this time on, the number of men on the welfare rolls regularly exceeded the number of those drawing unemployment insurance. To the District Employment Office in the old Army compound, almost fourteen thousand registered unemployed were making their dismal journey every week—double the adult population of Northeim. Two bankruptcies occurred in February, and a government proposal to lower the price of beer brought such heated protests from the Northeim County Tavern-Keepers Association that the authorities were forced to abandon their plans. Even the widows and orphans rose in protest. In early February a mass meeting of War Widows and Industrial Accident Victims was held to protest the lowering of pensions. Because the meeting was dominated by Socialists, World War I and not the Republic was blamed for the existence of so many widows and orphans, but the audience was in a bitter mood.[4]

It was also in March 1932 that the saddest blow of all came to some Northeimers when the Workers' Funeral Savings Society collapsed. It was a result of embezzlement by the Society's treasurer, though the loss could have been withstood if new subscribers had been joining. The 470 members were each reimbursed only a small portion of what they had put in over the years. As the older workers and their wives filed out of the hall they knew that in addition to everything else they now faced a pauper's grave.[5]

Such frustrations were easily channeled into aggression by the partisan press. The Nazis concentrated on accusations of corruption, even if there was none. By the opening of the election campaign, *Hört! Hört!* was being sued by the Northeim Senate for a libelous article on the City Hospital, by the County Prefect for having slandered a county official, and by the Health Insurance Office for publishing false reports. The *Volksblatt* was less clumsy but equally vicious. Among other things it took note of the fact that a leading Northeim conservative ("that great enemy of socialistic laws") had sent his daughter to draw unemployment pay. The *Volksblatt* expressed the fervent hope that the Employment Office would scrutinize this case with extra care. Similarly, fresh instances of Nazi crudity and bloodthirstiness were sought out and published.[6]

Though the SPD supported Hindenburg's reelection solely because he was the "lesser evil," it conducted a vigorous campaign in Northeim. On March 6, the new Iron Front staged a mass demonstration with the town band, the *Reichsbanner* fife-and-drum corps, and twenty-five flags and banners. At the Market Square little was said about the benefits of Hindenburg but much was said about the drawbacks of Nazism, including, according to a woman speaker who bolstered her assertions by quotations from the writings of Goebbels and Strasser, the probability that "women would be breeding-slaves in the Third Reich."[7]

The second SPD meeting for Hindenburg had to be held in the Riding Hall, since the *1910er Zelt* was unavailable. It was not available to the Socialists because the town's Nazis had taken the extraordinary step of renting it continuously themselves, just to keep anyone else from using it, despite the great cost involved.[8] Still, the Social Democratic meeting in the uncomfortable Riding Hall was a powerful one. Over 1,200 people were present to hear Carl Querfurt and Karl Deppe attack the Nazis and the Civic Association and also call for Hindenburg's reelection.[9] The People's party, officially backing Hindenburg, limited its support to advertisements in the NNN proclaiming Hindenburg to be above parties.[10]

The spur of electioneering even brought the Communists to Northeim. In February their district brass band came to town for a parade and a meeting in front of a tavern. Just before the voting the KPD staged another parade led by a ten-year-old boy wearing a red tie. The atmosphere became a bit tense when a strong contingent of *Reichsbanner* men joined the parade; the Communists rapidly decided to end their demonstration with a concert by the brass band instead of speeches in the Market Square.[11]

The Nationalists were in the campaign primarily to keep their identity before the voters. They also hoped, by increased activism, to regain the allegiance of their former followers who were drifting into the Nazi camp. Their first election meeting featured a lieutenant colonel who adopted a peculiar hedging stance on Nazism, saying that the DNVP was "against Hitler's politics, not his person." This was followed by a *Stahlhelm* "Theater Evening" with a century-old comedy of manners, and two other political meetings in the last week before the election. One, featuring a DNVP Reichstag member, who spoke of experiences during a trip to the USSR, drew a sizable crowd. The second meeting, poorly attended, heard a member of the *Stahlhelm* attack Hitler vigorously, claiming that he wanted to dissolve the *Stahlhelm* and institute Socialism.[12]

This extensive political activity was as nothing when compared to the Nazi effort. A month before election day the NSDAP brought the Nazi Minister of the Interior of Braunschweig to Northeim for a mass meeting.[13] But instead of following this up, Northeim's Nazis employed a new technique. No further meetings were held until early March, but then the Nazis used the *1910er Zelt* for eight days running. Mass meetings were held on four different evenings, and daytime demonstrations were used to keep the town saturated with Nazi propaganda. It was an all-out campaign and it completely eclipsed the efforts of the opponents of Hitler.

The Nazis' concentrated campaigning was not a premeditated tactic but came about because, for once, the *Gauleitung* had suffered a temporary breakdown in its propaganda delivery system. Already by early February, Local Group Northeim was beseeching the higher offices for help because they had no speakers booked for the upcoming campaign, now less than a month away. Then the speakers they were offered were second-rate; what they had really wanted were four speakers of national eminence plus two regionally famous ones. Other plans also showed how ambitious and extravagant Northeim's Nazis had become. For example, they ordered enough leaflets to give one each to half of all the eligible voters in the entire county. However, some of the propaganda material supplied was ill-conceived and had a boomerang effect—particularly some anti-Hindenburg stickers. The demands of campaigning in Northeim County as well as in the town were also complicating their problems, since by now there were about thirty other Local Groups under County Leader Steineck's charge. But eventually this was all sorted out and from mid-February to mid-March the Northeim County organization was to stage some forty mass meetings, including eight film showings.[14] By early March the town's Nazis were ready for their own saturation campaign. It would be all the more effective since the Nazis had preemptively hired all the meeting halls in town so that the opposition could hardly counter Nazi rallies.

The first mass meeting was held on Sunday, March 6; the speakers included the pastor who had spoken at the church-oriented gathering the previous month, and a Nazi member of the Provincial Parliament. There was an enormous crowd. The general theme was the desperation of the middle classes and corruption in Berlin. Two evenings later a mass meeting was directed toward workers with "the former red sailor, party-comrade Madel, and the former Communist miner, party-comrade Knauth" speaking on "The Treason of the SPD and KPD to the Workers. Marxism Our Death, Only National Socialism Our Salvation." Bad weather caused a poor turnout, which was probably just as well for the Nazis, since the second speaker had some nasty things to say about "indifferent bourgeoisie who won't help the workers," words of doubtful appeal to the overwhelmingly middle-class following of the NSDAP in Northeim. Both of these meetings had cut-rate admission: 30 *Pfennig,* and unemployed free.[15]

Thursday, March 10, was given over to the SA. By full use of all Stormtroopers in Northeim County and neighboring areas, the Nazis were able to stage an hour-long parade with band, fife-and-drum corps, and close to 1,500 SA and SS men. The streets were packed with friends, enemies, and the curious, and the marchers were greeted alternately by cheers and catcalls. At the Market Square numerous Communists were massed. The Nazis sang the "Horst Wessel Song" as they passed, accompanied by hoots and curses from the crowd and finally by the *Internationale* as a riposte. Northeim's police, heavily reinforced by state troopers, managed to get the Nazi parade past this narrow passage without incident. The Brownshirts wound up their demonstration in front of the *1910er Zelt* with a speech. But when the Nazis started to march back through the center of Northeim they found their way blocked at the railroad tracks by an enormous crowd, well-leavened with Communists. The crowd disdained police orders to clear the area, whereupon the police moved on them with nightsticks, arresting many. This led to new difficulties as the crowd attempted to recapture the prisoners. The police, almost powerless in the face of such a mob, finally released the prisoners in the Market Square, where they were greeted by cries of "Red Front!" Through all this the Nazi Stormtroopers kept perfect order in their ranks and eventually dispersed quietly.

Socialists were particularly incensed by the day's happenings because on the previous Sunday the *Reichsbanner* had been forbidden by the police to sing songs or wear uniforms in their parade, while on this occasion the Nazis were allowed to do both. The SPD contended that all difficulties could have been avoided if the police had been firm with the Nazis. This charge deftly obscured the main effect of the violence, which had been to make Nazi charges against the "Marxists" appear reasonable in the eyes of the bourgeoisie.

In any event, by evening the town had cooled off and there were no further difficulties. The NSDAP filled the *1910er Zelt* for film-slide lectures on "How They Lie" and "The Braunschweig SA March," plus a speech on "Money Measures in the Third Reich."[16]

Nothing had been planned for the following day, Friday, but nonetheless there was a big event when Adolf Hitler passed through Northeim at noon on his way to a neighboring town. He was met and cheered by a group of Nazis, and paused to express his thanks before driving on. Tempers were still high enough from the previous day so that the *Fuehrer's* reception was not altogether friendly. His car was forced to stop at the railroad crossing, where a crowd of unemployed greeted him with cries of "Red Front." His SS bodyguards cleared the way by displaying pistols, which prompted the *Volksblatt* to ask rhetorically: "Are we already in the Third Reich?"[17]

The final Nazi event was an "Evening of Entertainment" on Saturday night (election eve), with a band concert and the *Gauleiter* of Hanover speaking on "Into the Final Fight." It was well attended.[18]

This kind of electioneering—by last minute saturation—may or may not have won votes. It is impossible to say whether or not the votes gained by the Nazis in the election primarily reflected these tactics or the accumulation of other factors. In any event, it was a most impressive display of power, imagination, and energy. The mass meetings were varied and interesting, the street demonstrations were orderly and powerful, and the timing skillful (from straight speeches down to pure entertainment). This was an example of Nazi agitational and organizational ability at its best.

The resulting election statistics indicated for the first time how much the Nazis had gained since the Reichstag elections of September 1930. They had approximately doubled their support in Northeim. With 3,261 votes for Hitler, the Nazis now had 51 percent of the townspeople behind them. The parties of the so-called Hindenburg Bloc (the SPD, the Center party, the People's party, and most of the splinter parties) had together polled almost 4,000 votes in 1930; now they lost over 1,100 to Hitler. The Nationalists, despite vigorous electioneering, saw their voting totals cut in half. The Communists gained 67 votes (but were to lose them within a month). The Nazis had gained their increased support by winning at least three-quarters of the 300 or so "new voters" and by drawing from the other parties, especially those of the bourgeois center.[19] The NSDAP could now boast an absolute majority in Northeim.

It would be hard for the Nazis to surpass the impact of this campaign, yet this was exactly what they were then asked to do. In the March 13 election, Hindenburg had received a clear plurality, but not a majority (nationally, Hitler had received only 30 percent of the vote). Thus a second election had to be held, on April 10, four weeks after the first. Since Hitler ran for the presidency again, Northeim's Nazis had to begin their campaign all over again. Moreover, their campaign began under most inauspicious circumstances, since they had been discovered preparing for a *coup d'état.*

Rumors of an impending Nazi *Putsch* were especially numerous immediately before the first presidential election. The NNN declared that these rumors were unfounded but also pointed out that the police and state troopers had canceled all leaves and were on the alert to maintain peace and order. The *Reichsbanner* had by this time stepped up its campaign of readiness for a counterstroke. By the beginning of 1932 there were four hundred trained *Reichsbanner* members in Northeim, which was also the headquarters of the Tenth *Reichsbanner* District (Northeim County plus three other counties), which numbered about two thousand members. *Reichsbanner* strategy assumed that the workers would be armed by the undersized German Army in the event of an uprising by Nazi Stormtroopers. Hence they undertook frequent covert military maneuvers and rapid mobilization tests; within a half-hour they could assemble the entire Northeim force, without using telephones, automobiles, or bicycles, as their repeated "test alarms" proved.[20]

On election day, March 13, 1932, the Northeim *Reichsbanner* was in a state of alert, and watching Nazi actions very closely. In the evening a considerable number of Nazi Stormtroopers, instead of listening to the election returns, gathered in the woods above town in uniform. *Reichsbanner* men were dispatched to keep tabs on them and were able to creep within fifty feet of the assembled SA. The police were then informed and promptly came out from town and dispersed the Brownshirts. Some of the Nazis regathered at the SA soup kitchen where they were joined by a number of other Stormtroopers from neighboring villages. About three in the morning the police raided the soup kitchen and ordered the Stormtroopers to leave Northeim. The rest of the night was uneventful.[21]

This might be dismissed as romantic shenanigans except for a simultaneous event in a town about ten miles from Northeim. There, on election day, the police intercepted a truck loaded with five rifles, eighteen helmets, eighteen new rucksacks (each with two-day rations), two hundred rifle bullets, and a thousand cubic centimeters of explosives plus two detonating lines. The rucksacks were marked with the names of local Nazis; consequently the local NSDAP headquarters was searched, yielding twenty-eight additional helmets and several thousand more rounds of ammunition. The police also discovered that the town's Nazis had plans to assemble in a nearby woods. The whole story was prominently reported in the NNN.

By now the town began to take on an atmosphere of civil war. Over the previous weekend both *Reichsbanner* and SA had instituted "patrols" through Northeim's streets and had maintained standing forces at their respective headquarters, even after the election. The police became so nervous that they called in state troopers for reinforcement and cleared out both headquarters. In addition, the mayor of Northeim (and of the neighboring town) and the Northeim County Prefect joined to issue a blanket prohibition of "alerts" in political headquarters and of all "patrols." Henceforth both sides had to be more circumspect.[22]

Because of their suspicious actions on election day, the NSDAP was under a temporary cloud in Northeim. Official Nazi sources promptly disclaimed all knowledge of the arms discovered in the neighboring town and then later stated that they had expelled those guilty of the action. The leader of the local SA group issued a statement declaring that all SA actions were defensive, being designed solely to protect the lives of its members against the Iron Front. The SA *Oberfuehrer* gave his oath that no *Putsch* had been planned for the day of the presidential election. Within a few days Northeim's Nazis advertised that their district propaganda leader would speak on the subject, "Not Civil War; Rather the Renewal of the Republic." Though the meeting was to be in the *1910er Zelt,* admission was cut to 30 *Pfennig,* with unemployed admitted free. But Northeimers never heard this speech, since another speaker was substituted and delivered the standard diatribe against internationalism, freemasonry, conservatives, "Marxism," and the "system." There was a good crowd and the matter of the rucksacks, helmets, bullets, explosives, and nocturnal gatherings in woodsy spots was never brought up again by anyone but the Socialists.[23]

The new election campaign also served to draw attention away from the *Putsch* alarms. Hindenburg had come so close to reelection that the SPD did not put much effort into the second presidential campaign. It held only one meeting, under the auspices of an *ad hoc* "Hindenburg Committee." The speaker was a member of the People's party, Professor Percy Schramm of the University of Goettingen, who gave a calm talk entitled "Why Hindenburg?" During the discussion period Ernst Girmann, the local Nazi leader, gave a bitter speech in opposition. When he finished, all the Nazis present left the hall singing the "Horst Wessel Song." An eighteen-year-old Nazi called out "Croak Hindenburg," for which he was promptly arrested.[24]

The other parties were similarly inactive. The Nationalists, who had decided to back Hitler in the second elections, held only one meeting for this purpose. Apparently there was some grumbling over DNVP tactics at this time, since its "nonpartisan" women's auxiliary, the Queen Luise League, inserted the following unique advertisement in the NNN:

QUEEN LUISE LEAGUE
The Local Group leadership calls on its members to
PARTICIPATE IN THE REICH PRESIDENTIAL ELECTION
on this Sunday.
Even though the League officially withholds its voice and, on the basis of its constitution, which provides for a strongly anchored nonpartisanship, exercises no pressure, nevertheless this does not mean that you need not vote.

This second election also counts in the struggle against Marxism for the freedom of the *Volk*. Therefore, on April 10, EVERY VOTE TO THE CANDIDATE OF THE HARZBURG FRONT, *ADOLF HITLER*, no matter what national party individual members otherwise feel themselves drawn to.[25]

The lack of electioneering did not mean that the mood of violence had subsided. By 1932 Northeim resembled two armed camps bivouacked in one confined and tension-laden area. If constant police vigilance prevented most major battles, it did not eliminate individual violence, which hardly abated at all between the elections. Two days after the first election the police had to go to the Employment Office to rescue Tumpelmann (who had not yet been jailed for his part in the "Referendum Day Battle" of the previous August) from an angry crowd. Just as the police arrived, Tumpelmann clubbed a Socialist with his cane. The crowd followed the police all the way to the city jail and were dispersed only with difficulty. A week later there was a barroom brawl involving about fifteen people, which was prevented from developing into a major battle only by rapid police action. Both sides began carrying side arms. Early on the morning of the second presidential vote a Nazi was arrested for having fired his revolver at a Communist on the main street of Northeim. That same day, a *Reichsbanner* man was arrested for having an army pistol and five bullets on his person.[26]

Under these circumstances no political parades were permitted in Northeim, which prevented the Nazis from staging another SA spectacle. Nevertheless the NSDAP attempted to repeat its last minute electioneering tactics. A week before election day the first of the mass meetings was held, featuring the team that had spoken in the previous campaign, Knauth and Madel. This time the weather was good; they drew a full house. Both attacked "Marxism," which Madel characterized (in mirror image of Socialist charges) as being a threat to women, especially mothers. Knauth developed the thesis that "Marxism" was antinational rather than international and claimed that Hindenburg was being "duped into saving the system." Five days later there was an "evening of entertainment" with a four-act play ("1914, 1918, Corruption, Nazi Victory") plus song and dance. The final meeting came on election eve and consisted of a speech directed to the only group to whom the Nazis had not yet made a special appeal—pensioners and war widows. Such persons were admitted free and attendance was excellent.[27]

This was a commendable effort—four meetings, with three held in the week before election day—but it definitely lacked the punch of the previous campaign. Particularly missing was the pageantry of mass parades. Nevertheless, in the vote of April 10 Northeim's Nazis gained 435 votes over the election of a month earlier. Over half of the Nazi gain came from the newly won support of the Nationalist party (240 votes). The Hindenburg Bloc lost only 12 votes while the Communists lost 55; all of which must have gone to Hitler as must also the 106 new voters whom the Nazis had gotten out by vigorous campaigning. Hindenburg was reelected by a comfortable margin, but nationally the Nazi vote had risen to about 37 percent of the German people.

The electioneering of this incredible spring was not yet ended. There still remained the election of a new Prussian Parliament, scheduled for April 24, in which about three-fifths of the German people would vote.

The SPD, at last able to campaign for candidates they endorsed wholeheartedly, set to work for the Braun-Severing government. Two meetings were held in the two weeks available, both under the auspices of the "Northeim Iron Front" and both in the Riding Hall, since the Nazis' preemptive renting of the *1910er Zelt* continued in force. Over a thousand came to the first meeting at which a Reichstag member from Berlin spoke on the election, while Northeim's Carl Querfurt, himself a candidate in the election, attacked the "Northeimer Nazi lies." The second meeting had poor attendance because of rain. The speaker, an SPD Reichstag delegate, compared the Prussia of the three-class vote to that of 1932 and exhorted the audience to vote SPD so as not to lose all the good things gained.[28]

Two of the splinter parties also entered the campaign. The *Staatspartei* held a meeting entitled "We Want No Hitler-Prussia," but about the only people present were a strong contingent of *Reichsbanner* men who turned the meeting into an anti-Nazi demonstration. After this experience, the *Staatspartei* gave up activity in Northeim.[29] The other splinter party active in the campaign was the German Hanoverian party, a cranky and reactionary states' rights group. Their slogan for the campaign was "Against Prussia to the German Reich."[30] The faltering German Nationalist party also held a meeting during the two-week campaign, stressing its demand for a balanced budget and an end to the dominant SPD-Center party coalition in Prussia.[31]

The Nazis showed no signs of the weariness which might have been expected. They inaugurated their third campaign just four days after the final presidential election with a mass meeting featuring Gottfried Feder, who had done so well in Northeim the previous year. Advertisements announced "Password Prussia." There was a huge audience and the Nazi claque kept up a rolling applause as Feder used heavy sarcasm to attack the newly re-elected Hindenburg. The reaction of some townspeople to this was distinctly negative.[32] Eight days later, and just before the election, there was a final meeting, with a Reichstag member, at which all effort was given to attacking the SPD. Despite rain there was a full house. This made a total of ten meetings during the eight weeks of electioneering for the Nazis, almost all strongly attended.

Much Nazi effort was also devoted to their rural strongholds in Northeim County where, during the Prussian Parliament campaign they held at least twenty-five meetings.[33] The few Socialists who lived in the surrounding villages felt terrorized, so much so that the *Volksblatt* reminded its rural readers no fewer than three times during the two-week Prussian Parliament campaign that the vote was secret.[34] In Northeim itself the period of intense political activity came to a climax on election day with a major battle between Stormtroopers and *Reichsbanner* men. Teams of both were out hanging election posters that morning, and a fight involving about twenty-five men developed when the Socialists began to rip down Nazi posters. Neither side had weapons with them, but a picket fence was rapidly stripped to provide clubs. Contrary to explicit police instructions, both paramilitary forces had units on alert at different spots in town and within a few minutes each side was reinforced by sixty or seventy men. Fortunately the police arrived in time to limit the outbreak, though several men were badly wounded. Subsequently, five *Reichsbanner* men were indicted for assault, but four were acquitted and the fifth received a suspended sentence. This did not put an end to the destruction of opponents' placards, but it did lead to its being done more covertly.[35]

The voting showed little change from the second presidential election. The total vote dropped by only 15, while the Nazis lost only 76; in other words, they held tight to virtually·all the gains they had made in the presidential elections. With 3,620 votes out of a total of 6,585 cast, the NSDAP now represented 55 percent of the people of Northeim. Behind them were the Social Democrats with 2,024 votes or 31 percent (down 222 votes since 1930). The remaining 14 percent was divided among the Nationalists, Communists, and the splinter parties.

As these figures suggest, Nazi gains had come at the expense of the small parties of the center and the moderate Right. In 1928, these parties had had the backing of almost half the voters of Northeim. But these voters divided their allegiance among no fewer than ten parties, including such esoteric groups as the "Farmers, House-and-Landowners party." By the Prussian Parliament election of April 1932, these parties had been reduced to the point where, between them all, they controlled no more than about 450 votes. By the summer of 1932 they were whittled down to 200 votes, even though the total votes cast had been increased by over 1,200. Their erstwhile supporters were voting Nazi.

In Northeim the most important of the minor parties was the People's party, the DVP. In 1928 it was second only to the SPD in size, with 834 votes. In 1930 it withstood the Nazi onslaught better than all the conservative parties, losing only 46 votes. But by the time of the Prussian Parliament election the DVP too had to surrender its electorate to the Nazis and was left with only 154 votes. By the summer of 1932 it lost half of these, and with 69 votes became totally insignificant.

If the DVP was the most popular bourgeois party in Northeim during normal times, this was probably because of the civil service element in the town. The DVP's realistic acceptance of the Weimar Republic, its generally nondemagogic character, and its connections with Gustav Stresemann appealed to the solid burgher. Yet the DVP was unequivocally capitalistic and nationalistic. In Northeim the leading personalities of the People's party were very solid citizens: the director of the Grain Mill, the publisher of the NNN, and two highly respected teachers at the *Gymnasium*. In the eyes of most Northeimers, this was essentially the party of the middle way as exemplified in the persistently calm and generally moderate stance of the NNN.

What destroyed the DVP in Northeim was its ambivalent attitude toward democracy and its antipathy to the Socialists. When it combated the Nazis openly, as it did in the September 1930 elections, it was able to retain its followers. By the following spring, however, it joined in the drive to dissolve the Prussian Parliament, putting its enmity for the SPD ahead of its repugnance for the Nazis. A year later, the DVP switched sides again and allied with the Socialists to back Hindenburg.

The basic ambivalence of the People's party was well exemplified by a meeting which it held for the Prussian parliamentary election of April 1932. The speaker was a retired admiral who declared his opposition to splinter parties, to unscrupulous radical propaganda, to the Nazis, and to the Social Democrats. He was especially opposed to the Communists, to "emotion in politics," and he excoriated Brüning for not admitting Hitler to the government. It was not wholly clear what he favored.[36] In subsequent campaigns the DVP was more explicit. What it wanted was an authoritarian state based on the power of the president, which would "destroy the awful party politics of the Reichstag."[37]

The DVP's contribution to the cause of democracy was indeed dubious. It did oppose the Nazis, but mainly for their "radicalism." The NNN also clucked its tongue over excesses of every sort. This was, just as in the time of Aristotle, a good viewpoint, and one well suited to periods of normality. But these were radical, excessive times, as attendance at Nazi meetings showed. The NNN's prissy moderation served essentially to relax its readers after supper; it could not combat Nazism effectively. Had the DVP and its organ pushed for a reasoned and progressive democracy, the NSDAP might have found it a more dangerous opponent than the SPD. But by its fuzzy opportunism and blind "anti-Marxism," the DVP in Northeim not only proved incapable of dealing with the Nazi threat but also probably denied Northeim's middle class their only feasible alternative to the NSDAP.

In 1928 the third largest party in Northeim was the Democratic party. At that time it polled about five hundred votes, close to 10 percent of the total. Northeim was exceptional in this respect, for nationally the Democratic party fared so poorly that it went out of existence even before the great Nazi electoral surge. It had been the party of non-Socialist, non-Catholic backers of the Weimar Republic. At its demise some of its members voted for the SPD and some for the DVP, according to their feelings on "Marxism."[38]

There had existed in the Democratic party an extreme right wing which founded a successor party called the *Staatspartei* (State party). In Northeim it manifested itself as anti-Nazi but also as authoritarian, hyper-nationalist, anti-Socialist, and anti-Semitic—a poor imitation of Hitler's movement. Since Northeimers preferred the real thing, the *Staatspartei's* voting totals dropped from 246 in 1930 to 105 at the time of the Prussian parliamentary election. By autumn 1932, only 34 people voted for the *Staatspartei;* it served only to clutter the ballot.

The final splinter party of any consequence in Northeim was a peculiarity of the area formerly encompassed by the Kingdom of Hanover and reflected the xenophobia of some of its inhabitants. This was the German Hanoverian party (DHP) or "Guelphs," which was created in the Bismarckian era as a protest against Prussian dominance in Germany. The goal of the Hanoverians was to "rectify the crime of 1866," i.e., to separate the lands of the former Kingdom of Hanover from Prussia (which had incorporated them after the Austro-Prussian War of 1866). That this remnant of nineteenth-century particularism had no relevance to the problems of Weimar Germany goes without saying; nevertheless, the DHP did have views on other subjects and it did have a following. Its position was nationalistic, conservative, authoritarian, and anti-Socialist. Its following was provincial, cranky, and old-fashioned. What is amazing is that the DHP had so strong a following. In 1928 it had 455 votes—over 8 percent of the total cast. As the realities of the depression bore in on the people of Northeim, these rapidly melted away. By April 1932, the DHP registered only 62 votes in the town of Northeim, which represented the hard core of "Hanover Firsters." In the surrounding countryside the DHP gave even more to Nazism: its vote in Northeim County sank from 5,900 in 1928 to 200 in July 1932, which probably accounted for over a quarter of the Nazi votes by then.[39]

The DHP's contribution to the political struggle in Northeim was essentially negative. Being opposed to the SPD, it backed the Nazis at the time of the attempt to dissolve the Prussian Parliament, though it voted for Hindenburg in 1932. It publicly opposed a dictatorship and radicalism in general, but even in the momentous year of 1932 the DHP proposed, as its key plank, the separation of Hanover from Prussia.[40]

Thus by backing a program hopelessly out of touch with reality, the DHP provided the Nazis with some four hundred votes—its own followers who deserted because they had not been provided with an adequate political understanding of what was wrong with Nazism. Like the other splinter parties it had paved the way for Hitler by promoting nationalism and anti-Socialism. In fact the essential contribution of the splinter parties had become wholly clear by April 1932. They served as the repository of potential Nazi backers.

The failure of the middle-class parties to withstand the Nazi electoral drive was caused by many factors, some of which have been mentioned. But overriding them all was the inadequacy of their followers' commitment to (or understanding of) democracy. The German middle classes hardly wanted a nihilistic dictatorship, but their ideological heritage from the days of Bismarck and Kaiser Wilhelm II left them ill-prepared to appreciate what Nazism would mean or to develop a viable alternative to it. In the panic atmosphere of the depression they responded to the symbol manipulation that made up Nazi propaganda out of ideological poverty. In this sense the growth of Nazism was as much the product of two generations of the erosion of democratic values as it was of the constellation of circumstances present in the years of Hitler's drive to power.

One final item emerged from the voting totals for the three elections held in March and April 1932. The Communist party went into these elections with 115 votes, rose to 182, and then dropped again to 117 in the Prussian parliamentary election. From this it seems clear that at least 65 Northeimers switched from the Communists to the Nazis. Subsequent elections were to show increasing numbers switching back and forth between the two totalitarian parties.[41]

Obviously at least some Northeimers were ready, by 1932, for any dictatorship, as long as it guaranteed revolution.

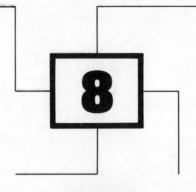

THINGS
FALL
APART

SUMMER
1932

Things fall apart; the centre cannot hold;
Mere anarchy is loosed upon the world,
The blood-dimmed tide is loosed, and everywhere
The ceremony of innocence is drowned;
The best lack all conviction, while the worst
Are full of passionate intensity.

W. B. Yeats, *The Second Coming*

When relative calm descended on Northeim after the elections of March and April, the average citizen (who had probably voted Nazi) could take time to consider what the depression had done to his town since 1930. The first fact to emerge from various newspaper reports was that people were spending less. In the town's two secondary schools the number of students had dropped from 472 in 1930 to 387 in 1932. This was clearly a matter of parents saving money, for there was a simultaneous rise in the number of students in the primary schools.* In the vocational schools, where tuition was only 16 marks a year, enrollment had fallen by a quarter since 1930. It was an ominous sign when parents saved at the expense of their children's future.[1]

Northeimers retrenched sharply on any unessential spending. The secretary of the Museum Society reported that membership dropped by 12 percent in 1932 because people were unwilling to pay the annual dues of 2 marks.[2] The number of passenger cars owned by Northeimers dropped to 143 by 1932, which brought the total back to the 1929 level.[3] Between 1930 and 1932, receipts from dog licenses fell by a third, as did entertainment tax receipts, and even the number of bath tickets sold at the public bath house. The townspeople even economized on the cost of gravestones and burial plots at the town cemetery, where receipts were cut almost in half between 1930 and 1932.[4]

A more serious manifestation of economic atrophy appeared in housing construction. In 1930 there were sixty-eight new dwelling units built; in 1932 there were only sixteen, twelve of which were publicly financed. This was despite a mounting housing shortage. Already in 1930 there were 136 families who needed new apartments either because they were living with relatives, or in condemned buildings, or had registered as "shelterless" and were housed by the authorities. Some of the latter paid 5 marks a month to live in the old Army compound. Others were put in emergency barracks and paid no rent at all. In 1930 a monthly average of 51 persons were so housed; by 1932 the average number rose to 114. Not only did this create an explosive social situation by compressing destitute people in a small area; it was basically irrational. There were many large apartments in Northeim too big to be rented, which the "shelterless" could have afforded had these been subdivided.[5]

---

*The *Gymnasium* and *Lyzeum,* university preparatory schools for boys and girls respectively, charged tuition. The primary schools, whose grades overlapped with the prep schools, were free.

Even more ironic is the fact that there was capital available in Northeim to finance the subdivision of apartments or the construction of new ones. In the City Savings Bank alone there were at least 1,500 accounts with over 100 marks each, and another 800 accounts with over 500 marks each.[6] Beyond this were the savings Northeimers had invested in stocks, bonds, and the other banks of the town. The more Northeimers became concerned about the depression, the more they curtailed their consumption in favor of savings. The depression thus affected their emotions more than their pocketbooks, and if spending in Northeim fell it was not because the middle classes were hurt; it was because they were hoarding their cash.[7]

Two groups were hurt by the depression—the small artisans connected with construction, and the workers. Artisans in the building trades were definitely pinched by 1932, though they were able to keep operating on a reduced basis. By the summer of 1932 a convention of craft masters in Northeim called for a public works program and bitterly denounced both illegal competition and the capitalist system. Few artisans were actually driven out of business, unless they were inefficient to begin with.[8]

It was different with the town's workers, especially those already unemployed. Customarily, unemployment crested in the winter and receded in the summer months. There was no quick summer recovery in 1932; the high level of unemployment persisted. The only change in the statistics was an ever-widening gap between the numbers of those unemployed and those receiving regular or "emergency" compensation. Furthermore, new rules went into effect in June 1932, limiting welfare payments to those who had previously been on regular payrolls. Many young people were thus excluded from all support and there were bitter protests.[9] By July only a third of those registered at the Northeim District Employment Office were actually receiving payments there. Most of the rest had been without work so long that they were wards of official charity—men who had forgotten what it was to work, men without a future.

For these men the summer of 1932 was dry and barren rather than fruitful. This was literally so since heat records of a hundred years were broken in July. There was also a major increase in the incidence of polio that summer.[10]

Despair was bound to register politically, even in the working class with its solid ties to Social Democracy. In the spring elections of 1932 the SPD showed its first losses of the depression era. Only 222 voters were lost (an eleventh of the pevious total, most of whom apparently voted Communist though some must have gone Nazi), but even this was portentous for a party that had been growing steadily for decades.

To the stolid Socialist leaders the solution had to strike at the roots of the problem and hence could only take the form of a massive public works program. But Northeim had no money for this. The town's budget had balanced for the first two years of the depression, but only because it was steadily cut. By 1932 the budget came to only one million marks, whereas in 1929 it had been a million and a half. Even then there was a fifty-thousand-mark deficit envisaged for 1932, and both the beer and head tax had been raised. Not only were welfare costs increasing enormously, but tax sources threatened to reduce their yield. In 1931 and 1932 the business tax percentage was the same, but the yield from the profits tax was only half as much in 1932 as it had been the previous year. The German tax system, which allowed the collector to charge on the basis of capital holdings where profits taxes were insufficient, kept this drop in profits taxes from cutting the total business tax yield, except by about 5 percent. But it was clear that tax receipts were not rising to meet the rising welfare costs, and that a continued tax on capital rather than profit might be dangerous.[11] Nor could the town borrow money for public works projects, since by 1932 the various emergency decrees of the central government prohibited this.[12]

Nevertheless, the Socialists constantly insisted that public works be inaugurated far beyond what had been done in previous years. In April 1932, the SPD faction on the City Council brought forward a new detailed works program involving mainly road construction and other projects which would require minimum outlays for materials and maximum opportunities for employment. Council members from the Middle and Right were dubious in view of the town's financial situation. In May the *Volksblatt* published a scorching editorial demanding that the Socialist plan be put into effect and asking what had been done with funds previously reserved for such a program. Finally and grudgingly, in June 1932, the Council approved a limited program involving three of the SPD's projects.[13]

Over that same summer some of the central government's plans for works projects began to be realized. A unit of the Voluntary Labor Service *(Freiwillige Arbeitsdienst)* was formed in Northeim. Its first project was to be a large sports field which would involve 5,500 workdays. This would begin to make a dent in the town's unemployment rolls, but it was too late to take effect in 1932. Moreover, the possibility of the Reich's financing large projects deterred local action. After desultory discussion the Northeim City Council finally postponed all works projects until government funds would be available. They were granted in January 1933—two weeks before Hitler became chancellor.[14]

The most promising public works scheme came from the unemployed themselves. This was developed by a "Settlement Club" which was founded in Northeim in the spring of 1932. The plan was to build inexpensive one-family houses on unused land belonging to the provincial monastery office, using unemployed workers for labor. The same workers who had built the houses would then live in them. An unemployed architect drew blueprints of a house which would be easy to build and would use very little material. The central government would lend each settler 2,500 marks if the city would provide materials and 500 marks per house. The only problem was that the monastery administration would not give up the land until the money was granted, and the Reich would not lend the money until the free land was assured.[15]

By August this impasse was overcome and the Northeim City Council voted funds for the first thirty houses, although it was stipulated that the cost per house must be within the amount of the government's loan. The city also agreed to supply free sand, gravel, and wood from its forest. Rightist members of the Council added a proviso that all other materials had to be purchased from Northeim business people. The next step was simple approval from the County Council, where the plan was backed by the SPD-Middle coalition. But the Nazis were very much against it.

The Nazi leader in the County Council condemned the whole settlement idea as "socialistic" and moved to postpone consideration of the plan indefinitely. The resulting debate was a violent one and at one point the whole SPD faction left the room in protest over the kind of language employed by the Nazis. At that moment the Nazis called for a quick vote and killed approval of the plan.

These tactics were then challenged by the Middle party and on a second ballot the plan was approved. An SPD motion to guarantee against a loan default by any settler fell, through Nazi opposition, since it required a two-thirds majority. At this, Carl Querfurt exploded and his speech against the Nazis was so strong that the County Prefect had to summon police to prevent physical violence.[16]

The Nazis later asserted that they actually favored the settlement plan but that the time was not ripe. As far as a county guarantee for the settlement was concerned, that was true, for at that point the county had an uncovered deficit of over 200,000 marks and was applying to the Prussian government for aid in view of the imminent collapse of its treasury. The deficit was mainly due to soaring welfare costs.[17]

It was now up to the town of Northeim to guarantee the loans since the county had refused. Again the Socialists backed the plan vigorously and the Right opposed it. Carl Querfurt called attention to the pressing housing shortage and pointed out how even this minor expenditure would be good for the town's economy. The only argument the Right brought against the settlement was that the children would have over a mile to walk to school. With the support of the Civil Servants party the SPD overrode the Right in the City Council and the town became patron of the settlement.[18]

But it was already autumn 1932; the days were growing shorter and the work could not begin. The unemployed would have to live on hope until the following spring. By that time the Nazis had seized power, inaugurated the settlement, and claimed full credit for its success.

If the town's workers were desperate over their economic plight, that was only half the story. The other half was that the Nazis, flushed with their electoral successes in the spring elections and armed with an absolute majority in Northeim, began to apply an inexorable political and economic pressure upon the SPD's followers which the Socialists were powerless to resist.

The process was the more excruciating because, in the beginning of the spring of 1932, the hopes of anti-Nazis were momentarily raised by an action of the Reich government. In April the Brüning cabinet issued decrees disbanding the SA. The day before this occurred the *Volksblatt* gave its opinion of the Stormtroopers:

> In *Hört! Hört!* we read a note by Hitler giving the Northeimer SA the tradition of the old Hanoverian *Garde-Kürassiere*. Should one laugh or cry? The ranks of the SA are filled with thieves, crooks, and worse. The old Guards would throw them all out if they knew about this.[19]

The following day the SA was officially prohibited. In Northeim the police, reinforced by state troopers, raided the Nazi headquarters and searched the homes of SA and SS leaders. No weapons were discovered, though perhaps some might have been found if a policeman had not tipped off the head of the Northeim SS a few hours before the raid.[20] But the Socialists had the satisfaction of seeing the Nazi soup kitchen-SA barracks closed, and the swastika flag that had fluttered over Northeim since the previous fall hauled down by the police.[21]

Any rejoicing was premature. Within a few days the police permitted the Nazis to reopen their soup kitchen and the swastika was promptly raised again. Furthermore, the SA was disbanded only on paper. Within a week of the dissolution decree the *Volksblatt* discovered that "the last emergency decree seemed to have no effect in Northeim where Nazis in SA, HJ, and SS uniforms stroll through the town. When will the long arm of the Prussian Ministry of the Interior reach into Northeim?"[22]

The Social Democrats nevertheless felt there was cause for extensive celebration on May Day. The *Reichsbanner* fife-and-drum corps marched all over town early in the morning to remind people what day it was. There was more music on the Market Square by the town band, and in the afternoon a stately parade wound through the town, with numerous flags and banners, to a beer garden. There the workers heard songs by the People's Choir, saw acrobatic acts by Socialist youth groups, and consumed much beer. A speech against capitalism brought loud hurrahs for German and International Socialism. The *Volksblatt* interpreted the event as "a turning point in the workers' struggle against Nazism."[23]

The NSDAP was subdued in its activities during the first weeks of May, but hardly because of Social Democratic militancy. One reason was exhaustion and disorganization from the spring's hectic series of campaigns. Another may have been impoverishment: in April and May, Local Group Northeim neither reported nor paid its required contributions to the higher offices of the Nazi party—a dereliction it shared with almost half the other Local Groups in Northeim County.[24] Excessive spending in reliance upon future growth had begun to catch up with the Nazis of Northeim. From this time on, they continued to have unpaid debts until the establishment of Hitler's dictatorship resolved their financial problems.

But even a letdown of Nazi efforts did not constitute complete inactivity. The first week of May they staged a relatively unpolitical "May Walk" in which about 250 men, women, and children made an excursion to the woods above Northeim and then returned to the City Park for coffee and *Kuchen* in the evening. Though the Nazis' next meeting, held a week later, was boldly advertised as "The Struggle Continues," it consisted only of a talk on how the Nazis hoped to overcome unemployment by a lightly inflationary credit program.[25] Violence also abated in Northeim, though in mid-May there was a fight between eight people in which one was seriously wounded, and in June a Nazi beat a young man into senselessness.[26] By late May, however, the interlude of hope was over and the Nazi juggernaut began to grind forward again.

Nationally a cabal of Junkers and Army leaders forced the resignation of Brüning. General von Schleicher then secured the appointment of the right wing authoritarian, von Papen, as chancellor in a cabinet which had not even a shadow of parliamentary support. One of von Papen's first acts was to rescind the ban on the SA, and for good measure he also tore up the decrees prohibiting the Nazis from wearing uniforms.

In Northeim the Nazis chose the late spring of 1932 to oust the SPD from its subsidiary positions of power, notably the School Advisory Councils. This was a telling blow since the SPD had long worried over the composition of Northeim's schools. As early as December 1930 the *Volksblatt* charged that students at the *Gymnasium* regularly greeted each other with *"Heil Hitler!"* Ten months later the *Volksblatt* reported that two Nazified *Gymnasium* students threw a stink-bomb through the open window of a house. It editorialized, "What are the school authorities going to do about all the Nazi ideas in the children's heads?"[27] Though the principal of the *Gymnasium* forbade students to give the Nazi salute and provincial authorities prohibited student membership in Hitler Youth, the SPD did not relax its concern. By the end of 1931 the *Volksblatt* charged that *Bürgerschule I* was a "Nazi stronghold." It implied that several teachers were Nazis and noted that the buildings and lampposts around the school were " 'decorated' with swastikas."[28] Thus the Nazi decision to expel Socialists from the School Advisory Councils came at exactly the moment when the Socialists were most concerned about the influence of Nazi teachers.

In the beginning of April 1932, the SPD initiated a campaign to purge the schools of Nazi teachers. The *Volksblatt* charged that Heinrich Voge, a teacher at *Bürgerschule I*, was a radical Nazi who read *Hört! Hört!*, taught politics in class, and wrote Nazi slogans on blackboards—all of which was true.[29] Since it was illegal in Prussia for teachers to belong to the NSDAP, this was a serious matter. A few days later the *Volksblatt* attacked two other teachers, charging one with being drunk at three in the morning and shouting *"Heil Hitler!"* as he staggered through the streets of Northeim, and the other with giving the Nazi salute during instruction and allowing pupils to carry swastika pennants on a school excursion. For the latter charge there was an eyewitness.[30] At the end of April the Socialists on the City Council formally demanded that Voge and another Nazi teacher from *Bürgerschule I* be discharged as subversives. The mayor ruled, however, that such action was beyond the competence of the Council.[31]

If the Socialists thought that these exposures would win them the support of the middle class, they were mistaken. The SPD tried to arrange a common list for the new School Advisory Council elections, but it was turned down. As the *Volksblatt* put it:

The bourgeoisie have decided on a "Christian-National" list made up almost exclusively of Nazis and also some former Communists who went over to the Nazis. Naturally a counterproposal must come from the workers.[32]

The Social Democrats contested the election only at *Bürgerschule I* and *II*, where their lists were called "Social-Republican Progress." Both the NNN and GGZ threw their weight against the Socialists. Both reported an SPD proposal to the City Council to curtail the town's subsidies to the Lutheran Church; both reported (in the *local* news section) that the SPD had voted for a Communist proposal in the Prussian Parliament to tax away all income above 12,000 marks.[33]

The Nazis led the attack. At the end of May a Lutheran pastor, who was also a Nazi Reichstag member, addressed a mass meeting in which he attacked the SPD savagely and demanded that it be outlawed in Germany. In addition to claiming religious support for Nazism he also insisted that the German Army was solidly behind Hitler's movement. A week later there was an "evening of entertainment" in the *1910er Zelt* which the GGZ reported was "truly Germanic." A week before the vote the Nazis demonstrated their concern for the young by holding a Hitler Youth conference in Northeim with parades, bands, and sports events. Then, on the eve of the election, another Lutheran minister spoke at a mass rally for the Christian-National list. The speaker declared that Liberalism and Socialism were poisoning the youth, that "Evangelical [Protestantism] and German Folkdom are inseparable," and that "in the National Socialist movement Christianity will celebrate its resurrection." The meeting closed with the singing of the "Horst Wessel Song" and repeated *Sieg Heils*. There had been an enormous turnout.[34]

The voting was heavy in both schools. At *Bürgerschule I*, located in the hillside residential district, the Nazis won ten of the fourteen representatives. At *Bürgerschule II*, located on the north side of the railroad tracks, the vote split and five representatives each went to the Socialist and the Christian-National list.[35] The impotence of the SPD had been demonstrated on its own ground. The following day, June 22, the Nazis celebrated by holding a mass march in Northeim County in honor of the old tribal-Germanic festival of the summer solstice. Three bands and twelve hundred SA men from three counties combined to make it an impressive event.[36] Within less than a week Local Group Northeim was writing frantically to the *Gauleitung* for more application forms to give to Northeimers pressing to join the Nazi party.[37]

The Nazi victory in the school elections was depressing but hardly catastrophic to the Socialists. What was serious was Nazi economic pressure. The core of Socialist strength in Northeim was the railroad workers. In 1930, the elections for Works Council members were won by the Socialist union with a ten-to-one margin. In the spring of 1932 the Nazis moved to break the union and coerce the workers into at least outward acceptance of Nazism.

The first indication of what was happening came in a *Volksblatt* report in mid-May. The Northeim Railroad Office was firing many men, some of whom had worked there as long as twenty years. Salaried workers with tenure were made to sign a release by which they became hour-wage workers and lost their tenure. Nine men refused to sign and were immediately fired. At the same time, wages were reduced to 50 *Pfennig* an hour.[38] A former railroad worker, Hermann Schulze, described the process:

In the spring of 1932 the Nazis made their first attempt to organize the railroad workers. Nazism was already strong among the directory, control offices, bureau workers, etc. It started with the highest officials and worked downwards. From 1931 on, the officials saw to it that those workers who belonged to the Brownshirts got privileged treatment. . . . There were often excited arguments and even some fights. When I argued with workers against the Nazis I was ordered by the directors not to speak during working hours. . . .
In the late spring of 1932 all Socialist workers were made to sign a release removing them from tenure. The bulk of them signed rather than lose their jobs. The pressure began to be applied to the other workers and the final step was "either join [the Nazi union] or be fired." I was the only one who held through and stayed [openly] with the SPD.)[39]

The process continued throughout the summer and in September there was a new wave of firings, including Schulze. For his obstinacy, Schulze was discharged without papers, which meant that he would be ineligible for either new employment or unemployment compensation. The yards director personally promised Schulze that he could keep his job if he joined the Nazi union, but Schulze felt safe because, as a Works Councillor, he could not legally be fired. When this happened nonetheless, and when the national offices of the union proved powerless to reverse the process, it convinced the other workers that they were defenseless.[40]

The struggle was a silent one, for apparently the Socialists were unwilling to expose their weakness, while the GGZ printed the official explanation of "seasonal layoffs." The Free Unions did arrange a mass meeting in July, where the workers might expect that some stand would be taken on the matter. Instead the speeches simply emphasized the need for a defense of the Republic and for the ultimate achievement of Socialism. The only reference to the immediate needs of Northeim's railroad workers was an appeal by a union secretary for proletarian solidarity.[41]

After the second wave of dismissals at the railroad yards, elections were held among *tenured* employees for the Works Council. The day before the voting the district railroad office announced it would hire a thousand workers in the Northeim area to replace 85 percent of those who had been fired. In the elections, Nazi representatives won four of the six seats and the Socialists won none. Results were the same throughout the district, and a man who was to become local leader of the "German Workers Front" in the Third Reich was named district representative from Northeim. In November 1932, thirty new workers were hired at the Northeim railroad station.[42]

The general economic situation rendered the Socialists helpless. With thousands of workers waiting for every job, a strike would have been impossible. Legal action, even in Schulze's clear-cut case, would have foundered through a lack of witnesses; the officials were in collusion, the workers already terrorized. As a result, the only action the SPD took was to call for a boycott against all Nazi stores. The *Volksblatt* published a list of shops owned by Nazis and suggested sarcastically that "Republicans will make sure that these stores survive."[43] The boycott never took hold. Since almost all of Northeim's merchants were Nazis, the workers had little choice. On the other hand the SPD's following of impoverished workers simply did not have the economic strength to make any decisive impact by means of a boycott, and the most politically conscious were already shopping through their consumers' cooperative.[44]

In any event one could hardly boycott the railroad, and it was there that the workers were suffering. The sense of hopelessness that the workers acquired through this experience engendered a mood of rage and despair over the summer of 1932 and led ultimately to a feeling of resignation that helped insure a frictionless seizure of power by the Nazis in Northeim after 1933.

There was one final blow which the Socialists received that summer. The inevitable result of von Papen's permissive attitude toward the SA was a wave of violence in Germany. Seizing this as a pretext, von Papen then executed a *coup d'état* in Prussia on July 20. The SPD-Center government was deposed and an authoritarian commissar replaced it. The Socialists chose to take the matter to court rather than fight. The bastion of German democracy was breeched without a shot being fired in its defense.

The Nazis not only attacked the subsidiary strongholds of the SPD in the summer of 1932, they also used their new majority to infiltrate the conservative Civic Association. It was simple: Northeim's Local Group merely required every party member to join the Civic Association and thereby acquired an instant majority.[45] Since the Socialists forced the resignation of Senator Mahner, a new executive had to be elected in July and Northeim's Nazis were there in force to see that it was the right one. At least six of the nine new executive committee members were Nazis, including the chairman, vice-chairman, secretary, and treasurer. The new chairman's first act was to call on all members of the Civic Association to vote NSDAP in the coming Reichstag elections. The new vice-chairman, who was Ernst Girmann, Local Group Leader of the Nazi party in Northeim, added that the Nazis were the sure defense of the middle class, while the Nationalist party was controlled by "big capital." The round of applause that he drew for this statement was probably not joined by the Nationalists, who had hitherto been the backbone of the organization.[46]

The final aspect of the Nazi attack came in July 1932, with the Reichstag election campaign. The voting was set for July 31, but Nazi preparations for the most coordinated effort they had ever designed began well beforehand. On June 20 the *Gauleitung* passed on to Local Group Northeim a request from the national headquarters in Munich for instances of wrongdoings in SPD-controlled health insurance offices, since "corruption" was to be a central theme of the campaign. (Northeim's Nazis could only report that their town's health insurance office was indeed dominated by the SPD, and its corruption consisted in having hired a Social Democrat who had previously been fired from another civil service job, and that sometimes its official automobile was used on Sundays.[47]) Shortly thereafter came clear directives on how to conduct the campaign: organization, financing, slogans, and the central theme to be stressed—corruption.

This directive went to some 600 leading Nazis in the *Gau* including 15 County Leaders, 430 Local Group Leaders, and 120 *Gau* speakers. It contained precise instructions for the use of a new technique: sending handwritten letters to voters selected according to their membership in specific categories, with different texts for each targeted group. Model texts were provided for war widows, pensioners, war wounded, rural workers, Communists, women, young workers, union members, bourgeoisie, wives of bourgeoisie, and for "an intellectually elevated woman." Each text was to be hand copied on good writing paper—made to look like an original rather than a copy, so that the recipient would be convinced that it was a personal letter—and signed by someone of the same category. Thus a Nazi union member would write to another union member, along the lines of: "As you know, I've never been much for politics, but this time I'm going to vote for Hitler because I'm sick of all this corruption. . . ."[48] Local Group Northeim ordered all the members of its various organizations to work on this, and by the end of the election campaign an appropriate letter had been sent to every single voter in the town.[49]

In addition, the Nazis did door-to-door leafleting plus the usual mass meetings and Stormtrooper parades, all well-tested over the past two years. Even so, as the voting day approached, the *Gau* speakers' organization was strained. By mid-July Walter Steineck was writing to the *Gauleitung* in panic because he had no "big gun" speakers and was afraid that both the SPD and DNVP would campaign more actively than the Nazis in Northeim.[50]

One result of the electioneering was predictable: violence.

The constant political activity of 1932 had already brought the town to the end of its tether. Political division had spread into all areas of life. The schools were disrupted by it. Families were split on the issue of Nazism. By summer, boys in the Hitler Youth were afraid to go home alone after meetings, yet to wear an anti-Nazi insignia (such as the three arrows of the Iron Front) was also to invite attack. Political violence was becoming a permanent institution.[51]

July 1932 brought with it not only the election campaign, but also hot, muggy weather. The SA, recently permitted to wear their uniforms, were in a belligerent mood. Socialist workers who had "hungered through" the winter found it impossible to pick up even short-term jobs. All over Germany violence erupted on a mass scale. Between July 1 and July 20 there were 461 political riots in Prussia in which eighty-two people were killed and over four hundred seriously injured.[52]

In Northeim a mood of arrogance settled over Hitler's followers. The SA readied itself for armed uprising. The *Volksblatt* reported in June that eighty uniformed Nazis were holding military maneuvers in the woods above Northeim and had roughed up a *Reichsbanner* man who "happened to be out for an evening stroll." Action was demanded of Northeim's chief of police.[53] The first Nazi campaign meeting stressed the mystique of the uniform:

Saturday, July 2, 1932, in the *1910er Zelt*. ARMY MARCH EVENING with SA RECRUITMENT. The Army March music will be presented by the 44-man strong Music-train of Standard 82. ***All kinds of [entertainment] presentations by the SA. ***Standard Leader X will speak on "The Will to Defense—The Way to Freedom."

The SA as bearer of the spirit of 1914.
It will be an experience for soldierly hearts.
The evening will begin by a Propaganda March through the city.

Sturmbann I/82
Standarte 82

Advance ticket sales at Spannaus's and at the Business Office of the NSDAP.[54]

The event fulfilled Nazi expectations as over five hundred SA and SS men marched. The *1910er Zelt* was crowded with an enthusiastic audience which applauded the SA's acts (gymnastic exhibitions) and especially the music, which, according to the GGZ, "had the true ring and high spirit of Nationalism."

Four days later the Nazis held another mass meeting geared directly to the impending elections. The speaker was a Reichstag member and the topic, "Brüning—Never Again! Von Papen—a Transition! Give Hitler the Power!" The speaker clearly dissociated the Nazis from the von Papen government, insisting that "without Socialism, Nationalism is impossible." He also swore that Hitler would come to power legally but that "the November criminals and SPD murderers" would "answer for their crimes." The *1910er Zelt* rang with applause and, finally, with the strains of the "Horst Wessel Song."[55]

The Socialists, struggling to retain the allegiance of the working class and to hold back the Nazi tide, responded with extreme militance. The day after the SA's "Army March Evening," the Northeim Iron Front held a countermarch led by the town band, two fife-and-drum corps, and many flags emblazoned with the three arrows. The speech on the Market Square was again in defense of the Republic. Five days later the Communists also held a propaganda parade with about fifty men and some red flags. The following day the Socialists marched again in an enormous demonstration sponsored by the Iron Front. The mood of militancy was reflected in advertisements for the event:

To all Republicans of Northeim County! On Saturday, July 9, 7 P.M. in Northeim: Demonstration of the Republican Workers of Northeim County against Fascism. The streets belong to the Republicans! Therefore all Republicans must march![56]

The parade lasted over an hour and a half and was led by thirty men carrying flags and by the two fife-and-drum corps. In the Market Square a speaker castigated the von Papen government and closed with the cry "Let us not be beaten by the swastika in the Reichstag elections!"[57] The next day there was another mass meeting, this time of the unemployed and sponsored by an *ad hoc* "Committee of the Unemployed" which was controlled by Socialists. Demands for better pay for the jobless were expressed and plans were made for a vast protest march in Northeim during the coming week.[58]

July 10 was memorable for more than the SPD's meeting, however, for this was the day that the swelling pustule of violence finally burst in Northeim. Early in the morning six Nazis beat up a member of the Iron Front who was wearing the "three arrows" pin. This set the stage for the real battle, which came about seven o'clock in the evening. About twenty-five *Reichsbanner* men were marching toward Northeim from the Employment Office and had just started across the "Long Bridge" when they were met by a column of sixty SA men who were crossing the river in the opposite direction. The heads of the columns passed each other without incident, but the rear ranks fell to exchanging curses. The passage on the "Long Bridge" was narrow and the insults led rapidly to a general battle. Clubs, canes, bicycle pumps and other improvised weapons were used by both sides. When the "shelterless" inhabitants of the old Army compound at the north end of the bridge saw what was happening they rushed out to help the *Reichsbanner*. By the time the police arrived and broke up the battle there was a surging crowd of about eighty persons pelting the Nazis with stones. Even while the police were trying to keep the opposing sides apart, individual fights broke out and the crowd began to hurl stones over the heads of the police into the ranks of the SA. This continued until a policeman drew his gun and fired over the crowd. Both sides were finally dispersing when two SS men rode up on the Employment Office side of the bridge and the crowd let fly the last of their stones. The SS beat a hasty retreat.

As a result of the battle, three men were hospitalized and many others received light wounds. By the time the wounded *Reichsbanner* men passed through Northeim, the news of the battle had brought out a hostile crowd and they were jeered all the way to the hospital.

In the subsequent trial, held in Northeim a month later, nine *Reichsbanner* members were indicted for assault with a deadly weapon. Four were acquitted; the others were given prison terms ranging from two to six months. In passing sentence the judge declared that neither side was exclusively at fault and regretted that there was insufficient evidence to prosecute some of the SA men.[59]

Four days after the battle of the "Long Bridge," on July 14, Bastille Day, the protest demonstration of the unemployed was staged. Though planned by the SPD, the march was infiltrated by both Communists and Nazis. The day before, the Communists held a parade with a hundred men and speeches calling for a united front with the SPD against Fascism. That evening the police arrested two Communists in the woods above Northeim; both had revolvers and ammunition.[60]

The July 14 demonstration of the unemployed involved about five hundred men and women. It was immediately dubbed the "Hunger March" by the newspapers. Its prearranged objectives were to protest the low dole rates and to make specific demands on the City Council, such as free baths and an end to compulsory labor.

The parade assembled at the City Hall after marching through the streets of Northeim with signs, placards, and a black flag (symbolizing a general mood of sorrow and extreme distress, as is still carried at funerals all over Europe). During the march the jobless grew restive and began to shout "Hunger!" and "Give us bread and work!" At the City Hall the cry went up for the mayor to come out and talk to them. When he refused, angry muttering commenced and one man cried out "What shall we do with the mayor?" The crowd shouted back: "Hang him!" Then the front line started up the steps into the City Hall.

The police immediately unsheathed their nightsticks, but some were grabbed and held while others were struck or kicked as the crowd surged forward with one man screaming, "We're coming in no matter what the cost!" When a policeman drew his gun he was told by one of the marchers, "You'll shoot only once."

Once inside the City Hall the jobless had no idea what to do next. There was a confused scramble and the police kept them from advancing beyond the first floor. One of the original leaders of the demonstration, a union secretary and local leader of the SPD, gave a short speech persuading the crowd to leave the building. Once outside they formed again and marched in an orderly manner to the County Prefecture where the Prefect came out and told them that he would like to raise the dole but that the county was almost bankrupt. Thereupon the parade dissolved.

The following day the jobless were still in an ugly mood. The GGZ had written a sarcastic account of the occurrence and an angry crowd gathered before its editorial office and began knocking on the window. The police arrived in time to prevent violence. Later in the day one of the *Reichsbanner* men who had been in the fight on the "Long Bridge" was released from the hospital and was immediately set on by a Nazi and brutally beaten. The same day also saw a political brawl between two women.

Eight of the "Hunger Marchers" were subsequently tried in Northeim before the circuit court. The trial dragged into November and was marked by more excesses. The courtroom had to be cleared repeatedly, and at one point the judge threatened to arrest the whole audience. Later he sentenced one of the defendants for contempt of court. Both the Nazis and Communists provided defense lawyers. Seven of the defendants were found guilty and given sentences ranging from six to nine months. When the sentence was pronounced one of the Communist defendants cried out from the dock, "The 'people down below' in Germany will soon give another judgment. You can lock up my body; my spirit stays free!" At this the audience in the courthouse broke into the *Internationale* and it was with extreme difficulty that the police were able to clear the room and disperse the crowd outside.[61]

After the tumult of the "Long Bridge" and the "Hunger March" the Nazis were relatively quiescent. Their sole activity came on July 18 when the SA staged a propaganda march through Northeim County after which their choir serenaded an SA man and his new bride with the "Horst Wessel Song."[62] This lack of activity was due to preparations for the biggest event in the Nazi repertoire—a speech by Adolf Hitler.

By the summer of 1932 Adolf Hitler had become Germany's major media star and a Hitler speech had become something like a combination carnival, rock concert, and major league championship game. It attracted the believers who sought mystical communion, the curious who just came to experience the happening, and the faddists who wanted to share what so many others were doing. Tickets were sold out from the moment the speech was anounced; usually they were rationed carefully among local Nazi bigwigs and went for premium prices. Walter Steineck, on an earlier occasion, begged the *Gauleitung* for a block of tickets to be given to invalids from World War I and considered himself lucky to be apportioned eleven at two marks apiece.[63] Steineck also wrote to the *Gau* in mid-June, when Hitler's itinerary was being set and the neighboring town of Goettingen had been selected for one of Hitler's speeches, with arguments as to why Northeim should have been chosen instead.[64]

But the locale of Hitler's speeches were not chosen lightly; by 1932 local Nazi officials were always sent, well in advance, a complete set of printed instructions as to how Hitler meetings must be conducted, down to the last detail—including the brand of mineral water Hitler insisted on and the curious requirement that on hot days Hitler had to have a bowl of ice on the podium so he could cool his hands.[65] A Hitler speech was also a major financial undertaking and a major income-generating event. This one, on July 21, 1932, in Goettingen, cost RM 11,470 to stage, but the 15,545 tickets sold (at prices of up to 3 marks each) grossed RM 19,222 for a net profit of RM 7,751. Even though the *Fuehrer* took half the profits, there was still big money to be earned.[66] But the main point was that a Hitler speech gave an enormous boost to the Nazi campaign wherever he appeared.

The town of Goettingen, where Hitler was to speak, was about ten miles away from Northeim. To bring Northeimers and others there, the railroad scheduled several special trains. The meeting was to be in the open air, with room for fifteen thousand in the audience. Hitler was to be preceded by Dr. Wilhelm Frick who would begin at eight o'clock in the evening. The grounds were to open at three. Hitler would arrive by airplane.

By early afternoon almost all seats were taken. The speakers' tribune was a mass of swastikas and flag after flag was visible behind it. The local SA served as ushers while squads of SS and Hitler Youth stood in groups. War injured were brought to the front for special places of honor; then the sick were carried in, including (it was announced) one dying man whose last wish was to see Hitler. During hours of waiting the tension grew. Suddenly at eight o'clock the crowd broke into shouts as Hitler's airplane flew over from Brunswick where he had spoken earlier. There were cries of *"Heil!*" and handkerchiefs were waved as the plane flew on to the airport.

Then Dr. Frick began to speak. "If the police say they can't protect the SA, we'll protect ourselves. Just give us the same weapons which our opponents have used against us for so many years." At nine forty-five he stopped and the crowd waited, murmuring restively. A light rain began to fall. Suddenly Hitler appeared on the platform, to be greeted with a roar of joy and spontaneous *"Heils."* With a few brusque words he ordered the umbrella over the rostrum removed so that, like the audience, he would stand with bare head in the drizzle. He spoke approximately as follows:

There are moments in the history of nations when a decisive instant comes. The coming vote is not an election but a decision between two worlds—the world of internationalism and that of the true German spirit. One must decide between a Germany riven by classes, parties, religions, and the Germany of one will, one goal. The last thirteen years have brought misery, destruction. No one else could have destroyed the national wealth, created millions of unemployed so well. These thirteen years have led to thirty parties all arrayed against one. All elements have their parties, only the German *Volk* has none. But the National Socialist German Workers party will never give up the struggle, for only it has the courage and will to act.

As he left the podium, there were rolling waves of furious applause interrupted by volleys of *"Heils"* and, finally, the spontaneous singing of the "Horst Wessel Song." "Everyone went home wet but full of hope," reported the GGZ; "street lamps were out near the railroad station—we hear that the Marxists cut the power." [67]

Although after Hitler anything would have been an anticlimax, the Nazis still had to fill out the remaining ten days of July with election meetings. They were able to hold two meetings, neither especially distinguished. On July 25 a Viennese Nazi was brought to Northeim for a talk against the Jews, and on election eve an "evening of entertainment" featuring "talkie" movies of Hitler, Goering, and Strasser was held in the Cattle Auction Hall.[68] To fill the gap the Nazis turned to slanderous accusations in their newsletter *Hört! Hört!*

It is probable that press vituperation had already reached a point of diminishing returns. A case in point is the clerks at the Northeim Post Office. A year before, the *Volksblatt* had labeled them Nazis but subsequently retracted the charge. Now, in July 1932, the Nazis attacked the same men for being Socialists. The clerks finally responded by instituting legal action against the Nazis, forcing them to publish a public correction and apology. The clerks then made a notarized declaration that they belonged to no political party, and were thus left in peace.[69]

But Nazi mudslinging worked in the case of the Northeim Health Insurance Office. This institution, controlled by the Socialists, had been under constant attack by the Nazis since the first issue of *"Hört! Hört!* in August 1931. A week before the Reichstag elections of July 31, 1932, the Health Insurance Office Directorate published an open letter explaining that its lawsuit against *Hört! Hört!* had fallen through because the court ruled that no reader could possibly find meaning in the tortured prose of the Nazi articles, but that since *Hört! Hört!* had renewed its attacks a new lawsuit had been instituted. The new charges, widely publicized in the NNN, were that the Health Insurance Office had permitted various labor organizations to use its mimeograph machine. *Hört! Hört!* discovered this from an employee of the office, who had subsequently been fired. The Socialists insisted that there was nothing improper in this, that the same thing had been done at the City Hall and County Prefecture for years, and that the use of the machine was paid for in every instance. The matter was speedily clarified when the County Prefect and a board of examiners went over the case and declared the Nazi allegations to be slanderous. The commission exonerated the Health Insurance Office completely on all counts and approved the dismissal of the employee who originally betrayed the matter to *Hört! Hört!* But this news was published only in the *Volksblatt,* and *after* the election. Northeimers went to the polls with the Nazi charges fresh in their minds and probably also with the impression that somehow, as a result of all the noise, there was something wrong with the Health Insurance Office and its Socialist directorate.[70]

The Socialists also indulged in wild charges on the eve of the election, including the claim that the Nazis would pay 3 marks to any worker who would walk around town in an SA uniform and 50 marks to any man who would become a Stormtrooper. In addition the SPD held two final meetings. One, sponsored by the unions and held six days after von Papen's coup in Prussia, sent protests to the government over this. The second came two days before the election. One speaker at this meeting was the chief Socialist candidate, who gave an objective analysis of the difference between Nazi promises and performance. The second speaker was a local union secretary who refuted in detail the Nazi charges against the Health Insurance Office. Thus the meeting differed considerably from the original advertisements which had proclaimed: "We are attacking! Up and at the enemy!" There was, however, excellent attendance.[71]

All other parties had been reduced to insignificance and hence did not campaign, with the exception of the Nationalists. Though von Papen was not a member of the DNVP, he certainly represented its point of view; hence it was the only party to back him in the Reichstag and the DNVP felt that this gave it renewed political possibilities. In Northeim the DNVP held one campaign meeting, two days before the voting, at which members carefully dissociated themselves from the NSDAP. The Nationalist speaker said he admired the Nazis for their patriotism but opposed their program, especially its "socialistic" aspects. He also condemned Hitler's wish to destroy all other parties, for "German culture has grown through diversity." The meeting was poorly attended.[72]

On Sunday, July 31, 6,730 Northeimers went to the polls—96 percent of those eligible. The Nazis received 4,195 votes: an increase of 500 over their previous high. They now represented 62 percent of Northeim's electorate. They had gained all of the "new" votes and had also drawn from all of the other parties. The SPD lost 385 votes in this election and now represented only a quarter of the townspeople. The only party besides the Nazis to register gains were the Communists, who doubled their vote; still they had only 285 votes, or 4 percent of the electorate. This made them the third ranking party in Northeim. Even allowing maximum switching of SPD votes to the Communists, at least 200 former SPD votes must have gone to the Nazis. Suffering and a sense of helplessness had begun to overtake the erstwhile followers of Social Democracy.

The Nationalists held their own in Northeim. With slightly more than two hundred votes they were climbing up from the nadir of the Prussian Parliament elections. While this was hardly a cause for wild rejoicing, there was much happening to encourage followers of authoritarian conservatism. Since von Papen's *coup* put the Prussian state under his control, he could now proceed to purge Prussia's administration of Socialists and replace them with Conservatives. In Northeim the Civic Association immediately arranged the removal of Carl Querfurt as deputy chief of police, with Senator Mahner taking his place. It also attempted to vote censure of the *Volksblatt* in the City Council, though unsuccessfully, since the Middle refused to agree. Most important, however, was the removal of the County Prefect, his replacement with a Nationalist, and the dissolution of the County Council.[73]

The previous County Prefect, Kirschbaum, though a Socialist, was a man of monumental calm; he was so objective that even the Nazis were sorry to see him leave in 1932. He remained unruffled even when Carl Querfurt, in the heart of a verbal battle, forgot that they were both Socialists and called him a dictator. The new County Prefect, Otto von der Schulenberg, was a conservative anti-Nazi with doubts about democracy and a distaste for Socialists. His appointment also meant the end of the Socialist majority in the County Council, since the von Papen government decided to join Northeim County with the neighboring one of Uslar, retaining Northeim as the county seat but dissolving the Council. A provisional committee took its place, composed of two SPD members, two Nazis, a Nationalist, and a moderate Rightist.[74] The Socialists had been expelled from yet another position of power.

The symbol of all these changes was the August 1932 celebration of Constitution Day. There was no parade. A small meeting was held in the auditorium of *Bürgerschule I*, but the schools were not even let out for the day. Late in the afternoon there were swimming races, but that was all for this chief annual holiday of the democratic Weimar Republic.[75]

In view of what had happened over the summer, there was little to celebrate.

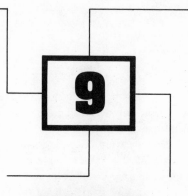

THE LAST WINTER

AUTUMN-WINTER 1932-1933

"I am hungry! I have hunger and nothing else!"

Shouted by an unemployed worker
arrested for disturbing the
peace, as reported in the
Northeimer Neueste Nachrichten,
December 6, 1932

Despite the crushing series of blows delivered to the Social Democrats, and despite the Nazis' decisive majority gained in the July Reichstag elections, the political situation in Northeim slipped into stagnation after the summer elections. There was little for the Nazis to do; they were at the apex of their popularity but still without power. The same situation existed nationally. The Nazi "triumph" of 230 seats won in the Reichstag in July proved, upon closer inspection, to be hollow. The NSDAP had only 37 percent of the vote—a proportion that had not increased since the second presidential election. When Hitler presented himself to von Hindenburg on August 13 with the demand that he be allowed to form a cabinet, the old man not only refused, he implied that he would never allow Hitler to become chancellor. If the "legal way to power" seemed bankrupt, force was equally out of the question. When the SA unleashed a wave of terror in August 1932, the von Papen government responded with emergency decrees under which five SA men were condemned to death for murder, and the Army told Goering that in the event of an attempted Nazi *Putsch,* they would shoot.

In this stalemate the Army seemed to have all the advantages. In Northeim the key event at the beginning of autumn 1932 reflected this, for it was a visit to Northeim of troop units from the Seventeenth Infantry Regiment, engaged in fall maneuvers. The town received four hundred soldiers and six officers with open arms. The newspapers were filled with descriptions of the maneuvers, the Regimental Band gave two concerts, and there were numerous "Maneuver Balls" held in various taverns. The NNN reported that the town's children were especially delighted to hear the old soldier songs, since they had a love of the military in their blood. To further their education, the children were all let out of school to watch the second day of the war games. In short, the town reveled in the pure military spectacle.[1]

On a minor scale the same sort of thing had occurred frequently before. In November 1930 a bicycle platoon visited Northeim and had a "comradely evening" drinking beer with members of the Northeim Society of Former Reserve Ninety-Firsters. In May 1931 a small motorized detachment spent two days in the town on simulated maneuvers. Apparently Northeimers were so desperate for military life that they were happy to see even police units come to town. In 1931 a party was given in honor of a troop of police who stopped in Northeim, and in June 1932 a "Maneuver Ball" was staged when police units visited the town. It should be noted, too, that several Northeimers were volunteer members of the illegal army *(Schwarze Reichs-*

*wehr),** for there was a unit stationed in the hills about fifteen miles east of the town.[2]

Commitment to militarism went beyond watching soldiers march. The fantastic celebration touched off by Field Marshal von Mackensen's visit to Northeim in 1930 demonstrates this amply. In 1932 the former field marshal passed through Northeim again, on his way to visit his old friend Count von Strahlenheim (a top local Nazi), whose estate was near Northeim. He requested that no fuss be made over him, but nevertheless he was met at the railroad station by 150 representatives of the *Stahlhelm* and presented with flowers by the Northeim Queen Luise Society. He drove through the town in the count's limousine (many houses had hung out flags in his honor), and was met by a *Stahlhelm* guard of honor at the "Long Bridge." The *Stahlhelm* marched behind the automobile all the way to Count von Strahlenheim's estate before being reviewed and dismissed. Later the local Cavalry Club was invited to tea at the count's mansion in order to meet the old warrior. Northeimers who delighted in this could hardly be pleased when the *Volksblatt* published a half-page photograph of the count's manor house, showing the servants' quarters, stables, etc., captioned: "Here lives the Count von Strahlenheim—leader of the workers—leader of the NSDAP—further commentary unnecessary."[3]

The persistent nationalism that Northeimers showed in the years of the depression must be taken as a political constant, but one which few could exploit as skillfully as the Nazis. Even entertainment was affected by it. The Lecture Society frequently had military speakers. Over the Christmas holidays, 1931–1932, the film "Reserves at Ease!" *(Reserve hat Ruh!),* a military farce, broke all records for Northeim's movie houses and ran a full two weeks. It outdrew such stalwarts as Tom Mix and Harry Piel. Nor was it a tolerant nationalism. In August 1931 the NNN reported that a small balloon from Belgium, with a postcard attached asking date and place of discovery, had been found near the town. "Many people think such things are a meaningless joke," editorialized the NNN, "but since so many of them come asking questions about wind, weather, and place of discovery, one can assume that the senders are seeking strategic information. Therefore do not send the postcards to France or Belgium. . . ." The GGZ noted that the Northeimer boy who climbed the tree to get the balloon had ripped his pants; it proposed seriously that the French pay for a new pair of trousers for him.

---

*The "Black Reichswehr" was a segment of the regular Army which was concealed from the public in order to evade the restrictions of the Treaty of Versailles.

The story drew no comment from the *Volksblatt*.[4] Religion was also used to foster nationalism; though the churches did not celebrate Constitution Day, they did hold services commemorating Bismarck's establishment of the Reich and in October 1932 they celebrated President von Hindenburg's birthday.[5]

It was in this atmosphere that Nazi appeals to nationalism and militarism, however crude, could have effect. Socialist charges that the Nazis were militaristic, on the other hand, were valueless, especially when they contained implied threats of violence. By late autumn 1932, the *Volksblatt* was driven to demanding action of the town government against Nazis wearing uniforms and marching through the town with flags. It called such activities "provocations to violence."[6] The town's Nazis knew, however, that these were precisely the kinds of gestures that appealed to their followers in Northeim. Thus, instead of attempting to combat the nationalistic, military-based government of von Papen, the Nazis turned the new emphasis to their own advantage.

On September 17 Northeim's Nazis held their first meeting after the July 31 Reichstag elections. It was advertised as a "Big Army March Evening" and featured a "Sport Show by the SS." A sizable crowd was on hand to watch the SS perform, though their "Sport Show" turned out to be an exhibition of what were euphemistically called "defense sports," i.e., military exercises. Two days later the SA held extensive public maneuvers in the forest near Northeim, followed by a "Maneuver Ball." Events of this type held much more appeal than another meeting, held a week later, in which "Workers of all classes! Businessmen! Artisans! Farmers!" were invited to "Storm with us with elemental rage against Marxism and Reaction!" According to the *Volksblatt*, the Nazis had only one-tenth of their usual attendance.[7]

Despite all their recent successes, Local Group Northeim was in trouble, as was the entire *Gau* of South Hanover-Brunswick. One component was financial. Money was still rolling in, but receipts had not risen while expenditures had—in anticipation of ever-increasing revenues. The "pyramid club" of 1931–32, whereby profits from mass meetings were fed into propaganda leading to higher profits from mass meetings, had reached its limit by the summer of 1932 and was beginning to collapse. There were no more floods of new Hitler followers to feed the cycle. Moreover, the incessant electioneering, with each campaign expected by starry-eyed Nazi leaders to be the one that would bring ultimate victory, led to reckless extravagances and debts that could not be paid because of the relative reduction in the rate of growth.

By August 1932 the *Gauleitung* was angrily dunning Local Group Northeim for dues remittances in arrears since June, amounting to RM 823.50.

At the end of August the Local Group paid that debt but then promptly slipped behind again. By the end of September Northeim was in arrears for RM 555.50, and in October it failed to pay the sum of RM 261 due for that month. On December 8 the *Gauleitung* reminded Local Group Northeim that it had not paid anything since August and demanded an immediate remittance.[8] Nor was it just Northeim that owed debts to the *Gau:* Local Groups all over South Hanover-Brunswick were not paying up.[9]

A second problem was that membership in the Nazi party was actually declining. At the end of September 1932 the *Gau* registered a net loss of 401 members for the month. There were 84 new members, but 330 had quit and 155 had been expelled (most probably for nonpayment of dues). Contributions and collections were also down.[10] This may have been because the NSDAP had simply squeezed too much already from its followers. But it may also have been because the party had turned "Left," in an attempt to distance itself from the von Papen government, and thus had alienated some of its middle-class followers. If so, there was a portentous political problem, too.[11]

By October 1932 Northeim faced a new election campaign—the fifth in eight months. The Reichstag elected in July had held only one business session, in which "no confidence" was voted against the von Papen government by a margin of over ten to one. Von Papen, who had no intention of ruling on the basis of parliamentary confidence, promptly dissolved the Reichstag and called for new elections on November 6. While it was clear that the government was supported only by the authority of von Hindenburg and the bayonets of the Army, there was no possible combination within the Reichstag that could have formed a government; 319 of the 608 seats were held by Nazis or Communists. They could not rule together, but together they could keep anyone else from ruling.

Thus in many respects the autumn Reichstag campaign was devoid of either hope or meaning. Yet the Nazis had to enter the fray and had to show gains if they were to maintain their aura of invincibility. Again the tactical directives went out and again the *Gau* queried Local Group Northeim about its propaganda needs. Walter Steineck was no longer the big spender of the summer and answered that he already had enough printed material. He no longer called, as he had for the July campaign, for "5 *Gau* Speakers, 3 Reich Speakers, and a big-gun for a 15,000-person demonstration on election eve."[12] The *Gauleitung* also devised new techniques that could be carried out with manpower rather than money: "missionary" speakers for door-to-door campaigning, each with a goal of converting (and selling literature to) fifteen to twenty families; renewed assaults on places where no Local Group existed;

a repeat of the personal letter writing tactic that had been used in July. And the campaign would still use tested agitational methods such as mass meetings.[13]

On October 8 the first Nazi mass meeting was held—again a mixed affair rather than a straight speech. There was a lottery, music by the SA band, and a play by the Hitler Youth entitled ''In the Enemy's Gold.'' Three days later a Nazi member of the Prussian Parliament spoke on ''Down with the Dictatorship of the Money-Bags.'' His whole effort was aimed at von Papen and the Nationalists, and he promised that the Nazis would crush this ''class-war party of capitalism.'' Attendance was good at both events.[14]

With the new campaign came the dreary increase of violence and vituperation. Throughout August and September the town had been quiet. The only exception came in early September when that inveterate Nazi brawler, Tumpelmann, beat up a Socialist, for which he was fined the token sum of 10 marks. On October 23, however, there was a fight between two *Reichsbanner* men and a Nazi, in which the Nazi's head was broken open. In the same week the courts fined an Iron Front member for insulting a policeman, and a Nazi for insulting a town councilman.[15] Comic relief was eventually supplied in the ''Battle of the Bands'' on October 10. The town band (which the Nazis considered Socialist since it frequently rented itself for SPD gatherings) was giving its usual weekly concert in the Market Square when the SA band arrived. Through police bungling, the Nazis had also been given permission to play at the same time and place. The audience on the square rapidly aligned itself politically and exchanged shouts of *''Freiheit!''* and *''Heil Hitler!''* To avert violence the police drew a line down the middle of the square and manned it while the bands attempted to out-blast each other. Under the urgings of the police, both bands finally packed up and the crowd dispersed quietly. Northeimers had probably had their fill of music that day anyway, since the Communist brass band had been through town earlier on a truck.[16]

The SPD began its campaign with a mass *Reichsbanner* meeting on October 22. The featured speaker was the national leader of the *Reichsbanner*, Karl Hoeltermann, and the meeting was preceded by a parade and a concert in the Market Square by the *Reichsbanner* band from Hanover. Since men from the entire Tenth *Reichsbanner* District came to Northeim for the event, the parade was impressive. Hoeltermann's speech, entitled ''Our Freedom at Stake,'' consisted of a vehement attack on the Nazis. The whole affair was a considerable demonstration of strength. A week later the SPD youth section held a demonstration with songs and an anti-Nazi play. The final demonstration came on November 4 and featured Otto Grotewohl, who attacked both the Communists and the Nazis in an extremely emotional speech.[17]

The Nationalist party held two meetings in the campaign, both in the final week, both attacking equally the Nazis and parliamentary government.[18]

The Nazis began the final electioneering with a mass meeting featuring the League of German Girls. A speech by the Northeim leader, Claire Denzler, stressed "love of Fatherland, Folkish Community, Germanic consciousness, and German morals." Three days later a dual meeting was held appealing to "Rentiers, Pensioners, and War Invalids" and to "German Artisans and Businessmen." Prices were cut to 20 *Pfennig*, the lowest amount ever charged for a Nazi meeting. In the morning the SA, SS, and Hitler Youth went to church *en masse*, and at noon the SA band gave a concert. Two days later a Lutheran minister spoke for the Nazis. Again the price was cut, though the Nazis were in such financial trouble, that for the first time they made a public appeal for funds. The minister attacked the von Papen government, though as usual he stressed religion and nationalism: "There is only one God in heaven whom we serve, and only one Fatherland that we love." There was a big, enthusiastic crowd. Finally, on election eve, the Hitler Youth and League of German Girls joined to sponsor an "evening of entertainment," with songs and a dance as well as speeches by local leaders.[19] That there was still money to be made from Northeim's burghers was indicated by the profits, after the cost of the beer, from this event: 400 marks.[20]

In this election for the first time since 1930, the Nazis supplemented their meetings with newspaper advertisements. For the week prior to the election, large advertisements appeared daily in both the NNN and GGZ, consisting of short slogans such as: "Fourteen Years Misery, Shame, and Dirt! Defend Yourself!" or "Our daily bread is the prime need. We want bearable living conditions!" In addition, all sections of the party were put to work distributing literature and tickets to meetings. The Nazis were clearly running scared.

The election, on Sunday, November 6, showed the first drop in Nazi support in Northeim. Some of this was attributable to "election weariness"; though only a hundred fewer people voted, these must have come from the NSDAP's totals, which fell by 267 votes. The main gainers were the People's party and Nationalists, though the Communists also added about 50 votes. The SPD seemed to have leveled off. Though it lost a dozen votes in Northeim, it actually gained in Northeim County. Yet despite the Nazi dropoff, they still controlled 59 percent of the popular vote while the Socialists had only 24 percent. Nationally the NSDAP seemed to have passed its zenith. It fell from 230 seats in the Reichstag to 196, while the Communists rose from 89 to 100. Yet the election solved nothing, for the Nazis and Communists still maintained their "negative majority" and authoritarian government continued.

As if to make this clear, von Papen issued a decree on election day prohibiting *all* political meetings, everywhere in Germany, for a twelve-day period. Even this did not prevent violence; two days after the election there was a fight between several SA and *Reichsbanner* men, though no one was seriously injured.[21] In the dangerous political sterility there was only one cause for optimism. By autumn 1932 it appeared that the depression had passed its worst period and recovery could now be expected, even without governmental action. Northeimers who studied the local unemployment figures that were published twice a month in each newspaper could see that the high point of unemployment reached in the spring of 1932 barely exceeded that of the previous year. They could note that unemployment was not increasing as rapidly in the fall as it usually did. Already, in October 1932, the district Industrial and Trade Council came to the conclusion that economic revival was underway. A statement to this effect, the first hopeful statement of the depression years, was issued to the press with evidence to back it up.[22]

This brought little cheer to the unemployed, however. Even those who found work at the sugar beet factory in autumn 1932 earned only 2 marks a week more than unemployment pay; the wage rate was exactly half of what it had been in 1929. In November 1932 a young woman welfare recipient began shouting "Hunger!" in the City Hall because her needs could not be met by the Welfare Office. She continued until the police expelled her. Later in November a local court sentenced a worker to a month's imprisonment for having cried "To the barricades! To civil war!" in anger over finding that the unemployment payments for his large family had been reduced. A near riot ensued at the City Hall when welfare recipients learned that the dole had been cut. Early in December an unemployed man became so incensed at the Welfare Office that he refused to leave and had to be arrested. All the way to jail he kept shouting: "I'm hungry! I have hunger and nothing else!" At the same time the Association of Industrial Accident Invalids and Widows sent a demand to the government for better and more equitable pensions.[23]

The city did what it could to help. The unemployed were offered inexpensive meat, or if one of them had a pig, the city would slaughter and dress it free at the town abattoir. Some potatoes were on hand for emergency cases, and those without any food could have free meals at the town's soup kitchen (an average of thirty-seven meals a day were given out in 1932). The city bath house offered warm baths at 10 *Pfennig* a person, and in especially needy cases the unemployed could bathe free. A warming hall was also established for the unemployed.[24] The city took such action partly because private charity failed. The "Charity Union" of 1931 was not repeated in 1932, "so as to avoid the difficulties they had last year." Exacerbated political rivalries made cohesion among the separate charitable societies impossible.[25]

In the last two months before Hitler came to power, the Socialists were gripped by a peculiar fatalism. Since the summer, they doubted their ability to control events. No public meetings were held, though the *Reichsbanner* continued its preparations for a fight in case the Nazis should seize power. In their Berlin headquarters a secret short-wave radio station was built and, after November, manned round-the-clock so as to be able to flash the signal when the Nazis struck. In Northeim the mood of the men became more belligerent the longer they waited. *Reichsbanner* leaders warned incessantly against precipitate action. They were eager to fight and yet they had little hope of winning. A union leader burned his membership lists in December 1932. A *Reichsbanner* leader from a suburb immediately adjacent to Northeim had difficulty holding his men back from an independent strike against the Nazis, but at the same time he took the precaution of destroying his membership rolls, also in December.[26] A common worker summed up the general feeling. He saw the Nazis possessing overpowering strength, mainly financial. He would not cower before them—in fact he was one of the leaders in a fight with some SA men, for which he was sentenced to jail—but he did feel that the Nazis would come to power and that he could not prevent this. After all, he was "just a small figure."[27]

The townspeople were also convinced of the inevitability of a Nazi victory. It was widely believed that the NSDAP had already compiled lists of how positions of power would be distributed in Northeim.[28] Non-Socialists did not believe the *Reichsbanner* would fight; they argued that its leaders were pacifistic and lacked personal courage.[29] This despite the fact that most of Northeim's *Reichsbanner* leaders had war medals to prove their courage (Karl Deppe held the Iron Cross, First Class). But while the town waited for the Third Reich in December and January, nothing happened.

The senseless round of political activity did continue, however. The Communists persisted in agitating and distributing leaflets among the jobless in the Army compound. Communist slogans were found traced on the sidewalks with a brown oil dye that caused city workers endless trouble to remove. In January the KPD led about eighty demonstrators in a parade with placards that bore the slogans: "Open the Cupboards! Out with the Coal,

Potatoes, and Bread!'' This also gave the townspeople something to think about. The *Volksblatt* twice issued vehement denials that the KPD was making inroads among the Young Socialist Workers.

Contrary to popular opinions about the Socialists, the Communists were considered serious revolutionaries who would fight if the Nazis came to power. This was not a viewpoint shared by the authorities in Northeim. In 1931 the town's police answered an official inquiry by stating: ''Our observations are that no one need worry about the Communists here. Their Local Group has only fifteen to twenty members and has been rather inactive up to now.''[30] Nor were Northeim's Communists ready to fight. When Prussian police searched the homes of leading Communist functionaries throughout the whole of Northeim County in August 1932, the total weapons from fourteen houses consisted of four ''clubs,'' two ''daggers,'' one revolver, and one pair of brass knuckles—the latter being the sole Communist weapon in the town of Northeim.[31] But the possibility of Communist growth in Northeim, in the depression environment, continued to provide the Nazis with a whipping boy, the middle class with new reasons for concern, and the Socialists with another cause for a siege atmosphere.[32]

The Nazis also continued their agitation throughout the dead winter months. Early in December they held two events, one with propaganda films and one with diverse entertainment. In January an SA propaganda march was held and also a mass meeting in which their speaker described the NSDAP as ''the last tortured cry of a *Herrenvolk.*'' Perhaps many of the unemployed, who were admitted free, came mainly because the Nazis had advertised that ''the hall is well heated.'' Finally, at the end of January the SA gave another ''Army March Evening'' coupled with a presentation of the play ''Brown Heroes.'' These activities did not stem from élan, as had been the case earlier, but from grim determination and inertia.[33]

Part of the Nazis' problem was the stalemated national situation. Another part was what Ernst Girmann (who had finally taken over on December 1, 1932, as official Local Group Leader for Northeim) called ''this momentary financial calamity,'' though it was actually a region-wide, if not national, crisis.[34] In any case, by December the Local Group was so strapped that rather than using the *1910er Zelt* for meetings, they had to rent the Riding Hall, to which they had previously and contemptuously relegated the SPD.[35] They had become so desperate for funds that they even resorted to *extorting* money from their own constituency. Girmann evolved a plan to issue a directory of all businesses owned by Northeim party members. Nazis would then be ordered to shop only from firms listed in this directory, two thousand copies of which would be distributed. To be listed, a Nazi businessman had to pay four marks. Girmann called it "cheap advertising," but he left his victims little choice: "How do you want your listing to read?" [36]

Meanwhile County Leader Walter Steineck was sick (with stomach ulcers that had plagued him for the past ten weeks), bedridden, totally without income, being maintained by the charity of relatives, and was receiving no reimbursement from the *Gau* for official expenses. He had an overdue telephone bill of RM 117 and his phone was about to be taken away. On December 19 he wrote to the *Gauleitung* to plead for his past-due expense money and mentioned: "Today I gave my last 20 *Pfennig* for 'postage due' on a letter from the *Gauleitung.*" The letter he had paid for was a reminder that he owed the *Gau* several past months' dues remittances and a request that he pay a *Gau* speaker the RM 57.50 he owed him, since the speaker was "flat broke." [37] It appeared that nobody in the Nazi party could pay anybody anything.

Ernst Girmann's solution, apart from plodding on with meetings and "evenings of entertainment," was to beseech the higher offices for "big gun" speakers. He asked the *Gau* for Hitler. He invited Goebbels to come to Northeim and described the town's charms to him. Eventually he begged his old comrades in the *Gauleitung* for *any* significant speaker, but none was promised. [38]

Meanwhile a faction fight broke out in the Northeim NDSAP. Dissident Nazis charged Girmann with cronyism, financial improprieties, and autocratic methods. He responded with summary expulsions. By January it looked as though the Local Group might be on the verge of breaking up. Also, the mood of the SA became increasingly ugly. A week before Christmas one of them beat an elderly Social Democrat so severely that he blinded him in one eye. [39] No one could foresee that Adolf Hitler was about to be appointed Reich chancellor and that the Third Reich was about to be launched. The town had long since given itself to the Nazi cause, but in January 1933 the Nazis seemed to have no idea what to do except resort to more of the same incessant propaganda and violence.

The factors that brought Northeim to the brink of the Third Reich with a three-fifths Nazi majority (almost double the national average) were not numerous, but they were complexly interrelated. Paramount among them was the depression. Though only the working class suffered physically in the three-year crisis, the town's middle class was more decisively affected through fears that an ultimate catastrophe would thrust upon it the same fate as the "shelterless," or that social revolution would destroy its status. More important than the actual misery caused by the depression was the constant flow of news items stressing that misery.

There were only seventeen bankruptcies in Northeim in the entire depression era, eleven of which befell small, marginal shop owners, and the other six for causes dissociated from the depression. But the bankruptcies were strung out over a long period of time and each involved lengthy and dolorous legal proceedings, all faithfully reported in the press. At the high point of unemployment, in April 1932, only 8 percent of the townspeople were unemployed, but the constant protests, fights, demonstrations, and the endless stream of gray-faced workers coming to the District Employment Office kept unemployment uppermost in the minds of the town's middle class. Nazi agitation drew upon this mood and intensified the unsettled atmosphere.

The despair of the unemployed not only terrified and repelled the middle class, it also destroyed the self-confidence of the workers. Years of idleness sapped their discipline; the destruction of the power of their unions left them exposed to crude economic pressures. Wage gains acquired over a decade were swept away, and even those who still held jobs lived in fear of losing them.

The depression not only created the climate of fear in which the Nazis throve, it also embittered political processes. Political rivalry in turn prevented the cooperation that was needed to mitigate the effects of the depression. In Northeim the politics of crisis took the form of a general class war. The town's middle class had never accepted the SPD as an institution; now with the rise of Nazism it was offered a method of destroying Social Democracy. One response by the SPD was to increase the viciousness of attacks in the *Volksblatt* against some of Northeim's leading citizens. Responses in kind by the GGZ and *Hört! Hort!* only succeeded in degrading politics and adding to the tension. Ultimately the Nazis proved the most capable at vituperation, which would have been held against them in normal times, but which was to their credit in the welter of mudslinging. Only the moderation of the civil servants' bloc in the City Council made effective city government possible amid the maneuverings for partisan advantage. It was hatred for the SPD that drove Northeim into the arms of the Nazis. Few of the conservatives realized that after the Nazis had destroyed the Social Democrats, they would turn on their erstwhile allies and smash them.

But the Nazis never would have been chosen as the instrument to subdue the SPD if they had not been otherwise acceptable to the burghers. The attributes which made the Nazis respectable were their intense nationalism, their manipulation of religion, and the support given them by the conservatives.

Northeim was a nationalistic town long before 1930, though as the depression wore on, commitment to nationalism and militarism increased.

Outside forces contributed to this, as did Nazi propaganda, but by manipulating the symbols of patriotism the NSDAP in Northeim associated itself with an important tradition. The same applied to the Nazis' exploitation of religious feelings, especially their use of Lutheran pastors as speakers in Northeim. The association of the German Nationalist party with the Nazis was also a reciprocal one. The DNVP and NSDAP were more or less in alliance throughout the entire pre-Hitler era in Northeim. The only period of real bitterness between the two came under the von Papen government, when countercharges of "reactionaries" and "socialistic radicals" filled the air. Then, at the end of January 1933, the Nazis and Nationalists acted in concert again, since the Hitler government was originally a coalition.

The Nazis and the DNVP had much in common: hyper-nationalism, fanatical anti-Socialism, and commitment to the destruction of the Weimar Republic. In Northeim, leading Nationalists were pleased by Nazi successes despite the frequent and clear signs of contempt which the Nazis showed them. The GGZ gave them editorial support, reported frequently and favorably on Nazi doings (the reporter being a Nazi), and apparently provided cut-rate or free advertising space. In the early years of the Nazis' growth the GGZ printing press was available for Nazi pamphlets and posters and its columns were the only way the Nazis could reach a mass audience.[40]

Though the DNVP had a small following in Northeim they had two assets that benefited the Nazis. One was money. In Northeim most of the members of the DNVP were either high-ranking civil servants, entrepreneurs, or noblemen. The other asset was respectability. Not only were the "best" people members; the party bore the tradition of having firmly supported the monarchy in the golden days of Germany's greatness. Finally, it seemed to have an intimate connection with the Army, through the *Stahlhelm,* whose honorary national commander was von Hindenburg. By giving enthusiastic support to the Nazis and by limiting its opposition (in the periods when the parties were at odds) to Nazi social goals, the DNVP helped pave the way for Hitler. To Northeimers it was clear that the best people were for the Nazis except where it might affect their moneybags.

A further factor which aided the rise of Nazism in Northeim was politicalization. The yearnings and needs created by the depression, class antagonisms, and resurgent nationalism all seemed capable of political solution. Constant elections meant constant campaigning and each campaign spurred bitterness and radicalism. From the local elections of November 1929 to the Reichstag elections of November 1932, there were nine major campaigns, five in 1932 alone. Northeimers voted heavily in all of these. This followed the pattern of the whole electoral district, which had the second highest voting participation record of Germany's thirty-five electoral districts.[41] In Northeim between 94 percent and 97 percent of those eligible voted in each of the major elections. Since registration was automatic, only the sick and feeble-minded stayed home. The rest were involved in politics, which is to say that political passion pervaded almost all areas of human existence in the town.

All of these factors contributed to the Nazi success in Northeim, but even favorable circumstances do not explain the remarkable Nazi leap from 123 votes to almost 4,200 votes in three years' time.[42] To understand this one must consider the skill and effort that the Nazis put into campaigning. Quantity was the first component. In the three-year period from January 1930 to January 1933, the Nazis averaged close to three meetings per month in Northeim. As the years went on, the number, size, and variety of the Nazis' public functions increased. High points were reached during election campaigns; in July 1932 there were six Nazi functions: three meetings with speeches, two parades followed by rallies, and one "evening of entertainment." Furthermore, activity was constant; throughout the entire three-year period there were only two months without Nazi meetings (July 1930, and August 1932).[43] Vigor was the strongest impression.

Nazi propaganda efforts in Northeim went beyond pure activism. Persistent, imaginative, and driving effort was coupled with a shrewd appreciation of what was specifically suitable for Northeim, and for each element in the town. Aside from general speeches on nationalism, Jews, and "Marxists," there were meetings devoted to artisans, businessmen, civil servants, pensioners, workmen, and other targeted groups. Northeim's local peculiarities were taken into account; there was little real anti-Semitism in the town, hence this was soft-pedaled. But the townspeople were strongly religious and this was exploited to the hilt. When there was no specific group to be appealed to, the Nazis relied on pageantry, "evenings of entertainment," film showings, plays, acrobatic acts, lotteries, dances, sport exhibitions, military displays, recitals by children, and other expedients from a seemingly inexhaustible bag of tricks.[44] They drew the tortured masses into the mammoth meetings where one could submerge oneself in the sense of participating in a dynamic and all-encompassing movement geared toward radical action in fulfillment of every need. The enemy was defined in similar terms: he was the Jew, the Socialist, the godless one, or, if one preferred amorphous generalities, the "System" which was to blame for everything from the collapse of the Enterprise Bank to the Treaty of Versailles.

In short, the NSDAP succeeded in being all things to all men. This was even reflected in the use of the name in advertisements, which were signed

"National Soc. German Wkrs. Party," "Nat. Socialist Germ. Workers Party," or other variations according to the needs of the moment. From the morass of propaganda the Nazis emerged as devout, serious, impeccably patriotic, the archenemies of "Marxism," "Socialistic" only so far as it served the needs of Nationalism, and (if you ever attended their "evenings of entertainment") obviously hail fellows. But the prime effect attained by the Nazi meetings was achieved simply by their numbers. If you wanted an energetic party this was it.

The energy and skill of the Nazis appears mysterious from a distance, but becomes quite understandable when one analyzes the motivation, composition, and mechanics of the party in its local operations. It is possible to speculate about the ideological and historical roots of Nazi fanaticism, the cult-like qualities of pseudo-religious movements, the daemonic release of energy produced by masochistic subordination to an all-powerful, charismatic *Führer*. But simpler explanations seem more likely to reveal the predominating factors in the frantic activism of the Nazis.

First of all, from the time that the Nazi party began to change from a fringe phenomenon to a mass movement, their goal became a very simple one. It was the acquisition of power. This was to be done by getting ever more members and votes. Everything else—such as doctrinal consistency or human decency—was subordinated to the single goal of mobilizing mass support to bring the Hitler movement into power. A goal as simple as that permits great concentration of effort and a very economical use of talent and energy.

Secondly, the composition of the Nazi party was such as to give them the talent to accomplish their simple goal with less effort then previous parties had to employ. The NSDAP was the first mass movement of the middle class. Its leaders, down to the lowest level, had the skills of the small businessman. They already knew how to get things down in the practical world with a minimum of effort. They thought in cost accounting terms (and understood how to keep account ledgers, as opposed to the proletarian followers of the SPD, for example, who had to learn this like a foreign language), and were familiar with such things as advertising, equipment leasing, fund-raising drives, and interoffice memos. They had the network of contacts (at least on the local level) to know where specialized skills could be located, to deal with practical problems like renting a microphone or getting a poster designed and printed overnight. Their middle-class background and business experience meant that they were already trained to punctuality, industriousness, disciplined task-solving, orderliness, and frugality. Those who had fought in the war also knew about ruthlessness, following orders without question, and exploiting opportunities rapidly. Nazi leaders also had the petty bourgeois qualities of intolerance, self-confidence, gullibility, and unreflective self-righteousness—characterological defects that Hitler knew only too well how to reinforce and employ.

Finally, the mechanism of propaganda and mass mobilization worked out by the Nazi party before 1930 through trial and error was simple, self-correcting, and self-reinforcing. By developing a diverse shopping list of written propaganda and a wide selection of speakers with varied themes (there were eighty *Gau* Speakers available to Northeim's Nazis by December 1932[45]), the higher offices of the NSDAP made it possible for local Nazi leaders to select virtually any combination suitable for local needs. Guesswork was required for such selections, but after a mass meeting had been staged the results could be rather precisely evaluated by counting ticket sales and collection proceeds. Future tactics were adjusted accordingly and could be constantly fine-tuned by this feedback system. Profits were the most easily measurable test for the success or failure of a particular speaker or his theme (each speaker also having a stake in his own top performance), and the profits made more activity and propaganda possible. Thus the Nazis' incessant campaigning may be primarily explained by the interlinkage between mass meetings and financing methods. And ultimately the most significant feedback system consisted of something else that was frequently recorded and easily counted: membership applications and votes. Since the quest for power was the single goal, these were also the prime reward and reinforcement elements for the whole mechanism.

None of this should be taken to suggest that the Nazis were invincible or that their juggernaut was unstoppable. A considerable portion of their success from 1930 to 1932 must be ascribed to their novelty and to the bandwagon effect. Once these factors stopped operating, the movement was in trouble—as exemplified by Local Group Northeim's problems in the autumn of 1932. By then the only sure way that Northeim's Nazis could get the townspeople to a meeting was to make it an "evening of entertainment." In other words, pure political propaganda had lost its pulling power for the average Nazi voter. Popular apathy and exhaustion had replaced curiosity and enthusiasm, the financial bubble had burst, and the party, denied the external focus provided by the expectation of imminent victory, had begun to attack itself. Nazi hyperactivism also exacted a toll from the leaders on the local level; they were burned out in a hurry, like Rudolf Ernst and Walter Steineck. The whole thing was like a death-or-glory cavalry charge, and by January 1933 it could just as easily have gone the one way as the other.

It seems clear that if a national leader of Germany had been found with the will and courage to outlaw both the NSDAP and the Communists (and perhaps to back that up by inducting the entire *Reichsbanner* into the Army Reserve), that would have been the end of Hitler. The party undoubtedly would have continued to exist, but, as was demonstrated by the Prussian ban in 1922, it would have atrophied through lack of agitation and money. Hitler was by no means irresistible, though by the beginning of 1933 the efforts and skills of his followers made it look that way.

Then too, the Nazis would never have succeeded in Northeim as well as they did had there been any effective opposition to them. The various right-wing splinter parties were no competition since they agreed with the nationalism and anti-Socialism of the Nazis and were at best highly doubtful of the merits of democracy.[46] Only two parties had an unqualified commitment to democracy and a clear appreciation of the dangers of Nazism. These were the Catholic Center party and the SPD. The Center party had a small following in Northeim because of the religious complexion of the town, but it was stable—180 votes in each election, give or take 10. The Socialists remained remarkably stable too, considering the fact that the depression bore directly upon their followers. They showed no losses at all until the spring of 1932. In the spring and summer elections of 1932 the SPD lost 28 percent of its votes but then stabilized itself. The social homogeneity that was the source of the SPD's strength was also the source of its inability to combat Nazism effectively. Had the Socialists mended fences with the non-Nazi bourgeoisie they might have prevented the growth of Nazism. The town's social traditions prevented this. Had the Socialists presented a revolutionary program they might have stolen the banner of radicalism from the Nazis. Their own reformist tradition prevented this. But the basic error in strategy was to assume that the threat of Nazism lay in its potential for armed uprising. The Socialists were prepared to counteract this; what they did not counteract was the Nazi *political* threat. Instead their approach was wholly negative.

The SPD emphasized the evils of Nazism but had no alternative program. It defended the Republic but could not promise a better future. The mood of SPD, *Reichsbanner,* or union meetings was wholly defensive, even to the extent of using mass rallies in national campaigns to deal with Nazi attacks on the local level. In the ideology of Socialism the SPD had a superb weapon for dealing with the depression, but in Northeim there was never any effort to use this weapon except for the crude vilifications of the individual bourgeois printed in the *Volksblatt.* Taken as a whole, the work of the SPD may serve as an example of the fecklessness of even the most dedicated activity, without an effective strategy behind it. Furthermore, the more the SPD strove to match the Nazis in determination the more they drove the middle class into the Nazi embrace. Socialist militancy simply increased the political tension in Northeim without diminishing the Nazi appeal.

The factors conducive to the rise of a radical mass party of the right were thus abundant in Northeim: economic misery which seemed to grow progressively worse, a traditional division along class lines which became exacerbated by political intolerance, intense nationalism and fervid militarism, an ineffectual but belligerent Left, and a splintered, indignant, insecure Right. In addition to its own propaganda the NSDAP contributed one other ingredient to this witches' cauldron—the breakdown of civil order.

From 1930 to 1933 there were no fewer than thirty-seven political fights in Northeim. Of these, four were general mêlées. These figures do not include the near misses—times when only the vigorous action of the police or the restraint of opposing leaders prevented fresh outbreaks of physical violence. There were also many times when the police forbade meetings, when contingents of state police had to be brought to Northeim as reinforcements, and when the newspapers reported the presence or lack of violence in almost the same tone as the weather or auto accidents. Police rules and regulations, government edicts and emergency decrees, none of these sufficed to eradicate the almost daily street fights in Germany, the classic land of tight laws and strict order.

The root of the problem was the division of the town into two groups of absolute opponents, each of which meant to destroy the other; the one to institute a dictatorship, the other to save the existing, if battered, democracy. This clash of views led to mutual vilification, first by the parties, then by individuals. Libel suits became commonplace. Taunts and insults by word and deed fostered arrogance. Terrorism, especially in Northeim County, became a standard weapon; knives, blackjacks, even guns became standard equipment. Beyond this there were the persistent rumors, some based on fact, of an impending Nazi *Putsch*.

From a sleepy provincial town, Northeim became an explosive center of violence. It is possible to construct a "fever chart" composed of political activity and street fights.[47] It would show a direct correlation between election campaigns, frequency of political meetings, and physical clashes. All three increased yearly. Furthermore, the courts were generally lenient so that hotheads on both sides were encouraged. The culmination of this attitude came on January 20, 1933, when a general amnesty was granted to all those convicted in the "Hunger March" and "Long Bridge" battles. Thus they were free to participate in the events following Hitler's accession to power.

The heritage of three years of violence, the fruits of numerous broken heads, split lips, and black eyes were manifold. Nothing, of course, was settled by any of the fights, which were the result rather than the cause of political tension. But from them the town accumulated a full measure of bitterness. Since peaceful settlements proved impossible, Northeimers grew accustomed to expect a violent resolution of political differences. Orderly minded people were sickened by the recurrent fights, but finally became inured to them. Thus the way was paved for the systematic use of violence and terror by the Nazis after Hitler came to power, and for their relatively indifferent acceptance by the people of Northeim. This was to be the prime factor in the Nazi seizure of power.

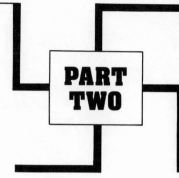

PART TWO

INTRODUCING THE DICTATORSHIP

JANUARY 1933
TO MAY 1945

THE LAST ELECTIONS

FEBRUARY- MARCH 1933

If this cancer of the German people was not all too obvious at the beginning, it was because there were enough healthy energies at work to restrain it. But as it grew and grew and at last, by a final piece of knavery, came to power, the cancer burst and made foul the whole political body. Then the majority of those who had opposed it went into hiding.

German Resistance Leaflet
Distributed in 1942

The month of January 1933—the last few weeks before Hitler became chancellor of Germany—was a hard one for almost all Northeimers. The weather was cold and damp with that peculiar marrow-chilling quality that one finds in the north German plain. The slate sky gave grayness to the old buildings and cobblestone streets and the very air itself seemed gray and dull. To the unemployed the barren branches of the trees and the frosty mud of the fields must have symbolized their own situation: stretched on the rack of despair, frozen in the mire of endless and pointless idleness.

Some had been unemployed for three years and more; others had found work only intermittently. Still others were perhaps more unfortunate: they had just reached the age when they would normally be getting their first jobs, but there were none, and it seemed as though there never would be any. To the store owner standing beside his idle cash register, to the artisan—with the proud title of "Master of his Craft"—sitting in his shop, waiting for the orders to come, it was an evil winter. Not even the children were merry, for there was a flu epidemic so severe that the schools closed, and to the ordinary man's worries were added the sight, at the end of his empty day, of his feverish children and his harassed wife.

What emotions were possible for the Northeimer in this, the last winter of the depression? Even the Nazi answer—hate—seemed lackluster, as attendance at Nazi meetings fell off and the SA men stood forlorn and miserable in their haughty uniforms, shaking collection cans on the street corners. In Northeim the Nazis appeared to have passed the zenith of their power. They had the votes of more than half of the town, but how long could they keep them when nothing happened? In the latest election (November 1932) it was all the town's Nazis could do to retain the electoral gains they had made. Nationally the Nazi tide gave signs of receding. In Northeim itself the Nazis seemed to be engaged in ritualistic acts: small meetings in the Cattle Auction Hall, plans for another of the repetitious speeches or "evenings of entertainment." Determination to hold on, not the élan of victory, seemed to be the characteristic note in January 1933.

Nor did the Social Democrats of Northeim have reason for elation. They had lost heavily in 1932. There were ominous signs of increasing interest in the Communist party among the unemployed of the town. Many expected a Nazi takeover. They planned to fight, but it was no longer fully clear what they were fighting for. For the Republic of General von Schleicher or von Papen? For democracy under rule by presidential emergency decree? During the gray January of 1933 Northeim's SPD held no meetings, sponsored no speeches. What was there to say?

The town government carried on, however, trying to deal with the depression. The City Council met on January 13, and Mayor Peters was able to announce that the budget would balance for 1933. This was accomplished by raising the town's taxes by 35 percent. In another effort to ameliorate the lot of the poor, rents on garden lands owned by the city were reduced 25 percent. Finally, Northeim's share of the central government's public works' money had come through and amounted to over 60,000 marks. Plans were in the making to put the money into employment-creating work. Before the meeting adjourned, Senator Querfurt took a moment to accuse the Nazi newspapers of slander.[1]

By January 27 the city administration had completed its plans for utilizing the public works' money. A new street would be built and several others would be repaired. The shooting societies asked the town for a new rifle range since this was a precondition for the expected holding of the North German Shooting Society convention in Northeim in 1933. The SPD was indifferent to pleas from the town's businessmen about the money this would bring into town and refused to allocate funds, thus provoking some bitter words.[2]

In the last days of January the NNN ran a curious story. An old Jewish cattle dealer named Moses had died. He had once been well-to-do, but his fair-weather friends helped him squander his wealth and now he was to lie in a pauper's grave. On this mildly anti-Semitic and moralistically lugubrious note, January 1933 was coming to an end in Northeim.[3]

Then, on the last day of the month, the news burst over the town that Adolf Hitler had been appointed chancellor of Germany. To all Northeimers it was clear that the pointless wanderings of national politics were over and that at last something was happening.

The news caught Northeim's NSDAP unprepared. The Nazis were not even able to organize a victory parade immediately after the event. However, on the weekend thereafter (Saturday, February 4, 1933) an "Evening of Entertainment" complete with speeches and a military concert had been planned. And on Sunday, February 5, a conference of all Nazi Local Groups in the county was to be held in Northeim. Now these plans took on new significance; listlessness was swept away and Northeimers flocked forward to buy tickets. A torchlight parade was hurriedly improvised for Saturday, February 4. The town's *Stahlhelm,* now in coalition with the Nazis, agreed to join. The victory parade was exceedingly impressive. In addition to the fife-and-drum corps and flags of the *Stahlhelm,* there were the flags, band, and fife-and-drum corps of the SA. Nazis and Nationalists from all over the county were in Northeim for the event. If the GGZ's figures are correct there were over eight hundred Nazis and two hundred *Stahlhelmern.* It took a quarter-hour for the whole mass to pass by. The streets of Northeim were packed with onlookers and in the Market Square there was an enormous crowd, "bigger than any heretofore seen," said the NNN. Speeches were given on the unity between Nazis and Nationalists and on the perfidy of Communism.

Most of those who had come into town for the parade left immediately afterward, but enough went on to the *1910er Zelt* for the "Evening of Entertainment" so that people had to be turned away. There was enthusiastic celebration, speeches by County Leader Steineck and other Nazis, and jubilant toasts by the *Stahlhelm* leaders on how good it was to be back with the Nazis as comrades. The Nazi talk of "reactionaries" and the DNVP charges of "dictatorship" and "proto-socialism" of the previous summer and fall were as forgotten as the vanished foam on the beer.

The following morning the Nazis sobered up to complete a strenuous series of activities connected with the county conference. In the morning the fife-and-drum corps marched through the town bright and early while a wreath was laid on the War Memorial by Walter Steineck. There was a parade and then conferences in the Cattle Auction Hall, two hotels, and a café. In the late afternoon there was a round of speeches, particularly against Communism, at the *1910er Zelt.* The Nazis gave the impression that the town was completely theirs.[4]

Repression went hand in hand with celebration. To Northeimers the justification was the prevention of violence: within the first ten days of February there had been two fights in the old Army compound.[5] With Goering in control of the Prussian Ministry of the Interior, however, there was to be no violence, except that which was officially sanctioned and directed. On February 2 all public demonstrations by the Communist party were forbidden. The following day Northeim's police, under orders from Berlin, raided the homes of local members of the KPD, though without finding, as the NNN reported, any "forbidden literature." By successive orders the Communists were forbidden to distribute any literature, solicit contributions, or hold meetings in homes or in public places.[6]

The Social Democrats were dealt with in a more piecemeal manner. On February 18 the Northeim police, prodded by new Nazi officials in the Prussian Ministry of the Interior, confiscated that week's issue of the *Northeimer Echo,* the organ of the "Iron Front." The grounds were that it had ridiculed Hitler in one article and called the swastika "the bankrupt symbol" in another. This was significant news for the timorous, especially since it was intimated that the paper would soon be suppressed altogether.[7]

The full meaning of the new order came to the SPD on February 19. On that day the "Iron Front" planned a demonstration in the Market Square in Northeim. As usual, the police had been notified beforehand. Early in the afternoon, members of the Northeim *Reichsbanner* gathered at the old Army compound near the Employment Office. By the time the parade started out for the Market Square there were about four hundred participants plus the usual flags and musicians. At the same time about one hundred and fifty SA men gathered inside the old town on Broad Street, "under alarm, and to protect the houses and the swastika flag from attack." As the Socialist parade came up to the old city walls, it was stopped by the police. Leaders of the SPD were told that there had already been clashes between SA men and *Reichsbanner* members in Northeim. The police suggested that public security and order were threatened and ordered the parade to turn around and meet at a nearby beer garden, rather than attempt to go to the Market Square.

At the beer garden (which had aspirations to respectability) the Sunday afternoon "Coffee Concert" was being held. The nodding burghers were rather shocked to have their repose broken by four hundred *Reichsbanner* men surrounded by the police. There, isolated by the high walls of the garden and by the police cordon, Northeim's Social Democrats held their last political meeting, while the Stormtroopers marched freely through the streets of the town.[8]

The effect of this occurrence upon the rank-and-file of the town's SPD was enormous. On the evening of this incident Hermann Schulze folded his *Reichsbanner* flag into a coffee can and buried it in a field. Others in the SPD knew the game was up, too. They pinned their hopes on the German Army. If the Army gave the word, they would fight; if not, Germany would go Nazi without organized armed resistance by the *Reichsbanner* or other worker organizations. The membership of the *Reichsbanner* was still willing to fight, but it was clear to them that unless the word was given soon they would be picked off individually by the Nazis.[9]

The Nazis now proceeded to harass the Social Democrats openly. On February 24 a Socialist pamphlet for distribution to the unemployed was confiscated by the police ". . . for ridiculing the Reich Chancellor" (i.e., Hitler). On the same day the police forbade outright a planned torchlight parade by the "Iron Front," on grounds that it would "endanger security and order." Nazi parades, of course, were permitted.[10]

Despite the absence of competition on the Left, Northeim's Nazis did not relax their agitational efforts. One of the Hitler government's first acts had been to arrange for new elections to the Reichstag, knowing that this time the campaign would be conducted on its terms. The party propaganda organization followed this up with directives stipulating that the campaign was to be aimed at the SPD and KPD, while the DNVP and Catholic Center party were not to be attacked (instructions hardly required by Northeim's Nazis).[11]

In Northeim the first mass meeting was held on Saturday, February 25. One speech was directed to war veterans and the second was entitled "Reckoning Up With the Marxist Criminals." The speaker called on all Germans to have the same kind of faith in Hitler as had been shown by "the men of 1914" who "went to death believing in victory." The *1910er Zelt* was jammed full. On the following day the Nazis made an appeal to the burgher's religious sensibilities by sending two hundred uniformed SA men to the town's Lutheran Church. After the services the SA band gave a concert in the Market Square, which attracted many Northeimers out for their Sunday constitutionals.[12]

The Nationalist party joined the campaign with a *Stahlhelm* parade followed by an "Evening of Entertainment" at the *1910er Zelt*. The speeches stressed the closeness of the Nazi-Nationalist coalition and excoriated the "Party-State," i.e., the Weimar Republic. Even the People's party held a meeting, though the message was, as usual, ambiguous. The speaker insisted that the DVP would continue to be important "under the Black-White-Red [Imperial] flag." He registered his opposition to "state socialism," stressed the need for "freedom from Versailles," and concluded with an appeal to "strengthen the Left Wing of the Black-White-Red Front." Twenty persons attended the meeting.

On March 2 the People's party took a stronger stand. In an advertisement in the NNN on that date, the DVP reminded Northeimers that "violence and force will neither bring economic peace nor solve the problem of unemployment." It called on Northeimers to help ensure a strong DVP representation in the Reichstag:

> That is the best assurance for the maintenance of a free citizenry and civil service, maintenance of the middle class and the working industry, maintenance of private enterprise, of a National and Liberal conscience. Those who want to hinder absolutism and want to close the ranks of all national forces, vote DVP.[13]

The allusion to "absolutism" was timely. The burning of the Reichstag building on the night of February 27 gave the Nazis a new excuse for repression of the Left, and the emergency decree which followed suspended all civil liberties in Germany and thus gave the police virtually absolute power. The beginnings of informal social reinforcement of the terror system date from this event. The morning after the Reichstag fire the son of one of Northeim's Socialists was overheard insisting to his classmates that the Nazis were responsible for the fire. Prompted solely by his awareness of the new atmosphere, the non-Nazi principal of the school suspended the boy. There were long telephone conversations with the mayor's office and it was nip and tuck as to whether the boy would be allowed to take his final examinations a few days later.[14]

The newspapers also did their part to help create an atmosphere of terror following the Reichstag fire. For example, the NNN, on March 3, reported:

> The blackest rumors have been continuously spread these days about Communist misdeeds, destructions, incendiary acts, etc. . . . They serve to increase the general tension which has already set in before the election. We have made inquiries to the proper authorities and have been informed that there is not a single word of truth in these rumors. One should strike energetically at such rumormongers. Naturally precautionary measures have been taken. The local police and the railroad guards have been strengthened and are in a state of preparedness, watching the bridges, buildings, and grounds of our railroad station, and also certain track stretches.[15]

In addition to the rumors there were concrete examples. On March 1 the police confiscated "forbidden newspapers and pamphlets of the SPD and KPD" after raids on private dwellings in Northeim. It was also announced that a worker had been arrested the day before for "distributing an SPD election leaflet despite the prohibition." The instruments of repression were also increased. On February 28 Ernst Girmann (in contravention of long-standing NSDAP directives) authorized the carrying of loaded firearms by the town's Stormtroopers, ostensibly to defend themselves against any attacks.[16] On March 1, thirty SS and SA men were deputized as police. Their uniform was the regular Nazi brown shirt with a white armband marked *Hilfspolizei* (Deputy Police). They immediately began patrolling the streets of the town. Since these were the same men who had repeatedly fought with *Reichsbanner* men in the previous years, it can be imagined what their concept of law enforcement was. The Stormtrooper achieved his dream: the chance to do violence without fear of police hindrance. The Nazis not only controlled the police—now they *were* the police.

The new police swung into action immediately. The very afternoon they were deputized, Stormtroopers raided the house of the local leader of the KPD. Though the house was thoroughly and violently searched, no incriminating material was found. Nevertheless a warrant was issued for the arrest of the Communist leader, since it was suspected that "he had distributed forbidden leaflets." Raids were also made on the homes of other Communists and Socialists.[17]

At the same time that force was being applied to silence the SPD, the Nazis undertook to spread slander about them. On March 3 and 4 the Nazis published the following advertisement in the NNN:

RESIDENTS OF NORTHEIM!

You want to continue your work in peace and quiet! You've had enough of the impudent behavior of the SPD and KPD! You want the red *Senators, Councilmen, and Reichsbanner Generals* with all their armed followers to go to the Devil! Remember the disgraceful behavior of these hordes last year! The red Messers Querfurt, Haase, Deppe [etc.] attempted a civil war! The distribution of packages of bandages from the Health Insurance Office was a clear sign of the bloodthirsty intentions of these members of an international *Criminal Party,* named SPD and KPD. The former red Police Senator lay heavily armed with his armed hordes ready. In the barracks were brutalized Communists, armed with military rifles—the comrade-allies of Querfurt and Co.—waiting for the bloody work in the streets of Northeim. *Northeim was to drown in blood and horror! Hitler was your savior!* The NSDAP, the SA, the SS are fighting for you, even here in Northeim!! *Tomorrow is the day of the awakened nation!* At the ballot boxes the German *Volk* thanks the great *Fuehrer* for its salvation in the last hour! A storm will sweep through Germany! Germany Votes List 1! Heil Hitler!

NSDAP, Local Group Northeim.

Deppe, Querfurt, and Haase immediately drew up a reply to this advertisement. The NNN, however, refused to publish it. Hence it appeared in a newspaper published in a neighboring town:

RESIDENTS OF NORTHEIM! A CORRECTION!

Through an election advertisement yesterday the Local Group Northeim of the NSDAP accused the undersigned of having intended a "Civil War" a year ago, manifested by "impudent," "disgraceful," and "criminal" behavior. We were supposed to have expected a blood bath in the streets of Northeim. "Northeim was to drown in blood and horror."

To this we declare, that we who were named in the advertisement are almost all "front-soldiers" whose bravery in action has been recognized by the awarding of Iron Crosses, first and second class, and other medals. Some of us suffered severe war wounds for the Fatherland.

It was we who, in the postwar days, regularly protected peace and order, and even in critical times restrained any of our comrades who became restive.

We and our friends have rejected civil war. We proved that not only in 1918 but also on every other occasion.

We call on our friends not to lose their calm reasonableness, despite this advertisement of the NSDAP.

We gladly leave the question of whether or not we belong to an "international criminal party" to the decision of the populace.

Northeim. March 4, 1933.
Carl Querfurt, Karl Deppe, Friedrich Haase [etc.][18]

There were some people in Northeim who read the newspapers from the neighboring town, but not many. The SPD's own newspaper, the *Volksblatt* (with its Northeim supplement) had been "temporarily" suppressed. Thus for all intents and purposes the Nazi charges went unanswered. Nor were there any other Socialist advertisements in the Northeim newspapers, nor public meetings, nor leaflets distributed. Social Democracy had been silenced.

The Nazis, on the other hand, were in a position to subject the town, in the week before the last free Reichstag election, to the most intense electioneering it had ever experienced. From March 1 to 4 (election eve) there were radio loudspeakers set up in the Market Square and on Broad Street, and every evening the voice of Adolf Hitler boomed across the town. During the days Stormtroopers passed out literature. On March 2 the *1910er Zelt* filled to hear Elisabeth Zander, the National Leader of the Nazi Women's Auxiliary. After Hitler's radio speech, Frau Zander spoke, affirming that now the whole world would know that Hitler was serious about "eradicating Bolshevism." Henceforth the task of women would be to buy only German goods when shopping and to instill "religion, morality, discipline, and love of Fatherland" in the children.

The great effort was reserved for election eve, March 4, a Saturday. On that night the Nazis held a torchlight parade with over six hundred uniformed SA, SS, Hitler Youth, and *Stahlhelmern*. The parade ended in the city park around a large bonfire. There the crowd listened to Hitler over the radio loudspeakers, which were playing also in the Market Square, on Broad Street, in front of the church and the Town Hall—in short, wherever there was room for a crowd to gather.

At the park the light of the fire illuminated the many swastika flags. There were also many Black-White-Red banners, and flags of both kinds were hanging in front of the stores and from the houses in the old town. Hitler's speech could be heard at the *1910er Zelt*, too, and after it was over the crowds sang *Deutschland über Alles* and the "Horst Wessel Song." Then a short speech was given by Ernst Girmann, after which Roman candles and multicolored rockets were fired. Finally, the crowds were allowed to go home to sleep before the voting.[19]

On election Sunday the town was, in the words of the NNN, "astonishingly quiet." The swastika and Imperial flags were still out. Nazi and *Stahlhelm* election autos brought people to the polls while units of SA and SS marched through the streets. About noon a three-plane squadron flew low over Northeim to advertise the Nationalist party. Otherwise there were no unusual incidents.[20]

The voting was the heaviest Northeim had experienced, with 6,802 people casting ballots—72 more than the previous record set in the summer of 1932. The Nazis surpassed their previous high (from the same election) by 73 votes, while the Nationalists polled 105 more than they had in November 1932. The other parties stood more or less as they had in the fall of 1932, except for the SPD and the KPD. The Communists lost 110 votes, but were still the fourth largest party in the town, with a total of 228. The Social Democrats lost 157 votes from their returns of November 1932. Both Communist and Socialist votes must have gone to either the Nazis or the Nationalists, though the numbers involved are so small that analysis is problematical. In any event the Nazi-Nationalists had a clear majority. The Nazis had 63 percent of the town's votes, the Nationalists 6 percent. The SPD still had 22 percent, while the KPD was fourth with 3.5 percent.

The figures are instructive in that despite intimidation and intense electioneering, the Nazis were unable to raise their percentage of support in the town from the previous high-water mark set in July 1932. Indeed, these figures probably represented the highest support the Nazis would ever have. This was nevertheless enough; it represented almost two-thirds of the town's voters, an ample majority for most purposes and wholly adequate for the Nazi purpose. For the Nazis knew that their goal was not to win elections but rather to secure enough popular support to work their will without serious public outcry. In Northeim this was the case, but the Nazis, being what they were, were not content with this expression of confidence. During the ensuing critical months every effort was made to maintain and increase public support. The recipe was the continued application of both force and propaganda.

Before the Nazis could relax their actual electioneering work they had to conduct one final campaign. This was the local election set for March 12, 1933, a week after the Reichstag voting. At stake was representation in the City Council, the County Diet, and the Provincial Diet. To some extent the Nazis could expect to ride the crest of the enthusiasm engendered by their victory on March 5. It was hardly to be expected that voting preferences would vary much in a week's time.

The mechanism of terror and the demonstrations of enthusiasm from the previous election campaign were still paying dividends. Thus the NNN reported, during the week between the elections, that seven Northeim Communists had been arrested. The arrests followed raids on the homes of these people, in the course of which ". . . sharpened iron bars, *Stahlruten,* rubber truncheons, sidearms, daggers, ammunition, etc., were confiscated." On the Tuesday following the Reichstag election the Nazis flew swastika flags from the Town Hall, County Prefecture, and other state buildings, by way of celebrating the victory. The following day, by order of von Papen, there was a school holiday all over Prussia in honor of the "national victory."[21]

In the week-long campaign before the local elections, Northeim's SPD was not allowed to hold meetings or pass out campaign literature. They did manage to place one advertisement in the NNN, but, doubtless because of their previous experience of being refused advertising space, the SPD made that a very cautious, almost perfunctory notice, in language that contrasted so sharply with previous Socialist advertisements that its publication probably did the SPD more harm than good:

> To the voters of Northeim! On Sunday, March 12, important elections will be held, namely for the Provincial Diet, County Council, and City Council. The SPD has presented its own list for all these elections, which bears the number "2." We call upon the populace all to vote, to vote early, and to vote, in each case, for the "List Querfurt," List number "2."
>
> SPD, Northeim Local.[22]

While the SPD entered the lists under its own name, the Nazis did so only in the case of the Provincial and County elections. In the elections for the

City Council, the Nazis ran under the name "National Unity List." Since the Civil Servants did not put up a separate list of candidates (as they had since 1924), the voters' choice was essentially between this "National Unity" slate and the SPD.

This represented a distinct advantage to Northeim's Nazis and one that they brought about through skillful manipulation. The local elections of March 12, 1933, were announced on February 6, only a little over a month before the voting was to be held. Parties were given three weeks in which to prepare their lists of candidates, the deadline being February 25. The Nazi executive committee of the Civic Association did not hold a membership meeting until eight days before the list of candidates was due. At the meeting, the Nazi chairman gave a short speech on how all members should vote *Bürgerlich* in the forthcoming elections and announced that the executive committee had drawn up a list of candidates called "National Unity" representing "workers, civil servants, craft artisans, craft masters, businessmen, farmers, white collar workers, and the free professions." He called on all members of the Civic Association to stick together so that the town could have "a bourgeois majority."

When this was announced there were cries from the older members: "Who are the candidates?" Thereupon the Nazi chairman announced that "for reasons of campaign tactics" he would not be able to divulge the candidates' names. This called forth vehement objections which Ernst Girmann then silenced by saying that anyone could make nominations from the floor if he wished. A number of nominations were made, but all those nominated refused to accept the honor, and the Nazi majority then voted to close the nominations (i.e., leave the matter in the hands of the Nazi-dominated committee). The conservative members of the Civic Association were clearly outmanuevered; though they protested strenuously, they had no choice but to accept the situation. One of the Nazi executive committee members closed the matter by remarking loftily that the names were not important; what mattered was the common viewpoint which would clearly be directed toward "German Community Spirit." After the sad news was announced that the North German Shooting Society would hold its annual meeting in Bremen rather than Northeim because the City Council had refused money for new target ranges, the meeting adjourned with the singing of the national anthem.[23]

The conservatives still had a week in which to get the list of candidates made public so that there might be a chance to get at least a few non-Nazis on it. Four days before the deadline the GGZ published a "Letter to the

Editor" signed by "several members of the Civic Association" demanding that the list of candidates be immediately announced. The GGZ also attempted to keep the matter before the public eye by pointing out that the DVP had recently decided to support "Bourgeois Unity Fronts" in the coming local elections.[24]

All of the protests of conservative members of the Civic Association were to no avail. The deadline passed and Northeim's conservatives now had no choice but to vote for a list of candidates handpicked by the Nazis. The GGZ did not take this without protest. When the "National Unity" list was finally printed, it was labeled "NSDAP (??)" in the GGZ. This brought a vicious letter from Ernst Girmann threatening the GGZ with legal action unless it printed a correction with the proper title. The GGZ blandly explained that it had gotten the title from the Northeim Senate, that the question marks signified the GGZ's own disbelief, and that by the time the error had been discovered, the edition had been printed and sold.[25]

Since the Senate at that time included two Social Democrats, a member of the Civil Servants party, and Senator Mahner, one can easily see how this little gibe was arranged. Thus the whole town learned that the Nazis had put one over on the conservatives, and that "National Unity" was a euphemism for "Nazi." This was counteracted by a shrewd Nazi maneuver. The list of candidates contained mainly Nazis, but there were also several non-Nazis. The non-Nazi candidates, however, were carefully picked; they were all men who could be induced to join the NSDAP, men who in fact were ready to join but had not yet done so. The town's conservatives could therefore vote for the "National Unity List" thinking that there were non-Nazis on it. But by the time the town council convened, every man who had been elected from the "National Unity" slate wore a brown shirt.[26]

This was the end of the Civic Association, whose *raison d'être* had been to oppose the SPD. By its vehement opposition to the only effective group in Northeim that was devoted to democracy, it had helped bring the Nazis to power. And once the Nazis had used the Civic Association for their own purposes, they promptly discarded it. It held only one more meeting in Northeim, in October 1933. The purpose of the meeting was to dissolve the organization since "its purpose had been achieved."[27]

Although they were running on a "National Unity" ticket, Northeim's Nazis conducted the campaign for the local elections under their own name. Apart from extensive advertising in the local press, the Nazi campaign in Northeim consisted of only one meeting, held the evening before the voting. The featured speaker was Ernst Girmann on "The Significance of the Communal Elections'' and on ''Political Matters in Northeim.'' It was also promised that ''the candidates you will elect'' would speak on their ''goals in the town hall.''

The *1910er Zelt* was overflowing and Ernst Girmann was in top form. He expressed the hope that this would be the last vote in a long time, but should there ever be another vote he hoped that people would be compelled by law to vote so that there would be no neutral Germans. In the new order there would be no more parliamentarianism but rather corporations, like those in the Middle Ages. That was an old Germanic custom and best for Germany.

A week ago, continued Girmann, a new Germanic spirit swept through Germany, that of National Socialism, for National Socialism and Germany were now coterminous. What was needed now was to cleanse Northeim, too, from Marxist corruption. There would be no more use of Health Insurance Office automobiles for private purposes and then setting back the speedometer. For the town's pool there would be no more diving tower from Amsterdam which cost 90 percent more than it should have. There would be no more false credit and big loans at the City Savings Bank. There would be no more cloak of silence over the brewery scandal. That would be completely hashed over and the guilty punished. Consumers' cooperatives, so injurious to the small businessman, would disappear. Polish Jews would be sent back to where they belonged, since Northeim's clothing goods stores had competition enough already. And the Jews who contributed money to the *Reichsbanner,* and thus to Germany's misery, would be taken care of.[28]

After Girmann was through the candidates spoke. One lamented the crowding in the schools. Another called for a better tax policy and for Northeimers to do their buying in their own town. A third revived some accusations against the SPD that had been made in 1929. Finally, the police secretary (also a candidate on the ''National Unity'' list) promised to make sure that the police did their duty. There were no other speakers, so Girmann led a *Sieg Heil!* for Hitler and Fatherland and the meeting closed with the ''Horst Wessel Song.'' It had been devoid of any positive program.

The final shot in the Nazi election campaign was an advertisement in the NNN the day before the voting. The advertisement was clearly an attempt to get non-Nazi elements in the town to back the ''National Unity'' list:

CITIZENS OF NORTHEIM!

For 14 years you were the plaything of the red Marxist system! For 14 years you had to look on while they governed Germany into the dirt! Last week's election cleared the way for recovery in the Reich and in Prussia! Tomorrow you must carry out your national duty in our town, Northeim. This is the last chance for a long time that you will have, by casting your ballot, to end the Marxist rule of force of Carl Querfurt and make the work of national recovery possible in Northeim. Personal crankiness must give way before this great goal. Tomorrow will see *nationalist Northeim* oppose the beaten remains of Marxism *in closed ranks! Away with Querfurt and his red clique! For Northeim's recovery in a Free Germany!* Vote the "National Unity List"—List 1!

Civic Association, NSDAP, *Stahlhelm*, DNVP, DVP, Hannoverian party, Small Businessmen's League, County Artisan League, Agrarian Society, Farmers Club, Tavern Keepers Society, German Nationalist Merchant Apprentice Society, National Railroad Employees, Local Cartel of the German Civil Servants League, Unemployed Committee for Northeim, town and county.[29]

After this only the voting remained. The results are given in the following table:[30]

PARTY	MARCH 5, 1933	MARCH 12, 1933		
	Reichstag	City Council	County Council	Provincial Parliament
Nazi	4,268	4,565 ("National Unity")	4,273	4,246
DNVP	406	("National Unity")	456	339
DVP	101	("National Unity")	—	49
SPD	1,470	1,677	1,650	1,592
Catholic Center	183	—	—	124
KPD	228	43	—	64
Other	146	("National Unity")	3	81
TOTALS	6,802	6,285	6,382	6,495

Outstanding in these elections returns is the failure of the Nazis to gain votes. This was perhaps because the total vote cast in the local elections was about 300 to 500 less than in the national elections a week before. But, although all three ballots (town, county, and provincial) were cast at the same time, the provincial votes totaled 210 more than the votes for the town council. Yet it was on the provincial ballot that the Nazis showed a drop.

This may have been because it was only on the provincial ballot that the voter had a full range of choice among parties. On the town and county ballots the choice was limited, and thus some two hundred people did not bother to mark their ballots. The same people did vote in the provincial election where they could cast a ballot for their own specific choice. And clearly, for some, where there was a wider choice, the non-Nazi parties were preferable to the NSDAP (though in local elections the Nazis were preferable to the SPD or Nationalists).

Secondly, one notices that despite the terror and adverse campaigning conditions, the SPD actually gained 207 votes (though, like the Nazis, they fared somewhat worse in the slightly heavier county and provincial balloting). Two facts emerge from this. One is that, in the town elections, the majority of people who voted Communist the week before, decided to vote for the SPD. The other is that there was a solid core of SPD voters unintimidated by the mounting terror and unimpressed by the intense propaganda and pageantry.

In the town election the ''National Unity'' list received 4,565 votes. This was 297 more than the Nazis alone had received a week before. But it was also 456 *less* than the parties endorsing the ''National Unity'' list had cast a week before. Thus it was clear that many of the members of the parties supporting the ''National Unity'' list had, when it came time to cast ballots, refused to back this Nazi-dominated slate of candidates. Some spoiled their ballots, some turned them in blank—altogether over two hundred people. Some did not even bother to go to the polls at all. But some went so far as to give their votes to the Social Democrats (though most of the gain made by the SPD can be accounted for by vote transfers from the Center and Communist parties).

If any generalization can be made on the basis of these two elections, held only a week apart, it would be that the Nazis were clearly not increasing their popularity, and that the SPD was just as clearly not losing its solid backing. The townspeople also showed some confusion in their voting, and some resentment over the Nazis' high-handed tricks with the ''National Unity'' list. Finally, the fact that over 90 percent voted should be weighed against the fact that voting participation fell off in just a week's time, despite all Nazi efforts. Was this the beginning of a reaction against the politicalization of life, or just a case of what the Germans call *Wahlmuedigkeit* ("election weariness")? It is hard to tell, since this was the last free election in Northeim for fifteen years.

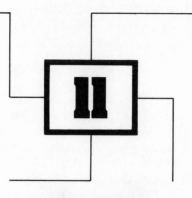

11

THE USES
OF ELECTORAL
SUCCESS

SPRING-
SUMMER
1933

*I run things here—all by myself—and
it's because I'm Local Group Leader!*

**Statement of Ernst Girmann,
Deputy Mayor of Northeim
and Local Group Leader for
Northeim of the NSDAP**

The first task of Northeim's Nazis after the local elections were over was to convert the town's mechanisms of power from democratic, pluralistic ones into instruments of dictatorship. This involved a purge—of the City Council, of the administrative officials, and of the rank and file city workers. The precondition was absolute control over the Council.

As a result of the March 12 elections, the Nazis received fifteen seats and the Social Democrats five seats in the twenty-man Northeim City Council. This was certainly a working majority for the NSDAP, especially since under the "Leader Principle" all Nazi representatives had to vote as they were told by the Local Group Leader. Nevertheless, a three-to-one majority was not enough for the Nazis, since if the SPD had even five seats they could legally demand that at least one Social Democratic city councillor be included in each of the standing committees. This would have been intolerable to the Nazis since their goal was absolute control over the town's affairs. If the SPD had only four representatives, though, they could, with complete correctness, be excluded from all committees.

The Nazis dealt with this problem with their customary thoroughness. On the one hand they were able to persuade one of the SPD representatives to declare himself "neutral," i.e., disavow the party under whose name he had run for office. How the Nazis managed to do this was never made clear. This particular Social Democrat had always been vehemently anti-Nazi; hence his defection was characterized by the other Social Democrats as the act of a Judas. It was a hard blow to them, though they realized that the Nazis had many means of persuasion.[1]

This reduced the Socialist delegation to four. As insurance, however, the Nazis arranged to have Karl Deppe (one of the four remaining SPD councillors) arrested the afternoon of the first meeting of the Council. Thus if the Social Democrat who had been persuaded to be "neutral" should change his mind in the actual session, the SPD would still have only four councillors and could still be excluded from committee seats.[2]

The first meeting of the new City Council took place on March 28. Contrary to all previous custom the meeting was not held in the room in the City Hall appointed for this purpose, but in the ballroom of Northeim's largest hotel. Long before the opening of the meeting the hall was packed with Nazis, including many SA men. The SS helped the police keep order.

Shortly before the Council session was to open, the fifteen delegates of the "National Unity" list arrived in a body, all wearing brown shirts. They were greeted with applause and then with *"Heil Hitler!"* Almost immediately thereafter the four SPD councillors arrived. On their way to the meeting from Carl Querfurt's house (where they had held a pre-session caucus) the police had seized Deppe. When the others arrived they saw the packed hall, well sprinkled with brown and black uniforms. The hall itself was draped with laurel boughs and on the back of the stage there were enormous pictures of Hitler and Hindenburg, flanked by the swastika and Imperial flags. Two tables stood on the stage: one long one for the Nazi councillors and, over to one side, a small one for the representatives of Social Democracy.

Twenty-five years later, Carl Querfurt still retained vivid memories of one incident. As soon as he sat down at his assigned place, Querfurt took out a big cigar and lit it. Immediately an SA man came over to the SPD table and said, "Put that out! You can't smoke here!" Querfurt exhaled slowly and surveyed the Stormtrooper. Then he leaned forward and said: "Now listen closely. Are you SA people running the City Council or are we city councillors? I'll smoke here if I like." The SA man turned on his heel and walked away.

Mayor Peters opened the meeting. He was a courtly man, noted for his dry and legalistic personality. After calling the session to order he spoke of his hopes that the new rise of patriotism would reflect itself in solid work for the good of Northeim. He enumerated the difficulties that lay ahead, mentioning especially the budgetary problems. After congratulating each new councillor personally, he gave the floor to Ernst Girmann for the first speech.

Girmann began by asking everyone to remember, in this hour, how Germany had been governed in the last fourteen years. The military collapse had brought unspeakable unhappiness to Germany. It was the SPD that had been responsible for the misery. Furthermore it had not even hesitated to rob its own workers. Today the time had come to settle up:

> We haven't forgotten a single thing. Nor will we hesitate to pay them back for every bit. In the reckoning up it won't be the poor people who were blinded by them, it will be the seducers themselves that we'll settle with, down to the smallest party hack. In locked concentration camps they'll learn how to work for Germany again!

There was more to say. Democracy was finished; from now on a dictatorship would rule and it would hit every enemy, no matter where he came from. The struggle against the Jews would be taken up anew. They would be met head-on. Remembering Hitler's campaign pledge, "The common good goes before that of the individual," National Socialism was moving into the

Northeim Town Hall, conscious of Germany's great past, to which Northeim had also contributed.

Next, Heinrich Voge, the new Speaker of the Council, read a list of committee appointments and senators as determined by the majority in its caucus. All were Nazis. The floor was then given to the SPD member who was to play the role of turncoat. He declared that he was now "neutral" and had left the SPD "since with the dawning of a new era I can no longer belong to this party." The audience cheered this announcement and it was to cries of "Bravo!" that the former SPD representative moved to the big table.

After the applause ended, Carl Querfurt rose to his feet and asked for the floor. Voge replied, "For fourteen years you wouldn't listen to the NSDAP and now we won't listen to you. I refuse to give you the floor." Querfurt spoke anyway: "You have a majority on the Council and in addition you won't even allow us to speak. I see, therefore, no further possibility of representing the interests of my constituents. If you will not give us the floor, then we will leave this session." The other two Social Democrats rose beside him and, accompanied by the hoots and catcalls of the audience, marched out of the hall. As they were walking down the aisle, SA men on each side spat upon them.

The rest of the meeting was more prosaic. The Nazi nominations for Senators, including Ernst Girmann as deputy mayor, were unanimously accepted. A loan for public works, which the old City Council had prepared, was approved and allocated in such a way that it appeared to have been done entirely by the new Council. Finally the new Speaker, Voge, closed the meeting with these words: "Everyone will surely have noticed that from now on a new wind will be blowing. The tasks ahead will require the entire strength of every individual, but we will fulfill them, inspired by the great idea, and by the spirit of Adolf Hitler." The crowd responded with the "Horst Wessel Song" and a triple "Sieg Heil!" The first session of the new Northeim City Council was ended.[3]

This session set the pattern for all that followed in the first four months of Nazi rule in Northeim. The features were to be persistent harassment of the Socialist members, apparent vigor in dealing with the economic situation, and the theatrical exposition of measures predetermined in the Nazi caucus.

Northeim's Nazis had a free hand in dealing with the Socialist councillors. According to a circular from Goering's Prussian Ministry of the Interior, representatives elected on an SPD ticket were not to be "hindered from fulfilling their duties," though this was not to preclude police action against them. If the SPD representatives were not "cooperative," however, then they were to be "furloughed immediately (if this has not yet occurred)." They were then to be replaced by temporary appointees, to be chosen by the appropriate Nazi District Leader.[4]

On April 7, Karl Deppe gave up his councillorship, since he was still in jail. On April 12 (the day before the City Council's second meeting), Carl Querfurt resigned. Querfurt and Deppe were replaced by two Nazis. Thus the SPD delegation was reduced from four to two.[5]

At the second session of the Council, the SPD turncoat requested that he be allowed to serve on the Council's Economic Planning Committee, since he had nine years' experience on it. Speaker Voge refused this but urged him to keep trying to cooperate with the Nazis. Next the NSDAP proposed, and it was unanimously enacted, that Hindenburg, Hitler, and Goering be made honorary citizens of Northeim. The NSDAP's second proposal, to change several of the street names, was also unanimously accepted. The new names were "Adolf Hitler Strasse," "Goering Strasse," "Hindenburg Strasse," "Darré Strasse" (for the Nazi Minister of Agriculture), and finally "Elisabeth Zander Strasse." It was announced that the next two new streets built in Northeim would be called "Schlageter Strasse" and "Horst Wessel Strasse." Before the session closed, one of the two remaining SPD delegates made two motions. One was for free books for school children whose parents were unemployed. The second was for a solution to the "settlement" question. Both motions were immediately tabled.[6]

Despite this kind of treatment, the two remaining SPD councillors continued to hold their posts. Thus they were present at the third meeting of the City Council on April 28. Most of the session was given over to listening to a report by the mayor on the state of the budget. The mayor explained how Northeim would be able to have a balanced budget in 1933 by dipping into the capital reserves of the various town-owned enterprises to the extent of about two-thirds of their total sum. By this expedient it would be possible to cut the business tax by about 16 percent, and to cut the town income tax by about 35 percent. This plan was accepted by the Council without discussion. Then they proceeded to vote subsidies. The Volunteer Labor Service, which was doing work for Northeim, was given 1,100 marks. The shooting societies were given permission to build their new rifle ranges and provided with free material for them. The Young Naval Society was given 70 marks' worth of wood for a boat they wanted to build, and 300 marks were given to the Hitler Youth so that they could attend a regional convention. The Council also voted 100 marks to help defray the cost of celebrating May 1 and agreed to pay for the use of the *1910er Zelt*. Finally, a salary of 50 marks per month was voted for each of the four Nazi senators. The entire meeting lasted only forty-five minutes.[7]

The next session took place on June 7. In the interim Mayor Peters had gone on his vacation and Ernst Girmann now presided over the meeting as deputy mayor. The first motion was to halt pension payments for city workers, "since the Reich intended to take over this cost." One of the two remaining Socialist representatives suggested that the town wait until the Reich had begun its payments and *then* cease. The original motion was then carried, over the opposition of the two SPD representatives, with Girmann remarking that the city would continue to pay pensions to some workers, he himself deciding which ones would get their pension money. The rest of the meeting was taken up with routine business, mainly granting financial aid to, or withholding it from, various organizations.[8]

This was the last session the Socialists participated in. Since the SPD had been dissolved in the interim, its remaining councillors had to resign by June 27, including "those who were elected as such but had since left the SPD"—in other words, the one turncoat. Nazis were appointed in their stead. Henceforth, sessions of the City Council were used solely for the purpose of announcing measures previously determined by the Nazi Local Group Leader and deputy mayor, Ernst Girmann. On one occasion, one of the handpicked Nazi senators actually spoke up, to the great embarrassment of Girmann. It was on July 18, 1933, and the session was being used to explain the new public works projects planned. After all the money had been allocated, Senator Ude, who had a farm outside of Northeim, suggested that some of the money be spent to build a sidewalk from the town out to his farm. This was voted down and the meeting was immediately adjourned by Girmann.[9] Henceforth, the councillors and senators kept absolute silence in session meetings.

A similar series of events took place in the Northeim County Council. The Nazis were unable to create a "National Unity" list, hence they were not in a position of overwhelming strength after the election. In fact, the Nazis were even incapable of presenting a united front for this election. The source of this anomaly was that during the previous summer the Prussian government had determined to unite Northeim County with the smaller neighboring county of Uslar. Local chauvinism was aroused by this measure, particularly in the neighboring county which was to lose its identity. Hence, when the time came to draw up a list of candidates, the members of the supposedly monolithic Nazi party presented two lists: the "NSDAP List" (Northeim County Nazis) and the "Hitler-Movement List" (Nazis from Uslar County). The SPD and the Nationalist party each managed to present a united front.[10]

The Nazis nonetheless gained an absolute majority with fifteen of the Council's twenty-five seats (ten from Northeim, five from the former county of Uslar). The SPD won eight seats, the Nationalists two.[11] Even before the County Council met for the first time, the Nazis began arranging affairs to their own benefit. Sixteen SPD village councillors in Northeim County were suspended from office. The county's contract for publishing official notices with the *Volksblatt* was severed. Publication of the *Volksblatt* had already been suspended, so this was mere legalistic neatness. It also enabled the county to award the contract to the new Nazi newspaper, the Northeimer *Beobachter*.[12] Finally, the Nazis forced the County Prefect, Otto von der Schulenberg, to join the NSDAP.

The Prefect's attitude toward the Nazis was mixed. He was convinced that increasing unemployment was driving people toward Communism and therefore that Nazism had saved Germany. But he would never have joined the NSDAP freely, because "previous experience led me to believe that its ranks were filled with incompetents and bankrupts." This aloof attitude was not long permitted him. On the afternoon of March 29, just before the County Prefecture was closing, Walter Steineck came into von der Schulenberg's office. Taking off his own silver swastika pin, Steineck tossed it on von der Schulenberg's desk and said, "Put that on. If you don't, you won't be County Prefect tomorrow." So von der Schulenberg joined the Nazi party.[13]

The first meeting of the new County Council was, like the first meeting of the Northeim City Council, largely a ceremonial affair, open to the public, and with the County Hall decorated with flags, pictures, and bunting. It did not have the tension-laden atmosphere of the Northeim City Council's opening meeting largely because the personalities of the Nazi leaders (Walter Steineck, the Nazi county leader was jovial and folksy; Count von Strahlenheim, majority leader in the Council, coldly aristocratic) were different from the personality of Ernest Girmann. Nonetheless, Carl Querfurt took von Strahlenheim aside before the meeting started and said, "Look, if we're going to have a farce like the City Council meeting, then the SPD is going home right now." He was assured by von Strahlenheim that decorum would prevail.[14]

The meeting opened with a speech by von der Schulenberg, in which he expressed himself in accord with the various Nazi measures and finished by calling for a triple *"Sieg Heil!"* for "the Fatherland, for President Hindenburg, and for Chancellor Hitler." Next a speech was given by von Strahlenheim, who declared that the Socialists were there on sufferance and would be tolerated only if they conducted themselves with extreme objectivity. (The position of the SPD was already tenuous. Two of their representatives had refused to take up their mandates and a third, Deppe, was in jail.) No "Marxist" would be allowed to hold any office in the county, and SPD representatives would not be allowed to serve on committees.[15] Then he read the committee assignments from a prepared list. All assignments went to Nazis.

Carl Querfurt limited his reply to stating that the SPD had no choice now but to bow to the will of the majority. What this was to mean was made immediately manifest, for von Strahlenheim's first motion was that all county contracts be taken away from Jews and that Jews be expelled from the County Old People's Home and deprived of other county services. The motion was "referred to committee" and the session ended.[16]

The County Council was only infrequently convened after that. Most Nazi sniping was directed at the Nationalist members of the County Council, von Strahlenheim making statements such as: "You're like a cork on a champagne bottle. We touch you, you fly into the air with a bang, and then you're finished." The SPD passed silently out of the picture. By the beginning of June there were only two SPD representatives left; the others had resigned except for one who joined the Nationalists. It hardly mattered because, like the City Council, the County Council had become primarily ceremonial, with all decisions resting with the Nazis, and all speeches being made by them too, since the other delegates were afraid to give speeches. By July all non-Nazi delegates were required to resign.[17]

With virtual control over the administration of Northeim and Northeim County, the Nazis undertook the first most obvious task: cleansing the city and county offices of actual or potential opponents. This was part of a prearranged plan, for as early as 1932 it was known that Heinrich Voge, the Nazi teacher, had a list apportioning the various offices and jobs among members of the NSDAP. There was no attempt to hide the fact that a purge was taking place, and the townspeople were clearly aware of it. The Nazis considered the "general cleaning action" one of their foremost accomplishments. It was so described in a special commemorative issue of the Northeimer Beobachter in 1936, and when Ernst Girmann made a report of his activities during the first two years of the Third Reich, it was the first thing he mentioned.[18]

Although the Nazis generally claimed to have dismissed a total of thirty workers and employees (Angestellter), the figure was actually higher. The sum of individual instances listed in contemporary newspaper accounts was forty-three, and this did not include persons edged out of their jobs with various other reasons given. In the latter category would be, for example, Mayor Peters, his assistant Thomas Galland, and probably others. Of the forty-five persons actually fired, most were workers but some were tenured employees, and a few were professional civil servants with full tenure. Together, they constituted approximately a quarter of the employees of the City of Northeim. The basis for the purge was Hitler's "Decree for the Reconstruction of the Professional Civil Service," promulgated under powers given the government by the Enabling Act, on April 7, 1933.[19]

The first wave of dismissals came in mid-April and involved Socialists in minor positions: a gas works employee, an accountant, and the manager of the city's swimming pool. At the end of April there was a second round of firings which affected fifteen workers from the Construction Office, seven from the brewery, and four more from the gas works. In addition, seven union shop stewards were dismissed. A week later the Nazi ax fell on the "red" Health Insurance Office. The board of directors was ousted and its functions taken over by Walter Steineck as "commissar." He immediately fired the business manager and two employees. To forestall resistance the offices were occupied by the SS. In place of the dismissed employees, three Nazis were hired and later a new board of directors was appointed with Walter Steineck as chairman.[20] The impact of this particular "cleaning action" can be judged by the recollections of a former reporter for the NNN:

> When the Nazis cleaned out the Health Insurance Office, they naturally fired the Socialist business manager, a competent fellow. In his place, Girmann put a Nazi named X. Now X had just been released from jail where he had served a term for—embezzlement! And his previous embezzlement had been from the State Sickness Insurance Office!
>
> Naturally this stank. It stank so much that [the head of one of the guilds] went in to see Girmann and raised holy hell and pounded on the table until Girmann took the job away from X. But later X got another job with the city as director of the *Ordnungsamt.*
>
> The Nazis were bankrupt people prior to 1933. Afterwards they all got jobs. The party in 1933 was full of the poor, the thieves, the morally and financially bankrupt. X is a typical example of the type of people the Nazis put in positions—people with the poorest reputations.[21]

The series of political dismissals was finally ended in mid-May with the firing of two city employees: a messenger for the City Savings Bank and a night watchman. There were, however, other dismissals which took place without political reasons being given. In April, a policeman was dismissed from service in Northeim with no reason supplied. Later, extraordinary promotions and reinforcements occurred. In June, the night watchman who had been fired in May was rehired, according to the official announcement, "since he petitioned for this giving certain assurances." His reinstatement necessitated the dismissal of his erstwhile replacement. Later in the same month, one policeman was promoted and three others given tenure. This was an unusual and unprecedented series of moves.[22]

Some of the dismissals may have been made less to get rid of politically undesirable people than to make room for unemployed Nazis. By the end of April, Girmann was sending the names of specific Nazis to his fellow senators and ordering the senators to find jobs for them at the earliest opportunity.[23]

A similar pattern took place in the county. The only person recorded to have been fired officially for his political opinions was Friedrich Haase. Nevertheless, a result of the union of Northeim County with Uslar County, a number of offices (and therefore jobs) became superfluous. The decision as to who would be retained and who would be transferred, pensioned, or simply fired lay with the all-Nazi executive committee on the County Diet. Needless to say, politics played a part in such decisions.[24]

To Ernst Girmann the most important single office to be transferred after the seizure of power was the mayorship of Northeim. As far as political control was concerned, it was hardly necessary for Mayor Peters to be removed from office. In fact Peters had even applied for membership in the NSDAP.[25] As Walter Steineck put it in a conversation with Thomas Galland:

> I can't understand Ernst Girmann. He and I are both businessmen and not civil administrators. I think we both have our hands full with just party matters. Now I'm sure that if I wanted to, I could have von der Schulenberg's job right now and be County Prefect myself. But I don't want to. As it now stands, he does what I tell him to in political matters and runs the administrative part quite well. Surely it is possible that Girmann could make some arrangement like that with Mayor Peters, don't you think?[26]

As a matter of fact, Girmann could even have eased Mayor Peters out of his position with very little effort if he had not tried to use underhanded tactics. Peters was sixty-one years old in 1933 and had been mayor of Northeim since 1903. In a private conversation with his assistant, Thomas Galland, he confessed that he would have retired voluntarily and instantly if he had been approached decently, but that he would not bow before a smear campaign.[27]

Since Girmann never tried anything except dirty methods, each new move he made simply hardened Mayor Peters' resolve. Peters could not be removed simply on grounds of "political unreliability." He was cold, objective, juristic. He was a conservative and in fact a member of the Nationalist party, but he suppressed his politics so completely that no one thought of him except as a professional administrator. Since Girmann could not use customary methods, he developed a complex attack upon Peters. It took the form of trying to provoke Peters into acts or statements that could be used against him, attacking his subordinates in order to frighten him, intervening with higher officers to have him removed by administrative fiat, slanderously charging him with incompetence and bringing him to trial on trumped-up charges of administrative malpractice, and finally, getting him and his assistant dismissed with the elastic (and patently false) reason, "in order to simplify the administration."[28]

In Girmann's plan of action, Mayor Peters was to be provoked into imprudent statements or actions through one of Girmann's good friends, August Ude. Ude, though a citizen of Northeim, had a small farm a short distance from the city. He was a rough and uncouth man, a peasant in the pejorative sense of the word. He was constantly involved in legal squabbles with the town of Northeim, which brought him into bitter contact with Mayor Peters. He was so well-known in Northeim for this that a joke went the rounds: "If August Ude ever forgets to put his boots on in the morning, they automatically find their way to the County Courthouse." One of the things he was supposed to have done was move the boundary stone on his farm so as to encroach on city-owned land. His dealings with the pre-Nazi Northeim Senate eventually became so acrimonious that the senators took the extraordinary step of refusing to rent him any land under the control of the town.[29]

This was the man who was to provoke the mayor. This became manifest by the time the Nazis composed their list for the division of elective offices in mid-March. At that time Ernst Girmann insisted that August Ude be made a senator. The other Nazi members of the City Council objected to this because of Ude's bad reputation. Ernst Girmann overrode their objections:

"I need Ude as a fighter. The era of Mayor Peters is absolutely finished. Ude will be the one to drive his fist to the mayor's heart."
And when the councillors still refused to do as he wished, the Local Group Leader declared: "As Local Group Leader I declare that Ude is Senator!"[30]

It was immediately apparent to many that this was Senator Ude's function. It was hard to imagine what other functions August Ude could possibly perform in view of his low-grade intelligence. It proved a problem what "areas of competence" to assign him as a senator. He was finally given only three: City Gardens, City Field Lands, and Garbage Collection. All this was clear to Mayor Peters and he maintained an attitude of cold correctness toward Senator Ude in the face of the most vile harassment.[31]

With the failure of these tactics, Girmann began to attack Peters' subordinates, primarily his protégé and right-hand man, Thomas Galland. Galland, as city inspector, was the town's second highest administrator. He had attained this position in 1932; in a rare moment of complete accord the City Council had voted unanimous approval of his selection. Shortly after the Nazis came to power, Galland learned that the Senate was petitioning Peters for his removal. Since each senator refused to explain why, Galland went directly to Girmann, who also refused to explain. When Galland expressed indignation over this, Girmann exploded. Pounding the table he shouted: "I want to tell you something! If you think you can hide behind the mayor's skirts, you're wrong! I run things here—all by myself—and its because I'm Local Group Leader!"[32]

This again hardened Mayor Peters' resolve not to be dislodged and not to permit Thomas Galland's career to be ended. Near the beginning of June, Peters went on vacation and Girmann, who now sat behind the mayor's desk as deputy mayor, was determined to make the vacation permanent. On June 28 Girmann took direct action. The minutes of the relevant Council meeting read, in part:

The National Socialist Faction, which today makes up the entire City Council, has determined in its meeting of today:

1. Mayor Peters no longer possesses the confidence of the City Council. The City Council refuses, therefore, any further collaboration with him.

2. The City Council concurs with the decision of the Senate to petition the *Regierungspraesident* to forbid Mayor Peters any further official activity and (in accordance with the decree of *Ministerpraesident* Goering) to strip him of police powers and to transfer these to Police Secretary Engelmann.[33]

This, plus some intensive lobbying by Girmann at the upper levels of the party and government, resulted in the repeated extension of Mayor Peters' vacation. In the interim Girmann used the supine Senate to lodge formal charges that Peters and Galland, as directors of the City Savings Bank, had conspired with Hugo Speissmann, the manager of the bank, to give improper credit concessions to various Northeim businessmen. Peters, knowing that Spiessmann (a March 1933 member of the NSDAP) might perjure himself under the kinds of pressure that the Nazis were capable of, finally permitted himself to be dismissed. Thomas Galland was suspended and then discharged "to simplify the administration." In return, the charges against both were dropped. (Hugo Spiessmann, an unwitting tool in the process, was dismissed as bank manager but given a job with the NSDAP.) Shortly thereafter, Ernst Girmann became mayor of Northeim.[34]

This resolution came in March 1934, but by June 1933, Girmann was already in the Mayor's office and Northeimers simply assumed that he was there to stay. Most Northeimers (excepting, as will be seen, a significant group) had no idea that there was even a struggle in the City Hall. What the townspeople did know was that by the summer of 1933 the local political situation was radically different from what it had been before Hitler. It was clear that, whether as deputy mayor or as Local Group Leader of the NSDAP, Ernst Girmann was firmly in the saddle. Not only had the Nazis gained absolute control of Northeim's Council, Senate, and Executive, they had also conducted a thorough purge of the city's administration. All actual or potential dissidents from Nazi goals and methods were eliminated or under control. The astute Northeimer, surveying his city government at the end of June 1933, could not but see clearly that it was exclusively a Nazi instrument.

THE TERROR SYSTEM

SPRING-SUMMER 1933

Cruelty impresses. Cruelty and raw force.
The simple man in the street is impressed
only by brutal force and ruthlessness.
Terror is the most effective political means.

Adolf Hitler

Control of the city government was one thing; absolute power in the town was another. Control of the city government made it possible to reward friends and punish enemies. It also involved control over the local police.[1] But that was not enough. The Nazis had to prove in the first months after the appointment of Hitler as chancellor that they were willing to use the power apparatus in a ruthless and effective way. If this could be done, if Northeimers came to believe implicitly that they might expect no mercy from their new Nazi rulers, then later terrorism would not be needed. The initial investment of terror would multiply itself through rumor and social reinforcement until opposition would be looked upon as wholly futile.

This is precisely what the Nazis of Northeim did. Roughly by July 1933, any Northeimer who had his wits about him knew that he no longer lived in personal freedom, that if he were even indiscreet the whole arsenal of the police state might be used against him. At the very least he might expect a raid and search of his house; at the worst the vaguely comprehended but deeply dreaded experience of the concentration camp.

It might have been possible for the Nazis to have created a system of terror without giving any justification for it, but this would have been risky. Hence, one of the first things that was done was to provide an excuse for the various repressive measures. Part of the justification had already been developed—the suggestion that the Communists and Socialists planned to overthrow the state by force. This had been bolstered by the Reichstag fire. Nevertheless, Berlin was far away from Northeim and a justification closer to home was needed. Northeim's Nazis provided this by finding various arms and weapons in and around Northeim and by publishing these findings in the local newspapers.

This was all the easier since there actually *were* many weapons in Northeim. There were, of course, the usual hunting rifles and shotguns that one might expect to find in any town. Since hunting tended to be a prerogative of the wealthy, such weapons were generally not found in the homes of supporters of the KPD or SPD.[2] Secondly, the shooting societies of Northeim also had arms—some very fine and expensive weapons. But again, these belonged mainly to middle- and upper-class people whom one could hardly connect with an attempt by proletarians to overthrow the state.

But there were also weapons belonging to workers. Some veterans of World War I brought rifles or pistols home with them, or acquired them in the confused period following the Armistice. Others, who were members of the *Reichsbanner*, took the threat of a Nazi *Putsch* seriously enough to gather guns and ammunition for the counterstrike. They did this without the consent of the *Reichsbanner* leaders, but nevertheless they possessed such weapons. And some of the workers who had weapons were extraordinarily careless about them. One worker frequently carried around with him a pocketful of high-caliber rifle bullets, and another boasted openly of having a dozen hand grenades at his home.[3]

Thus the Nazi police undoubtedly could point to bona fide reasons to justify their repressive methods. Whether or not all the weapon discoveries reported in the local press were authentic is unimportant. The newspapers reported whatever they were told by the police, and what people believed was more important than what was true.

In the week before the March elections the Nazi Deputy Police had already made a number of raids, especially on the homes of known Communists. According to the NNN, these raids yielded several weapons, mostly of a makeshift kind, but also some "sidearms." The report was extremely vague about the actual type and number of weapons confiscated by the police.[4] More concrete reports found their way into the press about the end of March. Then throughout April a series of specific discoveries was prominently publicized.

On March 30, 1933, it was reported that children playing near a beer garden had found sixty rounds of army-issue rifle ammunition. The speculation was that Communists had buried it there after the police raids began. On the same day it was reported that a *Reichsbanner* man voluntarily delivered to the police "a pistol, a saw, and a set of brass knuckles." Five days later police raids at the apartments of "Leftists" in the old Army barracks yielded "a carbine, a saber, a side-arm, and a revolver." This apparently spurred the police to greater efforts, for four days later a series of extensive searches was undertaken. But the only weapons found were old, and probably unusable. Two days after that the police ransacked the city Construction Office and found two pistols (one of military issue) and also "a large bundle of propaganda material, several flags, placards, etc." It was also reported that the police had established that a member of the *Reichsbanner* had thrown an Army rifle and several hand grenades in the Ruhme River. A week later new police raids yielded only rifle ammunition, but strollers along the Ruhme found a carbine and ten bullets. Four days later the police announced the discovery of an Army pistol under the woodpile of a home they were searching, though the owner of the home denied any knowledge of how the pistol got there. Four days after that the police dragged the Ruhme on the basis of a tip, but without success. Six days later, however, they fished sixty-one rounds of Army-issue rifle ammunition out of the river.[5]

Thus throughout a six-week period spanning April, Northeimers were given the impression that the town was a veritable arsenal. It was easy to reach two conclusions: first, that only vigorous action by the Nazis had prevented a civil war; and second, that it was extremely unhealthy to have any sort of weapon around the house.

After the rash of reports in April, there was hardly any further mention of finding illegal weapons. In July the Ruhme Canal was drained to be deepened and "a limited cache . . . of weapons and ammunition . . . was fished out. Probably these things were thrown into the water out of fear that they might be discovered." Finally in August a worker was given three months in prison for possessing a pistol. "The police discovered it through an anonymous accusation. . . ." Though the police claimed to have found 3,015 bullets in various places during that month, the great weapons' discovery was over.[6]

This was all first-class justification for the repeated police raids and arrests. Furthermore, the Nazis were able to point out that there were no more political fights; the violence of the pre-Nazi period had come to an end. That this was an excellent propaganda point can be seen from the following report (on Easter Sunday) in the NNN:

> . . . For the rest, the Easter celebration took place in peace and quiet within Northeim's walls, as it did everywhere in the Reich. There was not the slightest news of any political fights or other disturbances. The calmness in domestic politics, which the reordering of things has brought about, has shown itself here in an example as clear as it is beneficial.[7]

With the propaganda justification for police action firmly established, the Nazis in Northeim made use of the familiar tactics of repression and terrorism. The homes of potential or actual opponents were repeatedly ransacked and various people were arrested. This was done under the public eye, to increase its deterrent effect. In the first six months after Hitler became chancellor, the local press in Northeim reported, on fourteen different occasions, that house searchings had taken place. It also listed at least twenty-two people (most by name) who had been arrested for political reasons.[8]

Not all arrests and house searchings were reported in the press, but enough were made known so that the public received a good general impression of what was going on. Furthermore, the way in which police actions were reported was enough to give the townspeople an idea of the generally arbitrary nature of such actions.

Thus it was reported on March 14 that Deppe, the leader of the Northeim *Reichsbanner*, had been arrested "for reasons which in consideration of the investigation must be kept secret." The next day he was released with no further explanation. He was then arrested again on the afternoon of the first meeting of the City Council, and this time the reason given was that he was "suspected of having spread reports of an antigovernmental nature obtained from the newspaper from the Saar which he receives."[9]

Most persons arrested in the early months of the Nazi regime were taken to the county jail. Exactly what happened to them there was not clear to Northeimers, but it was clear that it was something extraordinary. In mid-March the GGZ reported:

> As we hear, eight of the eighteen *Communists* who are presently in our county jail (all from Northeim) have applied for membership in the NSDAP. Is it possible that the good influence of our hardworking jailer X who watches over them has succeeded in making itself felt? In any event, they seem to have "broken fully and finally with the unholy Bolshevism."[10]

Whatever went on in the county jail was probably considered preferable to other possibilities. Already in March the GGZ published a picture of the first concentration camp (at Dachau), with a text noting that there was room for five thousand political prisoners. By the end of that month the Northeim county jail was full and three Communists had to be taken to the "Moringen Workhouse." What this meant was only rumored, but by mid-July it was reported that "nine prisoners . . . were taken this morning by the Northeim police to Moringen where seven were delivered to the Concentration Camp and two to the Workhouse."[11] Henceforth Northeimers knew that there was a concentration camp within driving distance.

Actually, the press reports were considerably behind the reality. The Moringen Concentration Camp, located at the other end of the county from Northeim, was founded in early April 1933 to take the overflow of political prisoners from the city of Hanover and from other jails in the area. The immense number of persons taken into "protective custody" (a byproduct of the Reichstag Fire Decree whereby citizens could be arrested without being charged and held with no recourse to *habeas corpus*) in March were more than the regular jails could hold. Though the Moringen Workhouse was a state institution, the adjacent and newly created camp was, from its beginning, staffed by the SS. Originally the camp was to hold only Communists, including eleven from Northeim County, but by the end of April it had over three hundred inmates of mixed composition. The prisoners were forced to do road repair, read Nazi newspapers, attend church, hear Nazi speakers, and march in Nazi propaganda parades.[12]

The camp's population fluctuated over the spring of 1933 as prisoners were added, released, or transferred to other places. But overcrowding was an increasingly common problem to the point where the commandant insisted that, with 322 prisoners, there was no room for a single additional person. Yet by June the number was up to 356 (including about 20 from Northeim County). At that point the Communists organized a hunger strike in which 252 prisoners participated. The SS guards broke it within four days by turning off the drinking water and force-feeding the leaders. By August there were 381 prisoners.[13]

Though the numbers and composition of the Moringen Concentration Camp continued to change thenceforth (for a while it was exclusively a women's camp), it became a permanent fixture of the Third Reich and grew until by 1944 there were over seven hundred inmates.[14] Since prisoners from Northeim County were frequently added or released, and since at least two dozen of the SS guards were from Northeim County, some notion of what being condemned to a concentration camp signified must have gotten back to the people of Northeim. Such information was undoubtedly imprecise, but for purposes of creating an atmosphere of terror, vague knowledge was probably the most effective.

The press reports also made it clear that if the Nazis were after someone, they would get him on one account or another. Such was the only conclusion to be drawn from the case of a worker who was arrested and apparently promised his liberty if he revealed where guns and ammunition were hidden. He gave this information to the police and was then set free. The police were unable to find the guns at the place he indicated, however, and thus he was arrested again. A short time later he was sentenced to prison for "insulting a police officer."[15]

The reasons given for arrest were very minor, which created the impression that anything worse would be all the more severely dealt with. In June, for example, one of the two remaining SPD councilmen was arrested for saying that the *Stahlhelm* would soon be strong enough to "cut the SA to pieces." A few weeks later a woman peddler was arrested for "spreading false and agitational political rumors." It was suggested that she might possibly be a Communist and that perhaps this might be part of a Communist campaign "to make the people restive." At the end of the month a worker was arrested for "profane statements about National Socialism."[16]

Thus it seems clear that the public in Northeim had a good idea, by mid-summer 1933, that even to express oneself against the new system was to invite persecution. In fact, not only were Northeimers aware of this situation, but by their very awareness they reinforced the actual terror apparatus. Each time someone in Northeim cautioned his neighbor or friend, he was strengthening the general atmosphere of fear.

This happened frequently. A teacher remembered that the mother of one of his pupils complained about the book burning. He agreed with her but also warned her not to try to tell other people, lest she got into trouble. The principal of the high school remembers that he used to buy cigars at a certain store and along with the cigars usually received the advice to be careful. The general feeling was that the Gestapo was everywhere. At least five people were identified as being "Gestapo agents," though in point of fact there was probably only one for the whole town, Hermann Denzler, and that was considerably later.[17]

Other people claimed to know of the existence of a "list" (though they had never actually seen it) of people to be proscribed at some future date. "It was a blacklist; there were eighty people on it."[18] "It was made up of four groups: A, B, C, and D. The A people would be shot; the B people put in concentration camps, etc. . . ."[19] "I never saw the list myself, but everyone knew it existed."[20]

At least part of the reason for all the rumors was that in the first months of the Nazi seizure of power several elements in the Nazi party tried to play secret policeman. Individual members of the party and SA took it upon themselves to spy on potential opponents; others implied that they were doing so, for their own self-aggrandisement. The party's propaganda department decided to set up its own "intelligence service" and at the *Gau* level established a central card index with names and addresses of all SPD and KPD members. Individual county propaganda leaders were directed to select one Nazi, preferably a former police officer, to act as the local agent.[21] The Northeim SS also created an "intelligence troop" by June 1933, and began to report names of suspicious persons to the Local Group Leader, Girmann.[22] For a while, therefore, Northeimers were inundated by amateur "Gestapo" operatives.

Thus the Gestapo became extraordinarily efficient by reason of rumors and fears. It was unnecessary for the Nazis to suggest that someone who had no swastika flag buy one. Maria Habenichts, in her kind neighborliness, took care of that for them by cautioning the flagless person, "letting her in on what one had to do." Given the atmosphere of terror, even people who were friends felt that they must betray each other in order to survive. Thus very early in 1933 there was the case of a Dr. Kuno Ruhmann who went to a party and, after one drink too many, sought to entertain people by imitating Hitler's way of speaking. The next morning his hostess reported him to Nazi headquarters. Word of this spread quickly and soon Northeimers saw that it was better not to go to parties at all. "Social life was cut down enormously—you couldn't trust anyone any more."[23] Or as someone else put it:

> It wasn't so much that criticism was dangerous; it was pointless.
> Still I never felt free to say what I wanted, never felt a sense of
> personal freedom . . . It was well-known that Hermann Denzler
> kept himself informed on what Northeimers thought.[24]

Even if one were not actually arrested it was clear that one could easily lose his job or simply be excluded from any of the normal factors and considerations that ordinarily make society function smoothly:

> In general all people who were independent or who stuck to their
> own opinions were roughly handled or put to the side when the time
> came for favors. You could be boycotted; you could be driven out
> of business. These things were noticed by most people, who learned
> from the fate of others. It was pure force applied to politics and it
> meant that the Nazis got anything they wanted.[25]

From the moment the Third Reich was established, Ernst Girmann was relentless in using his position as Local Group Leader to hurt potential opponents of the regime. On March 3, 1933, he wrote to the Reich Ministry of Employment to get a Northeim Social Democrat who was employed there fired. A week later he wrote to Goering (as Prussian Minister of the Interior) to make sure that Northeim's former County Prefect, Kirschbaum, who had moved to another city, would be dismissed from the civil service because he was an SPD member and a "half-Jew."[26] And in the months to come he would write similar letters of denunciation to fellow Nazi leaders in any town where someone from Northeim had fled to escape Girmann's vengeance. Thus it became very clear that the Nazis had long memories and that any man who crossed them would be hounded wherever he went.

Under these circumstances the Nazis had very little to do to intimidate people. They created examples on the Left and Right (as will be shown) and let natural social forces do the rest. Conditions reached the point where one who failed to give the Nazi salute, who left a meeting early, or who ventured a cold look at Ernst Girmann, was thought to be displaying almost foolhardy recklessness. "There never was any opposition. The most there was was reserve. And even that was a luxury."[27]

And yet, one has to ask the question, what happened to those who had sworn resistance? What happened to the *Reichsbanner*, which had repeatedly asserted, in the years before Hitler came to power, that when the expected Nazi *coup* came they would be able to defend the Republic? In Northeim, at least, the Republic was destroyed without a single blow struck in its defense. The *Reichsbanner*, with all its plans for instant mobilization, had its members struck down one by one, its leaders imprisoned, beaten, hounded from their jobs and their homes without any resistance from the organization as a whole.

Perhaps the basic reason for this was that there was no Nazi *coup d'état.* Instead, there was a series of quasi-legal actions over a period of at least six months, no one of which by itself constituted a revolution, but the sum of which transformed Germany from a republic to a dictatorship. The problem was where to draw the line. But by the time the line could be clearly drawn, the revolution was a *fait accompli,* the potential organs of resistance had been individually smashed, and organized resistance was no longer possible. In short, the splendid organization was to no avail; in the actual course of events it was every man for himself.

The Northeimer *Reichsbanner* itself was ready to fight in 1933. All it needed was the order from Berlin. Had it been given, Northeimer's *Reichsbanner* members would have carried out the tested plan they had worked on so long—to obtain and distribute weapons and to crush the Nazis. But Northeim's *Reichsbanner* would not act on its own. The leaders felt that single acts would come to grief, would possibly compromise the chance when it finally did come, and would, in any event, be a betrayal of discipline. They felt that their only hope was in common action, all together, all over the Reich. Hadn't the former SPD governor of Hanover, Gustav Noske, said that *only* a counterattack should be made? So they waited and prayed for the order to come, but it never did. And while they waited the Nazis began tracking them down, one by one. Finally it was clear that there would never be an order and Karl Deppe and Friedrich Haase spread the word that the *Reichsbanner* was to be dissolved:

> We told them that every man would have to follow his own conscience now. If we could have maintained the organization we would have kept responsibility for our members. But when we no longer had the strength to protect them, we could no longer ask them to remain loyal.[28]

Yet most of the old *Reichsbanner* men did remain loyal to their ideals. According to Friedrich Haase, perhaps ten of the former four hundred went over to the SA. Carl Querfurt agreed with this estimation. He himself had little encouragement for the *Reichsbanner* men who came to him for advice. "Join the party," he usually said. "Think of your family. There's nothing to be gained by acts of heroism."[29]

This situation, where even heroism was denied the men of the democratic Left, came about in no small measure because of the failure of the Social Democrats to understand the nature of Nazism. Just as their basic premise in the years before Hitler came to power was the erroneous assumption that the Nazis were essentially *Putsch*-ists who could not possibly attract a mass following, so their basic premise after Hitler came to power was the equally erroneous assumption that his would be a government similar to the others of the Weimar period.

The most eloquent document on this was the set of instructions sent out to SPD Locals in District Hanover on March 23, 1933. It was filled with instructions about sending for handbooks on Socialist policy in communal affairs and filling out questionnaires; in short, carrying on business as usual. The only reference to the phenomenon of Nazism was contained in paragraph seven:

> *Will the election of our village and town representatives be approved?* That is a question which is repeatedly being asked. The question is unanswerable because we do not know what this government will do. However, in any case we must, now as always, select trustworthy comrades as village representatives wherever we have a majority. Should they later not be sworn in, then we will take a position on this. Under no circumstances should we value any of our rights cheaply.[30]

This at a time when SPD leaders were having their houses searched in the middle of the night for weapons! This when the officers of the *Reichsbanner* were being herded into jail by Stormtroopers, beaten in the prisons across Germany, cast into Nazi concentration camps! The SPD, the only defenders of democracy in Germany, the men who should have been gathering guns and calling the general strike, or at least developing an underground with passwords, false names, and the other paraphernalia of effective covert resistance, were instead being urged to keep the party files in order, to avoid bookkeeping errors, and above all to purchase the latest pamphlet on parliamentary tactics in village councils.

If the central offices of the SPD did not know "what this government will do," the local Socialist leaders in Northeim soon found out. The details of the personal experience of five Northeim Social Democrats will illustrate the general pattern.

Johannes Grote was a long-time Social Democrat, *Reichsbanner* member, and union official. He had been an SPD representative on the Northeim City Council from 1926 to 1930. He worked at the city gas works, where he had been employed for eighteen years in 1933.[31]

On May 12, 1933, Johannes Grote was dismissed from his job since "according to your previous political activity you do not give any assurance that you will, on every occasion, support the national state without qualification."[32] Twelve days later he was arrested and put in the county jail. He was held for three days and every day was questioned by the police for three to four hours. During the questioning he was forced to press his face against a wall and was then beaten from behind. This was some five weeks before his fifty-first birthday.

Both before and after this incident, his house was subjected to repeated searches, conducted by seven or eight armed SA men. Grote resented most that they stripped his library of some first editions by Marx and Bebel. His wife was also made to go to the police station once for two hours, but his children were never bothered.[33]

After these experiences, Grote found that most of his acquaintances in Northeim didn't know him any more. Furthermore, no employer was willing to hire him. Finally he found a job as a house-to-house salesman, selling soap. This was very satisfactory to Grote because he used it as a means of keeping in touch with fellow Social Democrats. "If I came to a Nazi, I just asked him if he wanted to buy soap and then went on to the next house. But if I came to a comrade or a fellow union man then we always talked about how to get rid of the Nazis. Many were for an open rebellion, but most were not."

Eventually, in 1934, Grote's travel identification papers were withdrawn from him, putting an end to the soap business.[34] The only job the Employment Office had for him was in a stone quarry, about forty-five minutes by foot from Northeim. The work was hard and Grote swallowed his pride and wrote, as a veteran of World War I, to the Nazi War Victims Aid Society (NSKOV), asking them to intercede for him. They did, but Ernst Girmann, to whom the matter was referred, refused to allow Grote to return to his old job, "since I do not intend to dismiss old SA and SS people in order to help leading SPD people."[35]

While working at the quarry Grote was arrested again, this time for having said that "von Papen and the capitalists would soon topple Hitler," but he was subjected only to an hour-long session with the Gestapo.[36] It was enough, however, to make Grote want to leave Northeim, which he did at the end of the year. Henceforth he was gone from Northeim until after World War II. His spirit remained cocky and buoyant, his repugnance for Nazism unabated, but he was, nevertheless, *hors de combat* as far as effective resistance was concerned.[37]

Another Northeim worker, who can be classed as a minor figure in the Socialist community, was Benno Schmidt. He had never even been a dues-paying member of the SPD, but he always thought of himself as a Socialist. As an unskilled laborer he had found employment only intermittently during the depression, lived mainly from the dole, and eventually he and his wife registered as "shelterless" and were housed in the miserable and turbulent rooms of the old Army barracks. A frequent participant in street fights against Stormtroopers, Schmidt was sentenced to prison for his part in the "Long Bridge" battle in July 1932, though he was covered by the general amnesty and never served his term.

In the autumn of 1932 he found work with the Northeim forest administration. When the Nazis came to power, Benno Schmidt did not think in terms of how to overthrow them but of how to keep from being forced into the SA. He was not fired from his job but was given the dirtiest work. His labor gang, which had been exclusively Socialist, became half-Nazi after the purge of city workers. Schmidt was struck by the growing distrust among the workers:

> After a while nobody wanted to talk any more because of all the Nazis. I can still remember the "second breakfasts" in the woods—everybody munching and nobody saying anything. It sure made the work worse.

At the same time he felt the growing power of the Nazis. He was beaten up one day for refusing to give the Hitler salute. ("I never could *Heil Hitler*—why should I? There was nothing special about the man.") In the summer of 1933 the police raided his apartment and seized the money and footballs of the Workers' Sport Club, of which he was treasurer, and also his pruning knife and a spring from the door, which were described as weapons and which cost him a fine of 8 marks, 50 *Pfennig*. He was also repeatedly pressured to join the SA, and as a consequence quit his job and left Northeim to work on the *Autobahn*. "They didn't bother me after that."[38]

With more substantial people, such as Friedrich Haase, the Nazis were more vigorous. His personal fate after the Nazi seizure of power included being thrown out of work, hindered in getting another job, prevented from drawing unemployment pay—in other words, deprived of all income. Furthermore, he was arrested, subjected to numerous house searchings, questionings and the like, and, finally, was repeatedly evicted from apartments by fearful or fanatical landlords.

The Gestapo were particularly anxious to get their hands on Northeim's *Reichsbanner* flags and membership lists. They refused to believe that Friedrich Haase had burned them until he actually led them to a field outside Northeim and showed them the cold ashes. Yet despite Friedrich Haase's prominent position in the *Reichsbanner* he was not arrested until the end of April 1933. He was then held for four days without charge, ineptly interrogated but not mishandled, released, and then arrested again a week later. This time he was made to sign a statement promising not to speak of his experiences in jail and not to sue for damages:

> I said that I wouldn't sign such a statement and Police Secretary Engelmann said: "If you don't sign that, you will be locked up again." So I said to him: "Engelmann! You know as well as I do that that's extortion and that you could be fined or imprisoned for it! It's right in the Civil Code Book—right there on your desk." Engelmann got up and went over to the window and looked out of it for a long time. Then he said: "I can't help it; sign or you'll be locked up again." So I said: "Give me the damned thing—I'll sign it."

While Friedrich Haase was in the county jail he received notice that he was suspended from his job at the County Prefect's Office, and after he was released he was permanently dismissed on the grounds of political unreliability.[39] From mid-April to mid-May his rooms were searched seven times by the police and SA. On April 27, two days before his first arrest, he was ordered to report to the local NSDAP headquarters. There Walter Steineck gave him a pen and paper and dictated a statement that Haase had resigned from "all Leftist organizations and [was] applying for membership in the NSDAP." When Haase ironically objected that the Nazis could scarcely desire a convinced Marxist and an ostensible subversive as a "party-comrade," Steineck simply replied: "Write what I tell you or it's the concentration camp."[40]

Friedrich Haase assumed that this extorted statement was used to demoralize Socialists in other towns. "The people around Northeim knew me well enough not to believe anything like that, and besides they could see that the Nazis were hounding me almost daily."

During the following months, Haase was frequently brought to the police station for questioning and had his rooms searched about once a month. Furthermore, he received a letter from his landlord who declared that he would no longer rent to an opponent of the regime. Friedrich Haase moved and after a few months was evicted again. After the third eviction he left Northeim. In the interim he had to live entirely on money given him by his father. He tried to find a job, but his chances were nipped each time by his record. Businessmen simply felt that hiring Friedrich Haase was a needless risk.

During this period Haase kept contact with other SPD people. Often they met at the river and talked while swimming. "The banks were flat and no one could sneak up on us." In the winter he took walks with his comrades in order to talk, and on one occasion was trailed and afterward questioned by the Gestapo. His main reason for keeping contact with other SPD members was political. But a second reason was that they were the only friends he had.

> After I was arrested most of my boyhood and family friends cut me. They just ignored my existence—didn't even say "hello." I lost good friends. Only the political friends remained true. The rest were living in a cloud. My fiancée remained true too.

Perhaps it was this as much as the frequent questionings and house searchings, the repeated evictions, and the financial distress that drove him from Northeim. In 1935 he left town to work in a factory in Hanover. He was not to return to Northeim, until 1949.[41]

Surprisingly enough, the arch-Social Democrat of Northeim, Carl Querfurt, had no really bitter experiences of the type related above. Perhaps it was because he was so well-known, perhaps because he was an astute enough politician to know that the SPD was temporarily finished and to act accordingly.

Carl Querfurt met the problem of Nazism with coolness and courage, as shown by his actions in the City and County Councils. His courage did not extend to what he termed "fruitless heroics"; hence, as soon as he saw what was going on in each of the organs he was elected to, he quietly resigned. In early April he learned the essential facts at a meeting of the Provincial Parliament. At its first session he was elected to the executive committee, but the new governor immediately declared him "furloughed." Thus within a short time after the elections, Querfurt either gave up or was stripped of all the offices he had held.

Apparently Northeim's Nazis originally intended to make an example of Querfurt. Shortly after the local elections in March, several truckloads of SA men from a neighboring town were brought to Northeim for a demonstration. The demonstration took the form of smashing the windows and office furniture of the "red" Health Insurance Office. Carl Querfurt's tiny tobacco shop was located across the street from the Health Insurance Office, and Ernst Girmann gave a speech to the SA men, attacking Querfurt. The most frequent oratorical gesture was a finger pointed across the street. Apparently Girmann's hope was that the SA men would ransack Querfurt's shop and drag Querfurt out to be a forced witness to the burning of Weimar flags, which was to cap the demonstration. But the SA, either sated or ashamed, refused to take the hint and Querfurt's shop was spared destruction.

The next Nazi action was to declare that Carl Querfurt's shop was under boycott. This hurt his business somewhat, especially when SA men stood outside and frightened people away, but Querfurt had many friends, and shopping habits became ingrained in a small town, so that his business survived. Eventually even Girmann forgot about the boycott.

Naturally the "Deputy Police" searched Querfurt's house repeatedly, but he anticipated their action by burning his files. Furthermore, he began counteraction. After the first searches Querfurt ordered a load of wood. Then he went to Girmann and demanded that policemen be detailed to observe the wood being stacked up so that they would not later search the pile for weapons and mess up the neat pile. He did the same when he first hoed the small vegetable garden in his backyard.

Finally he became even more aggressive. In the course of the boycott an SA man "stood guard" over Querfurt's back gate one night and the next morning Querfurt saw Girmann bright and early and told him:

Look, I know why you've got your Stormtrooper watching my back gate! One of these nights he'll throw a weapon over the fence and then the police will "find" it the following day. You know that mastiff I have? Tomorrow night at 8 P.M. I'm going to let him out for exercise—out the back gate. I'll feed him at 9 P.M.; that is, if he's still hungry.

The SA post was removed.

This kind of personal duel had its limits, and for Carl Querfurt the other side of his relationship with Girmann and the other Nazis was that he was absolutely dormant politically. He never said anything against Hitler or the Nazis and in general accepted the regime as an established, if unpleasant, fact. He was even willing to give in if pressed on minor matters. Thus the Nazis eventually determined that Querfurt would have to join one of their affiliates, the People's Welfare Society. Querfurt finally agreed but won a sort of personal victory by insisting that he pay half dues "since your boycott of my business has made me poor."[42]

In this peculiar role, a kind of tamed tiger, Querfurt lived out the Nazi era without ever suffering more than occasional petty chicanery from the Nazis. He was even able to wield some influence, as was the case when his interventions through von der Schulenberg secured the release from a concentration camp of two Social Democrats of Northeim County. Probably the main ingredient in Querfurt's survival was his coolness and his relationship with Girmann, for the two had grown up in the same block and understood each other.[43]

A final example of the personal experiences of Social Democrats may round out the picture. Hermann Schulze was a rank-and-file member of the SPD and also of the *Reichsbanner*. He had worked at the Northern railroad yards, had lost his job in the purge of 1932, and had furthermore been denied unemployment pay. Hence he entered the Third Reich fully engrossed with the problem of earning his daily bread.

During this period, Schulze and his family lived by working for the peasants around Northeim. He and his children worked all day and received their meals in exchange. His wife was lucky enough to find a job at the cigar factory, and thus they lived. His family was often hungry but his father helped out, sharing what little he had with them. Eventually the peasants refused to give Schulze any more work because they were afraid of what might happen to them if it were discovered that they were helping a Socialist.

During this period the Gestapo searched Schulze's house several times, very carefully. They cut open mattresses and thumped on the walls and even broke open a section of the wall that happened to be hollow. They confiscated Schulze's rifle, but Schulze hid the *Reichsbanner* flag so carefully that they never found it. The Gestapo were very angry about it. They questioned him on that and related matters at least twenty times.

In the summer of 1933, after he had been without work for several months, Schulze was given a job in the stone quarry near Northeim as a result of the intervention of Walter Steineck (who had once courted Schulze's cousin), and in return for a promise to give up political activity. He found many SPD officials from Northeim working there. Every morning they were all made to salute the swastika when it was raised. The work consisted of breaking stones with a sledge hammer and the pay was 20 marks a week, which Schulze said was like the old proverb: "Too much to die on and too little to live on." It was actually less than the dole.

For Schulze, who had worked as a track repairman, the work was quite tolerable, but for some it was brutal. Schulze's cousin, who had worked in a bureau in Northeim before the purge of the city employees, died as a result of exposure to the weather. Eventually, in 1935, Schulze found a better job with the *Autobahn* construction team.

During the intervening years the house searches continued. One Gestapo commissar searched Schulze's house at least seven times, and there were others, too. "The worst was hearing the knock on the door and wondering what was going to happen this time."

He was also watched in other ways. In the winter of 1933–1934, an unknown man knocked at Schulze's door and asked for him by name. Schulze took him in. It was raining and the man was wet. The man showed Schulze a *Reichsbanner* membership book and told him that he was a fugitive from the Gestapo. He told Schulze that the *Reichsbanner* had risen in the Ruhr and was fighting the Nazis. Would Schulze have any weapons? Could he supply the names of any loyal *Reichsbanner* men in the area? Schulze answered "no" to each question and added, "I'm through, I've had the s— kicked out of me. All I can do is put you up overnight and feed you, which I'd do for any human being on a night like this."

In the morning, after breakfast, the man went to the door and, just before he left, turned his lapel back and showed Schulze an SS button. Then he left wordlessly.[44]

From these five accounts—of a union official, a workingman, a *Reichsbanner* leader, the head of Northeim's SPD, and a rank-and-file member— the pattern emerges of how the Northeim Nazis dealt with avowed opponents to the regime. They were, first of all, economically hurt, as far as this was possible. Most SPD members who could be forced out of their jobs were subsequently given the choice of either no work at all or work in the stone quarry. The latter was work designed to break their spirits. In addition they were hounded by the police with arrests, questionings, and repeated house searches. Behind this lay the constant threat of the concentration camp, the very factor of uncertainty adding terror. For one never knew whether or not the latest house searching might, perhaps whimsically, qualify one for the half-mythical KZ. Then there were the petty nuisances: the demands to join the SA or some other Nazi organization, the calumny against one's name in speeches and the Nazi press, the pressure on the landlord and (subtly) on one's friends, the silence in the tavern when one stopped for a beer.

Poverty, terror, bureaucratic chicanery, social isolation—a potent formula. Perhaps one should add what might have been the most significant factor of all: the sense of futility. What was the Northeimer Social Democrat to do? Rebel? Even if one had weapons, whom was one to shoot? Policemen? Every Nazi (including those you went to grade school with)? And when? Which one of the various small acts exactly tipped the scale toward a dictatorship? And who was to rebel with you, since the factor of distrust entered in? And what then? Was Northeim to declare itself an independent entity in Germany?

Perhaps one should attempt first to prepare the population through effective propaganda. But Northeim voted for the NSDAP with a 63 percent majority, and if the SPD could not sell democracy when it had the advantages of free speech, its own press, and a party machine, what could it do with none of these?

Thus there was left only flight, internal conviction, irony, or little triumphs of the sort Carl Querfurt carried off. By the time the first six months of the Nazi regime were over, these were the alternatives open to the Social Democrats of Northeim. When it is too late, it is too late.

Under these circumstances it was only a matter of tidiness that prompted the formal outlawing of the SPD. Long before that step was taken, the membership had been broken and the organization smashed. In recognition of these facts the executive committee of Local Northeim met on April 29 and dissolved itself. The Northeim section of the *Reichsbanner* did likewise on the same date. Before the SPD was able to wind up its affairs, the police underscored the fact of the dissolution by seizing all SPD property (including 200 marks still in the treasury) on May 11. At the same time, former leaders were subjected to extensive grilling by the Gestapo, who were apparently amazed to find democratic Socialism so easy to destroy. The trade unions were dissolved and their buildings occupied on May 4. The other organizations in the complex SPD-worker system simply ceased to exist. Other parties had no local organization in Northeim to dissolve, with the exception of the DVP, which voted itself out of existence on July 14, 1933, after turning its treasury over to the "German War Graves Society."[45]

Thus ended all formal party organizations in Northeim whose ideology was opposed to that of the Hitler dictatorship.

WHIPPING UP ENTHUSIASM

SPRING-SUMMER 1933

What a Transposition Through Divine Disposition!

Title of the main speech at the Nazi Victory Celebration in Northeim, March 19, 1933

Vigor and thoroughness were the prime attributes of the Northeim NSDAP in the years before 1933. These qualities developed into frenzy after Hitler was named chancellor and the way to the Third Reich seemed open at last. Not only did the Nazis seize the whip of authority and use it to beat their former opponents into submission, they also intensified their propaganda efforts. Mass backing had been the Nazi forte before Hitler came to power; mass intoxication brought them their absolute majorities in Northeim in the March elections. Through every device in the Nazi repertoire the townspeople had been persuaded that a vote for Nazism meant a vote for new times, for a revolution which would sweep away all past difficulties and inaugurate the earthly millennium. But the Nazi revolution could not be accomplished overnight. So many things had to be done that the initial stage of the revolution (the establishment of the dictatorship) took at least half a year.

Hence a way had to be found to sustain enthusiasm over a long period of time. The enthusiasm not only served to make men *feel* that a revolution was occurring; it also served as mask and justification for the various components—many of them ugly—which made up the revolution. Finally, by seeming to involve everyone, the organized enthusiasm isolated anyone who might be opposed to, or even skeptical about, the introduction of the dictatorial state. Thus it was an essential reinforcement of the Third Reich.

A crucial prerequisite for effective propaganda was control of the press. By the creation of a system of terror the Nazis had already made sure that the local press would not oppose them. The organs of the opposition (the *Volksblatt* and the *Northeimer Echo*) disappeared by March; the GGZ had always been favorably disposed toward Nazism, and the NNN was at first ambivalent and then acquiescent. But Northeim Nazis wanted more. They wanted the existing local press to be a completely pliant tool and ultimately they wanted their own Nazi-operated newspaper.

The beginnings of a Nazi newspaper went back to 1931 when their bi-weekly newsletter *Hört! Hört!* was first published. By autumn 1932, *Hört! Hört!* began to appear as the weekly supplement to a larger Nazi newspaper which served the entire Hanoverian area, mainly because the *Gauleiter* ordered that to promote his regional newspaper. In this guise *Hört! Hört!* did not have a wide audience. There were some 54,000 inhabitants of Northeim County and the Nazi newspaper had only 1,000 subscribers there.[1] On April 6, 1933, the supplement's name was changed to *Northeimer Beobachter* (NB) and it was published three times weekly. By June it came out daily, but still as a supplement to the parent newspaper. In the intervening months the Nazis had taken over the *Volksblatt* printing plant and in July they began using it to publish the NB as an autonomous party newspaper to give the Nazi point of view for Northeim.[2]

While the Nazis were developing their own local press they sought to promote it in every way. Early in April the NB was made the official newspaper of the town of Northeim and the sole official newspaper in police matters. A few weeks later it became the only official organ of Northeim County. Naturally all party members were urged to subscribe to the NB, and SA men were put to selling subscriptions, apparently with phenomenal success. In May an order was sent from Walter Steineck to all Local Group Leaders of the NSDAP in Northeim County forbidding them to give any news to other newspapers and requiring them to support the NB with every means available.[3] In other words, one method of aiding the NB was to hurt the other local newspapers.

In the first six months of the Third Reich the Nazis turned their heaviest guns on the NNN, which then had the largest circulation in Northeim. While the NNN was either objective or ambiguous about Nazism in the local news section, it was an organ of the DVP and hence, in national news, anti-Nazi. This apparently made little difference to Northeimers before Hitler was appointed chancellor. Even the Nazis found it necessary to advertise their meetings in the NNN. After Hitler was appointed chancellor, many Northeimers suddenly decided, either through fear or conviction, that the NNN was not the kind of newspaper they wanted to read.

As a former reporter for the paper put it:

> Between Hitler's appointment as chancellor and the March elections, people quit reading the NNN by the hundreds. They didn't just drop their subscriptions—they came into the office and vehemently demanded that the paper never be delivered to their home again, beginning tomorrow. They said they never wanted to hear of it again. Advertising fell off too.[4]

Thus by March the NNN began to be very careful about what it printed. It even screened advertisements carefully. Nevertheless the future of the paper was in considerable doubt after the Nazis came to power in Northeim. In March 1933 Erhardt Knorpel, the local news reporter for the NNN, talked this problem over with his neighbor, Walter Steineck, County Leader of the NSDAP. Steineck told him, "There is a simple solution: you join the party and then the NNN won't get into any more trouble. The NNN will have a guarantee." So Knorpel, after consultation with the editor-publisher of the paper, joined the NSDAP. He did not feel enthusiastic about it, but it seemed a matter of economic necessity.[5]

But this by no means ended the NNN's problems. It lost its position as official organ of the town and county offices, to the undisguised glee of the NB:

> It was to be expected that the NNN should lose its official character. This, at the least, it deserved because of its record of struggle against our movement. In the last weeks the NNN has tried to put on a Nazi cloak, but they still accept ads from Jews and from the consumers' cooperative. The length of the NNN's future is indeed doubtful.[6]

After this the NNN became doubly cautious and refused advertisements from Jewish firms. But toeing the Nazi line was not an easy task, as Knorpel recalled:

> I remember my first mistake. I wrote a report on a meeting in which I mentioned the County Prefect first and the County Leader of the NSDAP second. There was a great stink over this—Steineck called me up on the telephone and bawled me out. That night the publisher told me the Nazis were going to close up the paper. When I got to work the next morning he was in a state of deep depression. So I went over to see Walter Steineck and apologized profusely and promised never to let it happen again. Steineck said: "Don't forget it! First comes the party, then its servants in office."[7]

In addition to these direct attacks, the NNN had other things to worry about, since circulation continued to fall off. The cause of this was the Nazi campaign to sell subscriptions to their own paper, the NB. Most Northeimers were afraid to refuse a subscription to the NB, and also felt they could not afford both the NB and the NNN. Hence they stopped buying the NNN.[8]

The NNN fought this the only way it could. In May it published a long article on the indispensable value of the local press. In July there was another article on the value of the local press, based on quotations from the Nazi provincial governor. At the same time it tried to buoy up its readers' courage. In June the NNN reported prominently that the Society of German Newspaper Publishers had passed resolutions against the "use of threats or boycotts to gain new circulation." The following month, under a big headline ("Boycott Measures Against Bourgeois Papers Forbidden"), the NNN reported that the *Reichsleitung* of the NSDAP had forbidden the use of economic sanctions against any bourgeois newspapers. A few weeks later there was another long article on unfair competition by the Nazi press against non-party newspapers. It criticized "terroristic methods of raising newspaper circulation" and bolstered this with frequent quotations by leading Nazis.[9] It is doubtful that any of this campaign was really effective.

In the course of building up the circulation of the NB, the Nazis also trod on the toes of W. A. Röhrs, owner and editor of the GGZ. As a nationalist newspaper the GGZ never made any attempt to hide its admiration for the Nazis in the years before Hitler came to power. Nazi advertisements were published in the GGZ (probably at a reduced rate), Röhrs printed Nazi leaflets at a time when the Nazis had no other means to get them printed, and he always reported Nazi meetings with enthusiasm. But while the GGZ was enthusiastic about the Nazis, the feeling was not reciprocated. To Northeim's Nazis the GGZ was to be used but not trusted, since its editor was a despicable reactionary. This attitude was made clear long before Hitler came to power.[10]

Nazi attacks on the GGZ abated after the formation of the Nazi-Nationalist coalition in the beginning of 1933, but increased again when the GGZ, like the NNN, began to try to protect its circulation against Nazi competition. In May the NB published the following article:

THAT'LL HAPPEN JUST ONCE

Printer and DNVPist Röhrs has attacked the . . . NB, not openly but nevertheless clearly. Talks about the value of the "Local Press"! We all agree on the value of the local press, but not on the value of the GGZ. Local press is not narrow "churchyard politics" but a vital connection with the basic opinions of its readers. The GGZ is too old. It clearly doesn't fit into the national community of Adolf Hitler.[11]

This stung Röhrs into a lengthy editorial reply. He insisted that he was proud of his role in helping to defeat "Marxism" and that he had spent his whole life combating "Marxists." He never accepted advertisements from the SPD or the consumers' cooperative "though they were repeatedly offered." As for the "churchyard politics," Röhrs said he could not understand this charge. He had reported every meeting the NSDAP held in Northeim and had even hired a Nazi party member to write the stories. He declared that "the GGZ was, is, and will be a Nationalist newspaper." As for the NB's report, it was clearly a pack of lies. If the NB attacked him again, Röhrs concluded, he would not stoop to answer them.[12]

This was strong talk and the Nazis obviously would not take this lying down. The GGZ's already small circulation began to dip. People who had subscribed to the GGZ asked that it no longer be delivered, but instead picked it up covertly at the paper's offices.[13]

Röhrs replied to this by publishing an enormous article on "illegal competition by newspapers" replete with quotations from the official Nazi *Völkisher Beobachter*. This then drove the NB into publishing an article against illegal methods of getting subscriptions. It suggested that people should demand to see identification papers from anyone who claimed to be selling subscriptions from the NB. Finally, it declared that it was publishing this "because of the many dirty accusations the GGZ is making against us." Furthermore the Prefect's office was brought into play to keep Röhrs from complaining about his having lost access to official notices.[14] Röhrs in short, was undertaking a fight he could not possibly win. By the close of the first six months of Nazi rule it was clear that the GGZ and possibly the NNN were going to be destroyed altogether. Thus the field would be left to the NB alone. But in neither case was this because Nazism had been challenged openly by the non-Nazi newspapers of Northeim. In fact, the more the GGZ and NNN feared for their existence the more eager they were to prove themselves enthusiastic champions of the new regime. Thus Northeimers were incessantly propagandized by their own trusted newspapers during the initial months of Nazi rule.

Press propaganda, useful as it was, was never the real Nazi method of stimulating support. To assure mass backing there had to be active participation, even more so after the Nazis had seized power and could require participation. Northeim's NSDAP began providing for this as soon as the March election campaign was concluded.

The first wave of mass demonstrations was connected with celebrating the electorial victory won on March 12. Election day itself had provided a foretaste, since it had also been designated a memorial day for the fallen of World War I. All public buildings were required to fly flags at half-mast, with the express stipulation that the Imperial and not the Weimar flag should be flown. In the morning, uniformed contingents of all the veterans' societies joined the SA and *Stahlhelm* in a memorial service which was also a tribute to the new *Volk** community of Hitlerian Germany. Subsequently there was a mass meeting in the Market Square at which the head of the County Veterans' Society spoke on how happy he was to see the old flag flying again. Flags were in abundance on the following days as the Nazis called for

* A term which can be variously translated as "national," "popular," or "racial," and thus connotes all three. It was a favorite Nazi expression.

three days of flag flying in honor of the electoral victory, featuring both the Imperial and Nazi flags. This began on March 13, with a general parade around Northeim to raise the two new flags and to burn the old flag of the Weimar Republic. The parade was composed of the *Stahlhelm*, the SA, and the SS, and was led by the SA fife-and-drum corps. It was on this day that Northeim's police force was made to put on swastika armbands.

The first place to undergo the change was the City Hall. The Imperial and swastika flags were raised and the mayor said a few words on the blessings of "unity" in Germany, followed by Ernst Girmann on a similar theme. After the speeches the Black-Red-Gold flag of the Weimar Republic was cast on a small bonfire which had been prepared, and as it was consumed by the flames, the crowd sang the "Horst Wessel Song." This same ceremony was repeated at the police station, the county building, and the post office, each time with a new speaker. Finally the parade marched to the Health Insurance Office where the flags were also raised and where Ernest Girmann outdid himself in condemning the Social Democrats "who considered this very building as their domain and propaganda institute." "The day is past," finished Girmann, "when such Social Democratic elements will have a chance to be active in this building." At last, exhausted by the orgy of symbol manipulation and speeches, the crowd dispersed.[15]

The next big event of the NSDAP was not held until the end of the week. In between, for those who wanted more, there was a patriotic speech by the poet August Winnig and a patriotic concert by the SA band. Then on Sunday, March 19, the Northeim NSDAP gave its victory celebration, fittingly held in the Cattle Auction Hall. The hall, decorated with swastika flags, was full to the bursting point with at least a thousand people. The chief speaker was the Nazi preacher, Pastor Muenchmeyer, and his topic: "What a Transposition Through Divine Disposition!" The whole tone of the celebration was conservative, solemn, and religious.[16]

As soon as Northeim's ceremonial inauguration of the Third Reich was completed, it was necessary for the town to repeat the process in order to be in line with the national ceremony staged by Hitler and Hindenburg at the Potsdam Garrison Church on Tuesday, March 21. In Northeim all public offices were closed for the day. Shops closed early and also during the period from eleven-thirty in the morning until one in the afternoon in order to hear the ceremony over the radio. Radio sets were brought into the schools where the children listened to the events in Potsdam and their teachers instructed them that "a new epoch in German history was beginning." Then they were given a holiday for the rest of the day. All houses and public buildings were to bedeck themselves with swastika flags. After dark came a torchlight parade that wound through the whole of Northeim. Participating were the various Nazi and Nationalist paramilitary units, all the sports clubs in Northeim, all the various veterans' and patriotic societies, all the schools, and such miscellaneous groups as the "Artisans' Training Club," the clerks and mail carriers from the post office, and the volunteer fire department. Led by the town band, the SA band, and the SA fife-and-drum corps, the parade finally came to a halt in the city park, where Ernst Girmann gave a speech in which he praised the new unity of Germany: "The individual is nothing; the *Volk* is everything! Once we unite internally, then we shall defeat the external foe. Then it will really be "Germany above all in the world.' " Upon this cue the crowd sang *Deutschland über Alles* and then dispersed. Some three thousand had marched; at least as many again lined the streets to watch. "Thus Northeim's citizenry," commented the NNN, "has proven, in its overwhelming majority, that it is ready to throw itself without reservation into the rebirth of our Fatherland." [17]

Mass demonstrations of loyalty and enthusiasm of this sort were the very breath of the propaganda campaign designed to convince Northeimers that they were entering a new era. But in the ensuing months it was impossible to continue having great parades and mass demonstrations simply to celebrate the advent of the Third Reich as such. Concrete occasions were needed. They were supplied by three great festive events, two of them new, a third traditional. These were the celebration of Hitler's birthday, the "Day of German Labor" (a reinterpretation of May Day), and the celebration of the tenth anniversary of the death of Albert Leo Schlageter,* on May 26. By emphasizing these events, it was possible to have a major celebration about every three weeks during those crucial first months of the protracted Nazi *coup d'état.*

The first of the three great festivals was the celebration of Adolf Hitler's forty-fourth birthday, held on April 20. The day's events began at seven in the morning with a march through the town by the SA and their fife-and-drum corps. Immediately thereafter there was a small ceremony connected with installing the new street sign on "Adolf Hitler Strasse." Next came participation in church services by all the various uniformed adjuncts to the NSDAP. The Lutheran church was decorated with Imperial and swastika flags, which were also to be seen on almost every house in Northeim. The sermon that morning stressed the heavy responsibilities that fell to Hitler and concluded by invoking the prayers of Northeimers for their *Fuehrer.*

---

* An otherwise obscure nationalistic hero who was put to death by the French during their occupation of the Ruhr in 1923.

After the services a parade was held, terminating at the Market Square, where a concert was given by the SA band. The Northeim Artillery Club contributed to the occasion by firing salutes from their miniature cannon, attended by two little boys dressed in replicas of the Prussian artillerist's uniform. The afternoon was then given over to drinking beer in the various taverns of Northeim. In the evening, festivities continued in the *1910er Zelt* with a concert of military marches, dramatic and humorous skits, dancing, and speeches. Every official in the town government, County Prefecture, *Stahlhelm*, and NSDAP was present. Ernst Girmann spoke on the theme "Unity Is Everything" and promised that Northeim would soon be 100 percent Nazi. The great hall was so full it was practically impossible to dance.

In an imaginative aftermath the newspapers announced that Northeim units of the NSDAP had been presented with cheese, chocolate, and sausage by Adolf Hitler. These were gifts that had been sent to him for his birthday and that he then redistributed to local units in his own name.[18]

The next great celebration came on May 1, a day which a party with the name of "National Socialist German Workers' Party" could not afford to ignore, but the character of which it was determined to alter. In Northeim, the method used to accomplish these goals was to put the May Day celebration under Nazi leadership and thus give it a Nazi tone, and to make the celebration so heterogeneous in character as to purge it of its previous class connotations.

Perhaps because this was thought to be a particularily sensitive problem, the planning for May Day was also the first instance during the Nazi seizure of power when the higher offices of the party intervened decisively in the local organization of mass propaganda. On April 15 the national propaganda headquarters sent out comprehensive and detailed instructions for the entire program of the day, coordinating it with the preplanned national radio schedule. Six days later, the district director of Goebbel's newly created Reich Ministry for Propaganda and Public Enlightenment followed that up with his own multipaged specific directions. Thus Northeim's actions on May 1 would be, for the first time, part of an explicit pattern that was the same all over South Hanover-Brunswick and, in all but minor details, exactly what would happen everywhere in Germany.[19]

Preparations for "The Day of National Labor" began almost immediately after the celebration of Hitler's birthday. The opening note was sounded by advertisements placed by Northeim's Nazi Local Group:

The "Day of National Labor," planned by the Reich government for May 1, will bear the spirit of National Socialism in its essence.

This day will bring the creative *Volk* to a recognition of the national state, as opposed to the international efforts of Marxism. At the same time it marks the beginning of the first years of planned work under the leadership of the Reich Chancellor, Adolf Hitler. We call upon representatives of all offices, economic groups, clubs, businesses, etc., to attend the planning session at . . .[20]

Shortly thereafter, Nazi County Leader Steineck announced that the theme for the May Day celebration would be "All Germans Are Workers." Hence, the whole of Northeim would have to be involved in the celebration. A simple system of control was devised. Every person in Northeim was to purchase a lapel button at the Nazi headquarters. The button would enable him to walk in the parade on May 1. A person who did not buy a button would draw attention to himself. The price for one button was 10 *Pfennig;* proceeds from the sale of buttons would finance the festivities.

In addition, the regular social and economic associations in Northeim were pressed into service to make sure that the celebration was well organized and well attended. There was a place in the May Day parade for every organization in the town, from the local office of the *Reichsbank* to the Teachers' Association. Naturally all the veterans' and patriotic societies, all the state and local government employees, all the sports clubs, all the artisan guilds, choral groups, fishing clubs, chess societies, etc., would march in the parade. Each one of these organizations was also asked to contribute 5 or 10 marks to cover the cost of the celebration. Contributions were payable at the county headquarters of the NSDAP.

The holiday was to be a busy one. The program prescribed the following schedule:

A.M. 6:30 Fife-and-drum corps gives the signal to arise.
8:00 Flag raising at all offices and places of business with all employees participating.
8:45 Church services.
10:00 Meeting of all officials of all clubs, businesses, etc., in the city park (for last-minute parade instructions).
10:30 Broadcast by the Reich government from Berlin.
P.M. 1:15 Parade begins (For the remainder of the afternoon there will be a carnival with booths and a midway at the parade grounds.)
7:30 Radio broadcast of Adolf Hitler's speech.
Thereafter until midnight: concert, dancing, etc.

Preparations for this fantastic program became frenzied in the last few days of April. Many organizations had to resort to newspaper advertisements in order to give all the details of what was required of their members. But thanks to these efforts the program was carried out with the precision of a Prussian drill squad. Most gratifying of all to the Nazi planners was that hardly a house or building in Northeim was not decorated with a swastika flag.

The parade—a miracle of organization—started only fifteen minutes late. This was, after all, excusable, since five thousand people marched in it. There were seventy-three vehicles and floats (roughly half the number of all the motor vehicles in Northeim), and the parade stretched out for nine kilometers. It took three hours for the parade to pass. Some sections were quite colorful since almost every occupation was represented by a float. The bakers' guild, for example, had a huge pretzel, while the Settlers' Club had a model house. The parade terminated at the parade grounds where the participants sang the "Horst Wessel Song" and *Deutschland über Alles,* and then were freed to complete the rest of the day's schedule. The press reported truthfully that Northeim had never seen anything like this before.[21]

After the exhausting experience of organizing the May Day celebration, Northeim's Nazis were inactive for over three weeks. Then came the last of the trilogy of Nazi celebrations, "Schlageter Day." This was a new holiday, commemorating the fact that ten years before that first Nazi spring, a former Free Corps volunteer and Nazi party member named Albert Leo Schlageter had been executed by order of a French court-martial for sabotage during the Ruhr occupation. Northeim would honor Schlageter by dedicating a stone inscribed: "Never forget! Albert Leo Schlageter. Murdered by the French on May 26, 1923."

The ceremony was to be a double one, for after the Schlageter dedication there was to be a burning of "filth literature" in the Market Square. The material for this literary *auto-da-fé* consisted of confiscated Social Democratic papers and pamphlets, plus other works taken from the public library, such as Erich Maria Remarque's *All Quiet on the Western Front.* Northeimers who thought they could contribute to the combustibles were urged to deliver their books to Senator Hermann Denzler.

The unveiling of the Schlageter memorial was aimed mainly at young people. Thus the Hitler Youth and League of German Girls took the leading role, though the SA, SS, and SA band also contributed. A large crowd came to witness the ceremony, including all children from the grade schools. Various poems and songs of a nationalistic nature were presented and then the main speech was given by Senator Hermann Denzler (supervisor of Northeim's Hitler Youth). After some general remarks on the significance of Schlageter and on the necessity for the Hitler Youth to emulate Schlageter's courage, Denzler came to the heart of the speech:

> But besides letting your courage be strengthened by his examples, let the name Schlageter cause you to increase your hatred against Versailles and against the French who murdered him because—despite persecution and danger—he dedicated himself to his Fatherland. *(Turning then to the boys and girls.)* Be you his avengers! Be you the German Youth that knows how to hate foreigners! Your way leads you daily by this stone; clench your fists and think: "Never forget, revenge is mine!"

Denzler was followed by the pastor of the Lutheran Church who chose, in his speech, to emphasize the heroism of Schlageter and the necessity of "being worthy of him and of our *Fuehrer,* Adolf Hitler." After a hymn was sung, the ceremony came to an end.

The crowd then repaired to the Market Square, where several hundredweight of books were piled up, and a red flag and a photo of Otto Braun, former Socialist Premier of Prussia, on top. After a few words on the "un-German spirit" and on the "Jewish spirit," Ernst Girmann concluded his speech by promising that no German books or newspapers would be written by "racially foreign elements" anymore. Then the flames crept over the pile of books while the crowd sang *Deutschland über Alles.* The double ceremony had been highly instructive for Northeimers.[22]

These three great celebrations do not by any means exhaust the list of propaganda activities undertaken by Northeim's NSDAP in the first six months of the Third Reich. In addition to these general activities there were other smaller events sponsored by the various Nazi suborganizations.

The SA and SS contributed much during the first months. In March they held a concert evening in the *1910er Zelt* and also field maneuvers. A month later they conducted maneuvers again, replete with symbolism. ("Red" attacked "Blue" and was annihilated by a counterattack in the woods west of Northeim.) These events undoubtedly helped satisfy the town's apparently unquenchable thirst for militarism. This was the case also in mid-May, when a member of Northeim's SA was married. In clear imitation of the approved military manner, Northeim's SA formed a passageway into the church with their arms upraised in the Hitler salute. Also in mid-May the SS band from a neighboring town provided a "Military March" evening in Northeim, and later in the month the SA formed a cavalry unit. With the coming of summer the SA began to emphasize "military sport." Early in June there was competition of this type in a neighboring town with twenty-six medalists from Northeim. In July, Northeim had its own SA "military sport" day, featuring the Motor SA of the entire district. There was a parade through the town, then an obstacle-course race for motorcycles, and finally a mock tank battle. In the evening there was a dance. Several thousand Northeimers watched the show. Later in the month the SA, SS, and *Stahlhelm* held a twenty-five kilometer pack-march race.[23]

In the general propaganda work during the period of the seizure of power, the Nazi youth organizations also did their part. The League of German Girls gave "Parents' Evenings," such as one in the latter part of April, designed to show that the League taught girls wholesome skills, such as singing and folk dancing. In May the League of German Girls undertook two well-publicized trips, one to a district Hitler Youth convention (at which the Northeim Local Group of the League was declared the best in the district), and another, a march to a neighboring town and back.[24]

The Hitler Youth's greatest contribution to the propaganda cause was a subdistrict meeting held in Northeim on June 6, 1933. Over 1,400 boys flocked to Northeim, camping out on the parade grounds and holding parades and sports competitions during the day. The NNN (and probably many of the townspeople) appeared genuinely charmed by "the little brown soldiers."[25] Naturally these organizations contributed most of their effort to making sure that the great demonstrations and meetings were successful. The Hitler Youth and the SA were constantly active during the Nazi seizure of power, while the SA and SS made a special contribution by working as deputy police for house searches, beatings, and arrests.

As in the period before Hitler became chancellor, the Nazis again made use of theatrical presentations and movies. One film they pushed especially was entitled "Bleeding Germany." In April the Northeim NSDAP provided special buses for people who wanted to see a play in a neighboring town. In July a Nazi road group gave a special showing of the play "Schlageter" in Northeim. It packed the *1910er Zelt*. Finally, even events outside Northeim were often used to provide propaganda spectacles. On the occasion of a general Nazi meeting in Hanover in June, for example, Northeim sent two special trains, with SA parades both on leaving and on returning.[26]

In the general propaganda effort, the DNVP (Hitler's coalition partners) and its uniformed adjunct, the *Stahlhelm*, also tried to ease the task of the Hitler government by whipping up enthusiasm. In March the *Stahlhelm* gave a series of film presentations. In late April the young *Stahlhelm* held field maneuvers and then gave a parade and a concert on the Market Square. The *Stahlhelm* also sponsored a minor imitation of the Hitler Youth Sport Day in July.[27]

During the first months of the Third Reich, many Northeimers joined the *Stahlhelm*. Generally they did so in order to avoid having to join the SA or some other Nazi organization. Between April and June, the town's *Stahlhelm* added almost 150 members.[28] While this activity was going on in Northeim, the DNVP was being maneuvered out of power in Berlin and Goebbels was beginning to charge that Communists were infiltrating the *Stahlhelm*. In Northeim, the DNVP Local Group bestirred itself enough to send a letter to Hitler expressing their loyalty to him but also insisting that "whoever fights Hugenberg fights the Hitler government."* Later in June someone removed the wreath that the *Stahlhelm* had placed on the new memorial to Schlageter. Finally the *Stahlhelm* in the Northern district declared (as of July 1, 1933) that they would accept no new members so that "applications could be examined more closely."[29] The Nationalists were beginning to discover the price of being fellow-travelers of the NSDAP.

While the Nazis and Nationalists were vigorously backing the new system, there was a continuation of the kind of nationalistic activities that had become so much a part of life in the town in the years before Hitler took power. Near the end of June all flags flew at half-mast in the town in sorrowful commemoration of the signing of the Treaty of Versailles. In April the *Reichswehr*, in accordance with its custom, sent a detachment to Northeim to give a military concert. There was considerable publicity, and backing by the NSDAP, but the event was unsuccessful—Northeimers were kept too busy by the Nazi celebrations to have time to enjoy their traditional amusements.[30]

Despite the drain imposed by the Nazis on the energies of nationalist-minded Northeimers, at least some of the pre-Hitler nationalist societies continued their work. In May the Northeim Navy Club sponsored a lecture by a former Navy officer, entitled: "With U-Boat 21 in the World War." On May 8 the town had its annual convention of the old guardists. As in prior years, there was a parade, a series of speeches, and finally a dance in the *1910er Zelt*. But now Nazi symbols and ideas were fused with the customary ceremony. Thus for the first time there were pictures of Hitler at the guardists' meetings, the singing of the "Horst Wessel Song," and speeches

---

* Alfred Hugenberg was the national leader of the DNVP. He was forced to resign from the Hitler cabinet and the DNVP was dissolved as a party on June 21, 1933.

by Ernst Girmann. For the rest, the ceremony continued its customary path of glorifying nationalism and militarism.[31]

By far the biggest event sponsored by the patriotic societies in the first months of the Nazi seizure of power was the joint celebration of the sixtieth anniversary of the Warriors' League and the tenth anniversary of the Navy Club. The celebration consumed a whole weekend, with speeches, pageants, and flag dedications on Saturday night, and church services plus a big parade on Sunday. As in the guardists' convention, Nazis made certain that Hitler and the NSDAP were given their due on each occasion. Because of the avid participation by Northeimer's Nazis, the celebration was extremely well organized and well attended. While it thus achieved a Nazi patina, the main effect of the anniversary celebration was, as had been true of the work of these societies before 1933, directed toward heightening feelings of nationalism and militarism. In the same vein, the Northeim Chapter of the Society for Germandom in Foreign Lands sponsored a marathon race and mass meeting on June 25, again with considerable Nazi overtones. This was also true of the celebration of the twenty-fifth anniversary of the founding of the Northeim Military Society, held at the beginning of August.[32]

In short, while the main Nazi propaganda drive was going on, there was also a continuation of the customary nationalist agitation. Simply by promoting the kind of background that made Nazism appear reasonable, this aided the course of the Nazi revolution. The individual events became charged with Nazi concepts and speeches. All helped to smooth the way.

In addition to the traditional nationalist groups in Northeim, two new movements aided the cause of Nazism. The first began before Hitler was named chancellor, but originally made itself felt in the town in February 1933. This was a civil defense program, designed to teach Northeimers how to protect themselves against air raids. Early in February 1933 a team of civil defense experts arrived in Northeim, led by the former *Freikorps* leader Rossbach. The assembly hall of one of the schools was placed at the civil defense team's disposal for a week, and lectures and demonstrations were given on types of bombs and measures to be taken to minimize their effects. The course of instruction was supported by the patriotic societies in Northeim, and the press gave it considerable publicity. The civil defense team itself staged a parade with muffled drums (a traditional call to arms) to promote its course of instruction. The total effect was to suggest that the town might soon be in danger from an air raid. By this means the atmosphere of a nation in arms was given a boost.[33]

The second new element was the building of gliders and training of glider pilots. This also began before Hitler came to power, but was strongly publicized by the NSDAP in the first months of Hitler's regime. The Northeim glider was prominently displayed in parades and commonly discussed as the kernel of the new *Luftwaffe*. Finally, in late June, the Nazis took over the operation and set up an "SS Flyer Group" for Northeim. Henceforth glider exercises were pushed vigorously.[34]

Thus in the first six months of the Nazi regime, Northeim was subjected to a veritable barrage of propaganda. While the NSDAP took the lead, all the various nationalistic and militaristic elements in the town were brought into play to support and generalize the Nazi appeal. In addition to the mass-participation events in Northeim, there was the steady stream of national news stories, radio speeches, and propaganda in magazines and books. The total effect was to create the spirit of a revolution and to justify the kinds of steps the Nazis took to insure themselves control over the people.

THE ATOMIZATION OF SOCIETY

SPRING-SUMMER 1933

*Behold how good and how pleasant it is
for brethren to dwell together in unity.*

Psalms, CXXXIII, 1

Very early in the Nazi era an event occurred in Northeim which effectively fused propaganda and terror. This was the boycott of the Jews, April 1 to 4, 1933. In addition to being the beginning of that ineluctable process which ended a decade later in the gas chambers of the SS extermination camps, this particular action was also a miniature example of what the Nazis intended to do to the entire German population. For the essential effect of the boycott of the Jews was to atomize them socially: to cut them off from the rest of German society so that normal human ties could not work to restrain the dictatorship.

Like the rest of Germany, Northeim had a very small Jewish population. The census of 1932 showed 120 men, women, and children professing the Jewish faith, out of a total population of ten thousand. There was no significant increase in their number; a generation before there had been 102.[1] Most Jews in Northeim were small businessmen: cattle brokers, grocery or clothing store owners, and artisans. One Jewish merchant celebrated, in 1932, the 230th anniversary of the founding of his haberdashery—during all of which time it had been located in Northeim. There was no Jewish section in the town; Jews were well assimilated into Northeim's society. The town had very little anti-Semitism before the advent of Nazism. What there was expressed itself only in jokes and slight feelings of generalized distaste—in other words, the usual heritage of medieval Europe. Jews belonged to the shooting societies, patriotic clubs, and choral groups, and if they were differentiated it was by class, not religion. Some were elected to offices in their clubs, some were very highly respected, all were accepted as a normal part of the town's life.

The Nazis were determined to change this, since anti-Semitism formed one of the cornerstones of their ideology. This was not generally realized by Northeimers, especially not by the Jews, who saw Nazi propaganda as an electioneering device or a manifestation of intellectual bankruptcy, but hardly as a concrete program.[2]

Until they took control of the town, most Nazi anti-Semitic actions were aimed at members of the Nazi party who continued to maintain economic relations with Jews. Girmann threatened such persons with expulsion, but that was not made public.[3]

There had been occasional anti-Jewish utterances in speeches by Ernst Girmann, but the real campaign against the Jews opened on March 29, 1933, with an advertisement in the NNN, sponsored by Local Group Northeim of the NSDAP. It declared that "International Jewry" was spreading "atrocity propaganda" against Germany and "mishandling our German brothers in foreign lands." In response to this, declared the statement, the NSDAP was calling a boycott against all Jewish businesses: "Germany will force Judah to his knees!" Three days later a second advertisement appeared which gave a specific list of individuals and businesses to be boycotted. The advertisement, marked "Clip and Save," listed thirty-five firms representing forty individuals (in other words, almost all the adult male Jews in Northeim).[4]

The itemized appeal for a boycott was followed by action. Beginning on April 1, SA men were posted before the doors of Jewish stores or offices. This "counteraction against the Jewish hate propaganda" was, according to the statement issued by the NSDAP, to continue "until the hate campaign and boycott against German goods ceases."

The boycott was also backed by the County Agricultural Society, which urged farmers to "crown your fight for nationalism by dealing a blow to the Jews." To provide farmers with an alternative to dealing with Jewish cattle brokers, a Cattle Brokerage Society was incorporated under the auspices of the County Agricultural Society, the only organization to openly support the Nazi boycott in Northeim.[5]

After three days the boycott was halted, ending with a parade featuring placards against the Jews. According to the NB:

> Upon inducement by the local action committee, the following telegram was sent to German consuls and embassies in New York, Warsaw, Paris, and London: "All agitation and hate propaganda of the Jews in foreign areas about Germany untrue. Peace and quiet in Germany. Halt hate and agitation propaganda immediately. The Jewish Synagogue Community, Northeim. The Chairman.[6]

Whether this telegram was extorted from Jewish community leaders or simply invented by the NSDAP is unclear. What is clear is that the connection between the six-score Jews in Northeim and an international conspiracy to besmirch the name of the new Third Reich existed only in the paranoia of the town's Nazis. But the effect of the telegram was a perfect solution to the propaganda problem that had been created earlier. And in the interim the position of Northeim's Jews underwent a radical change.

The application of the boycott varied in its effectiveness. One of the firms listed in the advertisement was A. H. Müller's Banking House, a solid and well-respected establishment. There were no SA posts before its doors on April 1, 1933, and business went on as usual. In most other cases there were SA posts, but only for a few hours. No violence occurred. Some Northeimers were actually unaware of the action. But all Northeimers eventually came to know that Jews were now outcasts and that the Nazis were deadly serious about this aspect of their program.[7]

The effect of the boycott upon the Jews of Northeim was cataclysmic. Gregor Ballin and his wife could not at first believe that it would take place. But when they saw the two SA men posted before their door the full significance of it broke upon them. They did not dare to leave their home at all that day and Ballin himself sat crumpled up in his chair for hours repeating, "Was it for this that I spent four years defending my Fatherland?"[8]

The economic effect of the boycott extended beyond the formal period. While Banker Müller's business apparently did not suffer at all, Gregor Ballin's medical practice declined rapidly and his income fell from 9,000 marks in 1932 to 6,000 marks in 1933. This was probably true of most Jewish businesses; as people became more fearful, dealing with Jews became more of a luxury.

The problem of Jew-as-pariah in Northeim was not simply one of the Nazis' attempting to impose a system of persecution upon an inert mass. The Jews themselves exacerbated the situation by withdrawing into themselves while the other Northeimers, even if they might be opposed to the persecution of the Jews, abetted the system by their own efforts at self-protection. The day after the boycott began, a chain store with branches in Northeim placed a large advertisement in the NNN which announced that theirs was a "purely Christian family-enterprise" with no "outside capital" to mar their "Economic Independence—the Pride of Our Firm." Shortly after the boycott more stores blossomed forth with signs proclaiming "German Merchant." Once the principle was accepted it was a short step to the poster, "Jews not admitted." Early in May the cigar factory in Northeim announced that "a thorough examination by the NSDAP has conclusively shown that the firm is a purely German enterprise." Astute Northeimers could also have noted that after April 1 no advertisements appeared in the NNN by any Jewish firms.[9]

As for the Jews themselves, they reacted in various ways. Banker Müller, a man who belonged to the uppermost circles of Northeim's society, ignored the whole matter as much as possible. On the occasion of celebrations he ostentatiously hung an Imperial flag before the bank. He was happy to do this anyway since he was a nationalist, a monarchist, and had served as an officer in World War I. Müller greeted friends on the street in a courtly manner by tipping his hat, thus circumventing the "German greeting" (i.e., *"Heil Hitler"* plus the Nazi salute). To the solicitous advice that was given him to leave Northeim, he replied, "Where should I go? Here I am the Banker Müller;

elsewhere I would be the Jew Müller." Secure in his position as a member of Northeim's upper class, he was convinced that the trouble would soon pass. To avoid unpleasantness he quietly resigned from his shooting society and singing club, giving "the press of business" as his reason.[10]

Others were not so self-confident. Gregor Ballin withdrew from all social contact and crossed the street to avoid meeting erstwhile friends. His own sense of persecution intensified the growing feeling among Northeimers that it might be inexpedient to be seen talking to a Jew. Soon Ballin received letters from the Veterans' Club and the shooting society dropping him from membership "for nonattendance at meetings" (a kindly euphemism). The chairman and the secretary of the Men's Singing Society of 1850 came to see him personally; Ballin was entertainment chairman of the club and therefore not to be dealt with by a simple letter. They urged him to attend meetings and help them keep the club going in these difficult times. Ballin had developed new sensitivity, and reading their faces carefully he told them that unfortunately his practice kept him so busy that not only would he have to resign his position as entertainment chairman, he could not even be a member any longer. They expressed profound regrets and left. Most of Northeim's Jews probably reacted in this way.[11]

Some townspeople, especially the Socialists, went out of their way to talk to Jews or to buy in Jewish shops. But to counterbalance this there were SA men to mutter insults at Jews when they passed by street corners, and yet other SA men who bought heavily at Jewish stores, running up bills which they never paid, sometimes perhaps because the bills were never tendered.[12]

Thus the position of the Jews in Northeim was rapidly clarified, certainly by the end of the first half-year of Hitler's regime. Every speech given by a Nazi leader on the subject of the Jew as a Marxist-Capitalist international poisoner of the *Volk*, every newspaper item in the same vein, every new joke or rumor reinforced the situation. The new state of affairs became a fact of life; it was accepted.[13]

Northeim's Jews were simply excluded from the community at large. At the same time the Nazis undertook their most Herculean task: the atomization of the community at large. Though the methods differed, the result was the same, and by the summer of 1933 individual Northeimers were as cut off from effective intercourse with one another as the Jews had been from the rest of the townspeople. The total reorganization of society was the most important result of the Nazi revolution. Eventually no independent social groups were to exist. Wherever two or three were gathered, the *Fuehrer* would also be present. Ultimately all society, in terms of formal human relationships, would cease to exist, or rather would exist in a new framework whereby each individual related not to his fellow men but only to the state and to the Nazi leader who became the personal embodiment of the state.

The usefulness of a general shakeup of social organization for dictatorial control can well be imagined. In the first place it would mean that people could be more easily observed, since all clubs would be Nazi controlled. Secondly, with old social ties broken down there would be less opportunity for the spreading of discontent. Thirdly, by giving a Nazi cast to all organizations, the members would become involved in the general Nazi system.

Facilitating dictatorial control was not the only reason for Nazi reorganization of social units. There was also a tendency to simplify social organization and thus provide more "efficiency" and less diversity. On the one hand, for example, it was thought that by lumping together the various sports clubs, one could arrive at the best combination of athletes. On the other hand, an attempt was made to amalgamate all clubs that had the same function but were formed along class lines, since the new criteria were to be German citizenship and good Nazism, not the old traditions or class distinctions.

In the case of mass organizations such as sports clubs, fusion did not take place in order to maintain control over the societies, since they were already well infiltrated. But in the case of small class-oriented groups, fusion might be needed to end their exclusive nature so that Nazis could bring the groups under control. Thus one of the elements of the Nazi reorganization of society was a consistent attempt to subordinate and join together all communal endeavors that had roughly the same goals or subject interests.

Clubs that pursued a definite purpose (for example, a chess club) continued to exist, though their form and composition may have been altered. It was their objective purpose that kept them going, perhaps with "N.S." in front of their name (for example, "National Socialist Chess Club"), but in any event, still extant. Those clubs that were formed for reasons of pure social intercourse, or that had only an incidental objective purpose, either declined, ceased to exist, or were absorbed. This was partly because of the Nazi desire to keep people from coming together merely for social reasons where discussion prevailed. It was also a side effect of Nazi mass participation propaganda, since the enormous demands on people's time and energies made purely social functions increasingly difficult. And finally it was a consequence of the breakdown of interhuman trust under the impact of terror and rumor. Nazi insistence on politicalizing all organizations poisoned the hitherto lively clubs. As one Northeimer put it, "There was no more social life; you couldn't even have a bowling club." [14]

Most of this was accomplished in the first few months of the Nazi era.

Clubs were dissolved; others were fused together; others lost their purpose and went into rapid decline. All organizations came under Nazi control since they were required to have a majority of NSDAP members on their executive committees. This gigantic process was all lumped together under the general term "coordination" *(Gleichschaltung)*.

Originally, *Gleichschaltung* was a term meaning the reorganization of political representation in the federated states of the German Reich, so as to make them reflect the political representation in the Reichstag, i.e., have a Nazi-Nationalist majority. Hitler justified his decrees on *Gleichschaltung* by claiming that they would reproduce the new "national unity" in every governmental body. But most Northeimers thought that the *Gleichschaltung* decree also applied to social organizations.[15] Even the GGZ and NNN occasionally suggested this. Ernst Girmann reinforced this falsehood by sending "official" notices to clubs instructing them that the national *Gleichschaltung* law required them to have an executive committee with at least "51 percent NSDAP or Stahlhelm members."[16] Thus, measures taken to control social organizations were accepted by Northeimers as being thoroughly legal, in the formal sense at least. If an organization was ordered by the NSDAP to dissolve its present executive committee and elect a new one with a Nazi majority, the assumption was that this would be necessary to comply with the law. They might have discovered differently had they challenged the legality of the order. But no one did this in the first few months of the Nazi rule, and after that it was too late. Thus the enormous social reshuffle took place without overt resistance.

The variety and number of Northeim's clubs made this a mammoth task. The Nazis approached it without hesitation, however, and carried it through with vigor and dispatch. In some cases the process began as early as March 1933. *Gleichschaltung* was in full flood by April and May, with organizations falling under Nazi control almost every day. By late summer 1933, there were practically no independent social entities left, and the great upheaval was almost complete.

The most basic organizations in Northeim were the economic ones: the unions, the business and professional societies, and the guilds. Of these the unions were clearly the most significant, not only because of the number of people involved but also because of the unions' Socialist orientation. Since one of the basic Nazi concepts was the idea that workers should be weaned away from "Marxism," the NSDAP was determined to supplant the existing Free Unions.

The way in which Nazis in higher positions at the Northeim railroad yards broke up the railroad union during 1932 has been described earlier.

Thus even before Hitler came to power much of Northeim's working force was enrolled at least nominally in the Nazis' own union, the NSBO *(National Sozialistische Betriebszellen Organization)*. Among the white-collar employees a parallel development took place featuring a Nazi front organization: the Working Society of Nationalist Railroad Officials *(Arbeitsgemeinschaft nationaler Reichsbahnbeamter und Anwaerter, Bann Northeim)*. In the first few months of the Nazi era, full control was established over this organization, with the leaders emerging openly as Nazis.[17] Northeim's Nazis moved rapidly to organize the city employees, too. Concurrent with the Nazi takeover of the City Council and the beginning of the purge, the NSDAP set up a professional employees' group of the NSBO and enrolled a few dozen members in it. A month later the existing Society of City Civil Servants and Employees, Local Northeim, was "coordinated" and a Nazi executive board elected by order of the NSDAP. The Nazi unionization drive was successful in two other areas as well. One was the organization of the Highway Repairmen *(Chausee und Landstrassenwaerter)*. These were mainly rural people and hence already Nazified. All that remained was to organize them into a branch of the NSBO. This was completed in March and April, 1933. Finally, the Nazis were able to win a preponderance of the thirty-eight-man regular work force at the sugar factory. During the depression years considerable political pressure had been brought on the workers at the sugar refinery. Thus the works council election held there on April 3 brought twenty-eight votes for the NSBO and only ten for an "unpolitical list" that was clearly Free Union.[18]

Despite these small successes it was clear that the Nazis were not really progressing with their own union. How far economic pressure and persuasion might have brought the NSBO is hard to say, since national events soon resolved the problem altogether. On May 4, following the pattern that had been set all over Germany on the morrow of the May Day celebrations, units of the town's SA occupied the offices of the Free Unions in Northeim, confiscated the books and furnishings, and declared the unions "coordinated." A few weeks later the NSBO moved into the old union offices. It was still so weak, however, that it required the services of at least two former union secretaries in order to carry out essential duties. The NSBO also found it necessary to call mass meetings in order to condemn the old unions. The memory of freedom was harder to expunge than the fact. To supervise the entire working force a kind of super-pseudo-union, the German Workers' Front, was later created. In the early months of the Third Reich in Northeim it was essentially a paper organization.[19]

The unions having ceased to exist, one vital group of social organization was completely smashed. Some small matters were left to clear up. The Railroad Officials' group was incorporated into a general Nazi Civil Servants' and Officials' Association, apparently for the sake of organizational neatness. The "Railroaders' Club," which had general social functions, though it drew its members from that economic sector, was "coordinated" in July with a new all-Nazi executive committee.[20] Other working-class organizations collapsed with the SPD.

Simultaneously with the smashing of the unions and the building of new Nazi structures in their place, the NSDAP moved to gain full control over the Northeim artisan associations. The County Artisan League was already favorably disposed toward the NSDAP, since so many craft masters were Nazis. In February 1933, the annual election of officers for the League resulted in the election of a Nazi chairman and in resolutions praising the new Hitler government. The NSDAP was not wholly satisfied with this, and in April the County Artisans' League was required to hold a new election "on the basis of the Gleichschaltung Law," which resulted in an all-Nazi executive committee.[21]

The NSDAP also coordinated each of the individual guilds that made up the Artisans' League. A mass meeting was held in mid-April at which the various guild leaders were told by Ernst Girmann that they must have their new executive committees elected by May 2. This touched off furious activity, since each guild had to draft proposals, negotiate with the NSDAP, work out new compromises, and finally elect the new Nazi-dominated executive board. Questions of personality became as important as ideological ones. Furthermore, many of the guilds were convinced that once "coordination" took place their treasuries would be siphoned off to benefit the Nazis. Hence several guilds held mammoth parties for their members at which they drank and ate up the treasury funds. Some guilds were able to complete the Gleichschaltung process almost immediately. Others had to wait until the day of the deadline. But by the beginning of May there was not an artisan organization left in Northeim that was not Nazi-dominated.[22]

"Coordinating" the Retail Merchants' Association took a little longer, primarily because the existing organization was completely broken and a new, purely Nazi one created—something that went far beyond the customary Gleichschaltung. The new organization of retail merchants was founded on May 2, with Ernst Girmann's brother taking the leading role. Proposing to enroll every merchant in Northeim County, Karl Girmann declared at the organizational meeting:

Admission into the new League is voluntary, but it will be expected that every merchant in town and county Northeim who feels himself a German *Volk*-comrade will place himself without reservation at the disposal of the new association. This will make clear his determination to aid the reconstruction of the German economy.[23]

The process of persuasion proceeded apace, but not quickly enough to please the Nazis. By June they adopted more direct tactics and, in one stroke,[24] forced the old Retail Merchants' Association to incorporate itself and all its members into the new. "Coordination" was complete.

Other economic associations suffered the same fate in rapid order. On April 18 a "National Socialist Physicians' League" was founded, incorporating the prior league. A month later the "Reich Society of Dentists" became the "National Socialist Professional Dentists' Group." In April a "National Socialist Teachers' League" was created which all Northeim teachers eventually joined in order to keep their jobs.[25] By summer of 1933 the only "uncoordinated" economic organizations in Northeim were the cooperatives. These were distinctly Social Democratic enterprises and contributed considerably to the economy of the town. A good example was the "Common Good Construction Club." Its function was to build low-rent housing. In 1932 it did over 600,000 marks' worth of business, reduced its rents by 10 percent, increased its capital, declared a dividend of 5 percent, and increased its membership from 112 to 128.[26]

Under these circumstances no one could complain that the "Common Good Construction Club" was poorly run. But the difficulty was that its chairman and business manager was a leading Socialist. Hence when the club received the order to "coordinate" itself, it manipulated the election so that the Socialist was left in a position of power, but otherwise made protestations of loyalty to the new regime. The club was especially vulnerable, however, since the Nazis looked on all cooperatives as "bolshevistic." Thus the NSDAP was able to demand still more. On August 7 it was "coordinated" again, with Ernst Girmann himself installed as chairman and with the Social Democrat resigning from the club altogether. It had been his life work, but he was sensitive to the possibility of the other members losing their investments if the club were dissolved outright.[27]

An even more important economic entity was the Northeim Consumers' Cooperative, with over 1,200 members. In the years before 1933 the Nazis had consistently railed against this "red" organization, because it competed with the local merchants. But after they came to power the NSDAP was in a dilemma. To dissolve the cooperative altogether would have disrupted the economy of the town rather seriously and would have embittered an enormous number of people. But to "coordinate" the cooperative would have been interpreted as a guarantee of its future existence, and would have embittered the burghers. Hence the Nazis tried a number of approaches. First, they spread various evil rumors about the consumers' cooperative, in the hopes that these would cause it to decline. Secondly, they brought the organization under control by putting a Nazi commissar in as "supervisor." And finally they suggested to private businessmen that they would "take care of" the consumers' cooperative "when the time is ripe."[28]

In contrast to the thoroughness and ruthlessness with which the Nazis dealt with the town's economic organizations, they were very cautious about the numerous patriotic societies. They created only one new organization, a National Socialist War Victims' Association (NSKOV). The previous Reich League of War Victims dissolved itself in May and merged with the new Nazi organization, but the Kyffhaeuser War Victims was able to maintain its independence, though the parent body was "coordinated." Only two patriotic groups were forcibly dissolved, the "Greater German League" and the independent boys' clubs (Boy Scouts, *Freischar*, and *Jung deutsche Orden Youth*). The latter were incorporated into the Hitler Youth. Of all the other military and patriotic clubs only the Kyffhaeuser League was formally "coordinated." There were enough Nazis in the other groups to dominate them already, and presumably the NSDAP did not want to stir up needless trouble. Propaganda seemed sufficient for control. In time the slower but equally effective social atrophy resulting from fear and distrust would destroy the patriotic societies as independent entities.[29]

The same general approach was used toward the various special interest clubs—the choral groups, shooting societies, and so forth. Most of the singing societies dissolved themselves rather than be "coordinated." As a former member put it, "Nobody in our club had either time or inclination for it any more."[30] Before *Gleichschaltung*, Northeim's choral societies reflected the town's class structure. The workers' singing club was the Northeim *Volkschor*. It had been founded in 1905 as the *Handwerkergesangverein* but became dominated by workers in the 1920s. In the three years before Hitler came to power the *Volkschor* frequently sang at SPD functions. In April 1933 the club, in an attempt to cleanse itself of ideological connotations, severed its connections with the German Workers Singers' League and promised a "complete reorientation." This was not enough for the NSDAP, which demanded that the choral director and the executive committee resign. Since these were the leading figures in the club it chose to dissolve itself completely and did so on April 22, 1933.[31]

At the other end of the social scale was the town's high-class singing club, the "Song Stave." It survived by quickly and unobtrusively Nazifying itself. Henceforth when the members altered the composition of their executive committee, they were careful to notify Ernst Girmann and to ask him if he had any objections to the new leaders. This may be considered an example of "preemptive coordination." [32]

Shortly after this all the town's other singing clubs were lumped together in one organization called the "Mixed Choral Singing Club of 1933." By bringing together all those from the defunct organizations who were actually devoted to singing, a decent membership was obtained. The new club made a point of stressing that social position was unimportant in this new club; only singing ability counted. [33]

The shooting societies of Northeim did not suffer such a shock, though their character was also altered. At the combined annual meeting of May 15, 1933, the clubs worked hard to maintain themselves. Declarations of loyalty to Hitler and *"Sieg Heils!"* poured forth. Ernst Girmann was elected an honorary member and immediately named Chief Captain. In his acceptance speech Girmann stressed the fact that the shooting societies could no longer exist just for enjoyment. They must promote the military spirit. They must also abandon their exclusive nature. The clubs promptly responded by voting a special Adolf Hitler Shoot, open to the general public, at the forthcoming shooting festival. When the festival for 1933 took place it was renamed a *Volk* festival and every citizen was invited to attend. Special competition was arranged for the SA, SS, and *Stahlhelm,* and no admission was charged. There were as many swastika flags as there were old club banners, and the most frequent music heard was the "Horst Wessel Song." [34] In short, the shooting societies were simply redecorated.

The other special interest clubs of Northeim (Red Cross, Museum Society, etc.) were "coordinated" in the more formal sense with new Nazi executive boards. In most cases this took place at the regular annual meeting and with little prompting needed. In some cases the stimulus came from the national or parent organization rather than from the local NSDAP. The only club given special treatment was the Beautification Club, a society which built paths in Northeim's woods and in general tried to promote the town's park system. Since this club had considerable money, Girmann was interested in it. The members anticipated him and invested all the club's funds in a hunting cabin just outside the city limits, and then dissolved themselves. [35]

The biggest special interest clubs were the sport clubs. Here the Nazi emphasis was on fusion. The process began in May 1933, when the town's two biggest gymnastic societies merged with the football club "VfB." This created an eight-hundred-man *Turn und Sport Verband.* At the same time the other football club *(Spiel und Sport)* strengthened itself by absorbing the Northeimer Swimming Club. The next step came in July when *Spiel und Sport* and *Turn und Sport* were merged to form one gigantic Northeimer *Sportclub* under the leadership of Hermann Denzler. Both clubs complained bitterly about this and, in an attempt to retain independence, accused each other of past political sins. But it was to no avail. The merger was forced upon them by Denzler, with Girmann's backing.[36]

Thus by July all the hitherto independent sports clubs had been fused into one. The new super-club was justified by the Nazis on the grounds that it would end "senseless competition" and provide the strongest sports club in the district. But it was also to be Nazi-oriented. Organization in the club was modeled after the NSDAP's "block" system and its chief stress was to be on military sport. The fusion was not well-liked by the component units. Despite Nazi efforts, membership in the club fell off by over 50 percent. After the end of World War II the old clubs reconstituted themselves independently and happily resumed their "senseless competition."[37]

Nazi efforts at social hegemony did not stop with the customary associations: economic, patriotic, special interest. The NSDAP also desired a dominant voice in religious and purely cultural matters. Nazi interest in religion predated the Third Reich. During the years before Hitler came to power one of the strongest appeals the Nazis had made in the town was through the Lutheran church, and their favorite speakers were Lutheran ministers. The Lutheran church in Northeim played a major role in Nazi celebrations during the first six months of Hitler's regime, and the town's pastors frequently urged Northeimers to pray for Hitler. For its part, the NSDAP promoted religion as an aspect of the struggle against the "religionless November-State" (i.e., the Weimar Republic). In contrast to the Socialist position ("religion is a private matter"), the Nazis proclaimed, "Religion is a matter for the *Volk!"* That this could cut both ways was not yet seen by Northeim's Lutheran pastors, nor were they as yet uneasy about such peculiar things as the application of Romans 11:36 to Hitler's role in the Nazi Revolution or the statement, "God is the Sun."[38]

Thus Northeimers were not shocked when the NSDAP began a campaign to "revitalize the church." As one letter to the GGZ put it: "The National Revolution in which we are now involved signifies a complete change of our German *Volk* in all areas of life. It is not surprising, therefore, that even church life is being drawn into the stream of this powerful movement."[39] The campaign took the form of an attempt to get Lutherans to join the "German Christian Movement." This was described as a nonpolitical movement led by religious men who were only incidentally Nazis and who were interested solely in unifying and regenerating Protestantism. The movement in Northeim was endorsed by a variety of active Lutherans, including both pastors of the church.

But this campaign on behalf of the "German Christians" was by no means a spontaneous local effort. Directives had come down to *Gau* South Hanover-Brunswick from the national Nazi headquarters and the *Gau*, in turn, had ordered its Local Groups to nominate and vote for Nazis in the church elections. Munich also provided, through the party's national propaganda office, complete guidelines on how to conduct the campaign, including instructions for speakers' themes. In short, this was a nationally coordinated Nazi effort.[40]

To push the campaign the customary Nazi publicity methods were used. In June, Pastor Jakobshagen, who had formerly been such a popular Nazi speaker, was brought in for a mass meeting at the *1910er Zelt*. About five hundred people were present, of whom about a hundred joined the movement immediately. A second meeting, held a month later, drew a very small attendance. In July 1933, elections were held for the Church Elders. In Northeim the German Christian Movement presented a slate of candidates. All were Nazis. The nominations were endorsed by the Evangelical Men's Club and the Evangelical Women's Club. Since these were the only nominations, the candidates were elected automatically, without a vote. Similar results were obtained in churches over the whole district.[41]

The men who backed the German Christian Movement were apparently sincere in their belief that it would aid Protestantism. In later years when the NSDAP became seriously antireligious, the same men were in the forefront of the struggle against Nazism and formed a courageous resistance. But by their blindness in the early months of the Third Reich they gave an enormous boost to Nazism.[42]

The only Lutheran organization to suffer during the first half-year of Nazi control was the "Friends of Evangelical Freedom," which dissolved itself in mid-May, possibly under threat of *Gleichschaltung*.[43]

The smooth relations between the Nazis and Northeim's Lutheran church were not paralleled by the party's relationship with the town's Catholic Church. The pastor was a firm advocate of the Center party and drew Nazi fire on that score. In March 1933, editorials were written against him on two occasions because he urged his parishioners to vote *Zentrum*. The situation was exacerbated in July 1933 when the Catholic Young Men's Society was dissolved and its property and flags were seized by the SA. Other Catholic clubs were not disturbed, but the NSDAP could still count on the enmity of the Catholic priest. Since only about 6 percent of the townspeople were Catholics, this was a negligible factor.[44]

In the schools, Northeim's teachers were drawn into a Nazi Teachers' Association. To make doubly sure, all other Teachers' Associations were "coordinated" in April 1933.[45] Full control over teachers would come only in time. To Nazi eyes, even more important than the teachers was control over the children. For this the Hitler Youth was the prime instrument. The chief weapon of the Hitler Youth was control over the school administration. This was manifest very early. In cases where both the Hitler Youth and the schools wanted to hold a celebration, the schools gave way. When questions of discipline arose, Hitler Youth members could not be punished. Even in academic matters the Hitler Youth reigned supreme. The principal of the *Gymnasium* was directly ordered by Ernst Girmann to advance any pupils who might have "suffered" academically because of membership in the Hitler Youth before the Nazi seizure of power. Girmann specified individual Hitler Youth students who were to be given preferential treatment in academic matters, including presumably higher grades for courses taken earlier. Nothing could have usurped the position of teachers more plainly. In all these matters school authorities acquiesced, for fear of losing their jobs. By the end of the first six months of the Third Reich it was questionable as to who was running the schools—the teachers or the Hitler Youth.[46]

The Hitler Youth was also aided by the dissolution of competing youth groups. By the end of the summer of 1933 it was the only existing youth group in Northeim.

The town's public library was also "coordinated." By mid-May over five hundred books were burned (one-quarter of the total number). This "un-German, foreign-to-the-*Volk*, and worthless literary trash" was replaced by a select list of books, beginning with *Mein Kampf*. The Free Unions' Lending Library was closed when the unions were forcibly dissolved in early May.[47]

One final cultural entity that was "coordinated" (after a fashion) was the City Band. For a monthly subsidy the City Band gave a concert every week on the Market Square. Since the subsidy was not enough, the individual bandsmen also played at dances and on other occasions. During the years before Hitler came to power the band frequently rented itself to the SPD for its parades and meetings. By these means the band clearly became tainted with "bolshevism" and therefore had to go. Furthermore, if the City Band were eliminated, the SA band would have a clear field. Early in March 1933 the City Band tried to adapt itself to the new order. Instead of the customary "Weekly Concert," a "Patriotic Weekly Concert" was given. But this did not suffice. The new City Council had hardly been elected before it cut off the band's subsidy. This upset the conservatives, who had gotten used to the weekly concerts. Furthermore, the Nationalists clearly felt that with a band of their own they could compete with the Nazis more successfully. Money was therefore quickly forthcoming and the City Band became the *Stahlhelm* Band. But since the *Stahlhelm* was not too active there was little for the band to do. Hence, every week, the *Stahlhelm* Band gave a concert on the Market Square. Things were back to normal. In this at least the Nazi revolution was unsuccessful.[48]

This rapid survey of Nazi inroads on the cultural and social life of the town has not included the organizations connected with the SPD. There were many, and all were dissolved. Some, like the Workers' First Aid Society, simply ceased to exist. Others with a more tenuous connection, such as the League for the Protection of Mothers, collapsed only when their offices were raided and property confiscated.[49] But the great and complicated group of sub-organizations connected with the Social Democratic party and the Free Unions were all destroyed. This put an end to all organized social life among the workers of Northeim.

Thus by the summer of 1933, the Nazis had either broken up, altered, fused, or brought under control most of the clubs and societies of Northeim. The complex and diversified social organization of the town had been almost completely uprooted. In most cases the Nazis tried to fill the vacuum, but often people simply stopped coming together. Either there was no more club, or the attractiveness of the club had been destroyed by *Gleichschaltung,* or people no longer had the leisure or the desire to continue with their club. What social life there was continued in the most basic groupings: the *Stammtisch,* the beer-and-cards evenings, or small social gatherings in homes.

Even these were threatened as people began to distrust one another. What was the value of getting together with others to talk if you had to be careful about what you said? Thus to a great extent the individual was atomized. By the process of *Gleichschaltung* individuals had a choice: solitude or mass relationship via some Nazi organization. None of the Nazi measures in the first six months of the Third Reich had a greater ultimate effect than *Gleichschaltung.* By it the externals of the rigid class structure were destroyed, and Northeimers were molded into the kind of unorganized mass that dictators like so well.

THE POSITIVE ASPECT

SPRING-SUMMER 1933

Everyone will surely have noticed that from now on a new wind will be blowing.

Heinrich Voge,
Nazi speaker of the City Council,
March 28, 1933

Of the factors responsible for the rise of Nazism in Northeim, none was as important as the depression. The fear it engendered made Northeimers amenable to radicalism in the first place. It was the Nazi claim that they had diagnosed the cause of economic difficulties (the Treaty of Versailles and the political leadership of the Weimar Republic) and could provide the cure (Nazi leadership) that made many Northeimers vote for the party of Adolf Hitler. Hence the Nazis knew that they must succeed on the economic front if they wanted to win solid allegiance.

Since the problem of the depression in Northeim was more psychological than economic in nature, the Nazis set out to provide an appropriate solution. A short-term solution could be quickly supplied—remove the outward sign of the depression by eliminating large-scale unemployment. It was also necessary to give Northeimers the feeling that the wheel of progress had begun to rotate again, that under vigorous leadership the town was beginning to move forward. These things the Nazis did. It was their only solid achievement.

The most visible sign of the depression was unemployment. The method of dealing with the unemployed had already been developed by the SPD faction in the City Council long before Hitler came to power: public works projects. A limited number of such projects had been carried out during the initial years of the depression, and in January 1933 the town had been allocated additional funds by the central government. What the Nazis brought to public works projects was the concept of applying them so as to eliminate *all* unemployment in the town. They were able to do this because the money previously allocated by the central government became available just at the time the NSDAP came to power and because the Hitler government rushed through new funds for public works.

In January 1933 the town had received 60,000 marks from the central government and had made plans to expend it on street repairs. By March the government gave its approval to a loan of 300,000 marks for Northeim County. In April, Northeim received an additional 100,000 marks from the government for public works. This money helped the town in many ways. First, it enabled the town to put the unemployed to work. By removing unemployed persons from the welfare rolls, this increased the amount of money Northeim itself could plough into works projects; it freed almost 4,000 marks a week from the town's treasury. Finally, by the multiplier effect, it increased the general spending in the town to the benefit of Northeimer's merchants.

But most important of all, it gave the new Nazi administration ample funds to carry out a crash public works program.[1]

At the end of January 1933, Northeim had 653 registered unemployed, of whom almost 400 were on the welfare rolls. It was estimated that there were an additional 100 "invisible" unemployed, bringing the grand total to 750 jobless persons. Despite the Nazi desire to put all these people to work, little progress was made throughout the spring of 1933. By June 30, 1933, there were still 506 registered unemployed in the town. The decrease was due almost solely to the customary seasonal upsurge in work.

In July, however, the great campaign began. Some 450 persons were put to work on a great variety of jobs. Roads were repaired, the town's forests were neatened up, and the old moat around the inner town was drained and converted into a ring of swan ponds and parks. New groups of unemployed were set to work almost daily. By July 24, Ernst Girmann was able to call a press conference and make public the news that all unemployed persons previously on the welfare rolls were at work. The only people receiving welfare payments on that date in Northeim were widows, old folks, and cripples. On the same date County Prefect von der Schulenberg announced that since March 1933, some 900 of the county's welfare unemployed had been put to work and that County Northeim too was free of welfare unemployed.[2]

This was astounding news, but more was yet to come. Throughout August the same effort was continued. By the end of the month every person in the town who had been registered as unemployed was at work. In the last few days of August over 130 people were drawn into the works projects. Even unemployed women were put to work planting flowers and pruning shrubs. What Northeimers could hardly believe possible had come to pass. There was not a single registered unemployed person in the town.[3]

The methods used by the Nazis in accomplishing this goal were similar to those used in their other actions. In the first place, preference in the works projects was given to Nazi party members, especially those with low membership numbers—the so-called "old fighters." Even private businessmen, if they were party members, were vehemently ordered by Ernst Girmann to hire Nazis first, and certainly not to hire any "reds."[4] Secondly, many jobs were opened through the purge of the Socialists and the arrests of the Communists. Those affected were either arbitrarily denied status as "unemployed," put to work at forced labor in the stone quarry, or taken to a concentration camp. In any case they were no longer listed as unemployed. Thirdly, many of the unemployed persons were actually forced to go to work.

All unemployed persons, regardless of their previous occupation, were put into what was, after all, hard manual labor. Some insisted that they be given work commensurate with their ability and experience, but the Nazi alternative was work on the works projects or no more dole. With much protesting, many of the previously unemployed persons climbed into the labor crew trucks each morning to be driven out to do road repairing.[5]

Nevertheless, many workers were pleased to be gainfully employed again, and Northeim's middle class was enormously impressed by the Nazi success on this level. Nor were the workers the only ones who benefited economically in the first months of the Third Reich. The artisans were also aided, primarily through a program of subsidies for household repairs. In the spring of 1933, the Reich granted 21,000 marks to Northeim for this purpose, especially to help refurbish apartments so as to ease the housing shortage. Furthermore, the Reich granted another 20,000 marks for subsidies to people who wished to divide large apartments into smaller units. The city led the way by repairing all the buildings it owned. At the same time, encouragement was given to new construction so that seven new dwelling houses were erected in 1933. Since construction and repair work had generally lagged during the depression, these programs and their vigorous administration were very welcome to electricians, carpenters, and painters. If the Nazi report can be believed, they were "swamped with work."[6]

Finally, the Nazis did all they could by way of propaganda and political pressure to end the depression spirit. Girmann was tireless in urging businessmen to expand and spend money. A "Book of Honor" was set up in the county building and the names of all employers who hired a previously unemployed person were inscribed.[7] In short, all that could be attempted in the economic sector was tackled with determination and vigor.

One measure that the Nazis pushed in the course of fighting the depression was later to become a permanent institution of the Third Reich. This was the Labor Service. Like the works' projects and the household repairs subsidies, it began before Hitler came to power but was pushed with greater vigor once the NSDAP assumed direction. Originally it was a "Voluntary Labor Service" with enlistment. The NSDAP set up the organization in Northeim in February 1933. Its goals were described as noneconomic in nature. The purpose was to enroll young people in order to "1) unite them with the Volk-community, 2) reinstitute their connection with the soil, and 3) reawaken a healthy military spirit." Nevertheless, the Labor Service did get young jobless men off street corners and the labor market, and it also carried out various conservation projects. By late April some 65 young Northeimers had enlisted. Most of them were housed in the old Army barracks. This necessitated expelling some of the "shelterless" who lived there. To provide housing for the displaced, the city offered to guarantee rent payments and to subsidize any alterations necessary to create new apartments. Eventually Girmann hoped to have 250 Labor Service men in the old barracks which, he pointed out, meant 250 new consumers in the town.[8]

In addition to its economic functions and its usefulness in indoctrinating youth, the Labor Service also aided in general propaganda work. It organized frequent parades through Northeim with a swastika flag in the forefront, and even gave a concert of classical music in the city park one summer Sunday.[9] All told, most Northeimers must have looked upon the Labor Service as a very good thing.

Despite their considerable efforts to end unemployment, the Nazis did not forget to push charity during their first few months in office. Some of this was purely for propaganda purposes, for example the special extra payment to welfare cases made on March 30 "in spite of the hard times, to show the social direction of the new government." Again, on Hitler's birthday, a special party with coffee and cakes was given for the unemployed. Charity collections for the Nazi "Winter Aid" brought in considerable amounts, and the SA soup kitchen reported that it had disbursed over 32,000 meals in the winter of 1932–33.[10]

During the first six months of the Third Reich, Northeim's Nazis attacked the town's economic problems with the same vigor and thoroughness with which they dealt with other problems. There is no gainsaying their effectiveness and success in this area. While they did not provide new ideas, they made the most of existing ones. By temporarily abolishing unemployment and increasing the disposable income in Northeim, the Nazis by no means ended the depression; in fact, they had to fight the battle of unemployment all over again in 1934. But there could be no doubt in the minds of most Northeimers that the Nazis were determined to master the depression. And to many Northeimers, appearance was more important than reality with respect to the economic crisis. In short, the NSDAP in Northeim did what it had promised to do in the economy; it exorcised the specter of the depression.

REACTION
AND
RESISTANCE

SPRING-
SUMMER
1933

The true supporters of government are the weak and the uninformed and not the wise.

William Godwin,
Enquiry Concerning Political Justice, and Its Influence on Morals and Happiness

In the first half year of the Nazi regime, Northeim underwent a revolution. Its main components were terror, dictatorial control, unremitting propaganda, the reconstruction of social life, and economic revitalization. Its total effect was to alter the basic structure of the town in an amazingly short period. Though six months may seem a long time, to Northeimers it must have appeared that everything happened at once, for all the elements of the revolution that have been compartmentalized here for analysis, were in actuality intermingled in a chaotic jumble. One day there were arrests and the next day a big, cheering parade. Here the city employees were purged and there the Labor Service team marched to work with shovels on their shoulders. First the singing club of ancient standing ceased to exist and then came the brassy SA band. Flashes of black-white-red flags, book burnings, blaring radio speeches, school children with swastikas, booted Stormtroopers dragging a man to jail, torchlight parades with voices singing hoarse songs, the pastor blessing the *Fuehrer,* rumors of the Gestapo, hammers pounding house repairs, rhythmic volleys of *"Sieg Heil!"*—all melded in a whirling kaleidoscope, and by the end of the summer of 1933 the town was so firmly in the grip of the Nazis that there was no possibility of reversing the process.

The majority of Northeim's adults voted for this. But in the years before the NSDAP came to power it was all things to all men. Thus most Northeimers had hardly any clear ideas of what the Nazis would really do, except change things for the better somehow. It is certain that only a few members of the NSDAP itself and some of the town's Social Democrats really expected what they got. Thus a question of considerable interest is: How did the townspeople react to the introduction of the Nazi dictatorship?

There were, of course, as one would expect in almost any society, those who simply used the Nazi revolution for their own profit. Immediately after Hitler came to power one of the town's taverns installed a radio and then advertised that all speeches of Adolf Hitler could be heard there, and that the price of beer was cheap. All through March and April there were daily advertisements in the NNN offering swastika flags for sale. The City Bank urged Northeimers to aid the great revolution by putting their money in a savings account. Even Ernst Girmann's brother was not above advertising his hardware store by proclaiming "Oldest Party Member in County Northeim." [1]

Many people also felt the need to protect themselves by joining the NSDAP. In several cases club leaders or artisan masters joined so that they could stay on executive committees. Others wanted job insurance. Mayor

Peters tried to join and so did Paul Hahnwald, publisher of the NNN—neither was pro-Nazi but each had something to protect.[2] Still others joined in response to the growth of terror.[3] A bureaucratic cause for the sudden influx of members was that Girmann began insisting, in early March, that every Stormtrooper must also become a party member ("as required by insurance regulations," he said).[4] The great rush to join the NSDAP began in February, immediately after the announcement that Hitler had been named chancellor. People who had been wavering or who had held back for fear of compromising themselves now submitted applications. In January 1933 there were only about a hundred dues-paying Nazis in Northeim. By March the Nazi Local Group swelled to almost four hundred. By mid-March there began a veritable flood of membership. This great climbing-on-the-bandwagon of March 1933 became so pronounced that old Nazis referred to the newcomers as the *Maerzgefallene*—with the sardonic double meaning of the "March favors" and "March casualties."

The NSDAP had so many applicants that it was forced to declare that it would accept no new applications after May 1, so that the existing backlog could be cleared up. This, of course, produced a still greater rush in April. Von der Schulenberg remembered seeing bushel baskets full of applications in the Nazi county headquarters on April 20. By May 1 close to 1,200 Northeimers had joined the Nazi party. Almost 20 percent of the town's adults had been enrolled.[5]

Not all of these new members joined as a result of commitment to Nazi ideas. One of the Nazi methods of bringing institutions under control was to require their leaders to become members of the NSDAP. This was the case with County Prefect von der Schulenberg and also with the NNN's reporter, Erhardt Knorpel. Both were exceedingly skeptical about Nazism and both joined because it was demanded of them. Others joined because they saw membership in the NSDAP as an indispensable prerequisite for personal advancement. This was admittedly the case with two teachers who confidently expected that by joining the Nazi party they would insure themselves a promotion.[6] Still others joined out of a pure desire to conform, i.e., to go along with the majority, as illustrated by the following story:

> Hugo Spiessmann was a curious case. Until the March Reichstag elections he was in an agony of indecision. I remember him frequently asking me for advice: Should he or should he not join the party? I always told him to do whatever he wanted, but this didn't seem to help. But the day after the Nazi electoral success the SA gave a victory parade which I witnessed. At the very end of the

parade was Hugo Spiessmann with a happy smile on his face. As he marched by he waved to me and yelled, "I've done it!"[7]

Many men were forced to join by the pressure put on them at home. As one man described it: "There were wives whose constant words were 'Think of your family!' There were wives who actually went out and bought a brown shirt and put their men into it."[8] Others claimed that they had wanted to join the Nazi party for a long time but were previously prevented from doing so by conflicting commitments: "I am free" wrote the owner of the Hotel Sonne to Ernst Girmann, on requesting an application.[9] Many such applications for party membership were actually rejected by the Local Group Leader, with the applicant being told that he was too lukewarm, or an obvious opportunist, or had previously opposed the Nazis, or just that Girmann was personally against admitting him.[10] Others joined the NSDAP at this time not because they approved of it, but because they disapproved and therefore thought that what Nazism needed was a leaven of decent people who would work from within to steer the revolution into moderate paths.[11]

Thus, at the very least, the level of commitment varied considerably among the new members. But once they had joined the NSDAP these people were trapped. They were now under party discipline and had to aid in the whole process. The organization of the party (in cells and blocks down to the smallest unit) kept them under constant surveillance. Instead of insuring their future, they became even more insecure, for if they were ever expelled from the NSDAP they would be marked men. And many were expelled that spring: for nonpayment of dues, for being impolite to the party "Block Warden," and for wholly unexplained reasons.[12] Whatever the reason, it usually spelled bad trouble for the individual for a long time to come. As will shortly be noted, Girmann had a long memory when it came to hounding those who had been found unworthy. Thus the "March casualties" discovered that joining the party heightened rather than diminished personal anxieties. They were not likely to resist the demands of the Nazi state. Furthermore, their consciences were hopelessly compromised, for as members they partook of responsibility in the most immediate sense.

But if many of the townspeople who joined the NSDAP were still dubious, there were also many Northeimers who never joined but were ardent supporters of the new regime. In general the burghers were enthusiastic over the parades and ceremonies and delighted by the economic action. The feeling seemed to be that an end had come to internal division and that real leadership would now be forthcoming. As one craft master put it:

I don't agree with everything that's been done, but I'm glad to see them trying things. The main thing is that people get work again and that they somehow learn to recognize a purpose and content in life again.[13]

Many of the concepts and slogans of the Nazi revolution appealed to Northeimers. In a nationalistic era the idea of national honor and revivification was exceedingly attractive. The vigorous, purposeful, and apparently immaculate direction of city government appealed to the civic-minded. Finally, there was fascination in the concept of the *Volk*-community, which despite its mystic connotations meant an end to class divisions.[14] The middle class was especially drawn to the idea that classes should cease to exist and that there should be only Germans. This may seem incredible in view of the burghers' repugnance for "Marxism," but it was the source and reason for ending a class war that was as important as the concept itself. Socialist efforts at social equality were examples of upstart leveling. The Nazi appeal was patriotic and charitable. While the SPD threatened, the NSDAP evoked *noblesse oblige* and was concerned with appearance rather than reality. This suited perfectly the emotional needs of Northeimers who were upset by the existing class structure; they were virtuously uplifted by the hope of creating a *Volk*-community, without actually sacrificing their own class status.

Naturally there were many aspects of the revolution that Northeimers were dubious about. Some, especially the conservatives, simply could not accept the Nazis because of their low class. As Maria Habenichts' husband put it, "How can a mere corporal lead the Reich?"[15] Others were disturbed by the arrests, the smashing of opposition, the destruction of social life, and especially the violence of the new anti-Semitism. But there were ways of rationalizing.

Was the SPD smashed and were the unions dissolved by force? They were upstart troublemakers and had it coming.

Were there arrests and house searches? Look at all the weapons that were found! The Marxists were clearly plotting violence, in accordance with their record.

Was all opposition stifled and the NSDAP made the sole legal party? The main trouble with Germany had been the senseless political strife and splinter parties. Anyone who wanted representation could join the NSDAP.

Were the clubs "coordinated"? This promoted national unity and economic revival. Germany must end internal division and pull together for once.

Were the Jews boycotted and outcast? This was an unfortunate but temporary excess similar to those which accompany any revolution. Besides, there were so few of them.

In short, there are two sides to every question: one should not make hasty judgments; give them a chance to prove themselves; you cannot make an omelette without breaking eggs; there is always some bad mixed in with the good. After all, in six short months the town had been unified, the economic problems were being dealt with, and nothing was more convincing than the shining faces of the Stormtroopers outlined by all the torches and silhouetted against the flags. The Nazi party was providing decisive leadership and was monolithic, dedicated, selfless, and purposeful.

In reality, however, Northeim's Nazi Group was rotten and festering within. The first and, during the initial period, the only resistance to the NSDAP came from within the ranks of the Nazis themselves. The leaders of the revolt were the old Nazis, particularly those gathered around Wilhelm Spannaus. Most of them were intellectuals; they included Heinrich Voge, the first teacher in Northeim to become a Nazi, and Dr. Edmund Venzlaff, the director of the Northeim Girls' *Lyzeum*. Ostensibly they were rebelling against the leadership of Ernst Girmann, but in actuality they were opposed to the violence, corruption, and dictatorial methods which they naively believed to be contrary to the true principles of National Socialism.

The Spannaus-Voge-Venzlaff "Idealists' Conspiracy" was long in brewing. Already in 1932 several Northeim Nazis grew restive under Ernst Girmann's leadership. The prime complaints against him were that he was rude and inconsiderate toward party members and that he protected the leader of the Northeim Nazi Women's Group, who apparently had misused party money (in one case to buy herself stockings). Girmann's rudeness kept many Northeimers from joining the party in the last year before Hitler came to power.[16]

Throughout 1932 the idealist group grew more and more dissatisfied. At the same time, Girmann proceeded to build up his own following, consisting mainly of rough and violent personalities such as Hermann Denzler and August Ude. Two separate Nazi groups were developing in Northeim, but of the two, Girmann's held the upper hand since Ernst Girmann himself was Local Group Leader and could maintain himself by appeals to the authoritarian discipline of the NSDAP.

In December 1932 the first storm broke. Several of the idealist group demanded an audit of the Local Group's finances. Girmann apparently had misused much of the party's funds. Whether they went into his own pocket or were simply lost through slovenliness is not clear. But donations had been taken and not entered in the books, entrance fees pocketed and the applications lost, and considerable unexplained debts had piled up.[17] At first, Girmann was conciliatory. He needed the idealist group because they were an important source of income through contributions. In January 1933 the idealists threatened to cut off contributions if explanations for the financial irregularities were not forthcoming. Girmann was forced to act. Using his position and combining bluster with lies, he expelled several of the idealists and at the same time, as a concession, withdrew his protection from the Women's Group Leader and expelled her, too. Girmann also took precautions against any possible future challenges: he purged the party's disciplinary committee, the Uschla, of its independent-minded chairman, August Schierloh, and packed it with people favorable to himself. That way he would have a reliable instrument for any further expulsions he might decide on.[18]

None of this mended the rift, however, and the Northeim Nazi Group was in danger of schism when the news of Adolf Hitler's appointment as chancellor of the Reich swept aside all internal squabblings and united the Nazis for the important work of February and March. During this time Girmann was able to strengthen his position substantially. Out of a spirit of enthusiasm the idealists came forward with new campaign contributions. The rush of Northeimers to join the NSDAP made it possible for Girmann to demand that new applicants pay increasingly higher entrance fees.[19] His financial problems were rapidly resolving themselves. At the same time, Girmann used his position as Group Leader to dispense patronage en masse in the form of jobs with the city, replacing those fired in the great purge of city employees. Other favors included his appeal to the Ministry of Justice to get a would-be lawyer admitted to the bar without examination (on the grounds that the applicant had previously been rejected because the examining board was prejudiced against Nazis), and his intervention to raise the grades of Hitler Youth high school pupils.[20] A great number of Nazis were becoming dependent on Ernst Girmann and still more were becoming afraid of him. Using his position, he turned the City Council into a supine instrument and packed the Senate. Protests were quelled by threats.

In February and March, Girmann also tried to mend fences with the dissidents. As a conciliatory gesture he rescinded some of the blocked applications and expulsions of persons who "agitated behind my back and tried to remove me." As he told the national registry office of the NSDAP, the dissidents had capitulated and their "grave offenses against party discipline" were really all fomented by the wife of one particular member. Others, such as the teacher Heinrich Voge, had risked their jobs to promote Nazism when that was prohibited. Besides, Voge had served in the army with Girmann during World War I. The time had come to exercise mercy.[21]

But dissidence was only dormant. In April the financial issue resurfaced. To settle the last of the debts Girmann arbitrarily raised membership dues and levied a special assessment on all members.[22] At the same time the idealists became aware of other matters. Girmann was exploiting his position as deputy mayor to distribute city contracts among relatives and friends. The NB was forcing people to subscribe by threatening them. "Contributions" were being extorted from merchants.[23] The dictatorial methods in City Hall were increasingly galling. And, worst of all to the idealists, the Nazi revolution was not producing that hoped-for utopian *Volk*-community, but rather a corrupt and brutal one-man rule. The idealist opposition began to rise again.

It exploded at the end of April in an incident where Ernst Girmann was publically accused of lying by one of the elder party members, August Döring. The response of the Local Group Leader was to assault the sixty-year-old Döring physically, whereon the latter called Girmann "a miserable brat." Girmann then demanded that his carefully reconstructed local *Uschla* expel Döring for publicly insulting the Local Group Leader and injuring the party's image and discipline.[24]

The whole incident enraged the party insurgents. In May the conflict became general, and by June, Girmann had launched a wholesale purge. *Uschla* proceedings were inaugurated against Voge, Venzlaff, Spannaus, and the erstwhile (uncooperative) head of the local *Uschla*, Heinrich Schierloh. All were expelled from the party.[25] The *Gauleiter* was informed that an antiparty conspiracy had been discovered in Northeim. The City Council was made to pass resolutions: it petitioned the provincial school authorities to transfer Venzlaff away from Northeim; the town's Senate was asked to institute a boycott against Wilhelm Spannaus's bookstore; the regional governmental authorities were informed that Voge had been removed from his position as speaker of the City Council.[26]

Wilhelm Spannaus was alert to what might happen. At almost the same moment that Girmann moved to squelch the conspiracy, Spannaus appealed to the *Gauleiter* for a complete investigation by the *Gau Uschla*. Spannaus was convinced that the *Gau* authorities would examine his charges closely since he had one of the lowest party-card numbers in the whole district. He was also certain that once the higher offices of the NSDAP discovered what was going on in Northeim, they would remove Girmann and "restore true National Socialism" to the town.

The higher officers of the NSDAP, however, knew what Spannaus did not know—that Ernst Girmann was just the kind of man they wanted. Just as Girmann could trust his tools in Northeim completely, so the *Gauleiter* could trust Girmann. The system of satrapies by which Nazi Germany would operate during the whole period of the Third Reich was being solidified. The only "true" National Socialism was the rule of men like Girmann. Anything else existed only in the minds of idealists like Spannaus and would never be compatible with the methods by which Nazism had established itself.

The *Gau Uschla* proceedings against Spannaus and Venzlaff, instituted at their request, were held in Northeim in the early days of July 1933. The defendants were exonerated and all reinstated as members. In other words, the charges made against Girmann were verified. But since these charges had concerned violations of both public and Nazi party law, Girmann should have been stripped of his office. Instead he was simply reprimanded verbally and allowed to continue his old ways. This convinced Wilhelm Spannaus that his hopes for a cleanup were wishful thinking. He remained a member of the NSDAP, because he still clung to the idea that the *Fuehrer* himself would take action some day. Voge was eventually transferred out of Northeim, though without loss of position. Spannaus continued to gather malcontents about him and to amass evidence against the Local Group Leader. But he was considerably more cautious, and his friends had learned a lesson.[27]

The lesson was firmly reinforced by Ernst Girmann's subsequent actions, for he conducted a vendetta against the party insurgents for years to come. He repeatedly called for investigations and trials of Schierloh and Döring. He made life in Northeim insupportable for Venzlaff, which was easy to do since Venzlaff was principal of a city school and lived in a city-owned house. When Venzlaff ultimately sought a position elsewhere, Girmann arranged to blacken his name with the Nazi officials of the other city and thus prevented him from getting the job. The point was thus driven home that anyone who defied the Local Group Leader, no matter what the justification, would rue it for a long time.[28]

These matters were shielded from the general public in Northeim. People heard rumors, but the struggle went on behind closed doors, within a relatively limited circle. Thus Northeimers could continue to believe that the NSDAP was monolithic and dedicated. And to many Northeimers the presence of Wilhelm Spannaus and his friends in the NSDAP was still reassurance that there was another side to Nazism and that once the "initial excesses" were over, the party would settle down to constructive, fruitful labor. Once again, as in the days before its acquisition of power, the NSDAP would be all things to all men.

What Northeimers believed about the NSDAP in the late summer of 1933 was fairly irrelevant anyway. For by the end of their first six months in office the Nazis had a stranglehold on the town. The city administration and the police were under the Nazis' thumb. Potential resistance had been smashed. Centers of social intercourse were dispersed or vitiated. The public was organized into a periodic cheering section. Numerous examples of terror had been provided and were spread by social reinforcement. The town had become the obedient instrument of the new dictatorship. The essential work of the Nazi revolution was complete.

17

FROM ENTHUSIASM TO RITUAL

SUMMER 1933- WINTER 1935

You had to go to the indoctrination sessions constantly and these ideas were drummed into you. And you had to learn them because you had to be very careful about what you said.

Northeim teacher

Certainly one of the reasons for the Nazi success in establishing a dictatorship during the first half of 1933 was the rush of events. So many different things happened so rapidly that Northeimers were stunned. But by the summer of 1933 the action slowed down from the breakneck pace of the spring. The new dictatorship began to find ruts and settle into them. Most of the destruction and construction had been completed and it was time to make the new system work. Yet despite the need for new approaches, there was a tendency to apply the same methods. Authoritarianism was increased, mass demonstrations were made all-inclusive, and force continued to be applied to the economy. Nevertheless there were modifications, for the town had a way of reasserting its corporate personality. The modifications worked within the new dictatorship, however, and not against it.

The momentum of the Nazi propaganda effort undertaken during the spring of 1933 carried well into the summer. While there were no great festivals, there was considerable activity on a minor scale. Some was spurred by the formation of new Nazi sub-organizations, or the rapid strengthening of existing ones which, in either case, seemed to demand some sort of demonstration of vigor. Thus, in August 1933, there were large demonstrations by the Nazi War Victims' Association, the League of German Girls, and the newly formed SS Reconnaissance troop. On the occasion of the first two events there were large parades and "field church services," with most Nazi sub-organizations drawn in. The SS affair involved "maneuvers" capped by a "Maneuver Ball."[1] Similarly, some of the new Nazi officials seemed determined to prove that they were important by setting mass events in motion. Hermann Denzler, the new sport director for Northeim, did this by proclaiming a vast sport program for the town in autumn 1933. Every day from September 10 to October 1 (except Sundays) there were athletic events in Northeim. Most activity consisted of shooting, gymnastics, and "defense sport," and to promote general sport-mindedness there were periodic parades, speeches, and other ceremonies. Naturally all buildings were beflagged during these days. No one could complain that the new regime was underemphasizing physical exercise.[2]

Meanwhile, the NSDAP, Local Group Northeim, preempted one of the free September Sundays for a general members' meeting. Ernst Girmann took the opportunity to declare that the revolution was over; the NSDAP was now the sole owner of state power. Nevertheless, he continued, the task of educating the new Germany would now begin. All members, especially the new ones, were reminded that they must attend their cell meetings, must join the SA, the SS, or the SA Reserve. They must participate in party functions.

They must go to the German Theater. Women must join the Nazi Women's Group. Above all, every member must read the NB, and not the newspapers of those who fought Nazism. In conclusion Girmann declared that he personally certified that the Local Group's treasury was in good order.[3]

Northeim's Local Group Leader was not the only Nazi worried about the quality of the new members who had flooded the party in the spring of 1933. The national party headquarters also prescribed a special two-week course to be taken by every person who had joined the party since January 1. It was essentially indoctrination in basic Nazi ideology. Attendance was mandatory and anyone missing a class was to be fined.[4]

In short, the NSDAP saw that the excitement was over and that now was the time to tighten discipline and organize the gains. With the enormous expansion of the NSDAP in the spring of 1933, it was questionable whether the Nazis could maintain élan and cohesiveness. Events were in the offing that would demonstrate that it could, but only under pressure.

In October 1933 Hitler withdrew the German Reich from the League of Nations. In the face of foreign reaction to this move, he felt it necessary to give a demonstration of home support for his leadership. The demonstration was to take the form of a plebiscite to which would be coupled elections for a new all-Nazi Reichstag. The first reaction set the tone for the subsequent campaign. Upon the request of the central government, County Prefect von der Schulenberg sent the following telegram to Berlin: "The population of County Northeim unanimously approves the Reich government's actions and calls for peace, bread, and work." Other organizations sent similar telegrams.[5]

The plebiscite campaign itself was an excellent example of Nazi methods. Even though the NSDAP could expect to report unanimous approval, since they alone would count the ballots, every effort was made to have Northeimers actually vote for Hitler's policies. The whole electioneering machinery that the Nazis had perfected over the past several years was cranked up again, as though this were going to be a free election. Soon County Leader Steineck began pleading with the *Gauleitung* for effective speakers; he even targeted specific villages that were trouble spots—two "nests of communists" and two SPD strongholds. For the last three days of the campaign he needed seven *Gau*-speakers, most of whom would address several rallies.[6] Very few Nazi leaders reflected on one obvious problem: since people were now compelled to attend Nazi meetings and were intimidated into demonstrating overt enthusiasm, there would no longer be any feedback system on the effects of Nazi propaganda. Before the dictatorship had been established, local Nazi leaders had been able to measure very precisely which speakers were "good" ones, which themes were attractive, and which rallies were successes. But now they were going to have to rely on memory, guesswork, or their own reactions. The creation of the dictatorship had broken the previous self-correcting mechanism that had been so important in winning the Nazis their mass backing.

The opening of the campaign for Northeim was Hitler's speech in Hanover, on October 25. Special trains featuring drastically reduced fares left Northeim for the Hanover event. Furthermore, Northeimers were advised that anyone who wanted to go could, if he applied to local Nazi headquarters. Four days later the SA and SS held a parade in Northeim with two fife-and-drum corps and their band.[7]

Then the campaign began in earnest. By order of the NSDAP, no meetings were to be allowed until after election day except those which had a political character. The first of these took place on November 2, ten days before the election. It consisted of a mammoth parade followed by a rally. From three o'clock on, the whole town was involved, one way or another, as requested by the NSDAP. ("The active participation of all inhabitants is expected! Out with the flags!") The parade itself was organized by groups, from the railroad workers to the Queen Luise Society, and included over three thousand people plus two bands, three fife-and-drum corps, and innumerable flags. The next big event was on November 9, a special day for the NSDAP anyway—the anniversary of Hitler's unsuccessful "Beer Hall" *Putsch* of 1923. In Northeim there was a full celebration with all the Nazi suborganizations participating and with a mass demonstration joined to the wreath-laying ceremony. All public officials were required to participate.[8]

The final surge came in the last two days before the voting. On November 10, Hitler was to speak on the radio, and in Northeim the NSDAP was determined that everyone would listen. All businesses were ordered to close during the speech and all of the town's civil servants were ordered to assemble in the largest hall in Northeim to hear it. The program was a masterpiece of synchronization:

1:00 to 1:01—Siren Signal. All work ceases; all traffic stops.
1:01 to 1:10—Report of Propaganda Leader Dr. Goebbels.
1:10 to 1:55—Speech of the *Fuehrer*.
1:55 to 1:59—Horst Wessel Song.
2:00 to 2:03—Sirens; work resumes.
The audience gathered in the Riding Hall will remove itself, in a closed column, to the Market Square where it will be dismissed.
    Out with the Flags!

Local Group Northeim NSDAP[9]

The following day, election eve, a totally inclusive demonstration was planned:

Northeim marches for peace! The entire population of Northeim is hereby summoned to participate in the demonstrations on Saturday at 6:30 which will end at the *1910er Zelt* where Party-Comrade Minister Klagges of Brunswick will speak. The order of clubs and organizations will be as on May 1. The appearance of each man is an unqualified duty.

Local Group Northeim NSDAP[10]

A circular memorandum from Ernst Girmann to all Nazi party members in Northeim reminded them to appear at the election eve meeting, with the words: "No excuses will be accepted."[11]

With this kind of preparation, the organization of the election itself was not overlooked. Each of Northeim's 1,200 Nazi party members was ordered to appear at the polls at nine in the morning on election Sunday, with the members of his family, his friends, and his acquaintances. After voting, each Nazi was to report to his cell leader and remain on call for further work during the entire day. Every business in Northeim was to fill its store windows with posters; every house was to display the swastika flag. Government offices and businesses were ordered to vote in closed ranks by noon. Various clubs were to meet and vote in closed ranks. Furthermore:

Strict control will be maintained by the NSDAP to make certain that everyone exercises his voting duty. After he votes, every voter will receive a lapel button which is to be purchased for 5 *Pfg.* at the polls. At the exits of the city, railroad station, etc., there will be posts set up, who will remind everyone without a button of his patriotic duty.[12]

To make certain that Northeimers voted in the right way there were large ads in the newspaper giving instructions: "This is how it looks if you voted correctly. The circle under 'Nein' should *not* be marked." And again: "ATTENTION! VOTERS! When you have given your vote for Hitler and voted with 'yes' at the polls, *then* you will receive a button."[13]

After such preparations the results were anticlimactic. County Northeim reported a vote of 98 percent for the NSDAP Reichstag slate (the only one on the ballot), and 98.5 percent voting "Ja" on the plebiscite. The significance of this becomes apparent when one looks at the figures reported for Moringen concentration camp, located in Northeim County. There it was reported that 252 prisoners had voted: 212 "Ja," 26 "Nein," and 14 had invalid ballots (in the Reichstag election the Nazi party was reported as having received 77 percent of the inmates' votes).[14]

In the town of Northeim results were similar. Only 94.6 percent voted and of these only 97.2 percent voted "yes." The published results stated that, of 6,942 voters, 193 voted "no" and 68 spoiled their ballots. Curiously, in the Reichstag elections held at the same time (for which only the Nazi slate of candidates could be elected), it was reported that 321 spoiled their ballots. How these figures were arrived at is hard to say since the NSDAP counted the ballots with no one to challenge its tabulation. But no matter how they were counted, it was treated as a victory for the cause of Hitler. Church bells were rung in Northeim when the results were announced.[15]

The significance of the election did not lie in the results but in the methods and techniques used. The campaign and the balloting showed that the dictatorial state was fully organized. For almost two weeks before election day practically all Northeim was forced to be involved in a ritual devoid of inner content. The function of the election was not to determine or register the will of the citizens of Northeim. It was to impress upon Northeimers the omnipotence and determination of the NSDAP. This was accomplished, but in the course of achieving this goal the NSDAP rapidly exhausted whatever capital of genuine enthusiasm they began with. In the last days of the campaign even the members of the NSDAP had to be whipped on by threats. The average Northeimer could not help looking upon the whole affair with increasing skepticism. The ritual was impressive but no longer genuine. After this campaign Northeim's NSDAP discovered that it was only by new threats that unified action could be achieved.

Yet despite the lack of widespread motivation, mass propaganda methods continued. The number of occasions when Northeimers were ordered to hang out their flags was multiplied and came to include such second-rank events as the birthday of Herman Goering and county congresses of the NSDAP.[16] Eventually Girmann began to insist that Northeim was known throughout Germany as a town with ingenious decorations. Instead of merely hanging out swastika flags, homeowners were urged to ring their balconies with a whole series of miniature swastikas, bunting, and other kinds of decorations.

In short, local chauvinism was brought into play to bolster whatever feelings Northeimers may have had for Hitler. The results were gratifying to the Nazis. Perhaps the high point was reached when a butcher on Broad Street contrived an effigy of Hitler in lard, parsley, and sausage-ends in his store window. The effort that had once gone into decorating the town for the shooting festivals and other ancient ceremonies was now redirected for Nazism. But Northeimers entered into the spirit of it and satisfied their aesthetic impulses in accordance with the new situation.[17]

Other native customs were also incorporated into Nazi methods in order to aid the propaganda effort. Long before the NSDAP appeared on the scene, Northeimers had been devoted to honoring the dead of previous wars. The NSDAP capitalized on this by holding frequent ceremonies. Special monuments were erected to honor such diverse groups as the fallen athletes of Northeim. A ceremony for the dead was even held on Christmas Eve and on other nontraditional dates. These events were superimposed on the by-now-customary Nazi celebrations (Hitler's birthday, May 1, etc.) Even charity fund drives were treated like propaganda campaigns. For the kickoff of the Winter Relief Fund drive for autumn 1933, the *Gauleitung* reported that it would employ 200 *Gau* speakers and hold close to 3,000 rallies.[18]

But already by 1934 enthusiasm for mass demonstrations had fallen off to the point where Northeimers made themselves conspicuous at the beginning of celebrations and then ducked down side streets to avoid having to listen to the speeches. Advertisements for Nazi-sponsored events made increasing use of absolute imperatives such as: "The *entire* population of Northeim *must* appear!"[19]

The apathy even pervaded the ranks of the NSDAP, and members were required to bring "control-cards" to meetings to be punched. Anyone who missed three meetings was threatened with expulsion. Members of the NSDAP were also required to bring others with them to meetings so that the halls would be filled. In a memorandum circulated in the summer of 1935 this concept is repeated several times:

Every member must look upon it as a *duty* to attend and to bring several other *Volk*-comrades with him. . . . Every party-comrade and comradess has the duty of making extensive propaganda for attendance at this meeting so that the very last of all citizens attends. . . . No citizen must be allowed to stay at home. . . .[20]

Despite these measures and despite the terror that was there to enforce compliance, the history of mass propaganda in the mature dictatorial structure in Northeim was one of increasing indifference. More and more Northeimers were bored and exhausted by Nazi dynamism and complained about the incessant meetings, parades, and demonstrations. As for the fanatical Nazis, they became increasingly convinced that the citizens of Northeim were hopelessly self-centered and apolitical.[21]

If enthusiasm was not voluntarily forthcoming, there were other means of evoking it. Of course the blacklisting of former Socialists from employment possibilities continued well into 1934, but that was through behind-the-scenes activity by Girmann.[22] The examples, however, remained as reminders. The most effective means of evoking external compliance was the continued system of terror. Even in the late summer of 1933 there were still arrests to be made, mostly for very minor offenses. Thus in late August it was reported that after a worker had shouted "*Heil Moskau!*" he had been sent to the Moringen concentration camp. Reports of similar arrests continued to trickle out. In September a worker was arrested for "making antigovernmental utterances." In November 1933, two Northeim women were arrested "for spreading false rumors about the NSDAP."[23] But eventually there were no more reports of arrests or other police action. As in other matters, the terror system was stabilizing itself. In September the NNN felt it advisable to publish an editorial against anonymous denunciations. Perhaps the last public manifestation of Nazi power came in September 1933, when the SA and SS carried out a roundup of beggars in Northeim. It was fruitless, but shortly thereafter the police conducted a similar action and managed to catch one unfortunate victim.[24]

Henceforth the operation of terror was undertaken by simple injunctions or by subtler and more effective means of social reinforcement. As examples of the former, there were commands not to listen to Radio Moscow, to give the Hitler salute, to maintain the graves in the town cemetery. Furthermore, there were injunctions to establish oneself as a good citizen by attending meetings, contributing to charity drives, and tracing "Aryan" ancestry.[25] More than anything else, rumor and social reinforcement maintained the system of terror. Occasionally, overt actions would be necessary. Thus after the struggle against the churches began in 1935, a police detective was placed before the church door every Sunday, ostentatiously taking down names and, after the services began, taking notes on the contents of the sermon.[26] But such measures were exceptional. Generally, Northeimers came to know very rapidly what was expected of them and acted accordingly. While fear was widespread, there were actually no incarcerations for political offenses in the mature dictatorship, at least not through 1935.

This was not because the regime had relaxed its commitment to internal terrorism, though it had systematized it. Since the spring of 1933 the Gestapo had been rapidly built up, and in April 1934 it came under the control of Heinrich Himmler and the SS. Simultaneously, most of the "amateur detective" networks that had sprung up in 1933 were phased out. By October 1934 the national headquarters of the Nazi party ordered all members to be on the alert for any suspicious activity that might be subversive, but to report it to the Gestapo rather than trying to handle it themselves.[27] But at the same time the party developed its own "intelligence service" to ferret out potential opponents. In March 1934 a Nazi named Ernst Reitz was appointed leader of this organization for Northeim County and he rapidly developed a network of informers in seventy of the county's seventy-eight towns and villages. In ensuing months Reitz reported that he thought there was a Communist cell in Northeim, that SPD people were joining the *Stahlhelm,* and that the latter were meeting regularly in the Hotel Sonne. There were no details behind these suspicions, but the very existence and activity of these Nazi snoopers doubtless helped to inhibit any thoughts of resistance by dissident townspeople.[28]

Not completely, though, for even the terror system accommodated itself somewhat to Northeim's peculiarities. There was the case of an old farmer who had been a member of the Hanoverian party. As long as anyone in Northeim could remember he had always spent his evenings in a tavern drinking beer, condemning the contemporary government, and extolling the good old days under the Hanoverian dynasty. When the Nazis came to power he included them in his curses as a matter of course. But he was so much a part of the general scheme of affairs that no one ever bothered him. Thus he had the distinction of publicly vilifying the government almost every day of the Third Reich, with a complete immunity.[29]

There were also a few Northeimers who were genuinely unaware of the terror system until the summer of 1934. It was after the *"Roehm Putsch"* that the "German glance"* and the general breakdown of trust appeared.[30]

In short, while threats, allusions, and rumor served to maintain control, there was no increase in actual terrorism in the first years of the Nazi regime in Northeim. A sort of equilibrium existed whereby Northeimers did what was expected of them and in return were spared the potential rigors of the police state. This kind of tacit agreement, based on the possibility of terror, was the essential prerequisite for the maturation of Nazi rule in Northeim. It was always held in reserve while the slow process of molding the various institutions in the town into acceptable instruments of Nazism continued. This process was as thorough as it was deliberate. The best example of it was in the school system.

The Northeim city government possessed extensive power over the operation of the elementary school system, from determination of the budget

---

*The "German glance" (a sardonic play on the "German greeting," which Nazi propaganda insisted was "Heil Hitler") consisted of looking over one's shoulder before saying anything that might mean trouble if overheard. The *"Roehm Putsch"* was a bloody purge of the SA in June 1934, in which hundreds of Stormtrooper leaders were murdered by the SS.

to appointment of teachers. It did not have the same kind of control over the *Gymnasium* and *Lyzeum*, since these were supervised by the Provincial School Board. After the NSDAP came to power, however, the determining factor was the Local Group Leader who not only controlled the Northeim city government but also had considerable influence, through the NSDAP, upon the Provincial School Board. It was not really necessary for Ernst Girmann to exercise this power after 1933, since almost all of Northeim's teachers cooperated fully with him. Only three teachers were removed: Voge and Venzlaff from the "idealist" opposition, one of whom was simply transferred and the other hounded out of town, plus another teacher from the *Gymnasium* with known republican sympathies who was also transferred away from Northeim.[31]

The NSDAP was not only interested in removing opposition, however. It was also concerned that education be enlisted as a positive support for the new regime. According to the town's official historian, writing in 1936:

It is no longer the sole task of the schools to impart knowledge; next to that stands the need to make out of the growing youth men and women such as the National Socialist State desires—adults who sense the meaning of "community" and want to join it. Thus the struggle for the unity of the nation has become the basis of education. . . . To develop men with hard bodies and hard wills, who can stand up to their man in the *völkisch* struggle of our era: that is the new task which the schools have taken over in addition to their customary promotion of general intelligence.[32]

Converting the schools into ideological bastions of the new state was a process begun almost immediately. New textbooks were brought in in 1933. The existing school libraries were stripped of "degenerate" literature and stocked with books glorifying nationalism and militarism. Teachers were given lectures laying down the general lines under which history and other sensitive subjects were to be taught. New courses were introduced in "Racial Theory" and Teutonic prehistory. The lectures and "schooling sessions" for the teachers continued incessantly. Frequently the same themes were reiterated session after session. Teachers were careful to get the general line down exactly, since the word was quickly spread that the Hitler Youth would report to the NSDAP on what teachers were doing.[33]

In addition to the new subjects and the new approach to old subjects, the schools were required to emphasize sport and physical education, especially shooting and "defense sport." In science classes, for example, pupils were put to building model gliders. Nazi propaganda films were used extensively and radios were installed in the classrooms so that propaganda speeches could be heard.[34] The extent to which life in the schools was changed can be gauged from the report of the Catholic Grade School on new acquisitions:

> Flags were acquired . . . every class put up a picture of the *Fuehrer* . . . reparations charts and hand grenades purchased . . . the school library was revised, among other things Graf Luckner's *Sea Devil* acquired. . . . School wall pictures were increased by racial tables, "Swastika in Four Centuries," genetic laws . . . a map of the World War 1914–1918 became our property . . . air rifles purchased . . . flagstaff . . . model gliders. . . .[35]

The process included all schools. The business and professional schools introduced courses in "Racial History" and "Political Education." Even the small school for the feebleminded did what it could do to indoctrinate its charges.[36]

The Hitler Youth played an active role in all these changes. In 1934 a drive was undertaken to enroll every pupil in the school system in either the Hitler Youth or the League of German Girls. Existing school clubs were driven out of existence. But as the Hitler Youth was exalted, the authority of the teachers was considerably diminished. In the words of a former principal, "It became almost impossible to teach."[37]

Despite this program, one aspect of Nazism did not enter the schools during the first two years of the Nazi regime. This was anti-Semitism. One principal recalls having had three Jewish children in his school: "There were never any difficulties with them in any way. The children graduated from school with the other children. And to the best of my knowledge the other children never insulted or harassed them in any way."[38] Later, Jewish children were systematically excluded from the schools, but not in the early years. In fact, even pupils sympathetic to Nazism felt enough of a sense of solidarity with fellow-students of the Jewish faith so that they refused to sing the "Horst Wessel Song" in their presence.[39] But in all other ways, the school children were intensively indoctrinated. More than any other institution in Northeim, the schools became active instruments of Nazism.

If their success with the schools was a source of encouragement to Northeim's Nazis, the same was not true of that other instrument of education, the daily press. It is true that the press was under firm control; both the NNN and the GGZ were well aware of the limits upon their freedom. But in Nazi eyes the press would cease to be a problem only when it was wholly Nazi-owned.

As noted above, Ernst Girmann declared on September 16, 1933, in a general meeting of the NSDAP, Local Group Northeim, that it was the duty of every member to subscribe to Northeim's own Nazi newspaper, the NB. The NB was quick to exploit this fiat. On September 23 every Nazi member received a letter from the NB reminding him of Girmann's command and informing him that he was therefore a subscriber as of October 1, 1933. An agent would stop by soon to formally take the order.[40]

This was part of a general campaign to increase the circulation of the Nazi press. Beginning in 1934 the NB did not have to be concerned with expanding its readership; this function was handled by a special official in each Nazi Local Group, the *Pressewart*. The *Pressewart* had the general task of overseeing all newspapers in his area, but his special and primary task was to build up the Nazi-owned press. He was to be a general reporter for the Nazi paper in his locality, covering every newsworthy event, ". . . so that he will have the possibility of informing our press, first, of all news . . . and so that the fat burgher will know that we have eyes and ears everywhere, and on this ground alone will fit himself into the new Germany." Furthermore the *Pressewart* was to do everything in his power to aid the Nazi press and weaken the non-Nazi press. He was especially to keep the nonparty press in line.[41]

In Northeim these general rules were interpreted to mean that the NNN and GGZ would be driven out of existence. With Erhardt Knorpel writing the news for the NNN, however, it was hard for the NSDAP to find anything to complain about in that newspaper. After his early brushes with disaster, Knorpel became exceedingly cautious. In fact, the NNN followed the Nazi line down to every twist and wriggle. Finally, however, Northeim's Nazi *Pressewart* found something so obvious that no one else had noticed it. Ever since the NNN was founded, it had borne the slogan, as a part of its masthead, "Fatherland above Party" *(Das Vaterland ueber die Partei)*. In Imperial and Weimar days this was presumably a statement of impeccable sentiments. In the Nazi state, however, it was treasonable, since it promoted the heretical concept that state and party were distinguishable. Had Erhardt Knorpel thought about it he would have whisked the offending slogan away immediately. But a masthead is something that everyone looks at but few see, that is, until the Nazi *Pressewart* for Northeim saw it one day in early December 1933.

The NNN was immediately suppressed. Knorpel and the paper's publisher had to make the most abject apologies and pull the longest strings to get permission to resume publication ten days later. Needless to say, the masthead had been trimmed. The NSDAP was convinced that this temporary suspension would be the death blow.

In point of fact it gave the NNN a new lease on life. Until the suspension, the NNN's circulation had fallen steadily. After the paper was suppressed, subscriptions came pouring in. The paper's reporter was convinced that this was the first sign of popular discontent with the Third Reich. In all likelihood it was simply that Northeimers had had their curiosity piqued. Whatever there was in the NNN that made it suppressable would surely make interesting reading in those days of censorship. Hence the NNN won back its readership and, since it was still well written, accurate, and first with the news, the subscriptions were maintained. Perhaps the reporter was right and Northeimers read it out of protest (a magnificent irony since the last thing the publisher was interested in was becoming a symbol of resistance), but in any event the NNN was economically secure thereafter. The Nazis threw up their hands in disgust and the NNN was tolerated, though still subjected to occasional harassment.[42]

While Northeim's Nazis were willing to tolerate the NNN, they were absolutely determined to exterminate the GGZ. This was partly because of antipathy for "reactionaries" such as the paper's owner and editor, Wilhelm Röhrs, and partly because Röhrs had the temerity to talk back to the Nazis. Although the GGZ was a dying paper anyway, Röhrs was convinced that his lagging circulation was due to Nazi pressure (which was certainly also true). He even went so far as to write to the District *Pressewart* for help against "illegal competition." This stung the NB to attack Röhrs repeatedly in editorials. He was charged with knowing nothing about National Socialism, with taking advertisements from Jews (he did), and with publishing erroneous reports about the doings of Northeim's NSDAP. He was also badgered in minor ways. By the summer of 1934 the NB refused the usual courtesy exchange of papers with the GGZ. Röhrs was urged by minor Nazi figures to publish scurrilous poems directed against himself. He was repeatedly found guilty of little indiscretions by the Northeim *Pressewart*.[43]

Eventually Röhrs began to write to friends for help. One editor in a neighboring town informed him that the editor of the NB had a past which included conviction as an embezzler, a perjurer, and a debt-evader, but that nothing could be done to aid the GGZ. A poet to whom Röhrs had written for aid went so far as to try to intervene with the Nazi *Gauleitung* but was told there was no hope for the GGZ.[44]

Thus no matter where he turned, Röhrs was trapped. The remnants of his family fortune enabled him to continue putting out the GGZ at a personal loss, but eventually the circulation shrank to the point where each issue became an exercise in futility. Early in 1937 he capitulated, sold the paper to the NNN for a pitiful sum, signed an agreement never to print anything again, and went into retirement. Shortly thereafter he died. He had contributed substantially to the Nazi seizure of power; he had rejoiced in their success and in their use of force against the "Marxists"; he was broken completely by them.[45]

The struggle waged by the NSDAP to establish its own newspaper in a monopolistic position occurred even though both the NNN and the GGZ printed only what the NSDAP wanted and printed it in the way the Nazis wanted it. And anyone who even mildly criticized the NB was threatened by Girmann with reprisal.[46] From the very beginning of the Third Reich all the newspapers in Northeim were active and effective instruments of propaganda for the Nazi dictatorship. In a similar way, almost all the organizations that were "coordinated" in the spring of 1933 were eventually made into instruments of Nazi propaganda. One group of organizations that had, in general, escaped *Gleichschaltung* during the first few months of the Third Reich were the veterans' and patriotic societies. This oversight was subsequently corrected. In November 1933 all former veterans in the *Kyffhaeuserbund* and similar organizations were incorporated into the "second reserve" of the SA. Thus they were placed under direct Nazi discipline and used for demonstrations, parades, and so forth.[47]

Other nationalist societies that served the Nazi purpose were systematically promoted. This was the case with the "People's League for the Care of German War Graves." The result of Nazi aid was apparent in their annual collections which yielded 31 marks in 1930, 37 marks in 1932, but 187 marks in 1933, when the SA helped solicit contributions. Similarly, the Society for Germandom in Foreign Lands was developed from a small group into a significant one. It was, of course, a perfect instrument for promoting Nazi claims in foreign policy.[48]

One of the main Nazi efforts went into expanding the glider group in Northeim. By September 1933 the town's second glider was built, and Girmann, in his dedicatory speech, laid emphasis upon the military importance of glider training. A Nazi glider group was created and a special flying show with mock bombing demonstrations was held. This was done by the express command of the government, though Northeim's Nazis showed some initiative. The Northeim Senate supplied close to 400 marks in financial aid.[49]

While gliders and air power were stressed, the NSDAP did not forget to promote civil defense. In September 1933 an Air Defense Society was created in Northeim under Nazi leadership, and all the town's schools, clubs, and newspapers were incorporated into it. The town was divided into four districts and organized for civil defense. By November the first courses began with 250 people attending lectures. Attendance was obligatory. The Civil Defense School was formally reorganized in May 1934, with eleven teachers. Belief in a coming war had become a permanent aspect of Nazi rule.[50]

Another institution that was used for propaganda and then eventually incorporated by the NSDAP was the *Stahlhelm*. This organization began its career in the Third Reich in partnership with the Nazis. The Nazis were determined to bring it under control, however, since it represented an independent mass organization which could be a potential gathering place for dissidents. Through August 1933 the Northeim *Stahlhelm* spent much of its time trying to convince the NSDAP of its loyalty and friendliness. For that purpose a special "Comradeship Evening" was given, with much drinking and dancing. By September it had been determined that the *Stahlhelm* would be unified with the SA, i.e., absorbed. The actual ceremony was turned into a source of propaganda for the NSDAP, with flags, bands, and a somewhat forced festive air. This process dragged into October, after which the *Stahlhelm* proper ceased to exist, being invoked occasionally in the next few months only for propaganda purposes. By incorporating the *Stahlhelm* into the SA, the danger of its becoming a rival group was obviated; moreover, additional numbers of Northeimers were brought under direct Nazi discipline. But at the same time, whatever communal spirit and enthusiasm had existed in this organization were destroyed.[51]

In short, the mature dictatorial structure in Northeim was monolithic and authoritarian, but also bereft of spontaneity. The terror system could evoke responses, but responses which were empty of inner enthusiasm. Propaganda became increasingly a matter of ritual. The Nazis were successful in stimulating genuine enthusiasm only in areas where Northeimers had always felt enthusiasm—in civic pride, for example.

It is even possible that one consequence of the deadening of human relationships was a rise in crime. Police statistics for the years 1933 through 1935 show that crimes of all sorts tended to rise. The following table gives the figures:[52]

	1933	1934	1935
Total investigations by Northeimer *Kriminal-Polizei* (excluding political offenses)	318	385	497
Misdemeanors: drunkenness, disturbance of the peace, etc. (excluding traffic offenses)	60	117	166

Crimes involving theft and betrayal of confidence rose especially sharply:[53]

	1933	1934	1935
Grand larceny	3	16	12
Petty larceny	57	69	76
Criminal fraud	11	17	14
Embezzlement	5	9	12

While the increases are relatively large, the numbers are still small. One can hardly speak of a crime wave in Northeim in response to the establishment of the dictatorship. Nevertheless, the figures are suggestive, as was Ernst Girmann's somewhat bewildered letter to school and youth authorities in the spring of 1934, protesting the recent wanton destruction by children of shrubs (and even the burning of evergreens) in the town's parks.[54] Girmann was undoubtedly also puzzled by the numerous cases of embezzlement involving members of the Nazi party, who then had to be expelled. Among others were the former editor of Northeim's Nazi newsletter and one of the town's SA leaders, both of whom stole party monies.[55] Others expelled for embezzlement were new Nazi appointees in the city government who had promptly dipped their fingers into the public funds under their control.[56] Girmann further found that he had to resort to threats of expulsion to get other party members to accept even the minor responsibilities of membership.[57] The evidence of both corruption and lack of commitment is not conclusive but it suggests that the Nazis were beginning to discover the consequences of creating a lawless regime and of forcing people to live a life of compelled insincerity.

All phenomena in Northeim in the years after 1933 must be put into a general context. The context was one characterized by the general breakdown of trust and by the destruction or perversion of hitherto unifying social organizations. The response of the individual was generally withdrawal, sometimes aggression. Both were useful to the dictatorship: withdrawal removed threats to the new system; aggression could be channeled against internal or external enemies of the regime. But the type of inner unity that the NSDAP had promised did not appear. Instead of creating the ideal *Volk*-community the Third Reich launched an era of deceit, distrust, and progressive spiritual decadence.

18

THE GREAT JUSTIFICATION

SUMMER 1933– WINTER 1935

You hear people saying: "Now we have work again; now we can buy something again."

A Northeim businessman

By 1935 Northeim had overcome all external signs of the depression. A visitor to the town in the summer of that year would have been considerably impressed by what he saw, especially if he had also passed through three years earlier and thus had a point of comparison. Construction was booming; there were no unemployed; work and purposefulness dominated the scene. Furthermore, the city undoubtedly looked better. There was a new and unified system of parks, the houses in the old town were freshly painted and repaired, and the streets were cleaner. It might even be that the visitor came to Northeim because of a new and vigorous tourist office which went out of its way to attract visitors to the small, charming town in the valley. All of these features must be credited to the Nazi record, and to a good extent to the imagination and energy of the town's Nazi leader, Ernst Girmann. The revival of the economy was the great and solid propaganda point of the NSDAP in Northeim. It was also the main justification for the dictatorship, since Girmann could argue that economic revival was made possible through the unity imposed upon the town, and because of the conversion of the city government into an instrument of personal authoritarianism.

For the city bureaucracy the great lesson in the implications of the new system was the personal fate of Thomas Galland. Galland, the second highest administrator in the city government when the Nazis took control, was subjected to a kind of harassment which could only demonstrate Ernst Girmann's virtually unlimited power within Northeim. This was not a result of Galland's political views, but solely because he was a symbol of independent thinking.

Galland was a democrat, but so wholly withdrawn in his political attitude that everyone viewed him as an unpolitical civil servant. The only ostensible reason for Girmann to hate him was that Galland had been closely connected to Mayor Peters and could have become a rival to Girmann. So the vendetta against Galland could only be interpreted as an expression of Girmann's personal attitude, though he occasionally invoked vague "political concerns."[1]

Throughout the summer of 1933 Galland was systematically stripped of his subsidiary offices. In August 1933 he was removed entirely from the city administration and his place was given to a rival. Then the vendetta began. Wherever Thomas Galland sought employment he was prevented from obtaining it by the personal intervention of Ernest Girmann. Girmann also let it be known that Galland had two alternatives: he could leave Northeim and sell his house at a loss, or he could find work as a ditchdigger in one of the works projects under August Ude.

To avoid either, the former *Stadt-Oberinspektor* was driven to taking a job in a neighboring town as a newspaper hawker at the railroad station. From this limbo he was ultimately rescued by the arrival of the Army in Northeim. The Army was beyond the reach of Girmann, and thus Galland found decent work with it as a civilian employee. Though Ernst Girmann made an annual effort for the next five years to have Thomas Galland dismissed as a security risk, the Army just as steadfastly defied him.[2]

Even though Girmann's campaign for the total degradation of Thomas Galland fell short of success, it was enough of a demonstration of power to turn the other members of the city administration into his complete tools. By 1935 Girmann was able to demand that city employees not only carry out their regular jobs in accordance with his commands, but that they place themselves at the full disposal of the NSDAP.[3] So far as it was possible, Northeim's administration became the expression of Girmann's will.

Ernest Girmann's authoritarian position had only two checks against it: the NSDAP which gave him his power, and the City Council which had elected him. As long as Girmann could depend upon support from the higher offices in the Nazi party, he could control the town's Nazi Group, and thus the City Council. By late summer 1933 it was apparent to the forces opposing him within Local Group Northeim of the NSDAP that Girmann did have the support of the higher offices in the party. This was reconfirmed when the national headquarters of the Nazi party rejected the dissidents' final appeal in December 1933.[4]

In September, Girmann took steps to weed out the opposition to him on the Northeim City Council. On September 21, 1933, at the public meeting of the council, the first order of business was a vote of "no confidence" in the then speaker of the council, Voge (the Nazi teacher and one of the leaders in the "Idealist Opposition"). Voge asked in vain for reasons and then tried to speak to individual members of the council. When they refused to talk to him, he had no choice but to leave the meeting room. Shortly thereafter he was transferred away from Northeim. At the same meeting it was announced that there would be no more meetings of the City Council, but that instead a committee of four members of the City Council would meet, in private, with the Senate.[5] The interim arrangement of the "Committee of Four" lasted until January 30, 1935, when the new uniform city code for Germany legalized the situation.

The new code (sections of which had been discussed as early as 1925) gave all power and responsibility to the mayor. He was to be advised and aided by boards of consultants and advisers. These organs were completely subordinate to him, and in no way limited his power. Thus Ernest Girmann became the sole and authoritarian ruler of Northeim.[6]

Girmann's absolute control over the city government was, of course, not the only weapon at his disposal for coping vigorously with the town's economic problems. Through his position as Local Group Leader of the NSDAP he could control all the various economic organizations in Northeim that had come under Nazi domination in the course of "coordination." In 1933 these various organizations were initially used for propaganda purposes. Thus the German Workers' Front, created to replace the Free Unions, limited its activities to holding mass meetings and enrolling members. The Artisan League provided an exhibition, demonstration, and parade. The retail merchants sponsored a week in which articles, advertisements, and editorials praised their function.[7] While these activities were perhaps psychologically gratifying, they did little to end the depression.

The real usefulness to the Nazis of the "coordinated" economic associations was that they could provide the lever to pry the economy of Northeim out of the depression. How the NSDAP proposed to do this became apparent by the fall of 1933. During the summer the town had been stripped of unemployed through a variety of public works projects. It was clear to the Nazis, however, that this was only a temporary expedient. The real need was to incorporate these unemployed persons into the regular economy. The Nazis seemed to be convinced that this could be accomplished if everyone in Germany did his part. If consumers purchased and employers hired, the depression would vanish. Thus the economic problem was viewed as one to be solved by organization and propaganda, fields in which the NSDAP felt it excelled.

The process began on October 5, 1933. On that date all employers, public and private, plus representatives of all clubs, met at one of the town's hotels. The city administration had composed a master list of all persons in Northeim capable of hiring workers, and triple-checked it to make certain no one was omitted. In his speech on this occasion, Ernst Girmann told the assembled businessmen that now was the time when they would have to do their part. The government had hired the unemployed temporarily, and it had money on hand in loans and grants. Now the private sector of the economy would have to begin hiring. The Northeim City Brewery would set the example by hiring four new men. The sugar factory had already agreed to keep its plant operating full time, with four shifts. Each employer would be visited in a few days, and asked to hire as many new men as his situation permitted. There was no immediate response to this speech. Only a few people rose to comment afterward. One suggested that the government should act firmly against illegal artisans. Another called on employers to hire old-time Nazi members first. But not a single businessman rose to pledge that he would hire a new worker.[8]

In subsequent days little was done publicly to realize the goals set forth in Girmann's speech. There were advertisements calling on people to buy more, to save more, and to patronize only legally licensed artisans. But by the end of October there were still 340 people employed in public works projects.[9] The situation remained relatively stable into the winter of 1933–1934.

In the spring the NSDAP began its drive in earnest. The new effort was to be called the "Battle of Work." The kickoff date was March 21, 1934—the first anniversary of the "Day of National Renewal" (when Hitler and Hindenburg had staged a ceremony in the Potsdam Garrison church).

But in Northeim the propaganda effort began three weeks before that. Late in February, letters were sent to all civil servants and heads of clubs and guilds, calling upon them to come to the *1910er Zelt* for a mass meeting. What Girmann would say to them would be the same thing that was being said all over the *Gau,* since a complete outline for material, contents, and presentation of speeches was forwarded to Northeim from the Nazi *Gau* Propaganda Division. Nevertheless, Girmann's speech was an excellent one: forceful, convincing, and inspiring, with an aura of beneficial purposefulness. The message was simple. Every Northeimer must consume, hire, borrow, spend, turn the wheels of the economy. Employers were told to raise wages and hire new men. If they did not, the state would force them to. House owners were urged to have all repairs done now, when interest rates on loans were low. In short, the speech was a mixture of threats and cajolery. It left Northeimers with the clear impression that the economy would revive and people would be rich and happy—or else![10]

This mass meeting was followed by a second smaller meeting of employers, craft masters, and civil servants a week later. Involved were the same people who had been addressed by Girmann the previous fall. But this time the atmosphere was entirely different. In the first place, Girmann no longer talked *at* the assembly; instead there was a general discussion. In the second place, practically everyone in the room *believed* that an economic revival was in the making. The best reports were from those in construction work. The Painters' Guild reported that a year ago there were only fifteen apprentices. Now there were forty. The Carpenters' Guild reported twenty new apprentices since January. Where there were gloomy reports, Girmann had positive things to say. The Shoemakers' Guild bemoaned the competition; Girmann promised that the Nazi Welfare Organization would order five hundred pairs of shoes to be made in Northeim. The grocery owners complained of competition from the consumers' cooperative; Girmann promised that this organization "will not be with us forever." The bakers could not see improvement; Girmann swore it would come in a matter of weeks. But most of those present had learned over the winter that the new government was trying to help. The Tailors' Guild reported that because of the sudden demand for uniforms, eighteen new apprentices had been hired. The Retail Merchants' head reported that the turnover in 1933 had been 11 percent higher than in 1932 and that it was still rising. He promised that merchants would be hiring new people: "You hear people saying, 'Now we have work again; now we can buy something again.' And I want to say that on the part of the NS *Volk*-Welfare much has been done for retailers."[11]

After the initial discussion Girmann spoke in summary. He promised to attack legal competition. He affirmed that Nazism was committed to the idea of decent profits. But he also swore he would crack down on anyone cutting wages, hoarding money instead of investing it, or working employees overtime. He set reasonable goals: sixteen new apprentices this month, a reeducation course for employees who had forgotten their skills. Then came the most enjoyable part of the meeting. Girmann declared that money in abundance would be forthcoming from the government. What should it be spent for? Pet schemes poured forth. Old dreams were dredged up. The meeting ended in a burst of enthusiasm and plans. There is no doubt that, psychologically at least, the depression was over.[12]

The mood was sustained. A few days later there was a short but magnificent advertisement in the NNN: "Who still has no job? Report immediately . . . at the City Hall." On March 15 there was a countywide convention in the *1910er Zelt* with speeches outlining plans for the "Battle of Work," pep talks, and so on. On March 21 the "Battle" was officially begun. Parades, demonstrations, bands, flags, a radio speech by Hitler—all the Nazi trimmings went into making it a memorable event.[13] But more significant for Northeim was the ceremonial groundbreaking for a series of new work projects.

Actually, despite all the discussion and propaganda, the depression was not defeated by every Northeimer doing his bit. Instead, the essential instruments were public works projects and a construction boom based on government pump-priming. The same week that Ernst Girmann was holding his remarkable discussion evening with Northeim businessmen, he wrote a letter to the city engineer outlining in detail a new series of works' projects for 1934. Since most of the money for these projects came from the central government, the town paid no more for them than it would have paid in dole money for the equivalent number of unemployed.[14] Many of the projects undertaken were not spectacularly apparent. These included work in the town-owned forest, repair of the extant park system, and repair of roads. But there was one project that transformed the whole face of the town. This was the "park ring." Circling the medieval inner city was a series of defense works dating from the era of Northeim's independence. By 1933 the wall was crumbling, the moats were filled, and the anti-artillery mounds covered with small vegetable gardens. Now, under the public works program, this was all rebuilt. The old wall was repaired where it could be and leveled completely in other spots. The moat was turned into a series of small swan ponds. The rest of the area was converted to pleasant parks with grass, flower gardens, and playgrounds. As a result, Northeim's park system was doubled in size and the town was given a delightful and distinctive aspect. Over eleven thousand workdays went into the creation of this "green belt." [15]

Northeim was made more attractive in many other ways. The two town-owned taverns, both in the woods above Northeim, were repaired and re-modeled, and new roads were built to them. Several run-down sections of the town were cleared and refurbished. Under the guidance of the museum director, houses in the old section of Northeim were repainted so that they again emphasized the medieval, half-timbered structural work. Much of this work was done by the town's own unemployed, but much was also done by the Labor Service. This was begun as a voluntary organization, but soon became compulsory. It was admirably suited to take up the slack in the economy by removing people from the labor market. Thus, when the North-eim sugar factory ended its seasonal refining in 1933, most of its three hundred temporary employees were taken into the Labor Service. Throughout 1933 the Labor Service undertook a number of random projects, from working on a football field and a shooting range to building paths in the town's forest. Beginning in 1934, however, they devoted full energies to creating a new asset for the town. This was an open-air theater, set in a natural declivity in the Northeim Forest.

It was originally conceived of as a meeting place for Nazi ceremonies and was first called the *Thingplatz* (from the old Teutonic term for a tribal meeting place), and then, even more significantly, the *Weihstaette*, or "Holy Place." When it was completed it did create an almost holy feeling in the beholder, since it was dramatically incorporated into the natural setting of ancient and majestic oaks. Almost 23,000 workdays went into the construc-tion of the "Holy Place" before it could be formally dedicated on June 7, 1936. The theater was useful for more than Nazi ceremonies, of course, and in 1936 alone lured more than sixty thousand tourists to Northeim. Further-more, Girmann arranged to have it turned over to the Nazi War Victims' Society, which responded by making Northeim its national headquarters and convention town. This drew considerable money into the town. Northeimers were very pleased over the building of the "Holy Place," though as usual with Nazi actions there was a flaw: the land on which it was built had been purchased—at a very favorable price—from Ernst Girmann's unpopular crony, Senator August Ude.[16]

The Labor Service was also involved in the other main ingredient for the cure of the depression: the construction boom. As a result of its occupation of the old Army barracks, some seventy-five families who had been living there as "shelterless" had to be relocated. The problem of finding apartments for these displaced persons brought into sharp focus the housing shortage in Northeim. The town had gone into the depression with a housing shortage, and the course of the depression only made it worse. From the beginning of 1930 to the end of 1933 Northeim's net population grew by almost four hundred persons. At the same time construction lagged seriously. Thus the situation was ripe for a building boom, if only money were forthcoming.[17]

One of the first measures of the Hitler government was to make that money available. By November 1933 close to 200,000 marks were ready for distribution in Northeim, and more was yet to come. The money was made available through grants and loans under extremely favorable circumstances. For repair or division of apartments, for example, the Reich would pay 20 percent of the cost and loan the rest of 4 percent for six years. Similar terms were available for new construction. Under these attractive arrangements, more than 63,000 marks were allocated by March 1934, for 728 different jobs. By 1936 over 1,300 applications had been approved totaling 175,000 marks. An additional 121,000 marks came from the government for new construction. This was increased again after the spring of 1934 when the Army returned to its old compound, forcing the government to erect new buildings for the offices previously located there and to build new barracks for the Labor Service. In short, by the spring of 1934 all the elements were at hand for a major construction boom in Northeim.[18]

The situation was made even more favorable by the actions of Ernst Girmann. He was considerably embarrassed by the fact that he could not find enough housing for the "shelterless" displaced from the Army barracks. This forced him to locate them in old railroad cars, which was undesirable for the town in many ways. Furthermore, the response of many Northeim landlords to his pleas for apartments for these people was to raise rents, which upset him greatly. For all these reasons, Girmann sought to accelerate the construction of housing in Northeim. By means of "coordination" he already controlled the "Common Good Construction Club," which was now made to increase its building rate. To supplement this organization,

Girmann founded a company called the "Northeim Housing Construction Company," with himself as head. The city treasury was required to put up 100,000 marks for capital, and some eighty-eight small businessmen, mainly in the construction trades, were induced to buy another 53,500 marks' worth of shares (and to elect an all-Nazi board of directors), with the City Savings Bank loaning them the cash for the shares.[19]

Thus, organization was also at hand to push the construction boom. Beginning in the summer of 1933, but gaining full momentum only in the spring of 1934, a whirlwind of construction encompassed Northeim. By the end of 1934, eighty-five new houses with 126 apartments were built. An additional 100 new apartments were fitted out in existing buildings. Over 1,200 were repaired. In the face of this effort, the town's economic problems melted away. By the winter of 1934–1935, public works were continued only to complete projects already begun. By 1936 Northeim had to import construction workers.[20]

The construction figures cited above do not include what the NSDAP considered the showpiece of its building projects—forty-eight new "settlers' " houses located on the northern edge of Northeim. Though the Nazis took full credit for this, the plans, money, and all other preliminaries were ready by the time the Third Reich was inaugurated. In fact, the main reason the settlement project was not begun in 1932 was that it had been blocked by the Nazis. This was conveniently forgotten in 1933. To the accompaniment of great ceremony, work was begun on the first two dozen houses in the project on August 16, 1933. Since these were simple houses to build, and since the project was also made a part of the public works program, these first houses were completed by early November. On the day of the opening of the "Battle of Work," the ground was broken for the second twenty-four houses in the "settlement." By the fall of 1934 those were also completed. Henceforth the settlement was commonly spoken of as the "Nazi Settlement."[21] It was that in one sense: no one was allowed to buy a house in the new settlement unless he could also prove "Aryan" ancestry, membership in a Nazi organization, and sponsorship by the Local Group.[22]

Since the depression was ended in Northeim by means of works projects and a construction boom, what was the role of all the propaganda, the discussions, the "Battle of Work"? It seems clear that at the time this was considered an essential part of defeating the town's economic woes. Though its direct *economic* contribution was minimal, its *psychological* contribution was crucial. It convinced the townspeople that the depression was over, and it convinced them that they had been the ones to end it, under Nazi leadership. Whether deliberately or not, the Nazis took advantage of the fact that what men believe happens is sometimes more important than what actually does happen.

In addition to conquering the depression, Northeim's Nazis made great capital out of the fact that they also dealt with the side effects of the economic crisis: hunger, want, and the other aspects of poverty. In mitigating distress they pushed two concepts, both of which proved popular. The first was that everyone should help; the second was that contributions were not charity but rather a rightful obligation to fellow Germans caught in a situation not of their own making. This effort at social amelioration was the closest the NSDAP ever came to promoting the promised *Volk*-community.

The primary instrument for Nazi welfare work was the NSV (Nazi *Volk*-Welfare Society). As was the case with other Nazi suborganizations, the main personnel for the NSV came from the ranks of the NSDAP itself: party members were simply required to join. But many Northeimers, who would never have joined the NSDAP or any other Nazi suborganization, found themselves willing to join the NSV because its work seemed so apolitical and beneficial.[23] The NSV was also able to make use of all the various clubs, societies, and other organizations that had come under Nazi leadership through "coordination." As in the case of the economic drive and the propaganda effort, the Nazis were thus able to use the entire social apparatus as a lever to move the masses.

The first project of the NSV began in September 1933 and was called the "Winter Relief." The specific campaign was called "The Struggle Against Hunger and Cold." It was kicked off by a series of mass rallies. In newspaper advertisements Northeimers were urged to give deeply. "Sacrifice" was the key word; those who contributed most generously were promised that their names would be inscribed in a special book of honor entitled *Northeim Sacrifices*. In a very short time the campaign demonstrated again the Nazi penchant for thoroughness. A list was drawn up of all merchants in town, and each was expected to contribute. The merchants were also advised that "the lists will be examined closely and contributions which are too small will be rejected." By mid-October the town was divided into six districts for intensive collection. In the collection process, all clubs and other social organizations were given target sums and made responsible for their members. Nor were benefit evenings overlooked. One of the customary "Evenings of Entertainment" with 30-*Pfennig* admission, turned its proceeds over to the "Struggle Against Hunger and Cold." The Hitler Youth was put to making special street collections. Finally, collection cans were set up in every public place, especially for small coins. They were marked with the slogan "When the *Pfennig* Wins, the Struggle will be Victorious."

But the most spectacular device was the *Eintopfgerichtsonntage*, or "Stew Sundays." The idea was that on selected Sundays (usually once a month) every person in Germany would eat stew instead of his regular meal and then contribute the difference in cost to the NSV. Stews were to be served in restaurants, homes, everywhere in Germany. By this means it would be proved that "all Germans are prepared to suffer together when the least of us suffers." These measures brought in considerable money. Collections on "Stew Sundays" regularly totaled in excess of 1,200 marks, and by January 1934 the *Pfennig* canisters alone brought in 342 marks. But from the Nazi point of view, the NSV work was even more important as a propaganda measure. Through it, every German was to feel that he had helped alleviate the misery caused by the depression. Nazi-imposed "unity" was again to be demonstrated as beneficial.[24]

The Nazis were also at pains to show the social direction of their government in other ways. Thus at Christmastime 1933, a Christmas tree was put up in the Market Square "so that everyone in Northeim would be able to enjoy one." Or again, articles appeared deploring the use of the term *gnaedige Frau*, in other words, opposing class distinctions.[25] Most Northeimers approved of these concepts. They were concerned about the class divisions that had rent the town so much in Weimar days, and they felt that the Nazis were doing something about this by attacking the externals of the class structure. They were excited by the possibilities of "national unity"— even so superficial a unity as that imposed by Nazism.[26]

Nazi contributions to Northeim's economy did not end with antidepression measures. Ernst Girmann was convinced that much could be done to help the town by promoting the tourist trade. One effect of the works' projects was to make Northeim a pleasanter place to visit, and this was frequently mentioned in explaining the repairs done on paths in the town forest and at the two town-owned taverns in the woods above Northeim. It was for this reason also that Girmann arranged to have sixty "historical tablets" affixed to buildings of note and other appropriate spots in the town.[27] The beginnings of an active campaign to bring in tourists came early in 1934 when Girmann fused two existing clubs, the "Tourist Club" and the "Improvement Association," to form a new "Club for the Promotion of Tourism." In subsequent meetings and by the usual methods, the club's membership was increased to about five hundred. Advertisements in big city newspapers and brochures praising Northeim's scenic location soon began to bring tourists to the town. In later years this added considerably to the town's income.[28]

Far more significant for Northeim's economy was the reoccupation by the Army of the former compound north of the Ruhme River. This was a project dear to the heart of Ernst Girmann and vigorously pushed by him. By the beginning of 1934, Girmann determined to begin negotiations with the Army and was prepared to expend up to 50,000 marks of the city's funds to buy additional land for the Army. The Army was also willing, and a contract was signed in April 1934. The main point of the contract was that the Army agreed to purchase the compound from Northeim for 285,000 marks. This represented a loss for Northeim, especially since the Army also demanded that the town's pool (located on land adjacent to the compound) be thrown into the bargain. There were howls of protest when the burghers learned that the town was going to lose its swimming pool, which Girmann had to quell by threats. Considering what Northeim had originally paid for both the compound and the pool, the town lost close to 2,350,000 marks in the deal.

But this was more than compensated for by the Army. In the first place, by 1937 the Army spent over 2,000,000 marks on new buildings and repairs, most of which went to contractors and workers in Northeim. Secondly, new buildings had to be erected by the central government to house the various offices hitherto located in the compound. Forcing an additional hundred-odd people out of the "shelterless" apartments also helped stimulate construction, especially since the Army granted funds for new apartments.[29] Most important of all was the economic gain to Northeim from the simple presence of an additional thousand consumers who were not a burden on the labor market. The soldiers spent money in the town, their relatives came to visit them and, above all, the Commissariat contracted for food and other items from local merchants. From every point of view the reoccupation of Northeim by the Army was a first-class economic *coup* by the Nazis.[30]

Naturally the arrival of the Army had other effects upon Northeim. While the soldiers had to be circumspect and the whole operation kept in disguise until 1935 (when Hitler announced to the world that he was defying the military clauses of the Treaty of Versailles), the townspeople soon knew that a battalion was located in the old barracks. In view of Northeim's great love for things military, as displayed in the pre-Hitler period, it can well be imagined that the arrival of the Army was greeted with joy. Furthermore, as exemplified by the personal experiences of Thomas Galland, the Army became a place of refuge for some Northeimers. There they were immune from Girmann's wrath. Since many officers in the Army were unsympathetic to Nazism, there soon developed a fine feeling between the "Idealist Opposition" and the Army. Thus the Army made the Third Reich much more tolerable for many Northeimers.[31]

In summary, the actions of the Nazis in the economic sphere did a great deal to redeem and justify Nazism in the eyes of the people of the town. Those who had the time and inclination to assess the nature of Nazism, by 1935, could set up a balance sheet. On the one hand, Nazism had apparently ended the depression, initiated an economic revival, beautified the town, provided vigorous and efficient leadership, and increased Northeim's economic assets. On the other hand, it had vitiated and regimented social life, introduced a system of terror and authoritarianism, attacked the churches, forced Northeimers to participate in a constant round of dulling and ritualistic propaganda events, and tied the fortunes of the town to the personal whims and dubious personality of Ernst Girmann. Obviously the balance did not resolve itself into a simple equation.

By 1935 most Northeimers were again unsure about Nazism. It is extremely hard to say what the results of a free election might have been. The odds are that in the minds of most Northeimers the bad outweighed the good. Given the chance, they probably would have voted to end or alter the Nazi regime. But long before 1935 the decision had been fixed.

Since Nazism had wrought the miracle of recovery, how could Northeimers have turned against it? In the first place, gratitude is short-lived among humans and many of the townspeople quickly accepted economic revival as normal and turned their concerns to other matters. Secondly, economic recovery was uneven in its benefits. The construction trades profited disproportionately, but small retailers merely stepped back a bit from the edge of disaster. In the long run they were headed for extinction; the Nazi regime did not repeal twentieth century economics. Besides, as has been shown earlier, the depression had not really hurt the middle classes in Northeim; economic issues agitated them mainly because of their political and social concerns. For the middle class, the great work of the NSDAP had been to destroy the Left. Once that was accomplished, the Nazis no longer seemed as necessary as they had once appeared.

Though the farm community around Northeim had been solidly pro-Nazi up to 1933, they rapidly became disillusioned with the regime's actions. Farmers were oppressed by the rigidity of Nazi controls over agriculture and burdened by the loss of hired hands lured away by Nazi construction projects. The farmer's discontentment was rapidly communicated to Northeimers because the town was a center for rural commerce. Thus the NSDAP undercut itself from the two main blocs that had supported it up to the seizure of power: the urban middle class and the farmers.

But outweighing the economic issues was that Northeimers had come to feel afflicted by the dictatorship: its destruction of social life, its pervasive threats, its capriciousness, its incessant demands. Above all, what disenchanted almost everyone in the town was the Nazi attack on organized religion (as will presently be described). In Northeim the Nazis had posed so strongly as devout Christians, when they were campaigning prior to the establishment of the Third Reich, that their abrupt turnabout, once they got into power, seemed like a crude betrayal of solemn promises. Which, of course, it was. It is a measure of the arrogance of power that Ernst Girmann would believe he could violate the basic values of his subjects without losing their allegiance.

Moreover, traditional political attitudes died slowly. In the spring of 1935 the Nazi sub-governor for the region that included Northeim wrote a curious report on the attitude of the people. The overwhelming majority are still behind us, he concluded, but there were a few trouble spots. Workers, for example, continued to oppose the regime. At the 1935 May Day celebration some workers in Northeim County made such disparaging comments about the *Führer's* radio speech that they had to be taken immediately to a concentration camp. Of course, workers had always been anti-Nazi. At the other end of the political spectrum, former *Stahlhelm* members in Northeim were no longer saying *"Heil Hitler,"* but instead ostentatiously greeted each other with *"Guten Tag."* And they were cautiously talking about the need for a change in cabinets, even for a "Fourth Reich." Intellectuals had turned anti-Nazi, too. As for Protestants, they were so dismayed by the regime's anti-church campaign that they were openly calling for an anti-Nazi Army dictatorship. "Some people are overtly saying that Russian conditions prevail here in Germany." And of course the Catholics were also anti-Nazi, though reserved about it. Having thus covered virtually all elements in society, he reiterated his initial point: the people are still for us.[32]

This particular Nazi official was a longtime, fanatical party member and his dismay might be attributed to unsatisfied expectations that had been excessive to begin with.[33] But the *Gestapo* was presumably colder in its assessment. Yet at the end of 1935 two *Gestapo* reports for Northeim's region were similarly dismal. The former Communists, especially in Northeim, were as active in opposing the regime as ever, despite repeated arrests, and had even established contact with dissident Nazis. The former SPD members were constantly undermining the regime through word-of-mouth propaganda. The Nazi party's own members, or at least the "old fighters," were very dissatisfied with the way the party had lost its "true spirit." Ordinary people were hoping for a purge to rid the party of its disreputable members. Many people noted the contemptuous attitude toward the party expressed by Army offi-cers.[34]

The next month's Gestapo report was even gloomier. Protestants were secretly circulating anti-Nazi writings; the Catholic Church was systemati-cally and ceaselessly trying to make its followers anti-Nazi. The lower classes were ripe for recruitment by the workers' underground. Ex-Social Demo-crats were hanging together and mutually reinforcing their opposition to the regime. People were still shopping in Jewish stores. Former conservatives were disgusted with the party and were seeking contacts with Army officers. Parents were turning against the Hitler Youth. And the old Nazis felt that they had been bypassed while the new members incessantly complained that too much was being demanded of them.[35]

Thus there were many elements dissatisfied with the Third Reich by 1935—for almost as many different reasons as there were identifiable groups. And that is one of the major reasons disaffection was not likely to produce any organized opposition or cohesive action against the NSDAP. The Nazis had been able to come to power in the first place because the people were divided, and they stayed in power at least partly because people were still divided. The work of the Nazi revolution, especially "coordination," kept people divided while the Gestapo dealt summarily with any publicly ex-pressed opposition. The Third Reich was firmly entrenched and, as events were to show, it would require foreign armies to dislodge Hitler's dictator-ship. But that does not mean that Northeimers liked the Nazis. It means that by 1935, no matter what Northeimers felt about the Nazis, there was very little that they could do about it.

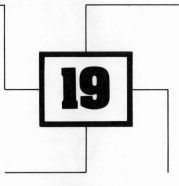

LIFE IN
THE THIRD
REICH

1935-
1945

For some time now, there has been an observable lack of interest by many party comrades, and also certain elements in the population, with respect to official party measures and functions. . . .

Memorandum (strictly confidential) from Local Group Northeim of the Nazi party to all Block Wardens of *OGN I & II*, 28 September, 1936.[1]

The history of Northeim from 1935 to 1945 has a curiously static quality about it. By 1935 the Nazi party had unquestioned control over the town, but it had lost its dynamic drive and its leaders were no longer certain that they had mass support, even from their own members. Consequently they began to move cautiously, except in areas where the rules of the dictatorship had already been established and accepted: clubs would be subordinate to the party, party members and city employees must be at the party's disposal, the townspeople would have to show outward enthusiasm for the regime on select occasions, and expressions of hostility would not be permitted. But otherwise the Nazi leaders became essentially administrators and the townspeople became passive objects. What was lacking in the mature Third Reich were revolutionary fervor, fanaticism, élan, or messianic goals. What was predominant, on the part of leaders and townspeople, was mutual accommodation to make daily life tolerable. When war came in 1939, the town lived through it stoically, suffered from bombing and the deaths of sons and fathers, and surrendered unheroically.

One component that contributed to the Nazis' reduced dynamism was that the local leaders got rich and comfortable. County Leader Steineck, who had been literally penniless in December 1932, began to draw a salary in March 1933 (when the flood of new members swelled the party's coffers beyond belief) and it was very substantial: 810 marks a month. Henceforth he devoted himself to ceremonial activities, to drinking, and to supervising the restoration of old buildings.[2] He turned over the actual administration of County Northeim to subordinates like Walter Baldauf, a mild-mannered clerk in his late fifties who had joined the party two months after Hitler was appointed chancellor, and to other cool-eyed professionals.[3]

Even the fearsome Ernst Girmann became comfortable in the Third Reich. After March 1934 he held a twelve-year appointment as mayor of Northeim at a salary of 880 marks per month.[4] Once the new municipal code of January 1935 went into effect, Mayor Girmann was legally answerable to no one in Northeim and his power could not be contested. Girmann felt so secure of himself that he decided to abandon his position as Local Group Leader, which he did in September 1935, though he was careful to pick successors who would not become potential competitors. In fact, he arranged to weaken the office of Local Group Leader by splitting it in two. For the town's twelve hundred party members, "Local Group I" and "Local Group II," were created. To head them, Girmann chose two accountants, each with a pallid personality.[5] One was forty-one and the other was forty-four years old; both had joined the party a half-year before Hitler came to power; neither showed any ambition beyond administering the Local Group punctilliously, under Girmann's general direction.[6] In 1938 Girmann spent RM 20,000 of the city's money to rebuild and enlarge the town's riding hall, and shortly after that he rejoined the Stormtroopers so that he could become a member of the "Mounted SA" and ride a horse around the new track.[7] It was his major action after 1938.

Another reason Northeim's Nazis became less dynamic after 1935 was that they were no longer sure of the support of the people. As previously noted, enthusiasm for the NSDAP in Northeim had begun to wane even before Hitler came into power; in the last several months before the establishment of the Third Reich, the only Nazi meetings to draw full attendance were their relatively nonpolitical "evenings of entertainment." After the dictatorship was installed Northeimers went to Nazi meetings, but mainly because they felt compelled to. The incessant Nazi meetings bored and exhausted them and they resented being forced to go to them. As time went on the townspeople showed increasing signs of apathy—their only nondangerous form of escape.

Coerced participation in Nazi propaganda activities also destroyed what had been a key element in the success of the party's propaganda up to 1933: a feedback system to register popular responses, plus local control over most speakers and topics in order to adjust propaganda according to that feedback. By 1935 the higher propaganda offices of the Nazi party were dictating to local leaders. For example, a directive sent to Northeim in November 1935 concerning a forthcoming meeting contained three pages of details on how it was to be staged, including a step-by-step program, complete down to the exact words to be used in introducing the speaker (with space for his name left blank in the mimeographed form).[8]

The national directives on local meetings were skillfully contrived. They also tried to provide variety. For example, there was a wide choice of slide shows, including such entertainment-oriented titles as "Winter Sports in Germany."[9] But no matter what the content, meetings lost their attractiveness when people were forced to attend them. Beyond that, there were simply too many of them. Over the winter of 1938–39, for example, the number of meetings that party members were required to attend averaged one every three days.[10] Schedules became so crowded that they had to be prepared eight months in advance and no other club in the city was allowed to hold a meeting without first obtaining the Local Group Leaders' permission.[11]

When Northeimers were careless enough to let their apathy become visible, the party could still show its fangs. Sub-leaders were ordered to keep records of all who were supposed to attend Nazi meetings and to send the Local Group Leaders lists of those who missed a meeting.[12] People who failed to show up were confronted about it.[13] Explanations were demanded of those who left a meeting early.[14] And anyone who did not show appropriate enthusiasm at meetings might be threatened with a beating, as exemplified by the following letter Ernst Girmann sent to a young woman in 1935:

> It has been reported to me that on the occasion of the *Führer's* birthday ceremony you did not raise your arm during the singing of the Horst Wessel song and the national anthem. I call your attention to the fact that by doing this you put yourself in danger of being physically assaulted. Nor would it be possible to protect you, because you would deserve it. It is singularly provocative when people still ostentatiously exclude themselves from our racial community by actions like yours. *Heil Hitler!*[15]

Under these circumstances Northeimers were generally careful not to reveal anything but approved attitudes, both by word and deed. But this obviously meant only that Nazi threats were credible. Consequently, Northeim's Nazi leaders grew increasingly uncertain about the true attitudes of Northeimers and the leaders' uncertainty made them cautious in pressing people any more than they had to.

The one set of events that drove this home to Ernst Girmann (and the biggest mistake he made during the Third Reich in terms of delegitimizing Nazism in Northeim) was his attack on the Protestant church. There was no objective reason for the Nazis to confront the church in Northeim. Its pastors had blessed the installation of Hitler's dictatorship and, before 1933, Lutheran ministers had been among the most popular and effective Nazi speakers in the town. In fact, a large measure of Northeim's support for the NSDAP had come because the Nazis posed as a devoutly religious party. But Ernst Girmann hated the churches and (as he wrote to a friend in 1934) he was privately determined to "vanquish all the faith of the preachers through our faith in Hitler."[16] However, he had no clear plan as to how he would accomplish this, except by general intimidation. So his original campaign, against the Lutheran church, turned into a fiasco.

Girmann let it be known that his goal was to make Northeim the first town in Germany to be completely without church members. But his fulminations and threatening measures only increased the quiet opposition of the intensely Lutheran community. He was apparently afraid to simply arrest the pastors or to forcibly prevent church attendance because the higher offices of the Nazi party would not permit that. So instead he had the Hitler Youth break up meetings of confirmation classes, pelt the crucifix on the town church with snowballs, and spy on the pastor—in hopes of recording an incriminating statement that would justify Gestapo action.

None of this worked. Church attendance increased and the internal party resistance clique around Wilhelm Spannaus showed its defiance of Girmann by singing in the church choir. It was wholly passive resistance, but effective, since there was nothing Girmann could do about it. His attitude never changed but his intimidation campaign petered out in futility, especially after the war broke out and the Third Reich absolutely could not risk any further alienation of its own people.[17]

Having learned his lesson, Girmann became slyer, and consequently more effective, when he set out to abolish the religious schools in Northeim. Instead of blustering, he used bureaucratic tricks and a circuitous attack. His caution thus exemplifies the limits that even this ruthless fanatic felt constrained to observe.

Shortly after Easter in 1937, Mayor Girmann summoned the parents of pupils attending the small Catholic grammar school to a meeting. He informed them that their children were getting an inadequate education since the Catholic school, with only seventy-seven pupils and two teachers, offered an insufficient variety of courses. He urged the parents to transfer their children to the Evangelical-Lutheran school, with its thirteen hundred pupils and ample teaching corps.

Thirty-four Catholic parents complied immediately. One Northeimer (Benno Schmidt, a Socialist and confirmed anticleric who never went to church, though a nominal Catholic) had his wife transfer their daughter *into* the Catholic school just to defy Girmann, but most of Northeim's tiny Catholic community did not react so clearly. In the following months the mayor brought personal pressure on the parents, one at a time, so that there was a slow but steady exodus from the Catholic school.

The Bishop of Hildesheim protested vigorously when he learned what was happening, but Mayor Girmann defended his actions by asserting that his sole argument was the superior educational opportunities available at the Protestant school. Girmann claimed that all he did was urge parents to think of their children's future, and the Bishop could not prove that anything else was said to the Catholic parents in the mayor's office. By Christmas 1937 Northeim's Catholic school had only sixteen pupils left and Girmann petitioned the provincial school authorities (in accordance with standing regulations) to close it as a "dwarf school," which they did. Thereupon the mayor again petitioned the authorities, in February 1938, to declare the Lutheran school "nondenominational," since it now had a substantial number of Catholic pupils. This, too, was according to the book and so his request was granted. By April 1938 Northeim had no more religious schools.[18] Ernst Girmann had won.

But note how this year-long campaign worked. Any use of force, or even overt threats, would have jeopardized it. Skillful maneuvering, not dictatorial fiat, enabled Mayor Girmann to reach his ideologically motivated goal. Admittedly, one component was a heavy measure of informal intimidation in the mayor's personal interviews with Catholic parents. No matter how "correct" Girmann was in his pose of solicitation for the welfare of the children, the parents knew full well what he could do to people on one pretext or another. He was hardly a reassuring figure, sitting in his Nazi uniform under the portrait of Adolf Hitler. But that was all unspoken suggestion. Essentially Girmann got his way through bureaucratic politics and calculated restraint. He had learned about limits, just as other Northeimers had.

One group of Northeimers that Girmann could bully overtly were the members of the Nazi party and its affiliates. It will be recalled that immediately after Hitler came to power hundreds of townspeople joined the party for a variety of (mostly opportunistic) reasons. So the party members came to be a sizable portion of the town's population. In fact, it took the NSDAP until spring of 1936 to issue membership cards to all Northeimers who had applied before May 1, 1933 (the cutoff date imposed at that time).[19] Every applicant was immediately considered a provisional member, however, in terms of paying dues and fulfilling other duties imposed on "party comrades."

Northeim had approximately 1,200 party members by the summer of 1933, plus 450 Stormtroopers, 150 SA reservists, 140 SS men, 150 Hitler Youth, and 300 *Jungvolk* (the pre-Hitler Youth children's organization).[20] About 600 of these people belonged to more than one party organization and so would be counted twice, but even so, the Local Group had at least 1,500 Northeimers under its direct control—a good fifth of the city's adult population.

These people were the prime targets of Girmann's demands. This was partly because he could expel them from the party, which was a very serious matter in Hitler's Germany. But it was also because he was extremely skeptical about their commitment to the Nazi cause, since they had jumped on the bandwagon only after the Nazi victory. While he was still Local Group Leader the overwhelming portion of his correspondence consisted of attempts to maintain the purity of the party and the SA. He wrote threats to members who missed party meetings, who failed to contribute to Nazi collections, who were slow in paying their dues, or who made improper statements. For those who behaved correctly (according to his standards), there were also rewards to be distributed, such as letters of recommendation.[21] But supervising fifteen hundred people's behavior was an enormous task for one man, especially since Girmann found out that the reprimands outnumbered the rewards by something like a ten to one ratio.

Long before Ernst Girmann discovered how difficult it was for one Local Group Leader to keep control over so many people, the Nazi party had developed a system to divide the task. Every Local Group was broken up into "cells," each of which was to contain several "blocks"; each block was to supervise a few dozen households. In Northeim there were 12 cells and 80 blocks. Since the town contained about 3,500 households, the average Nazi "Block Warden" was responsible for 44 households. By being in close and constant contact with such a limited number of people, the Nazi Block Warden was supposed to bear the prime responsibility for representing their needs to the party as well as conveying the party's commands to them. The Block Warden was thus a crucial figure in the party's apparatus; to many people he *was* the Nazi party.[22]

Like so many Nazi schemes, the Block Warden system was undercut by its own contradictions. A conscientious Block Warden could either win the trust of the people assigned to him and therefore represent their wishes, or he could impose the demands of the party upon his people. But he could not do both. Since it was the party that held him accountable, the Block Warden inevitably became the party's eyes, ears, and mouth. Just as inevitably, the people learned to distrust him; deceit became central to this relationship, too. But essentially, the Block Warden became a pest since his major assignments were to get people to join a party organization, attend Nazi meetings, read Nazi publications, and contribute money to the party's weekly collection campaigns.[23] Northeimers grimaced when they saw the Block Warden approaching, but they had to smile politely when they met him. Of course the Block Warden knew this.

Moreover, the system obviously hinged on the personality of each individual Block Warden and in Northeim those who filled that office after 1935 were mainly timeservers rather than zealots. When the two accountants took over from Ernst Girmann as managers of Local Group Northeim, they obviously believed that their mandate was to bring the party's affairs into businesslike order. So one of the first things they did was to replace most of the previously appointed Nazi cadre leaders with capable businessmen. Almost all of the fanatical "old fighters" who had been Cell Leaders or Block Wardens up to 1935 were now retired and their offices were assumed by

"March casualties"—the opportunists who had jumped on the Nazi bandwagon in March 1933, when it had become clear that Hitler had taken over
the country. What was expected of them was efficiency, not fervor. These
new Block Wardens were *appointed* to office (sometimes clearly against their
will, as a consequence of threats) and were obviously supposed to carry out
their duties with punctuality and precision.[24]

The goals were limited, the results easily measured by standard bookkeeping practices, but the duties were tiresome. At least once a week the
Block Warden had to visit every one of his forty-four households to collect
"Winter Relief Fund" contributions, or otherwise pester people. Periodically the Nazi party demanded more. For example, when it was discovered
in 1939 that Northeim had a relatively low number of subscribers to a certain Nazi newsletter, the Block Wardens were pressured, and in turn pressured their people, so that within eight months the number of subscribers
doubled.[25] At another point it was decided that Germans should drink more
German wine and the Block Wardens were put to selling sample bottles door-
to-door. They managed to unload one bottle for every second household in
town.[26] And then there were the party orders to convey—an impossible task.
By 1939 the *Gauleitung* had some twenty separate offices, each one issuing
regulations for everyone in all aspects of life. No human could have followed them all.[27] Finally, the Block Warden was required to spy on his
households and was often called upon to submit written reports on their po-
litical-ideological reliability.

Yet it is precisely these "Political Evaluations of Individual Persons"
produced by Northeim's Block Wardens in the years after 1935 that demonstrate most dramatically how far the Nazi party had retreated from its millenialist aspirations.

The evaluations were demanded for a great variety of reasons. If a
Northeimer applied to buy a house in the new "settlement," or wanted to
become an officer in a guild or a club, or hoped to get any sort of government job, or was eligible for any social welfare payment, or even needed a
marriage license, there had to be a "political evaluation" on file. The Block
Warden filled out the form and the Cell Leader countersigned it. The questions on the form were very specific about whether the individual belonged
to a party organization, subscribed to the party press, had prior political associations, attended Nazi meetings, contributed money for "Winter Relief,"
and whether his wife and children also belonged, contributed, attended, etc.
The key question was: "Political reliability?"[28] The Block Warden's response to that question could make or break an individual.

Yet in completing over a thousand of these forms between 1935 and

1944, Northeim's Block Wardens hardly ever listed anyone as "politically unreliable." Ex-Communists, former monarchists, dissident Nazis, erstwhile *Reichsbanner* militants, or whatever—all received a clean bill of health from their harassed Block Warden, as long as they did one thing, and that was to make their Block Warden's life tolerable by contributing a few coins regularly and cheerfully when he made his weekly collection rounds. Block Wardens were often vague in filling out many of the answers, but they were specific and complete, positively or negatively, when they came to the blank opposite the question on contributions. And this subject also dominated the "further comments" section.

Of course, by 1935 virtually everyone belonged to some sort of Nazi organization (usually the "N. S. *Volk*-Welfare Society" or the "German Women's Work"), virtually everyone attended meetings and subscribed to some Nazi publication, and above all, almost every Northeimer had sense enough to contribute at least a token sum to the "Winter Relief Fund." Where negative comments were put into the "political evaluations," it was often for such personality characteristics as "selfish" or "unfriendly," indications that they had made the Block Warden's dreary duties more burdensome once a week. For a while after 1935 some of the forms had negative comments if a person was strongly religious (though usually it was Catholics rather than Lutherans who were so stigmatized, as reflective of the town's religious prejudices), but overwhelmingly Northeimers were routinely listed as "politically reliable." [29]

Since quite a few of those so characterized were most definitely not "reliable" (*i.e.*, they were bitter opponents of the Hitler regime before, during, and after the Third Reich), the political evaluations indicate essentially that the Block Wardens were no more interested in causing trouble than anyone else. They were interested in getting their assigned tasks done as routinely and perfunctorily as possible, and they understood how to keep from complicating matters since they themselves were members of the Nazi party out of convenience rather than conviction. [30] Thus, even the Nazi control mechanisms adjusted to the needs of daily life.

One thing the Block Wardens did report was any sign of an emerging Social Democratic underground. If former SPD activists met at someone's home, the Block Warden could not help but notice (in a small town like Northeim everyone knew everyone else by sight) and they quickly notified the higher-ups in the Nazi party. But such meetings were increasingly rare after 1935. [31] Socialists were also often loathe to use the prescribed greeting of *"Heil Hitler!"* (Friedrich Haase, noted his Block Warden, *never* said that), but after a while this, too, was overlooked. Even Ernst Girmann limited his goals as he discovered that others did not share them; this emerges from a comment he made about a Social Democrat who applied in 1934 to regain his job with the state-owned railroad: "I do not believe that Herr Strohmeyer will ever become a follower of the National Socialist regime, but he will also not say anything against it."[32] He endorsed the man's application.

The only arrests of Socialists in the mature Third Reich came in 1943, when three former SPD leaders were sent to a concentration camp. This was not on the initiative of Northeim's Nazis, nor was it because of any particular thing these Socialists had done. It was part of a nationwide preemptive sweep by the Gestapo in the wake of the German Army's disaster at Stalingrad.[33] Apart from this, there were no political arrests in Northeim after 1935.

The Block Wardens were also only peripherally involved in anti-Semitic actions in Northeim. That is, they occasionally reported fraternization between members of the Nazi party and Jews, since a Nazi order of September 1934 expressly prohibited party members from being seen in public, or on social occasions, with Jews.[34] This, too, was impossible to hide in a place as small as Northeim. But apparently the only consequences were a letter of reprimand to the offending Nazi, plus the loss of preference in future government job opportunities.[35]

This was consonant with the generally mild anti-Semitism that had characterized both the people and the Nazi party in Northeim prior to 1933. Since Ernst Girmann's ideological focus was on the churches, he had a somewhat relaxed attitude otherwise. His personal conviction was that no radical action need be taken against the town's Jews. As he explained in a letter he wrote in 1934, it would "break the power" of the Jews if people would simply avoid business or social contact with them. And he never even stressed that, except with members of the NSDAP. Eventually he expected "Jewish businesses to vanish from here."[36] He was even occasionally willing to write letters of endorsement for individual Jews from Northeim.[37]

Consequently there was hardly any maniest anti-Semitic action by the Nazis in Northeim during the last ten years of the Third Reich. On two occasions in 1935, Stormtroopers threw stones through the store window of one Jewish businessman who had had the temerity to "insult" them.[38] During the night of November 9, 1938, several Jewish stores on Broad Street were pillaged by Stormtroopers as part of the nationally organized "Reichskristallnacht," but the reaction of Northeimers to this (as was the case all over Germany) was so openly negative that it was the last public anti-Semitic incident in the town.[39] By the time Hitler determined to murder all the Jews in his power, as his "Final Solution," almost all of Northeim's Jews had left the town for a bigger city and supposed anonymity, or had gone to another country for safety. Northeimers did not harass their Jewish neighbors, but they also did their best not to "know" what their government was doing to the Jews.[40] By then, apathy and psychological denial had become a way of life.

By the outbreak of World War II an equilibrium had been achieved in Northeim. The party expected only acquiescence and ritualistic responses from the people, who gave them just that, in measured amounts. In return, the Nazi leaders were careful not to push people too far.[41] On the other hand, the party leaders were nervous enough about popular attitudes so that by 1937 they began to give training in the use of small arms to the Cell Leaders and Block Wardens, and then issued them pistols to wear with their uniforms.[42] That was rather comic, in view of the Block Wardens' collective record. Their major concern with the pistols was how to get rid of them in a hurry when the Third Reich collapsed.

With the coming of war the Nazi party in Northeim took on new tasks that kept it fully occupied and diminished even further its demands upon the townspeople. The Stormtroopers became air raid wardens; the party officials became something like social workers. That was partly because it was decided, nationally, that the party would undertake to represent the wives and dependents of soldiers who were called to war. Since Northeim was a garrison town, there were a large number of soldiers' wives; their prime need was adequate housing. Much of the work of Local Group Northeim involved finding apartments for these women and then adjudicating the inevitable squabbles that arose between them and their landladies. The problems became even more numerous after refugee families from the bombed cities of the Reich began to arrive in Northeim.

For the rest, the work of the party in Northeim consisted largely of answering queries as to whether a townsperson was "politically reliable"; helping people get jobs, state financial aid, or a dwelling; dealing with complaints engendered by wartime strictures such as rationing; intervening on behalf of party members to assure them favors; and clarifying bureaucratic questions about party membership.[43] In short, it was work the average nineteenth century Tammany Hall ward heeler would have understood, and it kept the Nazi leaders busy enough so that they hardly had time to harass the people.

The war, and the consequences of having pledged allegiance to Adolf Hitler, came home to the townspeople as the casualty figures began to mount. By December 1944 the privilege of being part of the Third Reich had cost Northeimers 148 dead, 57 missing-in-action, and 14 captured sons, fathers, and brothers—or 6 percent of the town's male population, not counting the wounded. On December 12, 1944, Allied bombers destroyed the railroad yards in Northeim. In the process, they also hit several nearby houses. Ironically, these were working-class homes, so the victims undoubtedly included men who had fought the Nazis in the streets before 1933. In other words, the Allied bombs killed anti-Nazis. In any case, this very minor raid killed 6 men, 15 women, and 7 children. Two more died later, for a total toll of 30.[44]

When units of the United States' Third Armored Division entered Northeim County in early April 1945, Ernst Girmann ordered the local militia to defend the town to the death. He himself took off his Nazi uniform and drove away to the hills east of Northeim with a case of *Schnapps* in his car. The militia followed his example, rather than his orders, and so the town surrendered without a fight. The local German Army, under General Wenck, was also interested in retreating, though their rear-guard action cost the Americans five Sherman tanks. And so some American sons, brothers, and fathers also died because of what had happened before 1933 in this small town on the Leine River.[45]

Northeim had survived the Third Reich. April 12, 1945, marked the end of it.

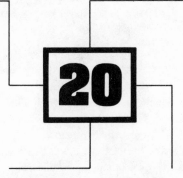

CONCLUSIONS

*The repetition of conditions is the
exception and not the rule, and when
such repetitions occur, they never arise
under exactly similar conditions.*

Friedrich Engels

Though Northeim was largely spared physical destruction in World War II, the town nevertheless underwent a radical change during and after the war. With the end of the Third Reich the Nazis, of course, vanished. Ernst Girmann was put in a P.O.W. camp for three years and then settled in a town near Northeim. In the late 1950s he returned to Northeim but lived a wholly withdrawn existence. The others had to go through "de-Nazification," which, at the least, stripped them of their civil rights to vote or hold office. After that they experienced collective amnesia about the Third Reich. The townspeople burned their swastika flags in April 1945, and shortly thereafter the British Army supervised the removal of all visible Nazi symbols. The occupation authorities also removed 853 Nazi books from the public library and pulped them for recycling. Wilhelm Spannaus made the selections.[1] The *Northeimer Beobachter* disappeared and the *Northeimer Neueste Nachrichten* (now subtitled "and Göttingen-Grubenhagensche Zeitung"), which had been shut down in 1942 as a "wartime economy measure," resumed publication and rapidly became again the most widely read newspaper in the town.

The occupation authorities appointed Carl Querfurt County Prefect for Northeim and he quickly and quietly reinstated a democratic local government. Thomas Galland became the town's chief administrator. The Social Democratic party reemerged practically overnight, and according to how the political currents have flowed, has governed Northeim whenever the conservatives have not. By the mid-1960s, the City Council's 21 seats were divided as follows: 10 SPD, 8 CDU, and 3 FDP. That was very close to how things had been before Hitler, but one major difference is that the conservatives and Socialists have learned to accept each other as legitimate; nowadays there isn't all that much to distinguish between them.

That is partly because, despite the apparent continuity, it was not the same town. During the war, refugees from Germany's larger cities poured into Northeim to escape the bombing and many of them stayed permanently after the collapse of the Third Reich. Even more refugees came to the little town from the areas occupied by the Russians. By 1950 the population of Northeim had doubled. By then probably only one out of every three inhabitants had been a Northeimer when Hitler had come to power.

Nor did the pre-Nazi social structure of rigid, mutually exclusive blocs, reassert itself. In the immediate postwar era economic misery was so evenly spread that, from 1945 through 1948, a truly classless society prevailed. Only status differentiations continued and, given the universal poverty, they no longer had much meaning. Then, with West Germany's subsequent economic miracle, income differentiations reappeared, but without the old im-mobility and chasms since a new economy created a new elite, while the mechanics of sustained full employment plus a strongly progressive income tax narrowed income gaps. There also emerged a new underclass of transient foreign workers so that, in contrast with them, the former German proletar-iat (earning close to the highest hourly wages in the world) moved up sev-eral social notches. Class lines became more fluid, too, partly as a heritage of the Nazi smashing of formal society, and partly because the massive in-flux of refugees scrambled the once precise and inflexible class associations and groupings. The result was that however Northeim's post World War II society might be described, it did not resemble the clefts and cohesions that had done so much to help Hitler into power. The old town was gone; it would never return.

Northeim is not now, and never was, a "typical" German town. The composition of Northeim in Weimar and Nazi days was not the same as the rest of Germany. There were an inordinate number of civil servants and the town was dominated economically by the railroad. Few places in Germany began the Third Reich with a two-thirds vote for the NSDAP, the national average being on the order of two-fifths. On the other hand, there were many places in Germany that saw more violence than Northeim in the early days of the Third Reich.[2]

What, then, is to be learned from Northeim's experience in the Nazi years?

In the first place, it is clear that an essential arena in the Nazi electoral surge and the seizure of power was on the local level, and that the critical figures were the local Nazi leaders. Northeim's Nazis created their own im-age by their own initiative, vigor, and propaganda. They knew exactly what needed to be done to effect the transfer of power to themselves in the spring of 1933, and they did it without more than generalized directives from above. Exactly how much was initiated locally and how much was promoted by the example of other Nazi groups in other towns or by the District and national Nazi leadership cannot yet be fully determined. Certainly there were no written orders from above, though there may have been verbal ones. But the major initiative clearly came from local leaders. It would be extremely interesting to know exactly what means were used by the NSDAP to instill the sense of purposefulness and initiative into its local groups, which were then used by the movement as a whole. It would be useful to know in explicit detail how coordination was combined with flexibility in this authoritarian instrument. The material available for this study of Northeim did not supply complete answers to these questions. It has, however, made clear that there would have been no Nazi revolution in Northeim, at least not of the totality that has been described here, without an active and effective local organization. Hitler, Goebbels, and the other Nazi leaders provided the political decisions, ideology, national propaganda, and, later, the control over the government that made the revolution possible. Hitler also gave his followers a simple goal that no other party shared: the idea of taking total and exclusive power at the first chance. But it was in the hundreds of localities like Northeim all over Germany that the revolution was made actual. They formed the foundation of the Third Reich.

As for the reasons behind the particular experience in Northeim, the most important factor in the victory of Nazism was the active division of the town along class lines. Though there was cohesion in Northeim before the Nazis began their campaigns leading to the seizure of power, the cohesion existed within the middle class or within the working class and did not extend to the town as a whole. The victory of Nazism can be explained to a large extent by the desire on the part of Northeim's middle class to suppress the lower class and especially its political representatives, the Social Democratic party. Nazism was the first effective instrument for this.

This is why Northeimers rejoiced in the gains of the Nazis and this is why they applauded the institution of the dictatorship. The antipathy of the middle class was not directed toward individual members of the SPD, but only toward the organization itself; not toward the working class as such, but only toward its political and social aspirations; not, finally, toward the reality of the SPD, but mainly toward a myth that they nurtured about the SPD. For a variety of reasons, Northeim's middle class was so intent on dealing a blow to the Social Democrats that it could not see that the instrument it chose would one day be turned against itself.

Exactly why Northeimers were so bitterly opposed to the Socialists cannot be answered on the basis of a study of this town alone; the answer lies in the history and social structure of Imperial and Weimar Germany, and possibly can be given only by a social psychologist. Nevertheless it seems clear that the nature of the SPD had something to do with the burghers' attitudes. Northeim's Socialists maintained slogans and methods which had little correspondence with reality. They maintained the façade of a revolutionary party when they were no longer prepared to lead a revolution. They never seriously attempted to mend fences with the middle class and frequently offended bourgeois sensibilities by their shortsightedness and shallow aggressiveness.

Yet it would be wholly incorrect to place all the blame upon Northeim's Social Democracy. The middle class responded to the existence of the SPD in ways which were almost paranoid. Its members insisted upon viewing the SPD as a "Marxist" party at a time when this was no longer so. They were determined to turn the clock back to a period when the organized working class was forcibly kept from exerting influence. They felt threatened by the very existence of this organization. This view of the SPD was not in accord with reality, since by any objective standard the goal of the SPD in Northeim was to maintain the kind of town that Northeim's middle class itself wanted.

What was needed in Northeim to stop the Nazis was a political coalition of the decent people, regardless of party, to recognize that—whatever it promised—Nazism was an indecent thing. That such a coalition never developed was the main reason the Nazis got into power. But it was the middle class that gave them their chance.

Perhaps the behavior of the good burghers of Northeim becomes more understandable when one realizes the extent to which they were committed to nationalism. The excess of patriotic feeling in the town during the pre-Hitler period was the great moral wedge for Nazism. In many ways the actions and beliefs of Northeimers during the last years of the Weimar era were the same as if World War I had never ended. It was in this sort of atmosphere that the SPD might seem treasonable and the Nazi reasonable.

A similar effect was wrought by the depression. While Northeim's middle class was not decisively affected by the economic crisis, the burghers were made desperate through fear and through an obsession with the effects of the depression, especially the sight of the unemployed. As for the effect of the depression upon the lower classes, it was equally large. There is no doubt that the progressive despair of the jobless, as reflected in the longer and longer periods of unemployment, weakened the forces of democracy in the town. It may be that this sapped the SPD's will to fight and led it into ritualistic responses to Nazism. It was hard for Socialists to bend all their efforts to combating Nazism when this involved defending a system that could produce this sort of economic misery. Had the SPD seriously undertaken to introduce democratic socialism in response to the depression, it seems likely they would have found new sources of strength among their own followers, and very likely might have won the votes of the many Northeimers who cast ballots for the NSDAP simply because the Nazis promised to end the depression. In short, intelligent and credible radicalism was a response the depression called for, but the Socialists did not offer it.

The depression exposed Northeim's Socialists in other ways, too. The use of economic pressure at the sugar factory and at the railroad deprived the SPD of much of its prestige and power. If it could not even defend its own people when the chips were down, how could it defend democracy, and how could it bring about the socialist society? The success of management's action at the railroad yards no doubt opened up several possibilities for the Nazis. It was there that they learned how economically vulnerable the workers were; it was there that they learned essentially that the SPD would not fight.

But the main effect of the depression was to radicalize the town. In the face of the mounting economic crisis, Northeimers were willing to tolerate approaches that would have left them indignant or indifferent under other circumstances. Thus the disgusting and debilitating party acrimony and violence mushroomed in the years before the dictatorship. The extent of the violence in Northeim was an expression of the radical situation, but it also added to it by making violence normal and acceptable. Along with the growing nationalism and increasing impatience over the depression, violence and political tension were significant factors in preparing the town for the Nazi takeover.

All these factors were exploited with considerable astuteness by Nazi propaganda. In the face of the senseless round of political squabbling and fecklessness, the Nazis presented the appearance of a unified, purposeful, and vigorous alternative. Their propaganda played upon all the needs and fears of the town and directed itself to almost every potential group of adherents. This was largely because the Nazis were willing to be programmatically flexible in their propaganda and because they had a simple feedback system to measure and adjust the effectiveness of their propaganda. By their own energy, adaptability, and effort Northeim's Nazis captured the allegiance of the town's confused and troubled middle class.

This set the stage for the actual seizure of power, but the revolution itself was also conducted in such a way as to insure success. The fact that this was, in the words of Konrad Heiden, a *"coup d'état* by installments" kept the *Reichsbanner* from responding decisively at any one point. By the time the SPD had been broken, the terror system had been inaugurated, largely through social reinforcement.

The single biggest factor in this process was the destruction of formal society in Northeim. What social cohesion there was in the town existed in the club life, and this was destroyed in the early months of Nazi rule. With their social organizations gone and with terror a reality, Northeimers were largely isolated from one another. This was true of the middle class but even more true of the workers, since by the destruction of the SPD and the unions the whole complex of social ties created by this super-club was effaced. By reducing the people of Northeim to unconnected social atoms, the Nazis could move the resulting mass in whatever direction they wished. The process was probably easier in Northeim than in most other places, since the town contained so many government employees. By virtue of their dependence on the government the civil servants were in an exposed position and had no choice but to work with the Nazis if they valued their livelihood. Especially Northeim's teachers—who formed the social and cultural elite of the town—found themselves drawn into support of the NSDAP almost immediately. As other Northeimers flocked to the Nazi bandwagon in the spring of 1933, and as terror and distrust became apparent, there was practically no possibility of resistance to Hitler.

Beyond this, the Nazis took considerable action to strengthen support, especially in the early months. There were the constant parades and meetings which gave the impression of irresistible enthusiasm and approval. There was the vigor in the economic area which more than anything else seemed to justify the dictatorship. But in addition to Nazi efforts on their own behalf, there were other factors that favored them. Many signs indicate that the depression was slowly curing itself by 1933. Moreover, there was the public works money allocated under the previous regime, but available just as the Nazis came to power. And one should probably also take into account the fact that the essential work of establishing the dictatorship came during the spring—a time when enthusiasm seems appropriate and revolution not wholly unnatural.

Thus many factors combined to make Nazism a possibility for Northeim. At the same time the town itself influenced the nature of Nazism as it manifested itself locally. It seems probable, for example, that the general lack of violence during the first months of the Third Reich was due to the nature of Northeim as a small town. Much as the Nazis hated all that the Socialist stood for, both sides knew each other too well for cold and systematic violence to occur. The SA might be willing to pummel their neighbors in a street fight, but they seemed to shrink from attacking the Socialists when they were defenseless. This is not to say that no violence took place, but it does help explain the fact that no one was killed and very few were sent to a concentration camp from Northeim during the early years of the Nazi regime. On the one occasion when Ernst Girmann seemed determined to turn the Stormtroopers loose on Carl Querfurt and his little tobacco store, it was not members of the Northeim SA who were to do the dirty work; truckloads of Stormtroopers from another town were imported for the occasion. The subsequent relationship of Querfurt and Girmann substantiates this again; it was hard for even the worst fanatic to be utterly ruthless against someone who had grown up in the same block with him.

The smallness of Northeim, the fact that many families had known each other for generations, undoubtedly modified the nature of the mature dictatorship. The Nazis could come and go but the "Club for the Defense of Old Northeim Privileges"—composed of old city dwellers of every hue in the political spectrum—continued to meet and work together to make sure they would receive their annual ration of free beer, their 18 marks' worth of wood from the town forest.[3] There were other things that seemed to stay the same after Hitler came to power. While the Nazis claimed uniqueness for their charity efforts, it can be shown that Northeimers gave just as much to their various separate charity organizations before 1933. While the Nazis felt they were doing something new by bringing the Army to Northeim, it should be remembered that the love of the military was something that the town had been noted for long before Ernst Girmann ever thought about it.

In fact, in many ways Girmann and his Nazi administration were simply the embodiment of the small-town chauvinism that Northeim displayed in the pre-Nazi period. When it came to a choice between Nazi ideals and promoting Northeim as a tourist center, Girmann had no hesitation. If important visitors came to Northeim he made sure they were lodged in the Hotel Sonne, because it was the best hotel in town, even if its owner was a former leading Nationalist party member and a master of the forbidden freemasons.[4] On the other hand, there were Northeimers who saw nothing new in Nazism, except possibly the chance to put into effect policies they had hoped for over a long period. To several leading members of the Northeim shooting societies, for example, the introduction of the Hitler regime simply meant that they could now have their 300-meter target range. To several of the town's businessmen, Nazism simply meant that now was the time to promote the concept that Northeimers ought to do their shopping at home. And no matter what their Nazi leader told them, Northeimers would not stop going to church, because that was what they had always done on Sundays.

Finally, it is possible to construe the actions of Ernst Girmann after he came to power as expressive of the class divisions of Northeim. Nothing is more difficult to discover than the truth about personal motivation, but many of the actions taken by Girmann and his closest friends suggest that they were a product of social resentment. Girmann was of the lower middle class and this undoubtedly made its mark upon him in a town where government and society were dominated by an elite that freely expressed its cool sense of superiority over the *petite bourgeoisie* as well as over the workers. When the Nazis came to power in Northeim they destroyed the SPD and its suborganizations and hounded Socialist leaders, but this is explicable because of the intransigent political opposition between Nazism and Social Democracy. What Girmann wanted of the Socialists was that they be rendered impotent, not degraded (except insofar as this would produce a sense of political futility). Thus he could endorse the job application of a Socialist who, in Girmann's estimation, would never support Hitler's regime.[5] And thus he was capable of producing one of his rare smiles when a common worker defied him; when he attempted to harass Carl Querfurt's brother, Querfurt was able to stop this by telling Girmann: "Look, if you want someone to pick on, try me—but leave my family alone."[6] This Girmann respected; what he hated were the upper classes of the town. In this he was seconded by his clique. As Hermann Denzler once said of Wilhelm Spannaus: "An honest Communist is more to my liking than such a *Scheiss-Akademiker.*"[7]

As a result, Girmann did things to the town's elite that he never did to outright political opponents. The methods used in the long and sordid process of ousting Mayor Peters were as unnecessary as they were disgusting. The attempt to degrade Thomas Galland falls in the same category. Girmann's treatment of the shooting societies and the Retail Merchants' Association went beyond customary "coordination"; they were a measure of his contempt. The same approach characterized all of his relationships with the town's upper crust, Wilhelm Röhrs of the GGZ being the most conspicuous example. The final expression of this attitude was in Girmann's struggle against the Lutheran church, which was more bitterly pursued in Northeim than in most other places in Germany. By attacking the citadel of the town's respectability with such extreme means and low methods, Ernst Girmann was possibly attempting to triumph over the environment in which he had grown up and which had condemned him previously to the condescension of his social betters.

Yet Northeim's people, even in the depths of the Third Reich, found ways to make Girmann and his followers accept the reality of the town's attitudes. Indeed, one slightly encouraging aspect of Northeim's experience with the Hitler dictatorship can be seen in the limits that even fanatical Nazis found they had to respect. Despite their arrogant supposition that they could challenge and change the nature of humanity, the Nazi leaders were forced to settle for external compliance rather than internalized commitment on the part of the townspeople. At least from 1935 to 1945, boredom and apathy were factors that the Nazi movement could not surmount. They could compel Northeimers to attend meetings and pretend enthusiasm, but that was largely a mutually agreed on charade and the great mystery was who was deceiving whom: those who pretended that their behavior had meaning or those who encouraged the pretense? In return for outward conformity, Northeim's Nazi leaders did not inflict much violence upon the townspeople in the mature Third Reich, but it is manifest that the Nazi leaders also knew that conformity depended on the unspoken threat of violence and was outward only. Acceptance of these rules made life temporarily tolerable in many aspects of daily experience.

This was a dubious triumph and should hardly be taken as an exoneration of the people of Northeim from the murderous deeds of their national government. Rather, when put in the broader context of the Nazi experience, it shows how ineffective cynicism, deceit, accommodation, apathy, denial, and determined indifference are as human survival tactics. The adjustments Northeimers forced upon their Nazi masters made it possible for the townspeople to live in the Third Reich, but popular passivity also made possible the crimes that the Nazis were able to perpetrate upon the human race. In some ways, the greatest Nazi crime was to encourage and justify moral numbness, even in those who did not agree with the Nazis. That is because this moral numbness was the prerequisite for all the other shameful crimes of Nazism.

Moreover, the Nazi dictatorship eventually afflicted even Northeimers who had made their peace with it. Ultimately almost every Northeimer came to understand what the Third Reich was bringing them. Most Northeimers learned what a dictatorship meant when they experienced the general breakdown of trust and of social communication. All became aware of it when Hitler's policies brought war to them—a war that the people feared and hated.[8] Despite the super-patriotism of the pre-Nazi years, there was no cheering in the streets of Northeim when the garrison marched out of town in 1939. The war brought hunger with it, especially after 1945, and the sons of many Northeimers learned to temper their love of militarism on the cold steppes of Russia. Their parents learned that Nazism meant death.

But no one foresaw these consequences in the days when Northeim's middle class was voting overwhelmingly for the introduction of the Third Reich. And that, perhaps, is the most significant lesson of all to be gained from this town's experiences during and prior to the Nazi seizure of power. Hardly anyone in Northeim in those days grasped what was happening. There was no real comprehension of what the town would experience if Hitler came to power, no real understanding of what Nazism was.

The Social Democrats failed to comprehend the nature of the Nazi appeal; so did the Jews and Lutherans, both of whom were to suffer bitterly under the Nazi whip. Even many convinced members of the NSDAP itself, such as Wilhelm Spannaus, had a completely false perception of what they were promoting. There was not even a teacher from Northeim's famous schools to ask why, if the German people were the *Herrenvolk* that Hitler kept telling them they were, they would have to be turned into a nation of terrorized serfs in order to achieve their supposed destiny.

Each group saw one or the other side of Nazism, but none saw it in its full hideousness. Only later did this become apparent, and even then not in the same degree to everyone. The problem of Nazism was primarily a problem of perception. In this respect, Northeim's difficulties and Northeim's fate are likely to be shared by other humans in other towns under similar circumstances. The remedy will not easily be found, but knowledge and understanding would seem to be the first step toward it.

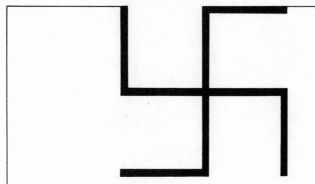

APPEN-
DICES

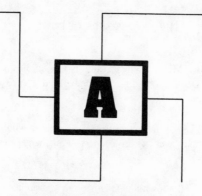

A DESCRIPTIVE LIST OF INDIVIDUALS INTERVIEWED FOR THIS BOOK

Quotation marks around a name indicate persons with pseudonyms. Order of information: occupation, political leanings, religion, age, chief activities, other.

"HANS ABBENRODE." Grade school principal, voted middle-of-the-road. Lutheran, aged 38 in 1930.

GREGOR BALLIN. Professional man, member of the Democratic party. Jewish, aged 45 in 1930. Veteran of and wounded in World War I.

RUDOLF BÜCKMANN. High school principal, member of the Nationalist party. Lutheran, aged 42 in 1930. University graduate.

HERMANN DENZLER. Owner of a dry-goods store, member of the Nazi party and of the SS. Nominal Lutheran, aged 30 in 1930. Later a senator for Northeim. Veteran of World War I.

THOMAS GALLAND. Civil servant in city administration, member of the Democratic party. Lutheran, aged 30 in 1930.

JOHANNES GROTE. Semi-skilled laborer in City Gas Works, union leader, active member of the Social Democratic party. Nominal Catholic, aged 48 in 1930. Past member of Northeim City Council. Veteran of World War I and holder of the Iron Cross. First Class.

FRIEDRICH HAASE. Minor civil servant in the employ of Northeim County, member of the Social Democratic party. Lutheran, aged 27 in 1930. Prominent leader of the local *Reichsbanner*.

MARIA HABENICHTS. Wife of a high school teacher who was a member of the People's party. Lutheran, aged 35 in 1930. Her husband was a Freemason and a veteran of World War I.

ANNA HUEG. Wife of the town's chief historian and author, Adolf Hueg. Slightly right-of-center in political beliefs, Lutheran, aged 33 in 1930.

"ERHARDT KNORPEL." Newspaper reporter for the *Northeimer Neueste Nachrichten* (a moderate newspaper), voted People's party. Lutheran, aged 38 in 1930. Veteran of World War I.

"HEINRICH LAMME." Assistant director of a private bank, voted for the Democratic party. Lutheran, aged 27 in 1930.

CARL QUERFURT. Small businessman (retail merchant); one of the local leaders of the Social Democratic party. Lutheran, aged 43 in 1930. Member of the City Council. Senator, delegate to the County Council. Veteran of World War I.

EVA RÖHRS. Wife of the owner-editor of the *Göttingen-Grubenhagensche Zeitung*, a Rightist newspaper. Voted for the Nationalist party, of which her husband was an active member. Lutheran, aged 48 in 1930.

"BENNO SCHMIDT." Unskilled day laborer, mostly for the city labor pool. Leftist, though never an actual member of the Social Democratic party. Nominal Catholic, aged 28 in 1930.

OTTO VON DER SCHULENBERG. County Prefect, 1932–45, member of the People's party. Lutheran, aged 42 in 1930. A professional government official of considerable ability.

HERMANN SCHULZE. Semiskilled railroad worker and union leader, active member of the Social Democratic party. Atheist, aged 31 in 1930. Leader of the *Reichsbanner* in a small suburb immediately adjacent to Northeim, Works Council member at the Northeim railroad yards.

WILHELM SPANNAUS. Owner of a bookstore, member of the Nazi party (first person in Northeim to join the Nazi party, but disenchanted with it after 1933). Lutheran, aged 43 in 1930. Former teacher in South America. An intellectual.

INDIVIDUALS INTERVIEWED

"HUGO SPIESSMANN." Civil servant, director of City Savings Bank, Rightist political convictions. Lutheran, aged 45 in 1930. Veteran of World War I.

"KURT ZEISSER." Printer's apprentice and member of the Hitler Youth. Nominal Lutheran, aged 13 in 1930.

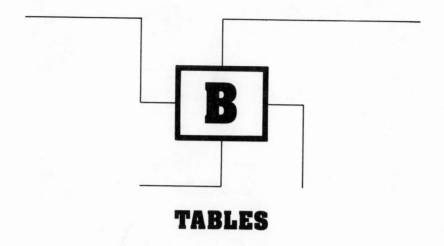

TABLES

TABLE 1

Unemployment, Northeim Employment Office District, 1930–1933*

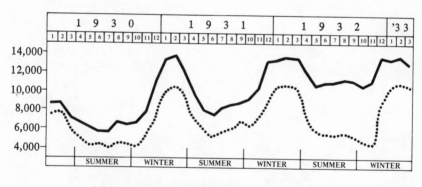

——— REGISTERED UNEMPLOYED

······ RECEIVING UNEMPLOYMENT OR "EMERGENCY" PAYMENTS

---

*Statistical base: monthly reports in the *Northeimer Neueste Nachrichten* and Oberamtmann Nolte, "Arbeit und Wirtschaft in Arbeitsamtbezirk Northeim, bearbeitet in Arbeitsamt Northeim, 1938/39" (ms. in files of the Northeim District Employment Office).

TABLE 2
Unemployment, City of Northeim, 1930–1933*

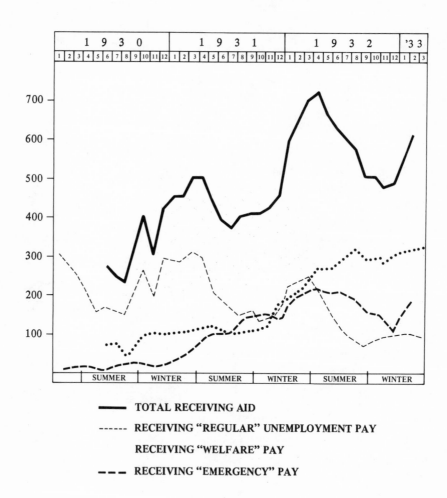

—— TOTAL RECEIVING AID

------ RECEIVING "REGULAR" UNEMPLOYMENT PAY

RECEIVING "WELFARE" PAY

– – – RECEIVING "EMERGENCY" PAY

*Same sources as Table 1.

TABLE 3
Unemployment, City of Northeim, 1930–1933
(Parentheses Indicate Incomplete Figures)

	Unemploy-ment Pay	Emer-gency Pay	Welfare Pay	Total
1930				
January	313	16	?	(329)
February	297	18	?	(315)
March	264	18	?	(282)
April	200	19	?	(219)
May	159	19	?	(178)
June	175	15	82	272
July	(149)	(22)	82	(253)
August	151	36	47	234
September	178	33	(75)	(286)
October	271	31	102	404
November	189	26	97	312
December	298	42	97	437
1931				
January	296	61	103	460
February	281	69	110	460
March	313	78	114	505
April	304	87	114	505
May	224	101	125	450
June	191	102	107	400
July	162	115	111	388
August	152	143	114	409
September	159	143	113	415
October	147	145	126	418
November	147	152	136	435
December	159	141	165	465

*Same sources as Table 1.

TABLE 3
(continued)

	Unemploy- ment Pay	Emer- gency Pay	Welfare Pay	Total
1932				
January	219	186	202	607
February	231	199	222	652
March	250	217	237	704
April	239	220	282	741
May	168	202	273	643
June	132	207	288	627
July	(103)	(193)	303	(599)
August	73	179	328	580
September	61	160	283	504
October	53	152	298	503
November	65	128	273	466
December	69	112	306	487
1933				
January	?	?	317	(317)
February	107	199	321	627
March	?	?	317	(317)
April	88	160	296	544
May	56	159	266	481
June	60	163	245	468

TABLE 4

National Elections in Northeim, 1928–1932*

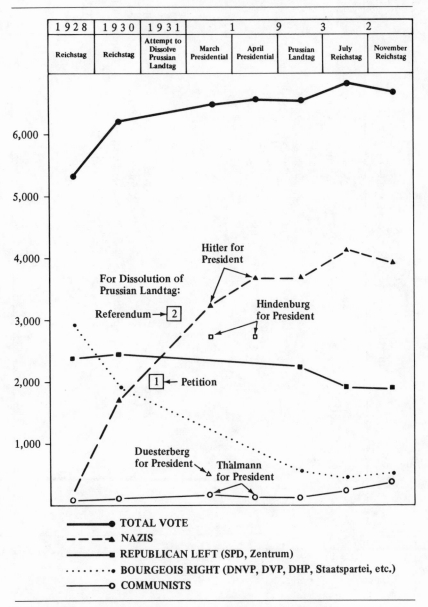

1 9 2 8	1 9 3 0	1 9 3 1	1	9	3	2	
Reichstag	Reichstag	Attempt to Dissolve Prussian Landtag	March Presidential	April Presidential	Prussian Landtag	July Reichstag	November Reichstag

- ● TOTAL VOTE
- ▲ NAZIS
- ■ REPUBLICAN LEFT (SPD, Zentrum)
- • BOURGEOIS RIGHT (DNVP, DVP, DHP, Staatspartei, etc.)
- ○ COMMUNISTS

*Compiled from reports in the *Northeimer Neueste Nachrichten*.

TABLE 5
National Elections in Northeim, 1928–1933*

Election	NSDAP	DNVP	DHP	Staatspartei	DVP	Zentrum	SPD	KPD	Other	Total
Reichstag 1928	123	475	455	505**	834	170	2210	28	572	5372
Reichstag 1930	1742	320	271	246	788	184	2246	115	275	6169
Petition to Dissolve Prussian Landtag April 1931 *Signers:* 2246	Backed by NSDAP, DVP, DNVP, KPD, DHP, Staatspartei, and splinters									
Referendum to Dissolve Prussian Landtag August 1931 "Ja": 3333 "Nein": 253 (not voting counts as "Nein")										

NSDAP—Nazis, DNVP—Nationalists, DHP—Hanoverians, DVP—People's Party, Zentrum—Catholic Center, SPD—Social Democrats, KPD—Communists

Election	NSDAP	DNVP	DHP	Staats-partei	DVP	Zentrum	SPD	KPD	Other	Total
	Hitler	Duesterberg					Hindenburg	Thälmann	Winter	
Presidential Vote #1 March 1932	3261	240				Backed by DVP, SPD, Zentrum, and splinters	2789	182	22	6494
Presidential Vote #2 April 1932	3696	NSDAP-DNVP Coalition				Staatspartei, and splinters	2777	127	—	6600
Prussian Landtag April 1932	3620	202	62	105	154	175	2024	117	126	6585
Reichstag July 1932	4195	212	41	66	69	191	1639	285	32	6730
Reichstag Nov. 1932	3928	301	51	34	136	176	1627	338	37	6628
Reichstag 1933	4268	406	62	67	101	183	1470	228	17	6802

*Same source as Table 4.

**Includes Democrats who thereafter voted DVP, SPD, or NSDAP.

NSDAP—Nazis, DNVP—Nationalists, DHP—Hanoverians, DVP—People's Party, Zentrum—Catholic Center, SPD—Social Democrats, KPD—Communists

TABLE 6
Political Meetings in Northeim, 1930–1933*

1930	Nazis	Nationalists	Socialists	Others
January	1	0	1	0
February	2	0	0	0
March	5	0	1	0
April	1	0	1	0
May	2	0	1	0
June	3	0	1	0
July	0	0	1	0
August	4	0	4	0
September				
(Reichstag Election)	3	1	2	3
October	3	0	0	1
November	4	0	1	0
December	2	0	2	0
1931				
January	2	0	2	0
February	4	1	5	1
March	2	2	2	1
April				
(Petition to Dissolve				
Prussian Landtag)	2	1	2	2
May	3	0	1	0
June	1	1	4	0
July	2	0	3	0
August				
(Referendum to				
Dissolve Prussian				
Landtag)	3	0	2	2

*Compiled from reports in the *Northeimer Neueste Nachrichten, Göttingen-Grubenhagensche Zeitung,* and *Göttinger Volksblatt.*

TABLE 6
(continued)

	Nazis	Nationalists	Socialists	Others
1931 (continued)				
September	2	2	0	0
October	2	0	0	0
November	3	0	0	1
December	2	0	2	0
1932				
January	2	2	3	0
February	2	2	2	3
March				
(First Presidential				
Election)	5	2	3	1
April				
(Second Presidential				
and Prussian				
Landtag Elections)	5	2	4	4
May	4	0	1	0
June	3	0	1	0
July				
(Reichstag Election)	6	1	5	3
August	0	0	0	0
September	2	1	0	0
October	4	1	1	0
November				
(Reichstag Election)	1	1	2	0
December	3	1	1	0
1933				
January				
(Hitler Becomes				
Chancellor)	3	0	1	1
February	4	2	1	1

TABLE 6
(continued)

1933 (continued)	Nazis	Nationalists	Socialists	Others
March (Reichstag and Local Elections)	12	1	0	0
April	6	1	0	0
May	6	0	0	0
June	6	0	0	0
July	4	1	0	0
August	5	1	0	0
September	7	0	0	0
October	5	0	0	0
November (Reichstag Election and Plebiscite)	7	0	0	0
December	2	0	0	0

Note: All parties other than the Nazis were outlawed on July 14, 1933. The "Nationalists" meetings of July/August were actually *Stahlhelm* ones.

TABLE 7
Political Meetings and Political Fights in Northeim, 1930–1932*

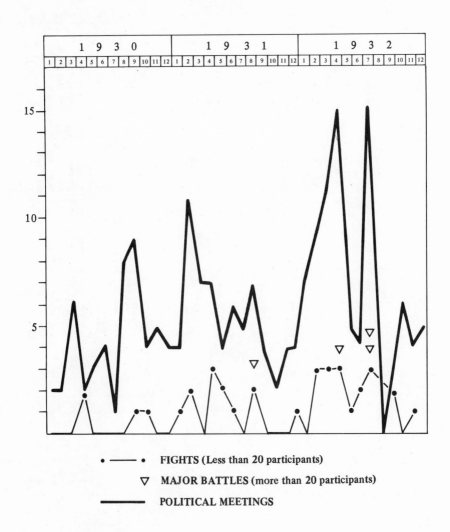

* Same sources as Table 6.

TABLE 8
Topics at Nazi Meetings in Northeim, 1930–1933*

	JAN	FEB	MAR	APR	MAY	JUN	JUL	AUG	SEP	OCT	NOV	DEC
1930	3	6, 7	5, 8, 11, 13, 14	5	10, 11	4, 13, 14		9, 10, 11, 12	12, 13, 13	11, 12, 13	6, 12, 13, 14	13, 14
1931	8, 9	4, 7, 8, 11	5, 14	7, 14	6, 9, 11	14	12, 13	12, 13, 13	4, 14	4, 14	10, 11, 14	2, 14
1932	7, 14	6, 12	7, 8, 9, 10, 11	1, 10, 11, 11, 14	10, 13, 14, 14	2, 14, 14	5, 8, 12, 12, 14, 14		9, 13	1, 3, 14, 14	3	14, 14, 14
1933	12, 14, 14											

Numbers refer to subjects: 1—Pensions (2); 2—Christianity (2); 3—Capitalism (3); 4—Youth (4); 5—Jews (4); 6—Foreign Policy (4); 7—Civil Servants and Middle Class (5); 8—Militarism (5); 9—The Republic or "System" (5); 10—General Economics (6); 11—"Marxism"—the SPD (10); 12—History and Theory of Nazism (10); 13—Unclassifiable (12); 14—Pure Pageantry/Entertainment (26).

Frequency (in parentheses) in ascending order.

*Same sources as Table 6.

TABLE 9
Terror Activities in Northeim
January 31, 1933—June 31, 1933
As Reported by the Local Press*

	House Searchings	*Arrests*
February 3	"at homes of Communists"	———
March 1	"at Communists and Socialists"	one Socialist
March 2	"at a Communist's home"	one Communist
March 6	———	seven Communists
March 14	———	one Socialist
March 29	———	one Socialist one Communist
April 4	"at several homes"	four "Leftists"
April 8	"at several homes"	———
April 10	"at several homes"	———
April 19	"at several homes"	———
April 24	"at one home"	one
April 28	"at one home"	one
May 5	"at several offices"	———
May 9	———	one "worker"
May 12	"at SPD offices"	———
June 2	"at Liga für Mütterschütz"	———
June 17	———	one SPD Councilman
June 19	———	one woman "Communist"
June 21	"at a Rightist office"	———
June 24	"at Union offices"	———
June 30	———	one "worker"
Total	14 different occasions	22 persons

*Note: This table shows only those actions reported in the press. Actual arrests and searchings were more numerous. Sources same as Table 6.

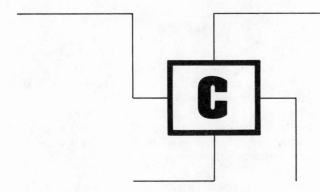

THE NORTHEIM NSDAP

A Formal Statement to the *Gauleitung* in defense of the assertion that "Dreadful Conditions Prevail in Local Group Northeim of the NSDAP." Submitted by Party-Comrade Edmund Venzlaff (Number —), June 20, 1933.

On Friday, June 16, 1933, *Kreisleiter* Walter Steineck and *Ortsgruppenleiter* Ernst Girmann demanded to know why I used the expression "dreadful conditions in the Local Group." In response to this I am sending the following formal statement to the *Gauleitung*.

1) *Financial Matters.* I accuse the *Ortsgruppenleiter* of not having assured the necessary cleanliness and order in party finances. On the contrary; he attempted to hinder this in many cases.

a) In the case of the irregularities in the Women's Group Northeim, Party-Comradess Meyer, he made the statement "I shall permit no clarification in this matter." (Witness: Party-Comrade Spannaus).

b) The receipts demanded by Party-Comrades E and F when they were examining the books last December, concerning election campaign expenditures, contributions, receipts from membership applications, etc., were never made available. (Refer report of Party-Comrade F to the *Gau-Uschla*.)

c) In December of last year many Party-Comrades met at the home of Party-Comrade C, discussed this, and laid the complaint before the *Ortsgruppenleiter*. He declared criticism to be healthy and asked for further cooperation in this sense. A few weeks later, on January 1, 1933, he expelled those Party-Comrades for plotting. (Witness: Party-Comrades C and Voge.)

d) In January 1933, the *Ortsgruppenleiter* called together a commission for the purpose of examining ways of covering debts incurred. Present were Party-Comrades

Spannaus, B, C, H, I, and J. The *Ortsgruppenleiter* was not present because of sickness, but was represented through his brother. The commission unanimously declared they would undertake nothing until a list of the debts, an explanation of how they were incurred, and a plan for the covering of them was presented. The commission was therefore never called again. The will to positive cooperation on the part of the members of the abortive commission is shown by the collections undertaken by them and the gifts made by them in connection with the election of March 5, 1933.

e) Concerning the holding back of registrations from the months of June, July, and August 1932, and the incorrect acceptance of donations, see my complaint to the *Gauleitung* of June 11, 1933.

f) To cover the debts of the Local Group, the *Ortsgruppenleiter* raised the monthly dues by 50 *Pfg*/mo. without having the approval of a Local Group meeting. In consideration of the financial misuses, many Party-Comrades refused to pay this.

g) The *Ortsgruppenleiter* demanded that every Party-Comrade in our Local Group make a special donation of at least RM 10.00 (see the enclosed). This was done arbitrarily.

h) On the same basis extra high entrance fees were demanded of new applicants, which were paid by most of them, since they feared that otherwise they would not be admitted to the NSDAP.

i) The present treasurer of the Local Group, Party-Comrade K, is reputed to have refused to do more than certify the amount of cash on hand when he took over that office because he did not want to be made responsible for his predecessor's malfeasance. I ask him to stand witness to this.

2) Unscrupulousness in the Choice of Methods.

a) On January 12, 1933, the *Ortsgruppenleiter* told the *Orts-Uschla* Chairman, Party-Comrade E, that he had been relieved of his post by action of the *Gauleitung* and the *Gau-Uschla*. This was untrue. (Witness: Party-Comrade E.)

b) Twice, on January 19 and January 28, 1933, the *Ortsgruppenleiter* asked the *Orts-Uschla* chairman, Party-Comrade E, to sign the expulsion of Party-Comrades Voge and C, and of Party-Comradesses L, M, and N, in spite of the fact that an *Uschla* trial had never occurred and in spite of the fact that he had already on January 12 declared Party-Comrade E removed from his office.

c) Shortly thereafter the *Ortsgruppenleiter* asked a member of the *Orts-Uschla* (Party-Comrade Schierloh) to sign alleged minutes of an *Orts-Uschla* trial according to which Party-Comradesses L and M were expelled from the Party, although such an *Uschla* trial had never occurred. Party-Comrade Schierloh refused to do this.

d) Later the *Ortsgruppenleiter* demanded that the documents concerning the case of Party-Comrade Döring be surrendered to him. This was refused. (Witness: Party-Comrade Schierloh.) (See below.)

e) The gravest suspicion exists that the *Ortsgruppenleiter* sets Party-Comrades to spying on other Party-Comrades who don't comply with his wishes. I ask the City Inspector, Party-Comrade Q, to say whether or not he was requested to spy on Party-Comrade R. But assure Party-Comrade Q that he won't lose his job, for the city employees stand under the constant dread of the dictatorial methods of the *Ortsgruppenleiter,* since, if they oppose him in any way, they will lose their bread. (See below.)

f) At the election of the senators, the city councillors expressed objections to the choice of Party-Comrade Ude because, owing to his fraudulent and illegal activities (of which I call Party-Comrade S to bear witness), he had a bad reputation. The *Ortsgruppenleiter* declared "I need Ude as a fighter. The era of Mayor Peters is absolutely finished. Ude will be the one to drive his fist to the Mayor's heart." And when the councillors still refused to do as he wished, the *Ortsgruppenleiter* declared: "As *Ortsgruppenleiter* I declare that Ude is senator." (Witness: Party-Comrade G)

g) Shortly thereafter, the *Ortsgruppenleiter* said to the witness above, Party-Comrade G, a city councillor: "If you won't obey, then you'll have to resign. You'll be surprised! I'll soon publish the first article against you in the newspaper. If you won't obey, I'll have your tavern boycotted and Voge (Speaker of the Council) will be transferred to East Prussia" (Party-Comrade Voge is a teacher.) (Witness: Party-Comrade G.)

h) A similar situation developed at the election for the Chamber of Industry and Trade. I refer to the complaint sent by Party-Comrade T to the *Gauleitung.*

3) *Untruthfulness of the Ortsgruppenleiter.* The *Ortsgruppenleiter* has a bad reputation for lack of truthfulness in Northeim. He himself once said to Party-Comrade Voge: "What is 'word of honor'? I recognize no word of honor." Here are some examples with evidence:

a) See cases 2 a, b, and c.

b) See cases 2 a, b, and c.

c) On January 30, 1933, he told Party-Comradess M that the *Gauleitung* had demanded her expulsion. The *Gauleitung* knows best that this is untrue.

d) A few weeks ago Party-Comrade Döring declared that the *Ortsgruppenleiter* lied not once but many times. He told Party-Comrade Ude to tell that to the *Ortsgruppenleiter.* Thereupon the *Ortsgruppenleiter* sought out Party-Comrade Döring and struck this man, 25 years his senior, to the ground. (See the complaint of Party-Comrade Döring to the *Gauleitung.*) To me, the *Ortsgruppenleiter* said on June 16: "I shouldn't have just knocked Döring down. I should have beaten him across the Market Square with a dog whip. And those other pigs who are spreading vulgar rumors about me will get even worse. The next in line is Spannaus."

e) While he constantly protected the then leader of the Women's Group, Party-Comradess Meyer, and declared: "I shall permit no clarification in this matter," he said privately to Party-Comrade U: "You're right, Frau Meyer is guilty of everything."

f) An inner untruthfulness is at least extant if the *Ortsgruppenleiter* at the burning of the "Filth Literature" on the market raged against the Jews while his own sister is married to a Jewish Lawyer in Einbeck without the *Ortsgruppenleiter* having ever ceased his friendly traffic with her.

4) *The Ortsgruppenleiter Permits Corruption and Graft.* Since the *Magistrat* in Northeim has consisted of four National Socialist senators one often hears the judgment: "The Nazis understand corruption and graft better than the reds."

a) The senators voted themselves a salary of RM 50.00/month each, through the *Ortsgruppenleiter* previously declared the offices of senator and councillor to be purely honorary. The city councillors have raised protest against this. (Witness: Party-Comrade C.)

b) The *Ortsgruppenleiter* arranged to have his father-in-law, in whose leather goods store he works, get the contract for the boots for the Labor Service camp. (Witness: Party-Comrade Spannaus.)

c) The *Ortsgruppenleiter* arranged for his brother, who has an iron goods store and who long ago ceased dealing in glassware, to be awarded the contract for beer glasses at the City Brewery. One of the *Ortsgruppenleiter's Dezernate* is the Brewery. (Witness: Party-Comrade Voge.)

d) The *Ortsgruppenleiter* arranged for his brother to be awarded the contract for garden chairs at the Brewery, although another ironmonger, Party-Comrade V, submitted a cheaper bid for the order. (Witness: Party-Comrade Voge.)

e) The *Ortsgruppenleiter* arranged for his brother to receive the order for caster-wardrobes for the city, although his brother does not stock such items and though other Party-Comrades in the town do. (Witness: Party-Comrade Voge.)

f) Senator Ude arranged to have the city drop its milk delivery contract with Party-Comrade W despite the fact that the contract with W was very favorable for the town. Ude's intention was to obtain the contract for himself.

5) *The Ortsgruppenleiter is not a True National Socialist.*

a) Party-Comrade Girmann has belonged to the party for a long time but was never active until March 1, 1931, when he appeared at a members' meeting and immediately took upon himself the office of deputy *Ortsgruppenleiter*. The general judgment is that he is motivated solely by ambition. Evidence includes a statement of his made last year: "If I don't become *Ortsgruppenleiter* then I'll go over to the others and oppose the Nazis, and then I'll give the *Gauleitung* a piece of my mind." (Witness: Party-Comrades Voge and Y.) One assumes that the goal of his ambition is to become mayor.

b) Party-Comrade Girmann sees only the power and not the responsibility involved in the *Fuehrer*-Principle. He wants to rule in dictatorial fashion and considers any criticism as sabotage or intrigue. (Witnesses: Party-Comrades Voge and C.) He does not want capable men as fellow workers—only tools.

c) As a result of his power as Brewery Senator, the *Ortsgruppenleiter* fired 25 city employees at the Brewery because they belonged to the SPD, although the *Fuehrer* has said that membership in the SPD or *Reichsbanner* is not sufficient grounds for firing people. The *Regierungspraesident* objected to this move. (Witness: Party-Comrade Voge) I put it to the *Ortsgrupplenleiter* on June 16 that this action was not in the spirit of National Socialism which wants to see the *Volk*-community of all Germans. He replied that " '*Volk*-community' was just a nice word." It was much more important, he said, to provide bread for the SA people who had been lying in the streets for years; with the word "*Volk*-community" you couldn't fill their bellies. At a special meeting last night the *Ortsgruppenleiter* mentioned this and said there were groups who wanted to put the newly employed SA people back into the streets. The SA leaders should tell their men about this and then let them decide whether it should be handled in a Christian way. (Witness: Party-Comrade Z.) I find this kind of inciting of the SA against their comrades and twisting of my statement to be in opposition to the spirit of National Socialism.

I respectfully request that the *Gauleitung* investigate these charges and clear up the situation in Northeim.

> Heil Hitler!
> *(signed)* Edmund Venzlaff
> Number, titles, etc.

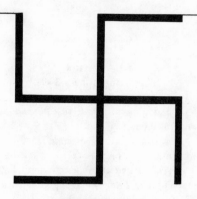

NOTES

Abbreviations used in these notes:

BAK: *Bundesarchiv Koblenz* (West German Federal Archives, Coblenz).

BDC: U.S. Berlin Document Center, Berlin-Zehlendorf.

GGZ: *Göttingen-Grubenhagensche Zeitung* (conservative newspaper).

GSHB: *Gau Südhannover-Braunschweig* (Office of the Nazi *Gauleiter* for Southern Hanover and Brunswick).

HSN: *Hauptamt der Stadt Northeim* (Administrative Offices of the City of Northeim).

KLN: *Kreisleitung Northeim* (Office of the Nazi Leader for Northeim County).

MVN: *Museumsverein Northeim* (Archives of the Museum Society of Northeim).

NB: *Northeimer Beobachter* (Nazi newspaper).

NNN: *Northeimer Neueste Nachrichten* (liberal newspaper).

NSAH: *Niedersächsisches Staatsarchiv Hannover* (Lower Saxon State Archives, Hanover and Pattensen repositories).

OGL: *Ortsgruppenleiter* (Local Group Leader of the Nazi party for the city of Northeim).

OGN: *Ortsgruppe Northeim* (Local Group Northeim of the Nazi party).

PK: Party correspondence of Local Group Northeim of the Nazi party (NSAH, *Bestand Hann 310 I/Nachtrag*).

PGSA: *Preussisches Geheimes Staats-Archiv* (Prussian Privy State Archives in Berlin-Dahlem).

SAN: *Stadtarchiv Northeim* (City Archives of Northeim).

VB: *Volksblatt* (Social Democratic newspaper).

CHAPTER 1
The Setting (pages 3–9)

1. Roger H. Wells, *German Cities: A Study of Contemporary Municipal Politics and Administration* (Princeton, 1932), p. 25.
2. Heinrich Eggeling, *Northeim: 700 Jahre Stadt, 1252–1952. Ein Festbuch zur 700-Jahrfeier* (Northeim, 1952), pp. 17–18, 74–75; Adolf Hueg, *Northeim: Ein Führer durch Vergangenheit und Gegenwart* (Northeim, 1938); Hans-Hennig Eggeling, *Die wirtschaftliche Entwicklung der Stadt Northeim i. Hann. vom Mittelalter bis zum ersten Weltkreig* (Northeim, 1960). See also Adolf Hueg, *Northeim zwischen Harz und Solling* (Hanover, 1939).
3. Verein für Fremdenverkehr, *Northeim: Führer durch Northeim und Umgebung* (Northeim, 1909), p. 41; Adolf Hueg, "Northeim 1933–36: Im Auftrage des Bürgermeisters auf Grund der Berichte der einzelnen Abteilung der Verwaltung dargestellt. Die Stadt Northeim und ihre Verwaltung 1933–36" (ms, Northeim, 1936, SAN); Adolf Hueg, *Chronik der Stadt Northeim, 1932: Northeim Einst und Jetzt* (Northeim, 1932). See also anon., *Northeim zwischen Harz und Solling: Stadt der Reichstagungen der N.S.K.O.V.; Verkehrsmittelpunkt Südhannovers* (Northeim, 1938?).
4. Stabszahlmeister Oessel & Zahlmeister Borgholte, "Chronik des Standortes Northeim, 26 August 1939" (ms., SAN). See also Adolf Hueg, *Northeim in Wandel der Zeit* (Northeim, 1928).
5. Hueg, *Northeim: Ein Führer* . . . (1938), p. 18. See also G. H. Vennigerholz, *Beschreibung und Geschichte der Stadt Northeim* (Northeim, 1894) and Adolf Hueg, *Aus Northeims Sturmzeit: 1625–1636* (Northeim, 1936).
6. Hans-Hennig Eggeling, p. 12.
7. Oessel & Borgholte, pp. 27–33.
8. Hueg, *Northeim: Ein Führer* . . . (1938), p. 24.
9. *Northeimer Neueste Nachrichten,* 1.III.32 (henceforth cited as "NNN." Issues from 1909–1933 in MVN, 1933– in HSN).

CHAPTER 2
The Anatomy of the Town (pages 11–22)

1. Heinrich Eggeling, pp. 76–78; Hans-Hennig Eggeling, p. 14.
2. *Göttingen-Grubenhagensche Zeitung: Nachrichtenblatt für Northeim und Umgebung.* (Northeim, 1831–1937; located in MVN), 7.X.32. Henceforth cited as "GGZ."
3. Interviews with Otto von der Schulenberg and Hermann Denzler.
4. Interview with "Hans Abbenrode."
5. NNN: 25.IV.30; 1.I.33.
6. This and the table to note 12 were calculated from the town address book: *Ein-*

wohnerbuch der Stadt und des Kreises Northeim i. Hann. (Northeim, 1932: in MVN).

7. NNN: 10.IX.31.
8. NNN: 4.X.30; "Vorbericht," *Rechnungs-Abschluss der Stadtsparkasse Northeim für den 31.XII.1930* (ms. in archives of Kreissparkasse Northeim).
9. NNN: 1.I.30; 1.XI.30; 6.V.31.
10. NNN: 22.X.30.
11. For material on the economic structure of the town see the sources cited in Chapter I, especially Heinrich Eggeling. Also, interview with "Hugo Spiessmann."
12. See above, note 6.
13. Notarized declaration made for *Entschädigungs Behörden* by Johannes Grote (private papers of Johannes Grote).
14. Notarized declaration made for *Entschädigungs Behörden* by Gregor Ballin (private papers of Gregor Ballin).
15. *Volksblatt: Organ für die werktätige Bevölkerung der Stadt Göttingen und der südhannoverschen Kreise Göttingen, Northeim, Einbeck, Duderstadt, Osterode a. H., Harzgebiete und Uslar* (Göttingen, 1921–1933, located in Stadtarchiv der Stadt Göttingen), 13.XI.30; 21.XI.32; henceforth cited as "VB." Also NNN: 18 XI.31; 18.X.33.
16. NNN: 6.II.33.
17. Interview with "Erhardt Knorpel."
18. GGZ: 1.XII.31; 6.III.32; 6.IV.32; NNN: 13.I.32; VB: 11.IX.30; 4.I.32.
19. Interview with the former chairman. Also NNN: 22.VII.30.
20. Interview with "Kurt Zeisser."
21. NNN: 21.VII.30.
22. NNN: 3.II.30.
23. Interview with "Erhardt Knorpel."
24. Interview with "Hans Abbenrode."
25. *Ibid.* Further data on Northeim's club life may be found in the *Vereinsregister, Amtsgericht Northeim.* See also anon., *Jahrbuch des Landesverbandes Niedersachsen im Deutchen Reichs-Kriegerbund "Kyffhäuser" 1936, 13. Jahrgang* (Braunschweig, 1936); Wilhelm F. Kassebeer, *Festbuch zum 75-jährigen Stiftungsfeste des Männergesangvereins Northeim vom 15. bis 18. Mai 1925* (Northeim, 1925); anon., (Fr. Renziehausen), *Festbuch für das 21. Kreisturnerfest am 11., 12., 13., und 14. Juli 1930* zu Northeim (Northeim, 1930); anon., *50 Jahre Volkschor Northeim: Ein Festbuch* (Northeim, 1955); Friedo Kopp, *Festbuch zur II. Deutsche Turnjugendtreffen in Northeim von 25. bis 27. VII. 52* (Northeim, 1952); Werner Schmidt et al., *Festbuch zur 100-jährigen Jubelfeier im Männergesangverein "Niedersachsen", Northeim, 10–11.IX.54* (Northeim, 1954); anon. (Friedrich Wilhelm Kassebeer), *Festbuch zur 100-jährigen Jubelfeier des Männergesangvereins von 1850, Northeim* (Northeim, 1950).
26. GGZ: 7.X.30.
27. Interviews with "Kurt Zeisser" and Rudolf Bückmann.

28. Interview with "Erhardt Knorpel." Further information on the schools in Dr. Ahrens, "Kaufmännische Berufsschule Grosskreis Northeim: Schulgeschichte 1887 bis 1937 (ms., 1937, in SAN); Oberstudiendirektor Dr. Rudolf Bückmann, *475 Jahren Städtische Corvinusschule in Northeim* (Northeim, 1952).

29. The name reflects the former feudal title of the district around Northeim and was already archaic by the 1920s.

30. Hueg, *Chronik der Stadt . . .* , pp. 46-48.

31. Interview with Friedrich Haase.

32. *Hört! Hört! Nachrichtenblatt der NSDAP, Northeim/Hann.*, Nr. 1, 8.VIII.31. (Complete run, 1931-32, located in the private collection of Mrs. Walter Steineck. The successor was *Nationalsozialistische Beobachter für Kreis Northeim und Duderstadt: Beilage der Niedersächsische Tageszeitung.* January 21 to July 18 are located in HSN. It was succeeded by the *Northeimer Beobachter: Parteiamtliches Organ der NSDAP für die Kreise Northeim und Einbeck*, 1933-1945 also in HSN.) *Hört! Hört!* sold for 15 *Pfennig* a copy while the *Northeimer Echo* sold for 20 *Pfennig.*

33. Circulation estimates from "Erhardt Knorpel" and Eva Röhrs.

34. NNN: 16.VIII.30; "Haushaltspläne der Stadt Northeim, 1933-45" (mss. in SAN, published yearly); information on the structure of the city government in Wells, pp. 34-51, 119-129, 257-258.

CHAPTER 3
Enter the Nazis (pages 23-40)

1. Interviews with "Erhardt Knorpel," "Hans Abbenrode," and "Heinrich Lamme." On the SPD and the staus quo see below, Chapter 4.

2. Interviews with "Erhardt Knorpel," Hermann Denzler, "Hans Abbenrode," and "Heinrich Lamme"; *Rechnungsabschlüsse der Stadtsparkasse Northeim* (31. XII. 30, 31, 32: mss. in archives of Kreissparkasse Northeim). Also Hueg, "Northeim 1933-36 . . . ," Tables "Sparkasse 1 und 2," untitled table on p. 89. Comparative national figures in Richard F. Hamilton, *Who Voted for Hitler?* (Princeton, 1982), p. 605, n. 45, show that the same pattern prevailed all over Germany.

3. Interviews with "Heinrich Lamme" and "Hugo Spiessmann."

4. NNN: 17.XI.29; 15.IX.30. For the 1929 local elections, however, the Northeim Nazi organization urged its followers not to vote in the city elections and therefore considered the voting for County and Provincial Diets as their true test. These were not much better in the city's voting: 320 Nazi votes for the county elections, 327 for the provincial. In Northeim County's votes however, there was significant support for Nazi candidates: between 1601 and 1797 votes. See NSAH Hann. 310 I/A-29 I, Nr. 90: OGN to GSHB, 18.XI.29.

5. NSAH Hann. 310 I/A-23, Nr. 3: GSHB to Pg. Ernst, 27.XI.28 and response, 10.XII.28. They were Rudolf Ernst, Ernst and Karl Girmann, Wilhelm Spannaus, and Heinz Weise. There had been a sixth, but he moved away. Fifteen was the minimum number for a "Local Group", as of 1929.

6. Jeremy Noakes, *The Nazi Party in Lower Saxony: 1921–1933* (London, Oxford University Press, 1971), p. 9.

7. *Ibid.*, p. 14. The ex-policeman was Gustav Seifert. The unemployed businessman was Bruno Wenzel. Both have left manuscript autobiographies. See BAK, NS26/141: Bruno Wenzel, "Zur Frühgeschichte der NSDAP in Niedersachsen" (Bremen, 1934) and Gustav Seifert, "Die Treue ist die Mark der Ehre" (n.p., 1934). Also *ibid.*, correspondence of 16.IV.21, 2.VII.21.

8. Noakes, pp. 19–23. The student was Ludolf Haase, later to become *Gauleiter* for *Gau* Göttingen until 1925, when he retired because of illness. He later played a minor role as a Nazi speaker. After Hitler came to power he was arrested by the Gestapo on suspicion of involvement in the "Roehm Putsch"; the Gestapo's interrogation of him broke his health and he played no further role in the Third Reich. See BAK, NS 26/1228: Gestapo Berlin an Ludolf Haase, 4.I.35, and Ludolf Hasse an Parteiarchiv, 11.I.35.

9. Noakes, p. 35; BAK, NS26/141, Wenzel ms.

10. BAK, NS 26/141, Seifert ms. He and Wenzel had to rerecruit their members in the wake of the Erzburger assassination (Aug. 1921) because of the atmosphere of intimidation.

11. NSAH, Hann 122a/XI, Nr. 76, Nr. 74: Städtische Polizeiverwaltung Einbeck, 29.VI.22; and Nr. 162: 10.VII.22; also Nr. 335: Landrat Uslar to Oberpräsident Hannover, 3.VII.22. The police blamed the *Jung deutsche Orden* for the riots and banned it in several towns near Northeim.

12. BAK, NS 26/141, Seifert ms.

13. BDC, Akten Ernst Girmann, geb. 1.VII.96.

14. Noakes, p. 23; BDC, Akten Karl Girmann, Heinrich Böhme, Rudolf Ernst, Wilhelm Spannaus.

15. Noakes, pp. 28 to 55, esp. p. 28, 35; BDC, Akten Heinrich Böhme; BAK NS 26/141, Wenzel and Seifert mss., see also "Vorträge des Pg. Bruno Wenzel, Hannover, in den Jahren 1921–24," *ibid.*

16. NSAH, Hann 310 I/A-2, Nr. 172: "NS Freiheitspartei, Landesverband Hannover-Süd, 25. VI. 24."

17. BDC, Akten Ernst Girmann and Heinrich Böhme; PK, OGN N-10: Grosskundgebungen in Northeim, 1935: OGN an den *Northeimer Beobachter*, 1935. Also: NSAH Hann 310 I/G-5a and /A-411; /A-83 II, Nr. 181: OGN an Gau Archiv, 25.V.37.

18. Noakes, pp. 104–05; BAK, "Slg. Schumacher," Nr. 202-I: Geschäftsführer NSDAP an Gauleitung Göttingen, 7.I.26; an Gauleitung Hannover-Süd, 29.I.26; Geschäftsführer Gau Göttingen an die Organisationsabteilung der NSDAP, München, 11.VIII.26; NSAH, Hann 310 I/A-8 I, Nr. 3–35 and /A-9 I, Nr. 1–66: "Mitgliederbestand, Gau Hannover."

19. BDC, Akten Rudolf Ernst, geb. 8.V.89; NSAH, Hann 310 I/A-83 II, Nr. 181: OGN an Gau Archiv, 25.V.37.

20. Noakes, pp. 108ff, gives a detailed analysis of "The Crisis of the Mittelstand in Lower Saxony, 1928–30." Pp. 118f describes how the rural middle class was alienated from the political system itself by 1928. In the Reichstag election of that year the vote for the DNVP, DHP, and DVP in Lower Saxony dropped from 48.4 percent to 31.2 percent, though the NSDAP, with 4.5 percent, was not yet the beneficiary.

21. *Ibid.;* also Larry Eugene Jones, " 'The Dying Middle': Weimar Germany and the Fragmentation of Bourgeois Politics," *Central European History,* Vol. 5, No. 1 (March 1972), pp. 23–54.

22. Noakes, pp. 5, 112–23, 118, 149–50.

23. Günther Franz, *Die politischen Wahlen in Niedersachsen, 1867–1949,* 2. Auflage (Bremen, 1953), p. 164. Also Noakes, p. 118.

24. Noakes, p. 105.

25. *Ibid.,* p. 121; Franz, p. 164.

26. NSAH, Hann 310 I/A-22 I, Nr. 36: Felix Kopprasch an GSHB, 28.X.28.

27. Noakes, p. 105.

28. NSAH, Hann 310 I/A-22 I.

29. *Ibid.,* /A-24: Mitgliederbestand. The figures do not correlate to those cited above, since the *Gau*'s boundaries had changed in the interim.

30. *Ibid.,* /A-29 I, Nr. 123: Versammlungsberichte OGN, 30.VII.29; Nr. 124–25: OGN an GSHB, 25.VII.29.

31. *Ibid.,* /A-27 II, Nr. 276: Ortsgruppe Göttingen an Gauleitung Hannover, 19.VI.29 and Nr. 279: ditto, 6.VII.29.

32. *Ibid.,* /A-29 I, Nr. 101–122: correspondence, OGN and GSHB, 14.VII.29–26.X.29.

33. *Ibid.,* Nr. 95–114: correspondence, OGN and GSHB, 24.IX.29–2.XI.29.

34. *Ibid.,* Nr. 91–93: correspondence, OGN and GSHB, 12–25.XI.29.

35. *Ibid.,* /A-27 II, Nr. 214: Monatsbericht, OGN.

36. *Ibid.,* /A-29 I, Nr. 81–86; correspondence, OGN and GSHB, 21.XI.29–18.XII.29; /A-27 II, Nr. 147: GSHB an Bezirk Göttingen, 14.XII.29.

37. Interviews with "Erhardt Knorpel," "Heinrich Lamme," Carl Querfurt, and Wilhelm Spannaus. Also NNN: 16.I.30, 15.II.30, 26.II.30, 11.III.30; GGZ: 17.I.30, 16 & 27.II.30; 2 & 15.III.30.

38. Interview with Maria Habenichts.

39. Interview with Wilhelm Spannaus.

40. Interview with Thomas Galland; also BDC, Akten Wilhelm Spannaus, geb. 29.XII.87. The *Parteistat. Erhebung* of 1939 gave his party number as 4,274.

41. NSAH, Hann 310 I/A-58 I, Nr. 83: OGN an GSHB, 18.I.30.

42. *Ibid.,* /A-28 I, Nr. 79: OGN an GSHB, 18.XII.29. The police, who were extremely well informed, gave the membership of Local Group Northeim as 50–55 and in the rest of the county as 232, as of January 2, 1930: *ibid.,* 122a /XI/79, Nr. 87: "Nachweisung der Ortsgruppen der NSDAP im LKP-Bezirk Hannover." See also *ibid.,* 310 I/A-58 II, Nr. 58–59: correspondence, OGN & GSHB, 4–6.III.30.

43. *Ibid.*, /A-58 II, Nr. 50: GSHB an OGN, 29.III.30 and /A-83 II, Nr. 222: OGN (list of members who quit), Aug. 1930.

44. *Ibid.*, /A-58 II, Nr. 74: GSHB an OGN, 12.II.30 and Nr. 40: OGN an GSHB, 16.IV.30.

45. *Ibid.*, Nr. 32: GSHB an OGN, 24.V.30; /A-83 II, Nr. 181: OGN an Gau Archiv, 25.V.37. Ernst was formally dismissed and Steineck's appointment made permanent on July 1, 1930. After recovering from his breakdown, Ernst returned to Northeim in 1931 and unsuccessfully agitated to become County Leader. Instead, he was given the minor position of "cell leader" and played no further significant role in events. See *ibid.*, /A-47, Nr. 125–126: Steineck-Maul correspondence, 1.XII.31.

46. BDC, Akten Walter Steineck, geb. 14.VIII.89.

47. *Ibid.*, Akten Hermann Denzler, geb. 31.III.00.

48. Interview with Maria Habenichts.

49. VB: 26.III.30 (Resolution of the Northeim County Conference of the *Reichsbanner*).

50. NNN: 16 & 19.IV.30.

51. NNN: 20.III.30.

52. NNN: 22.IV.30.

53. GGZ: 26 & 29.IV.30; NNN: 28.IV.30.

54. NNN: 29.IV.30; VB: 1.V.30.

55. NNN: 17 & 19.V.30; GGZ: 18.V.30.

56. GGZ: 16.V.30.

57. GGZ: 25.V.30; 1 & 14.VI.30.

58. GGZ: 22.VI.30; 1 & 2.VII.30; NNN: 30.VI.30.

59. NNN: 23, 25 & 27.VI.30; VB: 27 & 28.VI.30.

60. VB: 6 & 19.VII.30; NNN: 5.VII.30; 29.VIII.30.

61. VB: 9 & 24.VII.30.

62. VB: 7.VIII.30; 25 & 26.I.31; NNN: 26.VI.30; 5, 9, & 12.VIII.30.

63. NNN: 15 & 20.VIII.30; 26.IX.30.

64. GGZ: 9, 15, 21 & 25. VIII.30; NNN: 18, 23, 25 & 30.VIII.30.

65. NNN: 18 & 25.VIII.30; 2 & 4.IX.30.

66. NNN: 14 & 25.VIII.30; 13 IX.30.

67. NNN: 2 & 6.IX.30.

68. NNN: 29 & 30.VIII.30.

69. NNN: 21.VII.30; 23.VIII.30; 10.IX.30; VB: 10 & 23.IX.30. Interview with Johannes Grote, who was the object of one of the beatings.

70. NNN: 11 & 13.IX.30, for the Socialist meeting; NNN: 8 & 10.IX.30; GGZ: 17.IX.30, for the Nazi meeting.

71. Though I have expressed this voting analysis in positive language, so as to avoid cluttering sentences with qualifiers, it should be remembered that it is never possible to be absolutely sure where votes come from when the balloting is secret. My method for analyzing these and other election returns was to calculate the total number of votes lost by all parties (and then by each party), the total gained by all parties (and by each), and then to subtract from the total gained by all parties those votes gained by the non-Nazi parties. The remainder I took to be the minimum possible number of votes gained by the Nazis from their opponents. The same process was applied to the "new" votes.

My basic assumption has been that there were no complicated vote shifts, e.g., from the DVP to the SPD or from the SPD to the DNVP. This assumption is based on the fact that the Nazis were the net gainers over the three-year period, that "random voting" was rare, and that there were programatic affinities between the bourgeois parties and the NSDAP. For examples of voting analyses in several other German districts, see Karl Dietrich Bracher, *Die Auflösung der Weimarer Republik: Eine Studie zum Problem des Machtverfalls in der Demokratie* (Stuttgart, 1957), pp. 645–656; Alfred Milatz, "Das Ende der Parteien im Spiegel der Wahlen 1930 bis 1933" in Erich Matthias and Rudolf Morsey, *Das Ende der Parteien 1933* (Düsseldorf, 1960), pp. 743–793. The most sophisticated analysis is Richard F. Hamilton, *Who Voted for Hitler?* (Princeton, 1982). Full figures and a graph of election returns in Northeim are provided in Appendix B, Tables 4 and 5.

CHAPTER 4
Exploiting Victory (pages 41–52)

1. Interviews with "Hans Abbenrode" and Maria Habenichts.
2. VB: 30.IX.30.
3. Wells, p. 163; NNN: 1.VII.30; 3.XI.30; 1.X.31; 28.VI.32. See also Erich Roll, *Spotlight on Germany: A Survey of Her Economic and Political Problems* (London, 1933), p. 188.
4. NNN: 18.VII.30; 11 & 12.IX.30.
5. NNN: 5.XI.30.
6. VB: 17.IX.30; 7.X.30.
7. NNN: 1.VIII.30; 9.IX.30; VB: 29.IX.30.
8. GGZ: 14.IX.30.
9. VB: 24.IX.30.
10. Bertram W. Maxwell, *Contemporary Municipal Government of Germany* (Iowa City, 1928), pp. 11–19; Wells, p. 64.
11. Noakes, p. 130 & 136, describes the role of the *Bürgerblock* in other Lower Saxon towns.
12. NNN: 21, 23 & 25.X.30; GGZ: 24.X.30.
13. NNN: 24.X.30.
14. NNN: 24 & 25.IX.30; 3 & 9.X.30.
15. Noakes, p. 158, 201.
16. NNN: 18 & 27.X.30.

17. NNN: 7, 11, 13, 14 & 29.XI.30; 16 & 30.XII.30; GGZ: 12.XI.30; 7.XII.30.

18. BAK, "Slg. Schumacher," Nr. 202-I, GSHB: Monatliches Rundschreiben der Gau Propagandaleitung, 15.XII.30 and 27.I.31; also "Eiliges Rundschreiben an alle Redner," 27.XII.30; Noakes, pp. 143, 146, and 203 (but the date of the new speakers' certification system is incorrectly given as one month later).

19. NSAH, Hann 310 I/B-28 II, Nr. 27: OGN an GSHB, "Gegnerische Propagandatätigkeit"; /A-83 II, Nr. 244; KLN an GSHB, 4.I.31.

20. NNN: 6.X.30; 1.XI.30; VB: 4.X.30.

21. NNN: 11.X.30; 12.XII.30.

22. NNN: 22 & 23.XII.30.

23. NNN: 22.XII.30.

24. VB: 25.XI.30; 15.XII.30; NNN: 21.XI.30; 13, 15 & 16.XII.30. Also, interview with Friedrich Haase.

25. VB: 12.I.31.

26. VB: 2 & 5.I.31. The attack was unprovoked; the Nazis claimed that they were just trying "to shake the Querfurt boy back into the present."

27. NNN: 6.I.31; VB: 5 & 10.I.31. The exact quote: "Sitzt die Gesellschaft erst einmal drin, ist die Demokratie verloren." The speaker, Johannes Stelling, was subsequently murdered by the SA in June 1933.

28. NNN: 9.I.31. Actually, the topic was dictated by the *Gauleitung,* which was acting at the directions of the national Nazi propaganda office, and thus the weak effect is a good example of how top-down management of propaganda led to local disasters. See BAK, "Slg. Schumacher," Nr. 202-I: GSBH an alle Redner, 27.XII.30.

29. NNN: 16.I.31.

30. NNN: 19 & 23.I.31.

31. VB: 26.I.31; NNN: 26.I.31.

32. VB: 3 & 11.II.31.

33. NNN: 3.II.31; VB: 9 & 10.II.31.

34. VB: 17.II.31; NNN: 20 & 23.II.31.

35. GGZ: 19.II.31.

36. NNN: 3 & 7.II.31. The original title was "Die Bonzen im Speck, das Volk im Dreck."

37. NNN: 16 & 19.II.31.

38. VB: 18, 23 & 24.II.31; NNN: 23 & 24.II.31.

39. VB: 14.II.31.

40. NNN: 26.II.31.

41. GGZ: 27.II.31; VB: 28.II.31. The original article was from the *Niedersächsische Tageszeitung,* Nr. 20, 17.XI.30. The sudden increase in Nazi agitation was not a local reaction to the SPD's activity exclusively. In February 1931 the Nazis boycotted the Reichstag as a tactical gesture. Consequently the 107 Nazi Reichstag delegates no longer received their salary and were forced to recoup by earning speaker's fees. The competition also stimulated the usual Nazi speakers so that the local Nazi organizations suddenly went from scarcity to superfluity in their supply of speakers. The boycott lasted only about six weeks.

CHAPTER 5
Authoritarians Unite (pages 53–68)

1. Interviews with Maria Habenichts, "Erhardt Knorpel," "Heinrich Lamme," and "Hans Abbenrode."
2. Interviews with "Hugo Spiessmann" and Maria Habenichts.
3. Interviews with Friedrich Haase and Hermann Schulze.
4. Interviews with "Heinrich Lamme" and "Erhardt Knorpel."
5. Interviews with Johannes Grote, Friedrich Haase, Hermann Schulze, and "Benno Schmidt."
6. *Ibid.* Also interviews with "Hans Abbenrode," "Erhardt Knorpel," and Carl Querfurt.
7. Interview with Johannes Grote.
8. Interview with "Erhardt Knorpel."
9. Interview with Otto von der Schulenberg.
10. GGZ: 7.III.31.
11. NNN: 12.III.31; GGZ: 22.III.31; NSAH, Hann 310 I/B-9 II, Nr. 178: OGN an GSHB, 31.III.31.
12. GGZ: 21.III.31.
13. VB: 11, 12 & 14.III.31; 1.IV.31.
14. NSAH, Hann 310 I/B-9 II, Nr. 133 & 40: Monatlicher Propagandabericht, 30.IV.31 & 31.V.31; /A-83 II, Nr. 216: OGN an GSHB, 18.VI.31.
15. GGZ: 19 & 26.II.31; 18.III.31; 5.IV.31; NNN: 23.II.31.
16. NNN: 23.III.31.
17. NNN: 9.III.31.
18. Interview with Maria Habenichts, whose husband was the leader in question.
19. NNN: 5.VIII.31.
20. GGZ: 10.IV.31.
21. NNN: 13 & 16.IV.31; VB: 18.IV.31.
22. VB: 22.IV.31; 12.VIII.31.
23. VB: 24, 25 & 27.III.31.
24. NNN: 16.IV.31; VB: 17.IV.31.
25. NNN: 15.XII.30; 20.III.31; 10.IV.31; VB: 16 & 17.III.31.
26. VB: 9, 17 & 21.IV.31; NNN: 20.IV.31. The *Jungbanner* wrote to the NNN on April 21 denying the incident of the children going to church and pointing out that their organization was (1) interdenominational and (2) not open to school-children.
27. VB: 1 & 3.IV.31.
28. GGZ: 16 & 20.IV.31; NNN: 20 & 22.IV.31.
29. NNN: 2, 9 & 14.IV.31; 7.VII.31; 15.VIII.31; 29.IX.31; 31.V.33; VB: 22.XII.31;

5.I.32. Interviews with "Hugo Spiessmann," "Heinrich Lamme," and "Erhardt Knorpel."
30. NNN: 7.IV.31.
31. VB: 29.IV.31; interview with "Kurt Zeisser," whose father joined the NSDAP about this time after a threat of boycott.
32. NNN: 11.XII.30.
33. VB: 11.IV.31.
34. GGZ: 2.V.31; NNN: 1.V.31.
35. GGZ: 10 & 17.V.31; NNN: 11.V.31; VB: 22 & 24.V.31; NSAH, Hann 310 I/B-9 II, Nr. 40: OGN an GSHB, 31.V.31.
36. Ibid., /B-9 I, Nr. 257: OGN an GSHB, 30.VI.31; GGZ: 21.V.31; 7 & 16.VI.31.
37. GGZ: 10, 15 & 16.VII.31.
38. NNN: 17 & 20.VI.31; GGZ: 6 & 8.V.31.
39. NNN: 1.VI.31.
40. VB: 3, 4 & 9.VI.31; NNN: 3 & 5.VI.31.
41. NNN: 8.VI.31; VB: 15.VI.31.
42. NNN: 15.VI.31; VB: 15 & 18.VI.31.
43. Interview with "Heinrich Lamme."
44. VB and NNN: 14.VII.31.
45. VB: 16 & 22.VI.31; 8.VII.31. A Communist meeting held on June 28 had only 75 in attendance, according to a Nazi report. See NSAH, Hann 310 I/B-9 I, Nr. 257: OGN an GSGB, 30.VI.31.
46. For the sickle incident, VB: 15.VI.31. Both the NNN and the GGZ denied the story but the VB produced names in verification (see all three papers for 17.VI.31). For the *Reichsbanner* meetings, VB: 15, 23, 25 & 27.VII.31; NNN: 25.VII.31.
47. NSAH, Hann 310 I/B-9 I, Nr. 99: OGN an GSHB, 2.IX.31; NNN: 1 & 3.VIII.31.
48. NNN: 5.VIII.31; GGZ: 8.VIII.31.
49. VB: 7 & 8.VIII.31; NNN: 3.VIII.31.
50. Interview with Johannes Grote.
51. Interview with Carl Querfurt.
52. VB: 21.IV.31; 24.VIII.31; NNN: 29.VIII.31. In pronouncing sentence the judge lamented that the law would not permit him to impose stiffer penalties. In December 1931, the Nazis obtained a retrial before a sympathetic judge who acquitted ten of those previously sentenced and reduced the other sentences to token terms. This was jubilantly reported in the GGZ on December 21, 1931.
53. NNN: 20.IX.30.
54. GGZ: 12.VIII.31; VB: 14.VIII.31.
55. NNN: 3.VIII.31.
56. VB: 10.VIII.31.
57. Reprinted in *Hört! Hört!:* 15.VIII.31.
58. NNN: 10.VIII.31; 2.X.31; 6, 23, & 24.XI.31; 13.V.32; GGZ: 11.VIII.31; 25.XI.31; 14.V.32; VB: 11.VIII.31; 25.XI.31; 13.V.32. Also, interview with Hermann Schulze, a witness on the *Reichsbanner*'s side.

CHAPTER 6
The Depths of the Depression (pages 69–90)

1. GGZ: 12 & 15.VIII.31; VB: 14.VIII.31.
2. *Hört! Hört!:* No. 1, 8.VIII.31; NSAH, Hann 310 I/A-47, Nr. 136: Bericht der Kreisführertagung am 4.X.31 in Northeim. *Hört! Hört!* viewed attacking the SPD as its primary function: *ibid.,* /B-11 I, Nr. 104: KLN Tätigkeitsbericht für Mai 1932, 2.VI.32.
3. VB: 8 & 15.VIII.31.
4. VB: 8.VI.31; 13.VIII.31; GGZ and NNN: 12.VIII.31.
5. NNN: 28.VIII.31.
6. VB: 28.IX.31; NNN: 23, 24 & 28.IX.31; also Ch. 7, n. 8.
7. VB: 22.X.31.
8. NNN: 6, 7 & 17.X.31; 9, 27 & 28.XI.31; VB: 14.XI.31.
9. VB: 28.I.30; 5 & 11.II.30; 7.XII.31.
10. NNN: 15.IX.31; 8.X.31; 4.I.32; VB: 13.II.31.
11. NNN: 6.I.31; 12.II.31; 29.IX.31; 22 & 24.X.31; VB: 31.III.31; 30.XII.31. The manager of the sack factory, in an encouraging gesture of faith, bought the plant from the owner and reopened it ten months later. See NNN: 7.X.32.
12. NNN: 4.I.32; 2.XII.32.
13. NNN: 21.XI.31; 12.XII.31.
14. *Rechnungsabschlüsse der Stadtsparkasse Northeim, 1930–33* (see Ch. 3, n. 2); interviews with "Heinrich Lamme," "Hugo Spiessmann," and "Erhardt Knorpel."
15. GGZ: 28.VIII.31; 2, 12, 24 & 26.IX.31. One of the speakers (Dr. Buttmann) demanded and received an honorarium of RM 50, which was exceptional enough to cause Steineck to complain to the *Gauleiter,* who stated that Buttmann had overcharged by RM 20. See NSAH, Hann 310 I/B-28 II, Nr. 249: OGN an GSHB, 17.VIII.31 and /B-30 II, Nr. 132: GSHB an OGN, 20.VIII.31.
16. GGZ: 4, 18, 23 & 28.X.31; interviews with "Erhardt Knorpel" and "Heinrich Lamme," both of whom remembered the Feder speech as an "event" even after 25 years.
17. GGZ: 6 & 26.XI.31; 23.XII.31; NNN: 9.XII.31; NSAH, Hann 310 I/B-11 II, Nr. 156: KLN an GSHB, Tätigkeitsberichte, 4.XI & 1.XII.31.
18. GGZ: 12.X.31; interview with Hermann Denzler.
19. NNN: 27.XI.31; 19.XIII.31. Interviews with Hermann Denzler, who claimed that the kitchen fed people without asking any questions, and with "Benno Schmidt," who recalled being denied food because he was a known Leftist." The *Volksblatt* contended that the kitchen was being run for profit. On the extortion of food from farmers see NSAH, Hann 122a/XI/80, Nr. 292: Polizeipräsident in Hannover an Oberpräsident/Hann. d. 6.II.32, betr. N.S.Bewegung im Kreise Northeim.
20. NNN: 9.I.33; GGZ:6.I.32; 15.IV.32; VB: 11.I.32; 15.IV.32.
21. NSAH, Hann 310 I/B-28 II, OGN an GSHB, 15.IV.31; /B-11 II, KLN an GSHB,

4.XI. & 1.XII.31; /A-83 II, Nr. 203: OGN an GSHB, 28.X.31. *Ibid.*, 122a/XI/80, Nr. 292: Polizeipräsident in Hannover an Oberpräsident/Hann. d. 6.II.32, betr. N.S. Bewegung in Northeim.

22. Interviews with Maria Habenichts, "Benno Schmidt," and Eva Röhrs.
23. Interview with "Kurt Zeisser." For the attitude of the *Gymnasium* students, interviews with "Erhardt Knorpel" and Rudolf Bückmann.
24. GGZ: 19.III.32; VB: 6.VIII.32; 9.XI.32.
25. Interview with "Kurt Zeisser," corroborated by Hermann Denzler.
26. PK, N-16, OGN Ausgeg. Schreiben, N-Z, 1930–1932, BdM/OGN an Ortsausschuss f. Jugendpflege, 21.XI.32.
27. Interview with Wilhelm Spannaus; PK, N-16, OGN Ausgeg. Schreiben, N-Z, 1932–1933: OGL an KLN, 20.I.33.
28. See last item in note 21 above. Also NSAH, Hann 310 I /A-108 II, Nr. 141: OGN an GSHB, 30.I.32.
29. Interviews with Johannes Grote, Hermann Denzler, "Erhardt Knorpel," Friedrich Haase, Carl Querfurt, "Heinrich Lamme," and "Benno Schmidt." "Knorpel," the former newspaper reporter, made the most accurate estimate: forty.
30. Interview with Johannes Grote; the original text: "Unter diesen Zeichen wirst Du rote Schwein verbluten."
31. Interview with "Erhardt Knorpel"; the original text: "Schmeiss die Juden 'raus! Die Juden sind unser Unglück!"
32. Interviews with Friedrich Haase, Carl Querfurt, Hermann Schulze, and "Erhardt Knorpel."
33. VB: 12.VI.31; 21.IX.32; NNN: 28.XI.32; GGZ: 20.IX.32; 20.XII.32.
34. Interviews with Hermann Denzler and Wilhelm Spannaus. Also PK, N-14, OGN Eingeg. Schreiben, N-Z, 1932–33: Hermann Sebolde an OGN, 31.III.33.
35. NSAH, Hann 310 I/A 83-II, Nr. 241: GSHB (Kassenver.) an OGN. The SA was also never allowed to actually run a meeting, either: see below, note 42.
36. Noakes, pp. 105, 144. The dues charged varied over the years 1928–33; figures cited here were as of 1931.
37. PK, N-16, OGN Ausgeg. Schreiben, N-Z, 1932–33, *passim*.
38. NSAH, Hann 310 I /A 32-I (a collection of general memoranda and rules for GSHB, 1929–1931).
39. *Ibid.*, /A 83-II, Nr. 335–36: correspondence between GSHB and OGN, 7.III & 14.III.31.
40. *Ibid.*, /A 47, Nr. 136: Bericht der Kreisführertagung am 4.X.31 in Northeim; PK, N-16, OGN Ausgeg. Schreiben, N-Z, 1932–33: Erklärung am 19.XII.32 and *passim*.
41. Noakes, p. 123.
42. NSAH, Hann 310 I/B-5, Nr. 1: GSHB, Richtlinien der Propaganda Abteilung, 1.VI.31. The *1910er Zelt* had 1,200 seats; in a pinch the town's riding hall could be used for meetings. It could seat 1,800. See PK, N-10, OGN: "Grosskundgebungen in Northeim, 1935."
43. NSAH, Hann 310 I/B-5, Nr. 1: GSHB, Richtlinien der Propaganda Abteilung,

1.VI.31. By summer 1931, Nazi speakers' fees were fixed at 7 marks for a *Gau* speaker, 30 marks for a Reich speaker (plus costs in both cases). Before that, fees varied considerably. See *ibid.* /A 53-II, Nr. 64: GSHB Propaganda Abt. an OGN, 25.II.30.

44. See note 40 above, especially the circular numbered "9."

45. NSAH, Hann 310 I/A 53-II, GSHB an Kreisleitung Northeim, 2.VI.32 and *passim.*

46. Interviews with "Erhardt Knorpel," Rudolf Bückmann, Hermann Schulze, and Thomas Galland. Much of Steineck's personal attitude was gleaned in conversation with his widow. See also Ch. 3, n. 45–46.

47. Interviews with Thomas Galland, "Erhardt Knorpel," Hermann Denzler, Carl Querfurt, "Benno Schmidt," Wilhelm Spannaus, and Otto von der Schulenberg. The quotation is from "Erhardt Knorpel." See also Ch. 3, n.13.

48. Interview with Thomas Galland.

49. Interviews with "Hans Abbenrode," Wilhelm Spannaus, Hermann Schulze, and Otto von der Schulenberg; NNN: 8.XII.31; GGZ: 10.XII.31; PK: N-14, OGN Eingeg. Schreiben, N-Z, 1932–33: Hermann Sebolde an OGN, 31.III.33; *ibid.,* N-15, Ausgeg. Schreiben, A-M, 1932–33.

50. Interview with Hermann Denzler.

51. Letter from Dr. Edmund Venzlaff to the author, Jan. 14, 1967. His belief that Jews predominated in various professions is erroneous. The greatest overrepresentation of German Jews was among physicians and even there they constituted only one-eighth of that profession. By far the most common occupation of German Jews was tailor. Statistics are conveniently summarized in Karl A. Schleunes, *The Twisted Road to Auschwitz: Nazi Policy toward German Jews 1933–39* (Urbana, Illinois, 1973), pp. 37–44. See especially "Tables 5 & 6," p. 41. Venzlaff's misperception exemplifies how myths may lead to murder.

52. Interviews with Rudolf Bückmann.

53. Interview with "Kurt Zeisser."

54. Interview with "Erhardt Knorpel."

55. Interview with Otto von der Schulenberg.

56. Interview with "Erhardt Knorpel."

57. Interviews with Maria Habenichts and "Erhardt Knorpel." For the second statement, interviews with Gregor Ballin and "Heinrich Lamme" (whose employer was Jewish).

58. The editor, Max Herholz, was expelled from the Nazi party in January 1933 for having embezzled RM 40 from the newsletter's accounts. See PK, Nr. 16, OGN Ausgeg. Schreiben, N-Z, 1932–33: OGL an den Uschlavorsitzenden Pg. Peiters, 12.I.33.

59. VB: 4.II.32.

60. VB: 19.VIII.31; 6.II.32.

61. VB: 14.I.32.

62. VB: 20.XI.31; 26.III.32; 8 & 9.VIII.32.

63. NNN: 19.X.31; VB: 10 & 12.XII.31.

64. VB: 17.II.32; 1.III.32.
65. VB: 21, 25, 26, 28 & 30.I.32; 2, 10, 17, 20 & 23.II.32.
66. GGZ: 22, 26 & 27.I.32.
67. GGZ: 14.XI.31. By census count there were twenty atheists in Northeim.
68. GGZ: 12.II.32. The use of pastors as speakers and of religious themes as topics was a common Nazi practice throughout South Hanover (see Noakes, p. 207f). It was done partly in order to increase the women's vote for Nazism, by counteracting the party's neo-pagan image. See also NSAH, Hann 310 I/B-11 II, Nr. 186: KLN Tätigkeitsbericht für Feb. 1932, 3.III.32.
69. NNN: 13.II.32; GGZ: 11 & 16.II.32.
70. GGZ: 14 & 18.I.32.
71. VB: 4.XII.31; 20.II.32; 7.III.32.
72. GGZ: 27.II.32; NNN: 27.II.32; 9.IV.32.
73. VB: 23.IV.32; 4.VIII.32; 21.XII.32.

CHAPTER 7
Political Crescendo (pages 91-106)

1. VB: 4.XII.31.
2. VB: 23.II.32; NNN: 26.II.32; GGZ: 27.II.32.
3. NNN: 9.II.32; VB: 16.III.32.
4. NNN: 2, 3, 6 & 8.II.32; 12.III.32; VB: 10 & 21.II.32.
5. NNN: 9 & 26.III.32.
6. VB: 16 & 20.I.32; 6.II.32.
7. NNN: 7.III.32; VB: 5 & 8.III.32.
8. NSAH, Hann 310 I/B-11 I, Nr. 186: KLN Tätigkeitsbericht für Feb. 1932, 3.III.32; Nr. 133: für April 1932, 1.V.32; Nr. 152: für März 1932, 29.III.32.
9. NNN: 9 & 12.III.32; VB: 12.III.32.
10. NNN: 11.III.32.
11. NNN and GGZ: 13.III.32; NNN: 12.III.32.
12. GGZ: 17 & 21.II.32; NNN: 29.II.32; 7, 8 & 10.III.32.
13. GGZ: 12.II.32.
14. NSAH, Hann 310 I/B-21 I, Nr. 92: OGN an GSHB (Propaganda Abt.), 4.II.32; Nr. 89: GSHB an OGN, 19.II.32; Nr. 83: Fragebogen KLN, 1.II.32; Nr. 73: KLN an GSHB, 28.II.32. The propaganda boomerang came from stickers sardonically suggesting that the SPD was patriotic and religious.
15. GGZ: 5, 9 & 10.III.32; NNN: 7.III.32; VB: 9.III.32.
16. NNN: 11.III.32; GGZ: 12.III.32; VB: 10.III.32.
17. VB: 14.III.32; GGZ: 13.III.32.
18. GGZ: 15.III.32.
19. Table 5 in Appendix B gives the statistics of this and the next two elections covered in this chapter; for the method of analysis, see Ch. 3, n. 71.
20. Interview with Friedrich Haase. For the police alert see NNN: 12.III.32.

21. VB: 14 & 15.III.32; interview with Friedrich Haase, who was one of the *Reichsbanner* "scouts."
22. NNN: 16.III.32.
23. GGZ: 20 & 22.III.32; NNN: 18.III.32; 8.IV.32.
24. NNN: 8 & 11.IV.32. The words were a variation of the customary Nazi slogan, "Juda verrecke!"
25. NNN: 9.IV.32.
26. VB: 18.III.32; 12.IV.32; GGZ: 16 & 22.III.32; NNN: 15.III.32; 15.IX.32. A lenient court subsequently found Tumpelmann guilty of assault but fined him only 10 marks. NNN: 23.IV.32.
27. GGZ: 2, 5, 7 & 9.IV.32.
28. NNN: 5 13, 15 & 21.IV.32; VB: 15 & 23.IV.32.
29. NNN: 16 & 19.IV.32.
30. NNN: 14.IV.32; GGZ: 20.IV.32.
31. GGZ: 25.IV.32.
32. GGZ: 14 & 19.IV.32; interview with "Erhardt Knorpel."
33. NSAH, Hann 310 I/B-23 I, Nr. 191: KLN Fragebogen für GSHB, 19.IV.32.
34. VB: 12, 19 & 23.IV.32.
35. NNN: 25.IV.32; 27.X.32; 9.XI.32; GGZ: 26.IV.32; VB: 26.IV.32.
36. NNN: 18.IV.32.
37. NNN: 24.X.32.
38. Interviews with Thomas Galland, Gregor Ballin, and "Heinrich Lamme."
39. Guenther Franz, *Die Politische Wahlen in Niedersachsen, 1867-1949* (second edit., Bremen, 1953), p. 164.
40. NNN: 30.VIII.30; 2 & 13.IX.30; 4.VIII.31.
41. Table 5, Appendix B.

CHAPTER 8
Things Fall Apart (pages 107-127)

1. Hueg, "Northeim 1933-36 . . . ," Tables B-1, p. 76, and A-1, p. 27; also Rudolf Bückmann, *475 Jahren städtische Corvinusschule in Northeim* (Northeim, 1952), p. 12.
2. *Northeimer Heimatblätter*, herausgegeben von dem Heimat und Museumsverein für Northeim und Umgegend, Nr. 4, Jhrg. 9, Mai 1933:"Jahresbericht."
3. NNN: 4.X.30; 27.X.32. In July 1930 there were 162 autos in Northeim.
4. Hueg, "Northeim 1933-36 . . . ," tables to pp. 8 and 62; Table: "Städtische Warmwasserbadeanstalt."
5. *Ibid.*, table to p. 8; NNN: 21.XI.32; 1.I.33; VB: 21.XI.32.
6. "Rechnungsabschlüsse der Stadtsparkasse Northeim, 1930-33."
7. Recent research by Richard Hamilton (Ch. 3, n. 71) has shown that this was a national pattern: the middle classes were largely unhurt by the depression. See Hamilton, p. 604, n.45.
8. NNN: 29.VIII.32 Interviews with "Hugo Spiessmann" and "Erhardt Knorpel."
9. NNN: 15.VI.32.

10. NNN: 13.VI.32.
11. "Haushaltsplan der Stadt Northeim" (annual mimeographed copies in HSN); Hueg, "Northeim, 1933–36 . . . ," Table: "Gewerbesteuer nach dem Ertrag und nach dem Kapital." Because of the complicated formulae used in assessing taxes in German towns, the drop in the profits tax does not connote an equal drop in profits. Unless one examined each tax case individually, the most one could validly conclude from the figures cited is that profits were falling by some small and indeterminant amount in the course of 1932. A rapid drop in the *total* business tax yield would have indicated real trouble. In one sense, then, the tax returns simply show again that Northeim was not decisively hurt by the depression. The *general* reduction in the tax yield essentially reflected reduced spending, since the prime source of income for the town was, in addition to its various enterprises, indirect consumption taxes of various sorts. Thus the reduced budgets do not prove that Northeimers were actually suffering from the depression. My thanks, for assistance in fathoming the tax and budget issues, to Dr. Karl W. Roskamp, Economics Dept., Wayne State University.
12. Wells, p. 170.
13. NNN: 9.IV.32; 16.VI.32; VB: 11.V.32.
14. NNN: 28.IX.32; 12.XII.32; 13 & 27.I.33.
15. NNN: 17.II.32; 11.III.32.
16. NNN: 26.VIII.32.
17. GGZ and NNN: 27.VIII.32.
18. NNN: 30.IX.32.
19. VB: 13.IV.32.
20. At least one of Northeim's policemen was a secret Nazi from 1930 on. See PK, OGN Korrespondenz, H-K, 1936–43: Wilhelm Karcher an OGN, 10.VI.36. Also: interview with Hermann Denzler.
21. NNN: 14.IV.32.
22. GGZ: 15.IV.32; VB: 15 & 22.IV.32.
23. VB and NNN: 2.V.32.
24. NSAH, Hann 310 I/A-53 II, Nr. 40: GSHB an KLN, 2.VI.32.
25. GGZ: 8 & 11.V.32.
26. NNN: 17.V.32; VB: 13.VI.32.
27. VB: 10 & 13.XII.30; 1, 5 & 26.IX.31.
28. VB: 7.XII.31. There is little doubt that students at the *Gymnasium* were Nazified, though most of them out of adolescent rebelliousness rather than political awareness, according to the former headmaster. Interviews with Rudolf Bückmann, "Kurt Zeisser," and "Erhardt Knorpel."
29. VB: 2.IV.32. Interview with "Hans Abbenrode," Voge's supervisor in the school.
30. VB: 7 & 12.IV.32; 18.VI.32.
31. NNN: 29.IV.32; GGZ: 30.IV.32.
32. VB: 6.VI.32.
33. GGZ: 30.IV.32; 22.VI.32; NNN: 29.IV.32; 22.VI.32.
34. GGZ: 15, 21, 24 & 28.V.32; 16 & 19.VI.32; NNN: 13.VI.32; NSAH, Hann 310 I/B–11 I, Nr. 104: KLN Tätigkeitsbericht für Mai 1932, 2.VI.32.

35. NNN: 20.VI.32.

36. GGZ: 21.VI.32.

37. NSAH, Hann 310 I/A-108 II, Nr. 131: OGN an Wittenberg, GSHB, 28.VI.32.

38. VB: 15.V.32.

39. Interview with Hermann Schulze.

40. *Ibid.;* NNN and GGZ: 8.IX.32.

41. NNN: 25 & 29.VII.32; VB: 28.VII.32.

42. GGZ: 11 & 20.X.32; 15.XI.32; NNN: 12 & 17.X.32. Not one of these events was reported by the *Volksblatt.*

43. VB: 28.VII.32. The original text: "Die Republikaner werden dafür sorgen, dass diese Geschäfte lebensfähig bleiben."

44. Interviews with Carl Querfurt, "Heinrich Lamme," and Hermann Denzler.

45. NSAH. Hann 310 I/B-11 I, Nr. 61: KLN Tätigkeitsbericht für Juni/Juli, 4.VIII.32.

46. NNN: 20.VII.32; GGZ: 21.VII.32.

47. NSAH, Hann 310 I/A-37 I, Nr. 155: Sonderrundschreiben GSHB an alle Kreisleiter, 20.VI.32; Nr. 156: OGN an GSHB, 24.VI.32.

48. *Ibid.,* /B-6: Rundschreiben der Propagandaleitung GSHB 1932, *passim.* See Nr. 100 for the list of recipients; Nr. 107–120 give the texts for targeted groups; Nr. 121 (25.X.32), though for the fall elections, repeats the instructions in detail. For an example of the equally thorough, though quite different, SPD propaganda guidelines, see *ibid.,* /B-3 II, Nr. 211: Materialien f. d. Reichstagswahl 1932.

49. *Ibid.,* /B-11 II, Nr. 61: KLN an GSHB, Tätigkeitsbericht für Juni/Juli, 4.VIII.32; Noakes, p. 216.

50. *Ibid.,* /B-23 I, Nr. 151 & 152: KLN an GSHB, 14.VII.32.

51. Ahrens, "Kaufmännische Berufsschule. . . ." Interviews with "Erhardt Knorpel," "Kurt Zeisser," "Hans Abbenrode," "Heinrich Lamme," and Carl Querfurt.

52. Alan Bullock, in Baumont, Vermeil, *et al., The Third Reich* (New York, 1955), p. 514.

53. VB: 14.VI.32.

54. GGZ: 1.VII.32. Subsequent quotation from GGZ: 5.VII.32; also NNN: 4.VII.32.

55. GGZ: 13 & 16.VII.32.

56. NNN: 4 & 7.VII.32. The quotation is from VB: 7.VII.32.

57. VB: 12.VII.32.

58. VB: 8, 11 & 12.VII.32.

59. NNN: 11 & 22.VII.32; 10.VIII.32; GGZ: 12.VII.32; 12.VIII. 32; VB: 11, 12 & 13.VII.32. The *Volksblatt* claimed that it had a witness who saw the Nazis making obvious preparations for the fight during the afternoon of that day. No such witness testified at the trial, however. The heaviest sentence was given to "Benno Schmidt." At least one of the *Reichsbanner* men offered to testify against his comrades and also wept before the judge to get his sentence reduced (interview with "Benno Schmidt").

60. NNN: 13, 14 & 27.VII.32.

61. NNN: 14 & 16.VII.32; 12 & 13.VIII.32; 11, 21 & 22.XI.32; GGZ: 15 & 16.VII.32; 14.VIII.32; VB: 16.VII.32; 23.XI.32.

62. GGZ: 19.VII.32.

63. NSAH, Hann 310 I/A-108 II, Nr. 139: OGN an Wittenberg (Kasseleiter), GSHB, 6.III.32; Nr. 138: response, 7.III.32; Nr. 134: GSHB an OGN (requesting payment of RM 22 plus 25 *Pfennig* postage), 26.III.32.

64. *Ibid.*, /B-30 II, Nr. 121: Steineck an GSHB, 18.VI.32.

65. *Ibid.*, /B-2 II, Nr. 23: Richtlinien für Hitlerversammlungen. This also contained an explanation of why 50 percent of the net profits were to be paid into Hitler's private account.

66. *Ibid.;* also /G-3, Nr. 7–9, 15, and 50. Hitler also spoke in Brunswick and Hanover that day. In Göttingen the breakdown of ticket sales was 2,570 at 3 marks for a total of 7,710 marks; 10,046 at 1 mark for 10,046 marks; 2,929 at 50 *Pfennig* for 1,464.50 marks. Much of the costs that had to be deducted from the gross profits (for posters, ads in Nazi newspapers, payments to the SA, etc.) actually came back to the NSDAP, so that the true gain to the party was much larger than the net profits cited.

67. The content of Hitler's speech is a paraphrased summary, not a direct quotation. GGZ: 13.VII.32. Interview with "Kurt Zeisser."

68. GGZ: 21, 27 & 29.VII.32.

69. VB: 21.IV.31; 29.VIII.32; *Hört! Hört!:* 7.VIII.32.

70. NNN: 27.VII.32; VB: 27 & 28.VII.32; 5 & 18.VIII.32.

71. NNN: 25, 28–30.VII.32; VB: 28 & 30.VII.32.

72. GGZ: 31.VII.32; NNN: 27, 29 & 30.VII.32.

73. NNN: 19 & 23.VIII.32; 8.IX.32; GGZ: 27.VIII.32.

74. NNN: 1, 4 & 6.VIII.32.

75. NNN and VB: 12.VIII.32.

CHAPTER 9
The Last Winter (pages 129–147)

1. NNN: 13, 16, 18, 25 & 31.VIII.32; 5, 6, 8 & 9.IX.32.

2. NNN: 4 & 8.XI.30; 29.IX.31; 18.VI.32; GGZ: 14.V.31. Interview with Eva Röhrs, whose son was a member of this Black Army unit.

3. VB: 20.IV.32; NNN: 22.VI.32.

4. NNN: 20.VIII.31; GGZ: 21.VIII.31.

5. NNN: 16.I.31; 3.X.32.

6. VB: 4.XI.32.

7. GGZ: 17, 20 & 22.IX.32; VB: 21 & 26.IX.32.

8. NSAH, Hann 310 I/A-108 II, Nr. 119, 127 & 129, all GSHB an OGN. Nr. 124 shows, however, a remittance of RM 102 for 33 new applicants in September. See also *ibid.*, /A-53 II, Nr. 10 (November 1932) for a summary.

9. Noakes, p. 234f.

10. *Ibid.* Local Group Northeim, however, recorded 33 new members in this period (see n. 8, above). Noakes also points out that the net loss of 401 members must be measured against a total *Gau* membership of 39,336 (*ibid.*, p. 234, n. 2).

11. *Ibid.*, p. 236ff.

12. NSAH, Hann 310 I/B-26, Nr. 42: Fragebogen für die Propaganda durch Bild und Schrift, GSHB Prop. Abt., 3.X.32. The quotation is from Steineck's response to the questionaire of 7.VI.32 *(ibid.)*.

13. *Ibid.* /A-122 I, Nr. 165: "Richtlinien für die Propaganda durch Kleinarbeit," 26.IX.32.

14. GGZ: 5, 6 & 11.X.32; NNN: 10–12.X.32.

15. VB: 16.IX.32; 24.X.32; NNN: 24, 25 & 27.X.32.

16. NNN: 10 & 11.X.32; VB: 10.X.32. The Town Band's conductor was very upset by this and wrote a letter to the NNN insisting on his political neutrality.

17. NNN: 22 & 24.X.32; VB: 1 & 4.XI.32.

18. NNN: 1 & 4.XI.32.

19. NNN: 27 & 29.X.32; 1, 3 & 5.XI.32; GGZ: 1 & 4.XI.32.

20. NSAH, Hann 310 I/A-108 II, Nr. 116: OGN an GSHB, 21.XII.32.

21. NNN: 7.XI.32; VB: 9.XI.32.

22. NNN: 22.X.32.

23. VB: 28.XI.32; NNN: 1 & 26.XI.32; 6.XII.32.

24. NNN: 22.X.32; 21.XI.32; 4.I.33. Fourteen hundred free baths were taken in November and December 1932, suggesting that the unemployed were possibly the cleanest citizens of Northeim (see Hueg, "Northeim 1933–36 . . . ," Table: "Städtische Warmwasserbadeanstalt").

25. NNN: 1.XII.32.

26. Interviews with Johannes Grote, Hermann Schulze, and Friedrich Haase.

27. Interview with "Benno Schmidt."

28. This was probably based on the fact that in December 1932 the Local Group, in anticipation of the need to put up candidates for the next local elections, was proposing names of Northeim Nazis to take a course on local government in Göttingen. Given the division in the Local Group, however, there was no agreed upon "master plan" for the apportionment of offices. See PK, N-16, OGN Ausgeg. Schreiben, N-Z, 1932–33: OGN an KLN, 27.XII.32.

29. Interviews with "Erhardt Knorpel" and "Hans Abbenrode."

30. NSAH, Hann 8/Hild II, I, Bd. VI, Nr. 585: Polizeiverwaltung Northeim an Reg.-Präs. Hildesheim, 23. IX.31. The report was signed by the conservative mayor, Peters.

31. *Ibid.*, Landrat Kirschbaum an Reg.-Präs. Hildesheim, 15.VIII.32. See also NNN, 13.VIII.32; 27.I.33; GGZ: 13.XI.32; VB: 22 & 27.X.32.

32. The Socialists particularily had to worry about Communist "unity front" tactics, which had already won over one local *Reichsbanner* leader. See NSAH, Hann 80/Hild II, I, Bd. VI, Nr. 585: Landrat Kirschbaum an Reg.-Präs. Hildesheim, 16.VII.32.

33. NNN: 7.XII.32; 19 & 23.I.33; GGZ: 24.I.33.

34. Noakes, p. 243. The quotation is from PK, N-16, OGN, Ausgeg. Schreiben, N–Z, 1932–33: Girmann an Keunecke, 3.XII.32. Girmann attributed the financial difficulty to the hundred party members, mostly Stormtroopers, who could not pay dues; wealthier members had to make up for their missing payments.

35. PK, N-14, Eingeg. Schreiben, N–Z, 1932–33: Magistrat der Stadt Northeim an Walter Steineck, 18.XI.32.
36. *Ibid.*, N-16, Ausgeg. Schreiben, N–Z, 1932–33: OGN Rundschreiben, Nov. 1932. Similar tactics had been used earlier by a Nazi suborganization in Hanover, which is probably where Girmann got the idea. See Noakes, p. 171.
37. NSAH, Hann 310 I/A-108 II, Nr. 116: OGL an GSHB, 21.XII.32; /A-53 II, Nr. 4 & 6: KLN an GSHB (Pg. Wittenberg), 13.XII.32 and 19.XII.32; B-25 II, Nr. 98: GSHB an KLN, 17.XII.32. See also note 8, above.
38. NSAH, Hann 310 I/B-25 II, Nr. 108 & 109: OGN an GSHB, 15.XI.32, and GSHB an KLN, 18.XI.32; /A-83 II, Nr. 191ff: exchanges between OGN and GSHB, Jan. 1933; PK, N-15, OGN Ausgeg. Schreiben, A–M, 1932–33: OGL an Dr. Goebbels, 5.I.33. In January 1933 all the Nazis' famous speakers were being dispatched to the critical election in Lippe and Goebbels was busy trying to prove that a Nazi "victory" there meant renewed momentum. He never answered Girmann.
39. NNN: 15.XII.32. On the internal squabbling see Appendix C, paragraphs 1d, 2a, 2c, and 3c; also, below, Ch. 16.
40. Interviews with "Erhardt Knorpel" and Eva Röhrs.
41. J. K. Pollock, "Areal Studies of the German Electorate, 1930–33," *American Political Science Review*, XXXVIII. p. 93.
42. Nazi strength in Northeim reflected the general area in which the town was located. From 1930 to 1933, Northeim's electoral district was the eighth strongest, in percentage of Nazi votes cast, of Germany's thirty-five electoral districts. In the second presidential election of 1932, Northeim's electoral district gave the sixth highest percentage of votes to Hitler: 44.8 percent or roughly 8 percent higher than the national average (*ibid.*, pp. 60–63).
43. See Tables 6 & 8 in Appendix B.
44. For a schematic representation of this see Table 8 in Appendix B.
45. NSAH, Hann 310 I/B-11 I: Gau-Redner, 15.XII.32. Topics and specialties listed separately.
46. Nazi growth at the expense of the bourgeois right in Northeim is shown in Tables 4 & 5, Appendix B. For a striking portrayal of this phenomenon nationally, see the graph on page 119 in Richard N. Hunt, *German Social Democracy 1918–1933* (New Haven, 1964).
47. Table 7, Appendix B, shows such a correlated distribution.

CHAPTER 10
The Last Elections (pages 151–167)

Epigraph: Desmond Flower and James Reeves, eds., *The Taste of Courage: The War, 1939–1945* (New York, 1960), p. 400.
1. NNN: 13.I.33.
2. NNN: 27.I.33.
3. NNN: 26 & 28.I.33.

4. NNN: 28.I.33; 2 & 6.II.33; GGZ: 7.II.33.
5. NNN: 2, 3 & 11.II.33.
6. NNN: 2, 3 & 28.II.33; GGZ: 22.II.33.
7. NNN: 18.II.33.
8. NNN: 20 & 21.II.33; GGZ: 21.II.33.
9. Interviews with Hermann Schulze, Johannes Grote, and Friedrich Haase.
10. GGZ and NNN: 24.II.33.
11. NSAH, Hann 310 I/B-3 I, Nr. 176: Reichspropagandaleiter Goebbels an alle Gauleiter, 9.II.33. The SPD was to be the prime target.
12. NNN: 23 & 27.II.33.
13. NNN: 2.III.33. For the meeting, NNN: 15 & 17.II.33; GGZ: 18.II.33.
14. Interview with Rudolf Bückmann, through whose pleadings the boy was ultimately permitted to graduate.
15. NNN: 3.III.33.
16. PK, N-16, OGN Ausgeg. Schreiben, N-Z, 1932–33: OGL an Küchenverwaltung, 28.II.33; OGL an Standartenführer Schnepel, 28.II.33.
17. NNN: 1 & 2.III.33; GGZ: 3.III.33.
18. Interview with Friedrich Haase, text from his *Entschädigungsbehörden* documents, a clipping from the *Göttinger Zeitung*, 4.III.33.
19. NNN: 28.II.33; 3 & 6.III.33; GGZ: 6.III.33.
20. NNN and GGZ: 6.III.33.
21. NNN: 6 & 7.III.33. Apparently the Prussian Ministry of the Interior expressly ordered that there be no opposition to the flying of swastika flags from public buildings. Nevertheless there was some in Northeim. When the janitor at the City Hall hung a swastika flag on the building's flagpole, Mayor Peters ordered that it be taken down because he thought it improper to put a party symbol on a public building. The order to lower the swastika was actually delivered by Thomas Galland, the mayor's administrative assistant. This was later held against him by the Nazis. Thus, on March 7, the only public building in Northeim without a Nazi flag was the City Hall. Interview with Thomas Galland.
22. NNN: 11.III.33.
23. NNN: 6, 10 & 11.II.33.
24. GGZ: 21, 22 & 26.II.33. The GGZ later announced that Senator Mahner and another Nationalist wanted it known that they had not authored the "Letter to the Editor." The announcement about the DVP's decision was *not* reported in its own paper, the NNN.
25. GGZ: 28.II.33; 1.III.33.
26. Interview with Thomas Galland.
27. NNN: 23 & 24.X.33.
28. GGZ: 14.III.33. All the speeches were printed in paraphrase, but since the Nazis were watching the GGZ closely and suspiciously, and since they did not correct the account or otherwise comment on it, it was probably substantially correct. Furthermore, by this time the GGZ was employing a member of the Nazi party as its reporter for Nazi meetings.

29. NNN: 11.III.33.
30. NNN: 13.III.33.

CHAPTER 11
The Uses of Electoral Success (pages 169–181)

Epigraph: See note 32, page 355.

1. *Nationalsozialistischer Beobachter für Kreis Northeim und Duderstadt. Beilage der Niedersächsische Tageszeitung* (henceforth this newspaper and its successor, from July 18, 1933, *Northeimer Beobachter: Parteiamtliches Organ der NSDAP für die Kreise Northeim und Einbeck. Amtliches Organ sämtlicher Behörden für die Kreise Northeim und Einbeck*—both located in HAN—will be cited "NB"): 15.III.33, for the distribution of seats in the Council. Interview with Hermann Denzler for the operation of the "Leader Principle" in the Council; interviews with Thomas Galland and Carl Querfurt on the disaffection of the SPD councilman.

2. Interview with Carl Querfurt; NNN: 29.III.33.

3. This account is drawn from interviews with three eyewitnesses (Hermann Denzler, Thomas Galland, and Carl Querfurt) and from the extensive reports in the NNN (29.III.33) and the GGZ (30.III.33). Speeches are from the newspaper paraphrases, with the indented quotation from Girmann being a case where the two newspaper reports were identical. The difficulty in getting exact words may be illustrated by Voge's statement to Querfurt upon denying him the right to speak (quoted above from the NNN), which were remembered by Querfurt himself as: "For ten years you've made the people drunk with your tricks of speech; the people do not wish to hear you any more." The GGZ reported: "Herr Querfurt, in the years of your rule you plastered us with bile and scourges; we don't want to listen to you."

4. NNN: 6.IV.33.

5. NNN: 7.IV.33; GGZ: 14.IV.33.

6. NNN: 13.IV.33. Actually, these last two names were never used. The Nazis later changed the Market Square to "Platz der SA" and created a "Reinhard Strasse" in honor of the Nazi public works director. Later street changes came as a result of the ousting of the mayor ("Bürgermeister Peters Strasse" became "Karl Dincklage Strasse"—named for an early official in the *Gauleitung*), and attempts to discredit the church ("Kirchstrasse" became "Peter Hohmann Strasse"), which may have also been behind the creation of a "Tilly Strasse." For a complete listing of the streets, old style, see election district lists in NNN: 28.II.33. For new streets see the map in "Strassenverzeichnis Northeim, 1938" (SAN, no number). For typical names chosen before the Nazis came to power, see NNN: 11.XI.30. Through 1938 the names of eleven streets had been changed.

7. NNN: 26 & 28.IV.33.

8. NNN: 7.VI.33.

9. NNN: 27.VI.33; 19.VII.33.
10. Interview with Otto von der Schulenberg; NNN: 25. II.33.
11. NNN: 13.III.33. The prior County Council (old Northeim County) had 20 seats: 10 SPD, 2 "Middle," 2 NSDAP, 5 "Bürgerliche Unity," and 1 "Town and Country."
12. NNN: 29 & 30.III.33.
13. Interview with Otto von der Schulenberg; see also his record in the BDC, where his actual entry date is listed as 1.V.33—a common date for many who joined in the spring of 1933. Later, when Querfurt twitted him about "having a new shirt," von der Schulenberg simply replied that he could "do more within the party than if he were outside and powerless." Interview with Carl Querfurt.
14. Interview with Carl Querfurt.
15. "It was at this announcement," said von der Schulenberg later, "that I first realized that we were going to have a complete dictatorship." However, he was previously apprehensive enough to write his speech out and read it verbatim rather than speaking, as he usually did, from notes. Interview with Otto von der Schulenberg.
16. NNN: 1 & 3.IV.33; GGZ: 4.IV.33.
17. NNN: 9.VI.33. Interview with Carl Querfurt.
18. Interviews with "Hans Abbenrode," "Erhardt Knorpel," and Otto von der Schulenberg; NB: 30.I.36, "3 Jahre N.S. Kommunal Verwaltung;" Ernst Girmann, "Tätigkeits und Erfolgsbericht, 25.I.35," (Bürgermeister Girmann zum Landrat von der Schulenberg): ms. in SAN, Nr. C.
19. GGZ: 13 & 27.IV.33; NNN: 27.IV.33; 5 & 13.V.33; 24.VI.33. No extant document shows the number of persons employed by the town immediately before the purge. In 1937 Northeim employed 221 of whom 105 were hourly workers and the rest civil servants or *Angestellter*. Since new offices had been created in the interim (for example, the "Racial Ancestry Office," or *Sippenamt*), and since there were doubtless fewer workers at a time when the town was struggling to balance its budget, there were probably about 180 on the payroll before the purge. For the 1937 figures see "Stand 18.IX.37: Beschäftigte Arbeiter" and "Personalbestand am 17.IX.1937 (mss. in SAN, no number).
20. GGZ: 13, 14 & 27.IV.33; 5.V.33; NNN: 27.IV.33; 5.V.33; 24.VI.33.
21. Interview with "Erhardt Knorpel."
22. NNN: 19.IV.33; 13.V.33; 8, 9 & 29.VI.33.
23. PK, N-16, OGN Ausgeg. Schreiben, N-Z, 1932–33: Girmann an Senator Junge, 27.IV.33.
24. NNN: 10.V.33.
25. PK, N-16, OGN Ausgeg. Schreiben, N-Z, 1932–33, undated OGL form letter plus list of names.
26. Interview with Thomas Galland. Monetary greed could hardly have been a motive for Girmann since the deputy mayor's salary was only about 20 percent less than the mayor's and both were very substantial. See NSAH, Hann 174/Northeim 86: Magistrat Northeim an Reg.-Präs. Hildesheim, 10.XI.33.

27. Interview with Thomas Galland.
28. Interviews with Otto von der Schulenberg, "Erhardt Knorpel," Thomas Galland, Wilhelm Spannaus, and Carl Querfurt.
29. NNN: 13.I.33.
30. See Appendix C, paragraph 2f.
31. Interviews with Otto von der Schulenberg, Thomas Galland, and "Erhardt Knorpel." For Ude's *Dezernate*, NNN: 7.IV.33. Ude joined the party on 1.III.30. His post in the Local Group was "Local Peasant Leader." See PK, N-16, OGN Ausgeg. Schreiben, N-Z, 1932–33: OGL an KLN, 27.XII.32 and *ibid.*, Korrespondenz, S-Z, 1936–43: Kreisbauernschaft an OGN, 14.VIII.37.
32. Interview with Thomas Galland.
33. "Protokoll der Fraktionssitzung der Fraktion der NSDAP in dem Bürgervorsteherkollegium zu Northeim, dem 28. Juni 1933." Carbon copy in private files of Wilhelm Spannaus; excerpts in PK, N-15, OGN Ausgeg. Schreiben, A-M, 1932–33: OGL an Reg.-Präs Muss (*sic*, should be "Muhs"), 29.VI.33.
34. NNN: 7.VI.33; 15.VIII.33. Interviews with "Erhardt Knorpel," Thomas Galland, and "Hugo Spiessmann." After World War II, Girmann sued the City of Northeim for a pension and thus the whole matter of how he became mayor came before the courts. His suit was denied. See "Ausfertigung. Streitliste Nr. AH II 176/54. In der Verwaltungsstreitsache des Bürgermeisters a.D. Girmann in Northeim, Klägers, gegen den Rat der Stadt Northeim, Beklagten, wegen Berücksichtigung der Beamtenrechte," and "Ante Nr. II OVG-A 30/56, 24.X.56 Revisionsantrag." (Both mss. in HAN.) The formal clause used to dismiss Peters was section six of the decree of April 7, 1933; the postwar court found that Girmann had come to power illegally, as a result of political action. His letter of appointment is in NSAH, Hann 80/Hild. III, 18/76, Nr. 16; Girmann, Ernst (16.III.34). He was appointed for twelve years.

CHAPTER 12
The Terror System (pages 183–200)

Epigraph: Hermann Rauschning, *Gespräche mit Hitler* (Zurich, 1940), p. 81.
1. Control over the police was actually secured by informal means. Both local judges were Nazis even before the March elections. The effective administrative head of the town's police, Police Secretary Engelmann, depended on an annual bonus from the City Council to make ends meet and consequently had to conform to its will when it came under Girmann's control. But individual policemen were forced, some almost physically, to wear swastika arm bands about mid-March. In addition to being psychologically compromised thereafter, they risked losing their jobs if they did not obey Girmann. (Interviews with Friedrich Haase, Carl Querfurt, and Otto von der Schulenberg.)
2. For example, in 1930 only nine hunting licenses were issued in Northeim, all to business or professional men. See NNN: 8.I.30.

3. Interviews with Friedrich Haase and "Benno Schmidt." The latter was seriously compromised when his friend sat on "Schmidt's" couch one day with a pocketful of bullets and let a few slip down between the cushions. When the police later searched "Schmidt's" apartment, there were the bullets; it was only later and after conversations with his friend that "Schmidt" discovered how they came to be there.

4. NNN: 6.III.33.

5. NNN: 30.III.33; 4, 8, 10, 19, 24 & 28.IV.33; 5.V.33; GGZ: 4 & 5.IV.33.

6. NNN: 11.VII.33; 2, 9 & 22.VIII.33.

7. NNN: 18.IV.33.

8. For the distribution of these events, see Table 9, Appendix B.

9. NNN: 14, 15 & 29.III.33.

10. GGZ: 18.III.33.

11. GGZ: 29.III.33; NNN: 30.III.33; 12.VII.33.

12. NSAH, Hann 80, Hann II/752, Nr.51: Präs. des Straffvollzugsamts Celle, 30.III.33; Nr. 54: Reg-Präs. Hann Vermerk, 4.IV.33 and Nr. 60: 7.IV.33; Nr. 84: Moringen an Reg-Präs. Hann, 15.IV.33 and Nr. 102: 21.IV.33; Reg-Präs. Hann an Landräte, 27.IV.33. See also Nr. 112:28.IV.33 and Nr. 116:5. V.33.

13. *Ibid.,* Reports by Müller, Lagerkommandant, to Reg-Präs. Hann: Nr. 137 (8.V.33), Nr. 138 (11.V.33), Nr. 148 (19.V.33), Nr. 158 (26.V.33), Nr. 161 (29.V.33), Nr. 253 (2.VI.33), Nr. 273 (16.VI.33), Nr. 304 (30.VI.33), Nr. 307 (7.VII.33), Nr. 308 (14.VII.33), and Nr. 444 (4.VIII.33). On the hunger strike: Nr. 322 (23.VI.33), Nr. 385 (24.VI.33), and Nr. 387 (26.VI.33).

14. *Ibid.,* reports by Cordes, SS Sturmführer u. Lagerkommandant an Polizeimajor Bergin, Hann: Nr. 472–3, 499, 500, 529, and 545. Later satistical records down to June 1944 in NSAH, Hann 22a/XI, 104g.

15. NNN: 28.IV.33; 9.V.33.

16. NNN: 17, 19 & 30.VI.33; GGZ: 20.VI.33; 1.VII.33.

17. Interviews with "Hans Abbenrode," Rudolf Bückmann, "Erhardt Knorpel," Carl Querfurt, Hermann Schulze, Thomas Galland, and Wilhelm Spannaus. Hermann Denzler himself denied any connection with the *Gestapo,* but as Northeim's highest SS official he was doubtless also part of the "V-Männer" system. It should be noted, however, that the SS did not get formal control over the Prussian *Gestapo* until April 20, 1934.

18. Interview with Maria Habenichts.

19. Interview with "Heinrich Lamme."

20. Interview with "Hans Abbenrode."

21. NSAH, Hann 310 I/C-17, Nr. 192: GSHB Propaganda Abt. (Nachrichtendienst), Rundschreiben, 6.V.33.

22. PK, N-14, OGN Eingeg. Schreiben, 1932–33: Karl Schmikke, SS Nachrichtentrupp Northeim, an OGN, 20.VI.33.

23. Interview with Maria Habenichts.

24. Interview with "Hans Abbenrode."

25. Interview with "Erhardt Knorpel."

26. PK, N-15, OGN Ausgeg. Schreiben, A-M, 1932–33: OGL an das Reichs Arbeitsministerium, 3.III.33; *ibid.*, OGL an Goering, 10.III.33.

27. Interview with "Erhardt Knorpel."

28. Interviews with Hermann Schulze, Johannes Grote, and Friedrich Haase, from whose statement the quotation is taken.

29. Interview with Carl Querfurt.

30. "Kommunal-Politische Abteilung der SPD im Bezirk Hannover. Rundschreiben Nr. 6/35 (Hannover, d. 23.III.33), Wilhem Hess an die Ortsvereinsvorstände im Bezirk Hannover." Copy in private files of Carl Querfurt.

31. *Zeugnis*, 12.V.33. This and other documents cited for Johannes Grote's experiences come from his papers submitted to the *Entschädigungsbehörde* of the Federal Republic of Germany in support of his application for recompense of wages lost due to Nazi terror activities against him. The documents were verified and he received payments: *Der Beauftragte des öffentl. Interesses beim Niedersächsischen Landesausschuss für Sonderhilfssachen, Nr. 02/223, Hann. d. 17. Okt. 1952.*

32. *Ibid.*, form letter from the *Magistrat der Stadt Northeim*, 12.V.33.

33. *Ibid.*, notarized statement by a former Northeim police officer, 5.I.53.

34. *Ibid.*, "Der Bürgermeister als Ortspolizeibehörde an den Gasanstaltsarbeiter Herrn Johannes Grote" (Northeim, 3.I.34–v 1505–35); "Der Landrat des Kreis Northeim an Herrn Johannes Grote, Northeim, 6.X.34"; "Der Regierungspräsident Hildesheim an Herrn Johannes Grote, 28.III.35 (I.v.545)." The general point of these letters is that Grote could not have travel identification documents because he was not politically reliable.

35. *Ibid.*, "Der Bürgermeister an die Nat. Soz. Kriegsopferversorgung z. Hd. von Herrn Fritz Kaeppke," 9.III.34.

36. See note 33, above.

37. Interview with Johannes Grote.

38. Interview with "Benno Schmidt."

39. *Entschädigungsbehörde* documents, private files of Friedrich Haase: "Der Vorsitzende des Kreisausschusses an den Dauerangestellten Herrn Friedrich Haase, Northeim, d. 9. V. 1933"; "Der Preussische Minister des Innern an den Dauerangestellten Herrn Friedrich Haase, Berlin, den 20. Juli 1934."

40. *Ibid.*, "Friedrich Haase an den Entschädigungsbehörde, Hildesheim (18. April 1956)."

41. Interview with Friedrich Haase; all quotations: *ibid.*

42. BDC, Akten Carl Querfurt (NSV card).

43. Interview with Carl Querfurt.

44. Interview with Hermann Schulze. His account and documents to substantiate it were certified by the British occupation authorities in 1946.

45. NNN: 9 & 19.V.33; 15.VII.33; GGZ: 12.V.33.

CHAPTER 13
Whipping Up Enthusiasm (pages 201–216)

Epigraph: See note 16, below.

1. Subscription figures in NSAH, Hann 310 I/A-22 II, Nr. 112: Gau Presseamt, "Erläuterung zu der Karte über die Verbreitung der NTZ im Gebiet des GSHB." See also Noakes, p. 205.

2. Between Dec. 10, 1932, and April 6, 1933, this paper was also known as *Nationalsozialistischer Beobachter*. NNN: 18.VII.33; NB: 6.IV.33; 10.VI.33; interview with "Kurt Zeisser" whose father printed the NB from Oct. 1932 to July 1933.

3. "Runderlass der Kreisleitung Northeim an alle Ortsgruppenführer, 22.V.33"; "Landrat von der Schulenberg an GGZ, 24.IV.33" (both from the files of the GGZ, now in possession of Eva Röhrs).

4. Interview with "Erhardt Knorpel."

5. *Ibid.*

6. NB: 6.IV.33.

7. Interview with "Erhardt Knorpel."

8. Interview with Wilhelm Spannaus.

9. NNN: 9.V.33; 7.VI.33; 15, 22 & 29.VII.33.

10. *Hört! Hört!:* 6.IV.32; 22.X.32; GGZ: 26.IV.32; 1.V.32. The *Volksblatt* enjoyed this immensely, but continued to call the GGZ a "Nazi organ" and demanded that it be stripped of its status as official paper for the local governments (VB: 4.V.32; 2.VII.32).

11. NB: 21.V.33.

12. GGZ: 25.V.33.

13. Interview with Eva Röhrs.

14. GGZ: 9.VI.33; NB: 10.VI.33. Also, letter from von der Schulenberg to Wilhelm Röhrs, 20.VII.33 (from private files of Eva Röhrs).

15. NNN: 10, 13 & 14.III.33; GGZ: 15.III.33; NB: 15.III.33. It was on this occasion that Girmann tried to incite the SA to sack Querfurt's shop.

16. NNN: 11, 17–18 & 20.III.33; GGZ: 21.III.33. The title of the speech: "Welch' ein' Wendung durch Gottes Fügung." This was actually a statement composed by Prussia's King William I on the occasion of the capitulation of Sedan in the Franco-Prussian War. See: *Extra-Beilage, Magdeburgischen Zeitung*, 3.IX.1870.

17. NNN: 20–23.III.33.

18. NNN: 18–21.IV.33; GGZ: 21.V.33.

19. NSAH, Hann 310 I/B-6, Nr. 2–9: Reichspropagandaleitung, Richtlinien für den "Tag der Nationalen Arbeit," 15.IV.33 and Nr. 10–11: Huxhagen (Kommissar für Volksaufklärung und Propaganda für Wahlkreis 16, SHB) Rundschreiben Nr. 1/33–Betr. 1 Mai 1933, 21.IV.33 and ditto: 2/33.

20. NNN: 24.IV.33.

21. NNN: 24, 26, 27 & 29.IV.33; 2.V.33; GGZ: 28.IV.33; 3.V.33.

22. NNN: 24 & 27.V.33; GGZ: 25.V.33.

23. NNN: 23 & 27.III.33; 12, 15 & 20.V.33; 7.VI.33; 11, 17 & 31.VII.33; GGZ: 3.V.33.
24. NNN: 22 & 24.IV.33; 5 & 13.V.33; GGZ: 4.V.33.
25. NNN: 6.VI.33.
26. GGZ: 20.VI.33; NNN: 22 & 27.IV.33; 19.VI.33; 20.VII.33.
27. NNN: 17.III.33; 28.IV.33; 20.VII.33.
28. NNN: 5.V.33; GGZ: 7.IV.33; 5.V.33; 9.VI.33. Interview with Rudolf Bückmann, who joined the *Stahlhelm* at this time.
29. GGZ: 1 & 20.VI.33; NNN: 27.VI.33.
30. NNN: 15 & 28.IV.33; 2.V.33; 28.VI.33.
31. NNN: 8 & 29.V.33.
32. NNN: 12 & 26.VI.33; 7.VIII.33.
33. NNN: 8–10.II.33; GGZ: 11.II.33.
34. GGZ: 22.VI.33. Originally the glider group was sponsored by the Northeim members of ADAC (Germany's automobile club). Auto owners in the early thirties in Northeim tended to be both wealthy enough to finance a glider club and nationalistic enough to want to do so, as a means of training pilots and circumventing the clauses in the Treaty of Versailles that prohibited Germany from having an air force.

CHAPTER 14
The Atomization of Society (pages 217–232)

1. NNN: 1.I.33. The figure 102 is from 1900, when the town's population was approximately 8,000. Both figures were very close to the national average for cities.
2. Interviews with Gregor Ballin, "Heinrich Lamme," "Benno Schmidt," and "Erhardt Knorpel."
3. PK, N-16, OGN Ausgeg. Schreiben, N–Z, 1932–33: OGL an Pg. Mathäus, 24.II.33.
4. NNN: 29.III.33; 1.IV.33. The fate of these forty individuals up to the outbreak of World War II was:

Died by natural causes	4
Left Northeim	25
Taken from Northeim to concentration camps	8
Committed suicide	2
Fate unknown	1

Of the 120 Jews in Northeim in 1932, two returned to the town after 1945, both for economic reasons.
5. GGZ: 21.III.33; 2.IV.33. It was only in the farming communities around Northeim that there were real feelings of anti-Semitism, according to "Erhardt Knorpel."
6. NB: 6.VI.33.
7. Interviews with "Heinrich Lamme" and "Hans Abbenrode."

8. Interview with Gregor Ballin.
9. NNN: 3.IV.33; 4.V.33. Interviews with Friedrich Haase, "Erhardt Knorpel," "Heinrich Lamme," and Gregor Ballin.
10. Interviews with Eva Röhrs and "Heinrich Lamme."
11. Interview with Gregor Ballin.
12. Interviews with Johannes Grote and "Benno Schmidt."
13. A spark of the old way of acting flared up in 1937 when the banker Müller died, of natural causes. He was a conservative, an ex-officer, and a member of the elite of the town, which therefore simply could not ignore his passing even if his "race" made him a pariah in Nazi eyes. Despite having been warned not to, some sixty of Northeim's leading businessmen attended his funeral. An SA leader photographed this scandal and the picture was published in Julius Streicher's *Stürmer* over the caption "Judenknechte aus Northeim!" ("Jew-Serfs of Northeim!"). But apart from this national excoriation, the offenders received no punishment. Some of them were Nazis of the "idealist" group described in Chapter 16.
14. Interview with Otto von der Schulenberg.
15. Interviews with "Erhardt Knorpel" and Rudolf Bückmann.
16. PK, N-16, OGN Ausgeg. Schreiben, N–Z, 1932–33: OGL an Unterstützungsverein Northeim, 27.V.33.
17. NNN: 20.III.33; 8.IV.33. In addition to this the NSBO set up a cell in the railroad director's office. See PK, N-13, OGN Eingeg. Schreiben, A–M, 1932–33: Gau Hesse-Nassau-Nord an Ernst Hirmann (sic), 24.IV.33.
18. NNN: 27 & 30.III.33; 24 & 26.IV.33; NB: 6.IV.33; GGZ: 27.IV.33.
19. NNN: 5, 20 & 22.V.33; 24.VI.33; NB: 6.V.33. The temporarily rehired union officials were dismissed on June 6, 1933.
20. NNN: 22.V.33; 18.VII.33.
21. NNN: 13.II.33; 20.IV.33.
22. NNN: 18, 22 & 26.IV.33; 4.V.33. Interview with "Erhardt Knorpel."
23. GGZ: 21.V.33.
24. NNN: 4.VII.33.
25. NNN: 18.IV.33; 24.V.33; GGZ: 23.IV.33. Later, teachers were also required to join the NSDAP. In the whole of Northeim only one teacher refused to join the Nazi Teachers' League. She was an old maid who had been teaching in Northeim long enough to have boxed Ernst Girmann's ears when he was a little boy. She declared that the whole thing was "nonsense" and refused to have anything to do with it. Perhaps as a result of ancient fears, Northeim's Nazis never pressed the matter. But she was the sole exception (interview with "Hans Abbenrode").
26. NNN: 6.II.33.
27. NNN: 16 & 29.V.33; 8 & 9.VIII.33. Interview with Carl Querfurt.
28. NNN: 13.IV.33; 6.VI.33. Interview with Wilhelm Spannaus. The outstanding rumor was that the consumers' cooperative delivery truck had been used to carry a corpse.
29. NNN: 25.III.33; 3.IV.33; 8 & 30.V.33; 10.VIII.33; GGZ: 21.VI.33.

30. Interview with "Hans Abbenrode."
31. NNN: 8 & 19.IV.33; *50 Jahre Volkschor Northeim*, p. 39.
32. PK, N-14, OGN Eingeg. Schreiben, N-Z, 1932–33: Otto Klepper, Die Liedertafel, an OGL, 11.X.33.
33. NNN: 18.V.33. After World War II, several of the old clubs revived themselves (see Chapter 2, n. 25).
34. NNN: 16.V.33; 24.VI.33; 1.VII.33.
35. Interview with Wilhelm Spannaus. For an example of "coordination" from above, see *Northeimer Heimatblätter*, No. 5, June 1933: the "Museumverein."
36. PK, N-14, OGN Eingeg. Schreiben, N-Z, 1932–33: An die OGL, 25.VII.33 and response, OGL an Pg. E. Hentschel, 27.VII.33. Each club charged the other with being Jewish and liberal; both wanted to remain independent.
37. NNN: 15.V.33; 1 & 3.VIII.33; GGZ: 12.V.33. Members of the football club "VfB" actually hid their club flag during the Nazi era. See anon., *50 Jahre "Verein für Bewegungssport 1906, Northeim e.V.,"* Northeim, 1957.
38. NB: 10.VI.33. The Bible text is: "For of Him, and through Him, and unto Him, are all things. To Him be the glory forever. Amen."
39. GGZ: 11.VI.33; also, NNN: 15 & 26.VI.33.
40. NSAH, Hann 310 I/B-3 I, Nr. 56: Reichspropagandaleitung an Gauleitung Hannover (Telegram), 18.VII.33; Nr. 58: Reichsleitung Propaganda an alle Gauleiter; Nr. 115: Stabsleiter der P.O., Anordnung 28/33.
41. NNN: 10 & 17.VI.33; 11, 15, 20, 21 & 24.VII.33; GGZ: 18.VI.33.
42. Interviews with Carl Querfurt, "Hans Abbenrode," Rudolf Bückmann, and Wilhelm Spannaus.
43. GGZ: 12.V.33.
44. NB: 4 & 15.III.33; NNN: 3.VII.33.
45. NNN: 7 & 19.IV.33.
46. Interview with Rudolf Bückmann; PK, N-16, OGN Ausgeg. Schreiben, N-Z, 1932–33: OGL an Direktor Bückmann, 25.IV.33 (3 letters).
47. NNN: 20.V.33; Hueg, "Northeim 1933–36 . . . ," p. 23.
48. NNN: 9.III.33; 15.IV.33; 13.V.33; GGZ: 14.IV.33. Later, when the *Stahlhelm* was broken up, the band was also dissolved (see Chapter 17).
49. NNN: 2.VI.33.

CHAPTER 15
The Positive Aspect (pages 233–237)

Epigraph: See Chapter 11, note 3, page 353.
1. Stadtwohlfahrts- und Jugendamt Northeim: "Gesamtübersicht über die Entwicklung der letzten 3½ Jahre," 25 Aug. 1936, p. 2 (Nr. 7/71/VII in SAN). Also, NNN: 13 & 27.I.33; 15.III.33; 12.IV.33.
2. NNN: 20, 24–27.VII.33; also, letter and report from *Magistrat* Northeim to the *Regierungspräsident*, 17.VIII.33 (in SAN).

3. NNN: 29.VIII.33; 1 & 4.IX.33; also, letter from *Magistrat* Northeim to the *Regierungspräsident*, 31.VIII.33 (Nr. 4 in SAN).
4. PK, N-16, OGN Ausgeg. Schreiben, N-Z, 1932–33: OGL an Heinrich Schönewolf, 22.VI.33. The term used twice for hiring party members was "duty."
5. NNN: 17.VI.33; 20.VII.33. Interview with "Erhardt Knorpel." In Northeim there were only 15 NSDAP members with numbers below 100,000, of whom 5 were unemployed. Many Nazis had already been given work at the time of the purge of city employees.
6. Letter and report from *Magistrat* Northeim to the *Regierungspräsident*, 17.VIII.33 (in SAN). See also OGL, "Bericht über die Entwicklung des Führerprinzips in Northeim, 1933–37 (ms., 1937, in SAN) and NNN: 9.II.33; 25.VII.33; NB: 30.I.36 (special issue: "Drei Jahre N.S. Kommunalverwaltung").
7. NNN: 14.VII.33.
8. NNN: 25.II.33; 10 & 26.IV.33; 12.V.33; 3.VI.33.
9. NNN: 26 & 28.VII.33.
10. NNN: 30.III.33; 22.IV.33; 11.V.33; GGZ: 23.IV.33. The soup kitchen also supplied some 5,000 meals for various Nazi gatherings and to the standing SA guard kept at the kitchen in February and March.

CHAPTER 16
Reaction and Resistance (pages 239–248)

1. NNN: 25.II.33; 29.IV.33; NB: 6.V.33.
2. PK, N-16, OGN Ausgeg. Schreiben, N-Z, 1932–33 (section "N"). Both were a bit too ambivalent; they missed the deadline.
3. Interviews with Thomas Galland and "Erhardt Knorpel."
4. PK, N-16, OGN Ausgeg. Schreiben, N-Z, 1932–33: OGL an Stürmführer Pg. Fr. Dierbach, 8.III.33.
5. NNN: 22.V.33. Interview with Otto von der Schulenberg.
6. Interviews with "Hans Abbenrode" and Rudolf Bückmann. Abbenrode candidly admitted this about himself and Bückmann heard the same from one of his teachers. In the latter case the man actually was promoted.
7. Interview with "Erhardt Knorpel."
8. Interview with Thomas Galland.
9. PK, N-14, OGN Eingeg. Schreiben, N-Z, 1932–33: Otto Müller an OGL, 28.VI.33. He meant free from his commitment to the *Stahlhelm*. In July some six other former *Stahlhelm* members applied for Nazi membership; all this was because of the dissolution of the "Deutschnationalen Front."
10. PK, N-16, OGN Ausgeg. Schreiben, N-Z, 1932–33 (section "N").
11. Interviews with "Heinrich Lamme" and Maria Habenichts.
12. PK, N-16, OGN Ausgeg. Schreiben, N-Z, 1932–33: *passim*.
13. Interview with "Erhardt Knorpel." The man in question lost considerable money since he had to let his workers march whenever there was a parade and had to

pay them for that time, too. He was sure that if he refused to do either, he would be boycotted.

14. Interviews with Otto von der Schulenberg, "Hans Abbenrode," and Maria Habenichts.

15. Interview with Maria Habenichts. Despite these doubts her husband, who had been a local leader of the DVP, voted NSDAP in March 1933.

16. "Report of the Gau-Uschla proceedings in Northeim on July 4, 1933," p. 2. See also Appendix C. This and other documents cited for the "Idealists' Conspiracy" are from the private files of Wilhelm Spannaus.

17. "Report of the Gau-Uschla proceedings in Northeim on July 1, 1933." Interview with Wilhelm Spannaus; Appendix C. For an example of unrecorded applications, or at least a six month delay in processing them, see PK, N-14, OGN Eingeg. Schreiben, A-M, 1932–33: Ludwig Huch an OGL, 4.II.33.

18. On the expulsions, PK, N-16, OGN Ausgeg. Schreiben, N-Z, 1932–33: OGL an Frl. Maria Hermann, Lore Hartmann, 28.I.33 (both expelled for "defamatory utterances"); on the packing of the Uschla, ibid., N-15, OGN Ausgeg. Schreiben, A-M, 1932–33: OGL an Uschla-Vorsitzenden Göttingen, 22.II.33 and ibid., N-16, OGN Ausgeg. Schreiben, N-Z, 1932–33: OGL an Pg. Fr. Dierlach, Fr. Schoppe, 30.I.33. By summer it had to be purged again: ibid., OGL an KLN, 5.VII.33. The acronym "Uschla" stands for "investigation and reconciliation committee." Later in 1933 its name was changed to "party court."

19. PK, N-14, OGN Eingeg. Schreiben, N-Z, 1932–33: Friedrich Schrader an OGL, 26.IV.33; Hermann Sebolde an OGL, 31.III.33; ibid., N-16, OGN Ausgeg. Schreiben, N-Z, 1932–33: OGL an Rechtsanwalt (illeg.), 28.II.33. All are examples of the Local Group solving its financial problems by means of the election campaign.

20. PK, N-15, OGN Ausgeg. Schreiben, A-M, 1932–33: OGL an Justizministerium, 4.IV.33 (on behalf of the lawyer, Dr. Hermann Bartels); for the students see Chapter 14. n. 46.

21. Ibid., OGL an Reichsleitung der NSDAP (Karteiabteilung), 25.II.33 and 3.III.33; N-16, OGN Ausgeg. Schreiben, N-Z, 1932–33: OGL an Frau Regierungsrat Niemeyer, 28.I.33 and an Frln. Wilhelmine Dierking, 3.II.33. Girmann's troubles with Voge started when the latter refused to give party charity money to Steineck at the time of Steineck's illness in December 1932. See NSAH, Hann 310 I/A-108 II, Nr. 116: OGL an GSHB, 21.XII.32.

22. Mimeographed letter: "Ernst Girmann, OGL, an alle Parteigenossen OGN," 22.IV.33 (Spannaus files).

23. Ibid.; also NNN: 30.III.33; 31.VII.33. The former article speaks for itself: "The County Leader of the NSDAP has announced that collections, no matter what kind, without the written permission of the County Leader or approval of the Local Group Leader, are forbidden. Should collectors appear, their party card is to be immediately confiscated and the proper authorities immediately notified."

24. PK, N-16, OGN Ausgeg. Schreiben, N-Z, 1932–33: OGL an Pg. Peiters, 8.V.33 and Abschrift (Erklärung) Pg. August Döring, n.d.

25. PK, N-16, OGN Ausgeg. Schreiben, N-Z, 1932–33: OGL an Wilhelm Spannaus, Heinrich Schierloh, Dr. Venzlaff, Heinrich Voge, 28.VI.33; an August Döring, 8.VII.33; an Standartenführer Schnepel, 29.VI.33.
26. "Protokoll der Fraktionsitzung der Fraktion der NSDAP im Bürgervorsteherkollegium, 28. Juni, 1933" (Spannaus files, carbon); excerpted in PK, N-15, OGN Ausgeg. Schreiben, A-M, 1932–33: OGL an Reg.-Präs. Muss (sic), 29.VI.33. In all cases the reason given was that the individuals "no longer possessed the confidence of the City Council." In actuality the councillors were motivated mainly by fear of Girmann.
27. Interview with Wilhelm Spannaus.
28. PK, N-18, OGN Ausgeg. Schreiben, N-Z, 1934: OGL an Sturmbannführer der SA-Res. 91, Ehlers, 20.VIII.34; an Führer der SA Reserve Standarte 91, Schnepel, 28.IX.34; an Pg. Engelmann, Vorsitzender des OG Gerichts, 10.XII.34; an Gaugericht SBH, 20.II.35. Also letter from Dr. Edmund Venzlaff to author, Jan. 14, 1967. Venzlaff eventually found a job in Celle, where he stayed until 1945, "watched and distrusted by the party, but left in peace." Ironically, the British occupation authorities dismissed him from his job, 1945–48, for his former membership in the NSDAP.

CHAPTER 17
From Enthusiasm to Ritual (pages 249–264)

Epigraph: See note 33, page 365.
1. NNN: 7, 19 & 21.VIII.33.
2. NNN: 8 & 11.IX.33.
3. NB: 20.IX.33; NNN: 18.IX.33. The speeches given at other general meetings in Northeim County were identical in content.
4. NSAH, Hann 310 I/B-3 I, Nr. 127: "Richtlinien zur Schulung der nach dem 1. Jan. 1933 in die NSDAP eingetretenen Parteigenossen, München d. 18.V.33."
5. NNN: 16 & 17.X.33.
6. NSAH, Hann 310 I/B-53, Nr. 158–59: KLN an GSHB, 27. [X.] 33. The "Kommunistenneste" were Bishausen b/Norten and Bühle; the SPD centers were Suterode and Ertinghausen, according to Steineck.
7. NNN: 20 & 23.X.33.
8. NNN: 31.X.33; 1, 3–4, 6 & 8–9.XI.33.
9. NNN: 9.XI.33.
10. NNN: 10.XI.33.
11. Mimeographed circular: "Ortsgruppenleiter Girmann an alle Parteigenossen der Ortsgruppe Northeim" (n.d. [Nov. 1, 1933]), in private files of Wilhelm Spannaus.
12. NNN: 9 & 10.XI.33.
13. GGZ: 12.XI.33; NNN: 11.XI.33.
14. For the county vote: NSAH, Hann 310 I/B-53, Nr. 150: Landrat Northeim an

GSHB (telegram). For Moringen concentration camp: NSAH, Hann 80, Hann II, Nr. 752: report of 16.XI.33 an Reg.-Präs. Hannover.

15. NNN: 13 & 14.XI.33.
16. NNN: 12.I.34; 3.III.34.
17. Interviews with "Heinrich Lamme" and Maria Habenichts.
18. NSAH, Hann 310 I/B-31: GSHB an NSDAP Reichspropagandaabteilung München, 7.X.33.
19. NNN: 25 & 27.XI.33; 25 & 27.XII.33; 13.I.34; 26.II.34; interview with Wilhelm Spannaus.
20. Mimeographed circular: "Ortsgruppenleiter Girmann an alle Parteigenossen der Ortsgruppe Northeim, 21.XI.33"; mimeographed letter: "Ortsgruppenleiter Girmann an alle Parteigenossen der Ortsgruppe Northeim, 30.VII.35 (both from private files of Wilhelm Spannaus).
21. Interviews with Hermann Denzler, "Hans Abbenrode," and "Erhardt Knorpel."
22. PK, N-17, OGN Ausgeg. Schreiben, A-M, 1934: OGL an Verband mitteldeutscher Konsumvereine, 20.III.34 (in re: Robert Schnabel); ibid., N-18, OGN Ausgeg. Schreiben, N-Z, 1934: OGL an Post-Inspektor Jaep, 26.X.34 (in re: Hermann Lüdecke).
23. NNN: 29.VIII.33; 2.IX.33; 25.XI.33.
24. NNN: 19, 22 & 27.IX.33.
25. NNN: 10 & 30.VIII.33; 28.X.33; "Bericht des Stadtoberinspektors Horboth an dem Magistrat Northeim, 24.Aug. 1936," Nr.1A in SAN. By 1936 about 1,500 Northeimers had requested certification of ancestry.
26. Interview with Rudolf Bückmann.
27. PK, N-12: Veranstaltungen u. Tagungen in Northeim II, 1937–41: GSHB, Rundschreiben Nr. 53 (vertraulich), d. 13.XII.37 (repeating an order by Rudolf Hess of Oct. 20, 1934).
28. NSAH, Hann 310 I/C-16, Nr. 15: Kreisnachrichtendienstleiter an GSHB, 3.V.34; /C-15 I, Nr. 123: Kreisnachrichtendienst Tätigkeitsbericht, 4.VII.34; /C-10, Nr. 56–62: Kreisnachrichtendienst Tätigkeitsbericht, 5.VI.34, 3.V.34.
29. Interview with Carl Querfurt.
30. Interviews with "Heinrich Lamme" and "Erhardt Knorpel."
31. Wells, pp. 136–37; interview with "Hans Abbenrode"; NNN: 30.IX.33; 7.X.33.
32. Hueg, "Northeim 1933–36 . . . ," p. 16.
33. Ibid., pp. 17–19; OGL, "Bericht über die Entwicklung des Führerprinzips in Northeim, 1933–37" (ms., 1937, in SAN); interviews with "Hans Abbenrode" and Rudolf Bückmann.
34. Hueg, "Northeim 1933–36 . . . ," pp. 16–20.
35. "Verwaltungsbericht der Katholische Volksschule Northeim am 2.X.36" (Nr. 6/54/V in SAN).
36. "Bericht über die Hilfsschule Northeim f. d. Zeitraum 1929–36" (Nr. 6/53/V in SAN). Also: Hueg, "Northeim 1933–36 . . . ," pp. 19–20.
37. Interview with Rudolf Bückmann; "Verwaltungsbericht des Gymnasium Corvi-

nianum Northeim, 16.IX.36" (Nr. 6/54/V in SAN). Also, Bückmann, 475 *Jahre.* . . .

38. Interview with "Hans Abbenrode."
39. Interview with Rudolf Bückmann.
40. "NB an alle Parteigenossen, Northeim d. 23. Sept. 1933" (printed form letter in private files of Wilhelm Spannaus).
41. "Weigel, Gaupresseamtsleiter, GSHB, an alle Kreis- und Ortsgruppenpresse-warte, den Kreis- und Ortsgruppenleitern zur Kenntnis (Streng vertraulich!), Hannover, d. 5.IV.1934" (in private files of Eva Röhrs). Apparently there must have been a leak in the Nazi network, because the GGZ obtained an unauthor-ized copy of this.
42. NNN: 2 & 12.XII.33. Interview with "Erhardt Knorpel." The suppression co-incided with the issuance of the "Law for the Protection of the Identity of Party and State" which might have made the masthead catch the *Pressewart*'s eye. The NNN continued its independent existence until 1942, when it was merged with the NB as a "wartime economy measure." After World War II it resumed publication under its own name.
43. NB: 27.II.33; 27.VII.33; "Gaupressewart an den Herrn Wilhelm Röhrs, 14.XII.33"; "NB an GGZ, 27.VIII.34"; R.A.D. Unterfeldmeister (sig. illeg.) an Wilhelm Röhrs, 4.V.34"; "NB an GGZ, 29.I.34"; "NSDAP Kreispresse-wart für Northeim an GGZ, 21.IX.34"; "NB an GGZ, 25.IX.34"; P. Guss-mann, Reichsministerium für Volksaufklärung u. Propaganda an Wilhelm A. Röhrs, 26.III.35" (all from private files of Eva Röhrs).
44. "A. Schwertfeger an W. A. Röhrs, 2.III.34"; "Heinrich Sohnrey an NSDAP, GSHB, 6.VIII.34" (carbon copy enclosed in "Heinrich Sohnrey an Wilhelm Röhrs, 8.VIII.34"). All from private files of Eva Röhrs.
45. Interview with Eva Röhrs.
46. PK, N-18, OGN Ausgeg. Schreiben, N-Z, 1934: OGL an Gastwirt Dressel, 21.VIII.34, who was told that "Whoever attacks the NB attacks the party."
47. NNN: 30.XI.33; 26.I.34; 12.II.34.
48. NNN: 21.I.31; 13.IX.33; 27 & 28.XI.33; 10 & 13.II.34. Before the Nazis came to power, the war graves organization had 125 members and its collector was the Jewish banker, Müller (NNN: 13.V.33).
49. "Regierungspraesident Mühs an Magistrat Northeim, 9.X.33"; in reply, "Mag-istrat Northeim an Regierungspraesident Mühs, 16.X.33 ("Fach V" in SAN); NB: 8.X.33; NNN: 23 & 30.IX.33; 3 & 9.X.33.
50. "Tätigkeitsbericht der Luftschutzschule Northeim im Jahre 1935" (n.d., ms. in SAN, Nr. 121/XII). Also, NNN: 7 & 20.IX.33; 18.XI.33.
51. NNN: 31.VIII.33; 4, 23, 25–28.IX.33; 3.X.33; NB: 8.X.33; 3.XI.33; 27 & 29.XII.33.
52. Table constructed from Hueg, "Northeim 1933–36 . . . ," p. 33. "Political crimes" and "matters to be investigated secretly" are excluded.
53. "Statistik über die bearbeiteten Kriminal-polizeilichen Vorgänge bei der Kriminal Polizei in Northeim, Kriminal-Sekretär Meyer, Northeim 1936"; "Schutzhaft infolge Trunkenheit, Rühestörung, politisch pp." (both mss. in SAN, Nr. 2/VIII/c).

54. "Rede des Stellvertretener Bürgermeister Girmanns am 1.III.34 im 10er Zelt" (ms. in SAN, Nr. 74/VII/6).

55. PK, N-19, OGN Korrespondenz, A-K, 1935: Uschlavorsitzender Peiters an Max Herholz, 8.IV.33; *ibid.*, N-20, OGN Korrespondenz, L-Z, 1935: GSHB an Georg Meister, 4.III.35.

56. *Ibid.*, OGL an Karl Voss, 29.XII.34, and OGL an Vorsitzenders des Ortsgruppengerichts Pg. Richard Schmidt, 5.III.35, *in re:* Pg. Hugo Sauer.

57. PK, N-18, OGN Ausgeg. Schreiben, N-Z, 1934: OGL an Pg. Obermeister Ranberg, 26.X.34; *ibid.*, OGL an Pg. August Voss, 19.XII.34.

CHAPTER 18
The Great Justification (pages 265–279)

Epigraph: See note 11, below.

1. PK, N-16, OGN Ausgeg. Schreiben, N-Z, 1932–33: OGL an Pg. Ehlers, Führer der Reserve SA Standarte 136, 6.XII.33.

2. GGZ: 17.V.33; NNN: 7.VIII.33. Interviews with "Erhardt Knorpel" and Thomas Galland.

3. Order circulated among Northeim city employees, June 26, 1935 (copy in private files of Wilhelm Spannaus; also in SAN).

4. BDC, Akten Ernst Girmann: "Beschwerde des Uschla-Vorsitzenden der Ortsgruppe Northeim gegen den Ortsgruppenleiter von Northeim, Pg. Girmann, München den 4. Dez. 1933."

5. NNN: 22.IX.33.

6. Wells, p. 62. For Girmann's installation as mayor, NNN: 27.III.34 and Hueg, "Northeim 1933–36 . . . ," p. 2; also, OGL, "Bericht über die Entwicklung des Führerprinzips. . . ." The new institutions were "Ratsherrn" (previously "Bürgervorsteherkollegium") and "Stadtrat" (previously "Magistrat").

7. NNN: 3 & 5.VIII.33; 7 & 13.IX.33; 30.XII.33; 20 & 24.I.34 (for the DAF); 12 & 16.X.33 (for the artisans); 18.XI.33 (for the retailers).

8. "Bericht der Rede des Ortsgruppenleiter Girmanns am 5.X.33 im Deutsches Haus, Gr. Saale," including a form letter and attached list of names dated 30.IX.33 (all in SAN, Nr. 75/VII/b); NB: 8.X.33; NNN: 6.X.33.

9. NNN: 14, 25 & 29.X.33.

10. Form letter, with list of names attached, from Stellvertretener Bürgermeister Girmann, 27.II.34 (Nr. 74/VII/b in SAN) and "Richtlinien für die Redner in der Arbeitsschlacht des GSHB" (II 2640 Hu/wk in SAN); "Rede des Stellvertretener Bürgermeister Girmanns am 1.III.34 im 10er Zelt" (Nr. 74/VII/6 in SAN). The entire speech, covering four newspaper pages, was reprinted in NNN: 2 & 6.III.34.

11. "Versammlung, betr. Arbeitsbeschaffungs-Massnahmen, im Hotel 'Sonne' am Do., d. 8. März 1934, Abends 8:30 Uhr" (stenographic report, no number, in SAN).

12. *Ibid.*

13. NNN: 10, 15, 20 & 21.III.34.
14. "Stellvertretener Bürgermeister Girmann an Stadtbaumeister Nass, 12.III.34" (in SAN, no number); "Versammlung des Verein zur Hebung des Fremdenverkehrs Northeim in der 'Sonne' am 31.VIII.34. Ansprache des Herrn Bürgermeister Girmanns" (Nr. B/IIa in SAN).
15. "Merkmale über die Stadtforst Northeim seit der Machtübernahme durch unseren Führer [10.I.35]" (Nr. 8/91/IXc in SAN); OGL, "Bericht über die Entwicklung des Führerprinzips . . ."; Hueg, "Northeim 1933–36 . . . ," p. 23; NB: 30.I.36 (special issue).
16. NNN: 29.XI.33 (for the mass entry into the RAD from the sugar factory). On the theater, see "Bericht über den Bau der Weihstätte in Northeim, 1934–36" (unnumbered ms. in SAN); for a photograph of Girmann delivering the dedication address at the site, *Der Spiegel*, Nr. 49/1966, p. 59; NNN: 5.II.34; 7.VI.36.
17. Hueg, "Northeim 1933–36 . . . ," Table: "Bevölkerung der Stadt."
18. *Ibid.*, p. 7; NNN: 7.XI.33; 2.III.34.
19. NSAH, Hann 174/Northeim 86, Nr. 178: des Notariatsregisters, Jahrgang 1934, 26.V.34.
20. NNN: 21.XI.33; NB: 30.I.36 (special issue); Hueg, "Northeim 1933–36 . . . ," p. 7; Girmann, "Tätigkeits und Erfolgsbericht."
21. NNN: 16.VIII.33; 18.IX.33; 7.XI.33; 22.III.34; form letter with attached list of names, from Girmann, 19.III.34 (unnumbered in SAN); OGL, "Bericht über die Entwicklung des Führerprinzips. . . ."
22. PK, OGN Korrespondenz, S-Z, 1936–43: Bürgermeister Girmann an Herrn Schrader, 28.VIII.36.
23. Interviews with Maria Habenichts and Carl Querfurt.
24. NNN: 21–26 & 28.IX.33; 14, 25 & 30.X.33; 18 & 24.XI.33; 1.XII.33; 8 & 9.I.34; 12.III.34. NSV meetings were also used to promote Nazi policy in explicit ways. Shortly before the November 1933 plebiscite, one benefit evening was turned into an election rally and another, in January 1934, promoted German claims to the Saarland. See NNN: 25.X.33; 15.XII.33; 13 & 19.I.34.
25. NNN: 18.XII.33; NB: 20.II.34. "Gnädige Frau" ("gracious lady") may be used out of politeness or deference. What the Nazis opposed was the requirement that servant girls use it in addressing their mistresses.
26. Interviews with "Heinrich Lamme," "Hans Abbenrode," Maria Habenichts, and "Erhardt Knorpel."
27. NB: 30.I.36 (special issue); OGL, "Bericht über die Entwicklung des Führerprinzips . . ."; Hueg, "Northeim 1933–36 . . . ," p. 21.
28. NNN: 3.II.34; NB: 16.IV.34; "Versammlung des Verein zur Hebung des Fremdenverkehr . . ." (see n. 14, above).
29. Oessel and Borgholte, "Chronik des Standortes . . . ," pp. 29, 38–42, 59. Section 9 of the contract explicitly committed the Army to use Northeim artisans for most of its work and to hire townspeople for any extra jobs.
30. Hueg, "Northeim 1933–36 . . . ," pp. 10–11. For the protests when it was learned that the town was losing its swimming pool, see "Versammlung des Verein zur Hebung des Fremdenverkehr . . ." (n. 14, above).

31. Oessel and Borgholte, "Chronik des Standortes . . . ," pp. 40 & 55; interviews with "Erhardt Knorpel" and Wilhelm Spannaus. Many *Wehrmacht* officers conspicuously attended church after the Nazi antichurch campaign began. See Chapter 19.

32. PGSA, Rep. 90-P/3,4: Lagebericht des Regierungspräsidenten Hildesheim f. d. Monate April u. Mai, 1.VI.35.

33. BDC, Akten Regierungsassessor Dr. Hermann Muhs. Muhs had been in the party since the early 1920s and before 1933 had even been a *Gauleiter*, temporarily.

34. PGSA, Rep. 90-P/3,4: Lagebericht der Stapostelle Hildesheim, 2.XII.35.

35. *Ibid.*, Lagebericht der Stapostelle Hildesheim, 7.I.36. I was unable to find any additional Gestapo reports dealing with Northeim.

CHAPTER 19
Life in the Third Reich (pages 281–292)

1. PK, N-5, Rundschreiben der GL u. KL betr. Organisation, usw, 1935–36. Portions of this chapter were previously published in William S. Allen, "Totalitarianism: the Concept and the Reality," in Ernest A. Menze, *Totalitarianism Reconsidered* (National University Publications, Port Washington and London, 1981), pp. 97–106.

2. BDC, Akten Walter Steineck, geb. 14.VIII.89. The salary cited is what he earned as of April 1, 1936; he died on March 20, 1942. On his concern with local preservation see Walter Steineck, "Aufbau und Aufgaben der amtlichen Heimatpflege im Kreise Northeim, 22.X.35" (ms. in SAN).

3. BDC, Akten Walter Baldauf, geb. 30.XI.78; the "Parteistat. Erhebung 1939" gives Baldauf's entry date as April 1, 1933, and his title as "NSV Kreisverwalter." For other examples see *ibid.*, Akten Hans Blume, geb. 22.III.06, or Hans Böttcher, geb. 21.VIII.02.

4. NSAH, Hann 174/Northeim 86: Magistrat Northeim an Reg.-Präs. Hildesheim, 10.XI.33. As deputy mayor, Girmann had earned 700 marks per month.

5. They were Ernst Bartram (geb. 29.IV.94, party number 1,475,988, an accountant at the tax office) and Friedrich Bartels (geb. 2.IV.91, party number 1,475,985, a bank accountant). Both had joined the party on the same day in July 1932 so neither qualified as "old fighters." The interim head of OG II in 1935–36 was August Jörns, an ice cream dealer and another crony of Girmann.

6. PK, N-16, OGN Ausgeg. Schreiben, N-Z, 1932–33, *passim; ibid.*, OGN Korrespondenz A-B, 1936–43: OGN II an Industrie u. Handelskammer Hildesheim, 7.V.36, and Gauschatzmeister an Kassenleiter OGN, 2.XI.39. See also BAK, "Slg. Schumacher," Nr. 202 III: GSHB Ordnungsblatt, Gauorganisationsleiter, Ordnungsziffer 4, Blatt 11, Folge 7 (1.IV.39).

7. BDC, Akten Ernst Girmann. See especially his SA application form and the "Beurteilung für SA Führer (Hann., d. 16.VIII.43), SA Gruppe Niedersachsen, Standarte 136." See also NSAH, Hann 174/Northeim 89: Bürgermeister an Landrat, 27.IV.38.

8. PK, N-10, Grosskundgebungen in Northeim, 1935: GSHB Propagandaabt. an OGN, 28.XI.35.

9. PK, OGN Presse u. Film Rundschreiben, 1935–36: GSHB an alle OGL, 7.XII. 35. "Deutschland treibt Wintersport" was the exact title; there were also explicitly political slide shows such as "Adolf Hitler, unser Führer."

10. PK, N-12, Veranstaltungen u. Tagungen in Northeim, II, 1937–41: "Termin Kalender der OG Propaganda Abt.—gültig f. Sept. 1938 bis Mai 1939." The schedule had:

Oct. 9 events, all internal party.

Nov. 9 events, all internal party except 2.

Dec. 10 events, all internal party except 1.

Jan. 9 events, all internal party except 1.

Feb. 10 events, all internal party.

March 8 events, all internal party except 1.

This included the N.S. Frauenschaft, the SS, and the KdF, but excluded all other Nazi organizations. So it was a "minimum list" of required meetings.

11. PK, N-11, Veranstaltungen u. Tagungen in Northeim (I), 1936–37. For an attempt to punish the head of the town's Fishing Club for holding a meeting that conflicted with a party function, see *ibid.*, OGN Korrespondenz, A–B, 1936–43: OGL I (Pg. Bartram) an KLN, 21.X.36, betr. Angelsportverein.

12. PK, N-5, Rundschreiben der GL u. KL betr. Org., usw, 1935–36: OGL an sämtliche Blockleiter OGN I & II, 28.IX.36. This was after attendance had dropped to 50 percent.

13. PK, OGN Korrespondenz, H–K, 1936–43: Betr. Pg. Adolf Happe, 28.IX.36. This man compounded his problems by explaining that the town's middle class was boycotting Nazi meetings because of local corruption, especially the favoritism shown to August Ude. For examples of threats against nonattenders by Girmann, see *ibid.*, N-18, OGN Ausgeg. Schreiben, N-Z, 1934, *passim*.

14. PK, N-30, Politische Beurteilung einzelnen Personen, 1936–42: OGN an Friedrich Schrader, 17.XI.37.

15. PK, N-19, OGN Korrespondenz, A-K, 1935: OGL an Fräulein Albrecht, 14.V.35.

16. PK, N-17, OGN Ausgeg. Schreiben, A-M, 1934: OGL an Studienrat Meinecke, 4.XII.34. "So werden wir allen Glauben der Pfaffen durch unseren Glauben an Hitler überwinden."

17. PK, N-35, Vermerke über missliebige Äusserungen des Pastor Moritz, usw, 1937. Also interviews with Rudolf Bückmann, Wilhelm Spannaus, "Heinrich Lamme," and "Erhardt Knorpel." Information on the regime's reticence concerning action against the churches may be found in William S. Allen, "Objective and Subjective Inhibitants in the German Resistance to Hitler," in Franklin H. Littell and Hubert Locke (eds.), *The German Church Struggle and the Holocaust* (Detroit 1974), pp. 114–123. Hitler at one point threatened to personally shoot a *Gauleiter* (Wagner) if he resumed overt attacks on religion in Bavaria.

18. NSAH, Hann 80, Hild III/2631, *passim*. Girmann's campaign began on April 5,

1937, and the final action of the *Regierungs-Präsident Hildesheim* came on April 23, 1938. There were an estimated 750 Catholics in Northeim; for their pastor's protest, see *ibid.*, Fr. Meyer an Bürgermeister Girmann, 9.IV.37. Also: interview with "Benno Schmidt."

19. PK, N-1, Rundschreiben des Gauschatzmeisters, 1934–36: *passim.*
20. The latter figures are from November 1935: PK, N-10, Grosskundgebungen in Northeim, 1935: OGN an GSHB (Propagandaabt.), 28.XI.35. The most accurate count of party members is in NSAH, Hann 174/Northeim 85: Betr. Stadtbrief: Der Bürgermeister, d. 31.V.34.
21. PK, N-17 and N-18, OGN Ausgeg. Schreiben, A-M and N-Z, 1934: *passim.*
22. PK, N-6, Rundschreiben des KLN, 1935–36: "Rundschreiben 053/36, Hann. d. 27.VI.36, Org. Amt" (on the distribution of Block Wardens in Northeim). For the national directives: Aryeh L. Unger, *The Totalitarian Party: Party and People in Nazi Germany and Soviet Russia* (Cambridge University Press, 1974), pp. 99–104.
23. Unger, p. 101.
24. PK, N-18, OGN Ausgeg. Schreiben, N-Z, 1934: OGL an Pg. August Voss, 19.XII.34; N-22, OGN Korrespondenz, L-Z, 1935–36: OGL II an Pg. Otto Müller, 17.I.36; N-20, OGN Korrespondenz, L-Z, 1935, contains most of the material on the changeover in personnel.
25. BAK, "Slg. Schumacher," Nr. 202 III, GSHB: Verordnungsblatt Gauschulungsleiter, Ordnungsziffer 5, Folge 1, 1.I.39 (Blatt 1) and Folge 17, 15.IX.39 (Blatt 22).
26. PK, N-11, Veranstaltungen u. Tagungen in Northeim (I), 1936–37: Betr. Weinwerbewoche, 1936, 29.IX.36. There were 1,444 bottles sold.
27. BAK, "Slg. Schumacher," Nr. 202 III: GSHB Verordnungsblätter. This contains the orders and regulations for just the year 1939.
28. PK, N-29, OGN Politische Beurteilung einzelnen Personen, 1935–1943. The other files containing these are numbered N-28 through N-32 and go up through 1944.
29. *Ibid.*, especially *in re* Josef Eckermann, Luise Ahrens, and August Müller.
30. This seems to have been the pattern in neighboring towns, too. For example, in 73 pages of political evaluations in Bovenden, 1936–1941, not one person was recorded as "unzuverlässig," the chief comments were about contributions, and there was no sign of more than minimal accommodation to the regime. See NSAH, Hann 310 I/L-3, Nr. 36–7, 40–42.
31. PK, N-22, OGN Korrespondenz, L-Z, 1935–36: Zellenleiter Nahme an OGL, 15.IX.35 and Konrektor Hauk an Zellenleiter Hermann Nahme, 14.XI.35. (Both reporting meetings at the home of a Dr. Volkmann that included Karl Deppe, Friedrich Haase, and four other Socialists. It should be noted that Nahme was one of the few holdovers from the "old fighters"—his party number was 4,291— which may explain his exceptional zeal.) See also PK, N-32, Politische Beurteilung einzelnen Personen, 1936–43: Zellenleiter Fr. Schoppe an OGL, betr. Tischlermeister Gustav Knust, n.d.

32. PK, N-18, OGN Ausgeg. Schreiben, N-Z, 1934: OGL an Reichsbahn Oberin-spektor Pg. Schulze, 23.VIII.34. Girmann also noted that Strohmeyer had been "active and unpleasant in the SPD." Girmann's proviso was that of course Strohmeyer not be rehired until all the SA and SS men who had applied had been given employment.

33. Interview with Carl Querfurt.

34. PK, N-18, OGN Ausgeg. Schreiben, N-Z, 1934: OGL an Pg. Ernst Hilke, 26.X.34, and OGL an Pg. August Döring, 27.IX.34 (the latter probably prompted by Girmann's longstanding feud with Döring—see Ch. 16 and Appendix C); *ibid.,* N-22, OGN Korrespondenz, L-Z, 1935–36: OGL I an die Ortsgruppenverwaltung der DAF, 3.I.36.

35. PK, N-28, Politische Beurteilung einzelnen Personen, 1935–44: OGL an KLN, 15.VII.36; *ibid.,* OGN Korrespondenz, 1936–43: Betr. Gebr. Fricke Mode-waren, an OGL Lüchow, 8.I.38.

36. PK, N-18, OGN Ausgeg. Schreiben, N–Z, 1934: OGL an Frau Dorothea Bauer, Brooklyn, N.Y., 2.VIII.34 (for the former quotation); *ibid.,* N-20, OGN Korrespondenz, L-Z, 1935: Girmann an Ortsgruppe Bad Grund/Harz, 10.VIII.35 (for the latter quotation).

37. PK, N-15, OGN Ausgeg. Schreiben, A-M, 1932–33: OGL an N.S.Heilpraktikerfachschaft, 30.IX.33; *ibid.,* OGN Korrespondenz, L-R, 1936–43: An die KLN betr. Bankier Hermann Müller, 21.XI.36. Girmann took a similarly tolerant attitude toward Freemasons, another target of Nazi ideological wrath. See PK, N-18, OGN Ausgeg. Schreiben, N-Z, 1934: Betr. Pg. Dr. Gerhard Meissner (n.d.).

38. PGSA, Rep 90p/3,4: Lagebericht der Regierungspräs. Hildesheim f. d. Monate April u. Mai, 1.VI.35; Lagebericht der Stapostelle Hildesheim, 7.I.36.

39. Interviews with Maria Habenichts, "Heinrich Lamme," and Thomas Galland. For the negative response nationally see William S. Allen, "Die deutsche Öffentlichkeit und die 'Reichskristallnacht'—Konflikte zwischen Werthierarchie und Propaganda im Dritten Reich," in Detlev Peukert und Jürgen Reulecke, *Die Reihen fast geschlossen: Beiträge zur Geschichte des Alltags unterm Nationalsozialismus* (Wuppertal, Hammer Verlag, 1981), pp. 397–411. Virtually all foreign diplomats and reporters found extensive opposition by the German people to *Kristallnacht.* So did both the Social Democratic underground and the *Gestapo.*

40. Interview with Gregor Ballin.

41. There were some exceptions: city employees or contractors, who were forced to demonstrate exceptional zeal for the Nazi cause, and young people, who were told they would have "no future" unless they were active in the Hitler Youth. For the former, see NSAH, Hann 174/Northeim 86: Stellplan für Northeim, 26.X.35 (which lists "Aryan descent" and political commitment as the first requisite in the job descriptions of every salaried city employee), and PK, N-29, Politische Beurteilung einzelnen Personen, 1936–43: OGL betr. Milchhändler Bünger, 13.V.37 (one of a series compelling contractors to join the party). For the latter, see *ibid.,* N-11, Veranstaltungen u. Tagungen in Northeim (I), 1936–

37: BM Girmann an die Elternschaft der Northeimer Jugend, 9.XI.36; N-21, OGN Korrespondenz, A-H, 1935–36: OGL I & II an Amt für Erzieher in der NSDAP, 12.XI.35; OGN Parteikorrespondenz, L-R, 1936–43: Girmann an OGL, 8.XI.41.
42. PK, N-11, Veranstaltungen u. Tagungen in Northeim (I), 1936–37, *passim*. The weapons were Walther PK-9 automatics.
43. PK, OGN Korrespondenz, 1936–1943, A-M and L-Z, *passim*.
44. PK, N-1, OGN Gefallenen von Northeim, Band 1.
45. On Girmann's actions, interviews with Carl Querfurt and Thomas Galland. Dr. Heinrich Eggeling has pointed out in Girmann's defense that he exchanged his Nazi uniform for an Army uniform, since he was a reserve officer. In some nearby towns the militia fought to the bitter end and the towns were destroyed; Einbeck is one example. On the capture of Northeim on April 12, 1945, Third Armored Division, *Spearhead in the West* (Frankfurt a/M, 1945), pp. 247–49; Charles B. MacDonald, *The Last Offensive. U. S. Army in World War II: The European Theater of Operations* (Washington, D.C., 1973), p. 391; Vincent J. Esposito, *West Point Atlas of American Wars*, Vol. II (New York, 1959), map. 70. Citations courtesy of "Historica" World War II Reference Service.

CHAPTER 20
Conclusions (pages 293–303)

Epigraph: Edmund Wilson, *To the Finland Station* (New York, 1953), p. 187.
1. Wilhelm Spannaus and M. Luders, "List of 853 Books Removed from the Northeim Public Library on the Order of the Allied Control Council" (ms., January 12, 1946, located in Northeim City Hall, Room 8).
2. For comparitive local and regional studies of the Nazi experience, apart from the works already cited, see Waldemar Besson, *Würtemberg und die deutsche Staatskrise 1928–33* (Stuttgart, 1959); Martin Broszat et al, *Bayern in der N.S.-Zeit: Soziale Lage und politischer Verhalten der Bevölkerung im Spiegel vertraulicher Berichte* (multi-volume: Munich, 1977–); Wilfried Böhnke, *Die NSDAP im Ruhrgebiet 1920–1933* (Bonn/Bad Godesberg, 1974); Bernd Burkhardt, *Eine Stadt wird Braun: Die nationalsozialistische Machtergreifung in der Provinz: Eine Fallstudie* (Hamburg, 1980); Ursula Büttner, *Hamburg in der Staats- und Wirtschaftskrise 1928–1931* (Hamburg, 1982); John Farquharson, "The NSDAP in Hanover and Lower Saxony, 1921–26," *Journal of Contemporary History* (1973), pp. 103–120; Ellsworth Faris, "Takeoff Point for the National Socialist Party: The Landtag Election in Baden, 1929," *Central European History* (June 1975), pp. 140–171; Elke Fröhlich and Martin Broszat, "Politische und soziale Macht auf der Lande: Die Durchsetzung der NSDAP im Kreis Memmingen," *Vierteljahrshefte für Zeitgeschichte* (1977), pp. 246–72; Norbert Frei, *Nationalsozialistische Eroberung der Provinzpresse: Gleichschaltung, Selbstanpassung und Resistenz in Bayern* (Stuttgart, 1980); Hans Graf, *Die Entwicklung der Wahlen und politischen Parteien in Gross-Dortmund* (Hanover, 1958); Johnpeter H. Grill,

The Nazi Movement in Baden, 1920–1945 (Chapel Hill, 1983); Hans-Peter Gör-gon, *Düsseldorf und der Nationalsozialismus* (Düsseldorf, 1969); Reiner Ham-brecht, *Der Aufstieg der NSDAP in Mittel- und Oberfranken 1925–1933* (Nur-emberg, 1976); Gertrud und Erwin Herrmann, "Nationalsozialistische Agitation und Herrschaftspraxis in der Provinz: Das Beispiel Bayreuth," *Zeitschrift für Bayerische Landesgeschichte* (1976), pp. 201–250; Franz-Josef Heyen, *Nation-alsozialismus im Alltag: Quellen zur Geschichte des Nationalsozialismus vor-nehmlich im Raum Mainz-Koblenz-Trier* (Boppard, 1967); Gerhard Hoch, *Zwölf wiedergefundene Jahre: Kaltenkirchen unter den Hakenkreuz* (Bad Bramstedt, 1980); Werner Jochmann (ed.), *Nationalsozialismus und Revolution: Ursprung und Geschichte der NSDAP in Hamburg 1922–33* (Frankfurt/Main, 1963); Ger-hard Kirsch et al., *Berliner Alltag im Dritten Reich* (Düsseldorf, 1981); Kurt Klotzbach, *Gegen den Nationalsozialismus: Widerstand und Verfolgung in Dortmund 1930–1945* (Hanover, 1969); Claus-Dieter Krohn and Dirk Steg-mann, "Kleingewerbe und Nationalsozialismus in einer agrarisch-mittelstän-dischen Region: Das Beispiel Lüneburg 1930–39," *Archiv für Sozialgeschichte* (1977), pp. 41–98; Karl Kühling, *Osnabrück 1925–33: Stadt im Dritten Reich* (Osnabrück, 1969); Edward N. Peterson, *The Limits of Hitler's Power* (Prince-ton, 1969); Henner Pingel, *Das Jahr 1933: NSDAP-Machtergreifung in Darms-tadt und im Volksstaat Hessen* (Darmstadt, 2nd Edition, 1978); Sigurd Plesse, *Die nationalsozialistische Machtergreifung im Oberharz: Clausthal-Zellerfeld 1929–33* (Clausthal-Zellerfeld, 1970); Günter Plum, *Gesellschaftsstruktur und politisches Bewusstsein in einer katholischen Region 1928–33: Untersuchung am Beispiel des Regierungsbezirks Aachen* (Stuttgart, 1972); Geoffrey Pridham, *Hitler's Rise to Power: The Nazi Movement in Bavaria, 1923–1933* (New York, 1973); Horst Rehberger, *Die Gleichschaltung des Landes Baden 1932/33* (Hei-delberg, 1966); Ernst-August Roloff, *Bürgertum und Nationalsozialismus: Braunschweigs Weg ins Dritten Reich* (Hanover, 1961) and *Braunschweig und der Staat von Weimar: Politik, Wirtschaft und Gesellschaft 1918–1933* (Bruns-wick, 1964); Paul Sauer, *Würtemberg in der Zeit des Nationalsozialismus* (Ulm, 1973); Jürgen Schadt (ed.), *Verfolgung und Widerstand unter dem Nationalso-zialismus in Baden* (Stuttgart, 1976); Hans-Dieter Schmidt, *Die nationalsozial-istische Machtergreifung in einer Kreisstadt: Ein Lokalmodell zur Zeitgeschichte* (Frankfurt/Main, 1983); Eberhard Schön, *Die Entstehung des Nationalsozialis-mus in Hessen* (Meisenheim am Glan, 1972); Herbert Schwarzwälder, *Die Machtergreifung der NSDAP in Bremen 1933* (Bremen, 1966); Hans-Josef Steinberg, *Widerstand und Verfolgung in Essen 1933–1945* (Hanover, 1969); Gerhard Stoltenberg, *Politische Strömungen in Schleswig-Holsteinischen Land-volk 1918–33* (Düsseldorf, 1962); Lawrence D. Stokes, "The Social Composi-tion of the Nazi Party in Eutin, 1925–1932," *International Review of Social History* (1978), pp. 1–32, and "Der Fall Stoffregen: Die Absetzung des Eutiner Bürgermeisters im Zuge der NS-Machtergreifung 1928–1937," *Zeitschrift der Gesellschaft für Schleswig-Holsteinische Geschichte* (1979), pp. 253–86, and "Das Eutiner Schutzhaftlager 1933/34: Zur Geschichte eines 'wilden' Konzentrationslagers," *Vierteljahrshefte für Zeitgeschichte* (1979), pp. 570–625; Hans Teich, *Hildesheim und seine antifaschistischen Widerstandskampf gegen den Hitlerfaschismus und demokratischer Neubeginn* (Hildesheim, 1979); Robert Thévoz *et al.* (eds.), *Pommern 1934/35 im Spiegel von Gestapo Lageberichten und Sachakten* (two volumes, Cologne, 1974); Timothy Alan Tilton, *Nazism, Neo-Nazism, and the Peasantry* (Bloomington, 1975); Harald Voigt, *Der Sylter Weg ins Dritten Reich: Die Geschichte der Insel Sylt von Ende des 1. Weltkriegs bis zu dem Anfängen der nationalsozialistischen Diktatur* (Münsterdorf, 1977); Vereinigung der Verfolgten des Naziregimes, *Peine unter der NS-Gewaltherrschaft* (Peine, n.d.); Friedrich Walter, *Schicksal einer Deutschen Stadt: Geschichte Mannheims 1907–1945* (two volumes, Frankfurt/Main, 1950); Falk Wiesemann, *Die Vorgeschichte der nationalsozialistischen Machtübernahme in Bayern 1932/33* (Berlin, 1975); Bettina Wenke, *Interviews mit Ueberlebenden: Verfolgung und Widerstand in Südwestdeutschland* (Stuttgart, 1980); Gerda Zorn, *Stadt im Widerstand* (Frankfurt/Main, 1965).

3. See Chapter 2 for a description of this club.
4. Interview with Rudolf Bückmann.
5. Chapter 19, n. 32.
6. Interviews with "Benno Schmidt" and Carl Querfurt.
7. Minutes of the *Gau-Uschla* proceedings against Wilhelm Spannaus on July 1, 1933 (in private files of Wilhelm Spannaus).
8. Marlis G. Steinert, *Hitlers Krieg und die Deutschen: Stimmung und Haltung der deutschen Bevölkerung im Zweiten Weltkrieg* (Düsseldorf, 1970); in abridged translation as *Hitler's War and the Germans*.

INDEX

William Sheridan Allen was born in Evanston, Illinois, and studied at the universities of Michigan, Connecticut, and Minnesota, and in Germany at the Free University of Berlin and the University of Göttingen. *The Nazi Seizure of Power* was his first book. He has also written *The Infancy of Nazism* and is at work on studies of the effectiveness of Nazi propaganda and of the Social Democratic underground in the Third Reich. Dr. Allen is now professor of history at the State University of New York at Buffalo.